Marketing Logistics

The Wiley Marketing Series

MARTIN ZOBER, *Marketing Management*

ROBERT J. HOLLOWAY AND ROBERT S. HANCOCK,
*The Environment of Marketing Behavior—
Selections from the Literature*

GEORGE SCHWARTZ, Editor
Science in Marketing

EDGAR CRANE
*Marketing Communications—
A Behavioral Approach to Men, Messages, and Media*

JOSEPH W. NEWMAN, Editor
On Knowing the Consumer

STEUART HENDERSON BRITT, Editor
*Consumer Behavior and the Behavioral Sciences—
Theories and Applications*

DONALD F. MULVIHILL AND STEPHEN PARANKA
Price Policies and Practices

DAVID CARSON
International Marketing: A Comparative Systems Approach

BRUCE E. MALLEN
The Marketing Channel: A Conceptual Viewpoint

RONALD R. GIST
Management Perspectives in Retailing

JOHN K. RYANS AND JAMES C. BAKER
World Marketing: A Multinational Approach

JOHN M. BRION
Corporate Marketing Planning

NORTON E. MARKS AND ROBERT M. TAYLOR
Marketing Logistics: Perspective and Viewpoints

Marketing Logistics:

PERSPECTIVES AND VIEWPOINTS

NORTON E. MARKS
Associate Professor of Marketing
University of Notre Dame

ROBERT MARTIN TAYLOR
Chairman, Department of Geography
Texas Christian University

JOHN WILEY & SONS, INC.   *New York · London · Sydney*

Library of Congress Catalog Card Number: 67-19784

Printed in the United States of America

Contributors

Andersen, R. Clifton
University of Texas

Barrick, B. B.
General Sales Manager, Raytheon Company

Baumol, William J.
Princeton University

Baumback, Clifford M.
State University of Iowa

Bowman, Edward H.
Massachusetts Institute of Technology

Brown, Robert G.
Arthur D. Little, Inc.

Browne, L. O.
Director of Distribution,
Burroughs Corporation

Blumenthal, Lassor
Vice-President
The Charisma Organization,
Marketing and Communication Consultant

Brewer, Stanley
University of Washington

Catlin, Yates
Public Relations Consultant
Specializing in Transportation

Dearden, John
Harvard University

Dillon, Thomas F.
Associate Editor, Purchasing

Dommermuth, William P.
University of Texas

Drucker, Peter F.
New York University

Flaks, Marvin
Booz, Allen and Hamilton, Inc.

Fredericks, Ward A.
Michigan State University

Hamburger, Michael J.
Carnegie Institute of Technology

Heskett, J. L.
Harvard University

Hohorst, Henry G.
New York Central System

Ivie, Robert M.
President, Guild Wine Company

Jolivet, Vincent M.
University of Washington

Konopa, J.
State University of Iowa

Kuehn, Alfred A.
Carnegie Institute of Technology

Lazer, William
Michigan State University

Magee, John F.
Vice President, Arthur D. Little, Inc.

Marks, Norton E.
University of Texas

Meehan, William J.
General Manager, Ryder Bonded Warehouse

Mossman, Frank H.
Michigan State University

Napolitan, Arthur W.
Manager, Procedures and Computer Operations,
Coats and Clark, Inc.

Parker, Donald D.
Portland State University

Plowman, E. Grosvenor
Vice-President, United States Steel

Reese, Bud
Associate Editor, Industrial Marketing

Roberts, Merrill J.
University of Pittsburgh

Rosenzweig, James
University of Washington

Ruppenthal, Karl M.
Director of Transportation Management
Program, Stanford University

Shabecoff, Philip
Correspondent, New York Times

Shiele, Irene
Michigan State University

Smykay, Edward W.
Michigan State University

Stewart, John B.
Massachusetts Institute of Technology

Weigand, Robert E.
De Paul University

Whiteman, Irvin R.
Director of Operations Research,
Computer Concepts, Inc.

Wolfe, Philip
The Rand Corporation

Zusi, Charles J.
Packaging Consultant

Contributing Periodicals

American Transportation Research Forum

Business Horizons

Business Management

Business Topics

California Management Review

Distribution Age

Dun's Review & Modern Industry

Factory

Fortune

Harvard Business Review

Industrial Marketing

Journal of Marketing

Journal of Retailing

Managing Materials Function, American
Management Association, Report Number 35

Management Review

Management Science

New Decision Making Tools for Manager,
Harvard University Press

New York Times

Operations Research

Purchasing

Social Responsibilities of Marketing,
AMA Proceedings, 1961

Transportation Progress

University of Houston Business Review

University of Washington Business Review

Preface

Marketing Logistics represents an attempt to tie together several of the related aspects of the administration of the economic firm. For several years the American Marketing Association's Committee of Definitions has persistently, if not successfully, tried to shift academicians and practitioners away from the use of the term, "distribution" toward the use of the generic term, "marketing." Professor J. L. Heskett has suggested that "marketing" subsumes the functions of promotion and logistics, whereas "promotion" refers to the demand-creation segment of the whole. Logistics then encompasses "the movement and handling of goods from the point of production to the point of consumption or use."[1]

Presenting promotion and logistics as dichotomous is a cogent approach to the study of marketing logistics, and is one with which this book will be concerned. However, this approach tends to present the reader with a dilemma. Are these functions actually separable? Can we sever them one from the other? Although both theory and practice have attempted to do so in the past, the solution is probably more complex. For example, the astute student finds himself hardpressed to separate the tightly interlocked promotion and logistics functions of packaging, inventory, order processing, plant and warehouse location, and many other elements. Promotion and logistics so thoroughly interact upon and with each other as to defy precise separation. Certainly a sharp-penciled accountant may be capable of determining the cost of the color material that goes into the package, but is he or anyone else likely to be capable of separating the cost incurred in making the Quaker Oats package perform its logistics function from the cost of making that package attractive to a child as a toy drum? At what point is the package then a promotional device and when is it merely a means for conveying the product to the consumer?

The manager of a major business consulting firm once told an audience his method of training analysts in making a presentation to their clients. His first suggestion was to present the client with an overview—an idea of how the firm fits into the economy, then how the individual segments of the firm function severally, and finally, how the segments interact to comprise the total.

Following this sage advice, we have taken a similar approach in *Marketing Logistics*. The reader is presented with material which attempts to fit the discipline into its proper position in the economy. Peter Drucker's article introduces the book by demonstrating the need for further study into marketing logistics. Next, J. L. Heskett's important study re-emphasizes Drucker's point by dramatically illustrating the macroeconomic cost of physical distribution.[2]

After the reader has acquired the requisite background material to acquaint him with the role of marketing logistics in the economy, a discussion follows that investigates the integral parts which constitute the discipline. Functions discussed in this part of the book include customer service, facility location, information flows, packaging, material handling, storage, inventory management, and movement services. Each is discussed as a separate function in its respective section as well as being considered in its relationship with other logistics functions.

[1] Definitions Committee of the American Marketing Association, "1948 Report," *The Journal of Marketing*, October, 1948, p. 202.

[2] Marketing logistics and physical distribution will be treated as interchangeable terms throughout this book.

The last section presents the best of the synthesizing articles in the discipline. Here are found the studies whose central themes are the interrelationship that exists within marketing logistics. "Rhocrematics and Organizational Adjustment," by Brewer and Rosenzweig, describes the impact upon management when the "new science of material and information flow, Rhocrematics" cuts across traditional organizational lines. The Andersen, Dommermuth, and Marks article describes the interfunctional exchange which takes place between promotion and marketing logistics. In general, the articles in this section describe marketing logistics as a process which refuses to respect traditional functional organizational lines.

The readings in this book represent the thinking of the greatest scholars in the field. A balance between works by academicians and practitioners has been achieved to give the reader an opportunity to see that the theoretical material is actually applied in practice, and that practitioners in fact first theorize. Articles have been collected from a wide range of publications in order to achieve the same purpose.

Marketing logistics is rapidly developing into an extremely important aspect of the firm. Authors such as those whose works appear in this book are continually generating articles which bear an impact on the business community as a whole and which will assist in making the discipline an important emerging science of the 1960s.

NORTON E. MARKS
ROBERT M. TAYLOR

February 1967

Contents

xi

Section I. Distribution Economics

The importance of Marketing Logistics activities in the national economy as well as in the individual firm is boooming more and more evident as logistics scientists gather the demonstrating data. Quoting Professor Heskett, "The statement is often made that transportation and/or physical distribution are gaining current attention because their costs are rising rapidly. In dollar terms we know this is true." Heskett further concludes that the macroeconomic cost of physical distribution as a percentage of gross national product declined from an estimated 16.4% in 1950 to 14.9% in 1960.[1]

It is evident from these data that those involved in marketing and/or management—students, academicians and practitioners alike—should become knowledgeable in the field. Peter Drucker's, *The Economy's Dark Continent,* challenges the reader to investigate the profit potential available in the change from the disjointed approach to the overall view. The remaining articles in the section are intended to acquaint the reader rapidly with how physical distribution in the economy is linked with the marketing success of the firm. The articles by J. L. Heskett and E. W. Smykay are particularly pointed in this direction.

[1] See Professor Heskett's article, "Macroeconomic Cost of Physical Distribution," Article 2.

1. *The Economy's Dark Continent**

Almost 50 cents of each dollar the American consumer spends for goods goes for activities that occur after the goods are made, that is after they have come in finished form off "the dry end of the machine," to use the papermaker's graphic term. This is distribution, one of the most sadly neglected, most promising areas of American business.

The activities that are encompassed by the broad term distribution include sorting and cutting, invoicing, billing, and other paper work; labeling, packaging, storing, moving, shipping—plus wholesaling, retailing, financing, and insuring. Physically, distribution contributes little; it can only mar, soil, tear, scratch, or otherwise damage or downgrade the product. Economically, however, distribution is the process in which physical properties of matter are converted into economic value; it brings the customer to the product. But how much of the distributive cost is really "value added," how much is merely "waste added"?

We know little more about distribution today than Napoleon's contemporaries knew about the interior of Africa. We know it is there, and we know it is big; and that's about all. There are plenty of experts on individual phases: on transportation and warehousing, on retailing and consumer buying habits, on labeling and packaging, on factoring and insurance. But when a major government department recently looked for two or three men to advise it on distribution, none of the many people consulted in industry, government, and the universities could name even one qualified candidate.

To reach a real understanding of the role and structure of distribution in the American economy we need new concepts of economic theory and economic analysis. Most of our present concepts focus on production or on the stream of

money and credit, rather than on the flow of physical goods and its economic characteristics. We also need new data; our figures today, such as those of the Census of Business, obscure distribution rather than report on it. (And only the high-speed computer can analyze anything as complex as the distributive system.)

G. M.'s Grand Design

Business need not wait until this work is done. An industry or a company can make its own distribution manageable. This was proved more than a generation ago by the automobile industry and especially by General Motors. Henry Ford, in building River Rouge, had had the premature but great vision of the manufacturing plant as the central switchboard in a flow of physical matter from mine to customer (and from there to scrap heap and back into the furnace as raw material). With this as its starting point, General Motors, in the middle and late Twenties, built its business around the economic characteristics of the distributive process—beginning with the customers' buying habits, proceeding thence to the structure and characteristics of dealer finance, dealer inventories, and dealer compensation, going back further to the design, location, size, product mix, and scheduling of assembly plants, and finally all the way back to corporate organization. For well over three decades General Motors' distribution system has made the automobile the highly engineered mass-consumption product with the lowest total distribution costs.

By now this system may be obsolescent in important parts. How much economic sense, for instance, does the "franchised dealer" still make in a world of supermarkets and discount houses? How meaningful is his fixed commission? But G. M.'s achievement still stands as a useful example of how distribution can be brought under control. The example has been only too rarely followed. Only lately have things begun to stir

* Reprinted by permission from *Fortune*, April 1962.
† New York University.

—mildly. The American Management Association, for instance, has run a number of conferences on physical distribution. A few large consumer-goods companies have made distribution a specific corporate responsibility; H. J. Heinz of the "57 varieties" has a vice president-distribution. The results are encouraging. It does help, for example, to have someone around who points out that a proposed new packaging design will double freight costs, instead of having this come to light only after millions of the new packages have been made—as happened a few years ago at one of the big soap companies.

Why Distribution Lags

But even at their most successful, the new approaches attempt only to do a little more systematically and a little more cheaply the old jobs of transportation, inventory keeping, and warehousing. And they are still isolated attempts rather than a broad trend. A recent study by Professor Michael Schiff of New York University (to be published on May 1 by the Financial Executives Research Foundation under the title *The Financial Management of the Marketing Function*) found that the importance and cost of distribution are recognized in fewer than half of the twenty-eight large companies analyzed.

Getting at the distribution problem requires cutting through a hard-rock overburden of legal, managerial, and organizational concepts. Few companies think of their distributors when they speak of "our business." Their horizon is set by the legal boundaries of their corporation. Few companies, for instance, know how large their distributors' inventories are and what is in them; this ignorance is a major cause of the persistent inventory booms and inventory busts that beset our economy. Distribution is no respecter of legal corporate boundaries. In industry after industry the price the consumer pays for the merchandise delivered and installed can be double the manufacturer's factory price or more. This means that perhaps half of the dollar the consumer pays for "our products" goes to distributors who are not legally part of "our business." The competitive position of industry and company, the reputation and availability of its products, and the use the customer makes of them, all depend more and more on events outside the legal business boundaries than on what the manufacturer does within his legal four walls. Perhaps the single most im-

portant lesson the generation-old G.M. approach still has to teach us is that distribution policy and distribution system must take into account the entire flow of the product regardless of lines of ownership and legal responsibility.

For example, the manufacturers who make the bulk of the products sold by Sears, Roebuck are legally and financially independent, as a rule. Yet every Sears buyer is expected to know as much about the making of the product —the manufacturer, his plant, his process, his materials, his people, and his costs—as he knows about selling it in the Sears stores. He often gets into product design. He is, in other words, responsible for the entire process even though he legally controls only a small part.

As restrictive as the legal boundaries are organizational and managerial boundaries within the manufacturing business itself. These tend as a rule to keep distributive costs out of sight and distribution activities unmanaged. Even in the few companies that have such a title, the "manager of distribution" usually takes over only when the product is ready to be loaded and shipped away. The major distribution costs within the manufacturing business tend, however, to lie before this stage—and so do the major opportunities for significant savings.

The Mob in the Shipping Room

In a well-managed manufacturing plant the machine areas are—and should be—quiet places. There aren't too many people in sight. They don't rush around. They do not seem to exert themselves unduly but move with measured calm. There is a good reason why the "drama of industry" so rarely comes through in paintings or photographs: in a well-managed plant there is no "drama."

But even in the best-managed plant things change drastically as soon as one goes through the door labeled "Finishing Room" or "Shipping Department." There is suddenly a mob of people. Everybody seems to rush and no one seems to know why and where. If the machine areas are soporific, the areas where products are sorted, cut to size, packaged, labeled, stored or shipped, are pandemonium.

The board of directors tends to hit the ceiling whenever the monthly scrap figure in the plant goes up by one percentage point. But few boards, to my knowledge, have ever been told how much spoilage there is in the distributive activities under the plant roof, and they have not been very interested in finding out. Yet this area is where the costs are in a modern plant—for this is where the people are. An aluminum rolling mill, for instance, may employ four workers in distributive plant jobs to every one actually employed at "making." To be sure, this distribution work is unskilled work, done usually with the simplest tools. But no matter how unskilled the job, there are no more "unskilled wages." Yet the costs of these distributive activities are rarely known and almost never shown. They disappear in general catch-alls: "allocations," "indirect labor," "administrative expense" or "burden." The industrial engineers sweat to pare one mill off the costs of making. But they rarely pay any attention to the dollars that might be saved in finishing, cutting, packaging, and shipping. I know of one company where a small team of industrial engineers put in ten days of routine work on the areas between the machines and the loading dock. As a result of the study, the company was able to reduce its fleet of forklift trucks from over 200 to fifty, to cut its manpower needs by half, and to speed up shipping time of the finished products from seven to four and a half days.

Typically, no one is individually responsible for these distributive activities in the plant. Organizationally these activities normally come under manufacturing management. They are lucky, however, if they are treated even as stepchildren. For people with a technical orientation—the production man, the chemical engineer, the plant manager—these activities are low-grade nuisances. And because, to a technically oriented man, most of the distributive work is donkey work, he tends to put a donkey in charge—more often than not a man of proved incompetence for "more demanding" work as a manufacturing supervisor.

"Solutions" That Don't Solve

As we apply management science and data processing to segments of the distribution process it becomes even more important to make sure that distribution is seen and managed as something that crosses legal and organizational boundaries. I have a suspicion—strengthened by a good deal of the work I have seen—that high-powered operations-research "solutions" for inventories, warehousing, transportation, order handling, and so on often increase the costs of distribution. For many managers tend to try

and fit operations-research into the existing legal and organizational boundaries as if these were physical facts. In straightening out one kink in the stream they may only create expensive, new turbulences some place upriver or downriver, in what may be somebody else's job, if not "another business," but is still part of the same distribution process and part of the cost structure of the same product.

I have seen one example of this in a steamship line, where an operations-research team overhauled the entire loading and scheduling process. The team produced what the operating vice president wanted: a schedule that gave the fullest possible utilization of ships, that is, of expensive capital equipment. But no one told the team that there are different rates for different kinds of freight, and that therefore freight-mix has even more to do with final results than turnaround time. And the new scheduling system put such a substantial premium on getting a rather unfavorable freight-mix that total earnings plummeted even though the rate of capital utilization went up by half.

To get control of distribution, therefore, requires seeing—and managing—it as a distinct dimension of business and as a property of product and process rather than as a collection of technical jobs. Whenever this has been done (with or without a separate "manager of distribution") substantial benefits and savings have resulted.

The Discount House and Its Lessons

But effective and economical distribution also requires, in many cases, that an entire business be run differently. This is evident in three big areas in the American economy where we know distribution to be ineffectual and costly: retail selling, the new multibillion-dollar scientific-equipment market, and the buying of industrial supplies.

The discount house, it is commonly said, can sell at a lower price because it concentrates on the brands with fast turnover. Plausible—but simply not true. Many brands that turn over slowly in the ordinary retail store turn over rapidly in the discount house. In different discount houses the same brands often perform quite differently. And even the retail store's best seller turns over much faster as a rule in the discount house (or at Sears, Roebuck). The truth is that concentration on staple items is what gives the discount house both low costs of distribution and fast turnover.

Ninety per cent or so of all business in a given line—for a manufacturer as well as for a retailer—is contributed by a very small percentage of items, 5 to 8 per cent as a rule. The remaining 90-odd per cent of all items, however, account for 90-odd per cent of the costs. For while revenue is roughly proportionate to volume, costs tend to be proportionate to the number of items or transactions. A slow seller requires just as much shelf space as a fast seller and ties down just as much capital. One requires as much paper work as the other—and paper work is so expensive that a major wholesaler has concluded that orders with a net profit of less than $10 do not even cover their ordinary paper-work expenses. In transportation, as everyone knows, the smaller the unit the higher the cost—and the same goes for crating, for collection, for inventory control, for insurance, and so on. Even spoilage and losses in transit, according to the meager figures available, seem to be higher proportionately, the smaller the unit of transaction or shipment.

Markets Without Middlemen

For the last two years I have watched the building of a fair-sized medical center. The buying of a good many million dollars worth of hospital and classroom equipment—from beds to benches—was a reasonably well-organized job. Ample technical help was available both to design facilities and to choose equipment; there were a good many distributors, well equipped with products and competent to give technical advice; and information enabling the center to weigh the consequences of decisions—say between initial costs and cost of upkeep—was reasonably easy to obtain.

But when it came to buying the scientific equipment for laboratories and testing facilities—in biology, chemistry, bacteriology, pathology, electronics, and so on—chaos took over. No one apparently had the faintest idea what would be needed, how much, and where. No one seemed to know what was available on the market and from whom. The laboratories took at most one-tenth of the total equipment budget. But in time, they took more than all of the other equipment together. And worse, a score of men who should have been getting on with their scientific work spent months as amateur lab designers and purchasing agents. Even so, no one is very happy with the results: there is too much stuff that

will be needed only rarely, and not enough of the bread-and-butter items; the wrong equipment is centralized, creating bottlenecks; and far too many pieces are not where they are needed the most.

Scientific equipment has become a multibillion-dollar market, with thousands of producers and with a multitude of customers: government agencies and industry, hospitals and schools of all kinds. But it is still organized as if it were a small "specialty" business in which one or two manufacturers supply a few odd customers. No wonder that the cost of equipment is going up twice as fast as the number of qualified research people—to the point where equipment costs may soon force us to cut back research. No wonder that, even on some apparatus in standard use, distribution costs take 80 cents of the customer's dollar.

This is a peculiar market: each individual buyer buys once in a lifetime—but then he buys a great deal at once (though there is, of course, also a constant replacement and expansion demand). Yet there are enough buyers to provide a constant order flow. Such a market, more perhaps than any other, needs a middleman—and it has none. A middleman knows both the market in an area and the available supply. Typically, the middleman of such a market is an adviser to the buyer—either the architect type who receives his pay as a fee from the buyer, or the advertising-agency type who receives his commission from the supplier. But out-and-out wholesale distributors also can supply such a market—as they do in many other hospital and school supplies. And there may be room for a cooperative buying organization of major users, such as the design and purchasing cooperatives some of the major universities are talking about. But without effective middlemen this rapidly expanding market cannot be supplied properly, let alone cheaply.

The scientific-equipment situation gives a conclusive answer to the old charge that the middleman is a "parasite." So, by the way, does the paperback book market, our fastest-growing market in the last few years. Cheap, paperbound books have been around a very long time—at least since the days of the Haldeman-Julius "Little Blue Books" more than forty years ago; the "serious" reading public was there all along too—though in smaller numbers. What created the industry was the discovery and development of new distribution channels, such as the campus bookstore, and the bookrack in drugstore and supermarket.

The Semi-literate Buyer

A good deal of work has been done these last ten or fifteen years on the marketing of industrial goods. Yet marketing men all say that selling and distribution in this field still leave much to be desired. Above all, they would increasingly agree that the key to efficient and effective industrial marketing is not the supplier but the buyer. And the buyer of industrial products and supplies is in many cases semi-literate, or even illiterate, in a business sense.

One example is paper. For many a business, paper is a major supply: the carrier of its communications, of its "image," its relations within and without; the carrier very often also of its product, its product appearance, and its product message. It is also a substantial cost item. But few companies buy paper as a major supply—if indeed they even know that they buy paper at all. Thus, in some very big banks the paper bill may be the second-biggest expense item after wages. Yet not only is there no accounting for the costs of paper, there is usually no one who knows anything about paper or about the graphic arts, no one who supervises the bank's paper buying, no one who knows what papers are available and what they can and should do in terms of end results, such as graphic representation, easy control, or accessible information. Typically, forty or fifty people in as many different departments buy paper as an "incidental" office supply—and through whatever printer, merchant, or stationer they happen to have come across (check paper is an exception—it is bought as a highly engineered product for a specific end use). As a result the bank is likely to end up with far more varieties of paper than it needs, and yet with little paper that is really right for the job. This is costly for the bank—if only because it pays retail prices for wholesale quantities. It is costly above all for the manufacturer, who has to maintain a meaningless product variety with its high expenses, both in making and in distribution. What the bank needs is a paper buyer who knows the needs of the bank and the end results it aims at, as well as the paper industry's technical and economic structure. The "old battle-ax" in accounting who, only too often, places the paper order for her

department knows none of these; as a paper buyer she is illiterate.

Another example is the ordering of generating equipment for electric-power companies. Technically these buyers are extremely highly qualified. But economically they know little—especially about the economics of their supplier, the equipment producer. As a result many buyers tend to insist on their own special designs—rather than ordering by performance specifications, most of which can be satisfied by standard designs. If the apparatus producers could build standardized models to performance specifications and on a planned even-flow basis, their costs would tumble. It is probably not entirely accidental that one major utility system which manufacturers say really understands the economics of equipment production, American Gas & Electric, also has turned in a truly superior performance in respect to growth, technical performance, and profits.

An Urgent Job

The industrial purchaser has to know his own business, of course—and the progress made here in the last few years is all to the good. He has to know what the product or supply he buys is supposed to contribute to his company's end results, has to buy it as cost per unit of his own output rather than just by the price tag. But he also needs to know just as much about the structure of the supplier industry and its economics.

This sketch of the distribution challenge oversimplifies and overgeneralizes, of course. There are countless exceptions to its sweeping statements. But my purpose is to point to distribution as an area where intelligence and hard work can produce substantial results for American business. Above all, there is need for a new orientation—one that gives distribution the importance in business design, business planning, and business policy its costs warrant.

At a time when American business faces great competitive pressures from abroad—especially from a unified Europe whose industries can hold their own in technology, manufacturing knowledge, equipment, and salesmanship—raising the effectiveness and cutting the costs of the American distributive system may be a more important and a more urgent job than most managements yet realize.

2. Macroeconomic Cost of Physical Distribution*

J. L. HESKETT†

Recently transportation has come to be recognized as an integral part of a wider range of activities, in the managerial sense, than was formerly thought to be the case. Rather than concerning himself with only transportation matters, the enlightened manager must now consider the management of inventory levels, storage procedures, and customer and supplier relations and service as activities directly related to, and interrelated with, transportation. All of these responsibilities make up the long-existent but newly-recognized managerial function of business logistics.

Two concepts of cost are important in the field. First is the cost of logistics to the individual organization, those costs of physical supply and distribution which each firm or government organization incurs. Second is the cost of physical distribution to the economy as a whole. Cost figures, although fragmentary, are rapidly appearing for the former. It is with the latter that this paper deals.

What is a valid measure of physical distribution cost in the economy? What is the current magnitude of costs of physical distribution? What is the estimated trend of these costs between the years 1950 and 1960? An attempt will be made here to provide tentative answers to these three questions. Beyond answering the questions, this paper is intended to: (1) suggest the magnitude of inaccuracies in past estimates of transportation cost to the economy, (2) provide a comparison of costs of physical distribution with estimated costs of the two other major activities in the economy, production and promotion, and (3) further thought to elaborate and improve upon assumptions, methods, and information inputs used in this analysis.

* Reprinted by permission from *Transportation Research Form*, 1962.
† Harvard University.

Measurement

The statement is often made that transportation and/or physical distribution are gaining current attention because their costs are rising rapidly. In dollar terms, we know this is true. But these figures are meaningless unless related to a measurement of cost increases in, or incomes derived from, all types of economic activity.

The measurement employed in this analysis attempts to determine, on a year-by-year basis, imputed revenue derived from physical distribution activities as a proportion of gross national product. A relationship such as this can provide one measure of the relative costs of our physical distribution system and of trends in this measure. For purposes of measurement and discussion, physical distribution costs in the economy have been broken into three major categories, transportation, inventory carrying, and non-carrier management costs.

Transportation Costs

Misleading statistics have been used to present the importance of transportation activities in the economy. This has been caused partially by the dearth of information available, partially by a lack of definition of the scope of transportation activities.

For example, the Interstate Commerce Commission is able to compile revenue reports only for those types of freight carriers under its jurisdiction, i.e., motor common carriers and contract carriers of property, pipelines, inland and inter-coastal water carriers, freight forwarders, electric railways, Railway Express, railroads, and private rail car fleets. This excludes almost all consideration of private or exempt transportation. Data that are available, for example, show that private and exempt for-hire motor carriers performed nearly two-thirds of the total intercity ton-miles of transportation by highway in 1960.[1] In addition to private and exempt for-hire intercity operations, there is a great deal of transportation volume carried out by manufacturing, wholesaling, retailing, and service establishments for local delivery of materials. The income-producing activities of these transporters is measured nowhere by federal agencies. Therefore, Interstate Commerce Commission statistics greatly understate revenues received for transportation services.

Previous Estimates. The Department of Commerce, Office of Business Economics, has published a breakdown of our national income by industrial origin over a long period of years. This type of data is obtained by the "establishment approach."[2] As such, it should include a greater number of transportation firms in its figures than I.C.C. reports, because theoretically it surveys exempt for-hire carriers and classifies their statistics as highway freight under the transportation category in the break-down of national income. But again, activities of transportation, particularly trucking, which are carried on by manufacturers, wholesalers, retailers, or service firms are classified under the major activity in which the firm engages, not transportation. In addition to important omissions resulting from this type of information presentation, statistics relating to the proportion of national income originating in transportation contain a negative bias. They place undue emphasis on revenues of the mode for which the most complete statistics are collected, rail transportation. The magnitude of the bias is indicated

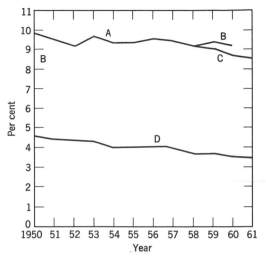

KEY:

A = Trend in freight movement costs as a proportion of G.N.P., estimate of this study.
B = Employment in transportation as a percentage of total employment, presented in Harold Barger, DISTRIBUTION'S PLACE IN THE AMERICAN ECONOMY SINCE 1869 (Princeton, N.J.: Princeton University Press, 1955).
C = Trend in freight transportation, loading and unloading, and traffic management costs as a proportion of G.N.P., estimated by the Transportation Association of America.
D = Trend in income derived from freight transportation as a proportion of national income, reported in SURVEY OF CURRENT BUSINESS, National Income Number, Department of Commerce, Office of Business Economics, for appropriate years.

FIG. 1. Various measures of the relative importance of movement (transportation) activities in the economy.

by the relative rate of decline of the trend lines in Figure 1.

Two major studies investigating the magnitude and the trend of importance of all distribution costs in our economy adapted figures compiled by the U.S. Bureau of the Census for size, in numbers, of employment groups engaged in distribution, among other activities.[3] The Twentieth Century Fund study concluded that transportation and public utilities accounted for

[1] Estimated by the American Trucking Associations, Inc., Research Department, American Trucking Trends, 1961 Edition (Washington, D. C.: American Trucking Association, Inc., 1961), pp. 8–9. This figure apparently has been disputed recently by a report on private and unregulated transportation, prepared by Walter Y. Oi and Arthur Hunter of the Transportation Center at Northwestern University, the preliminary findings of which indicated that private intercity ton-miles by highway approximated only 32% of the total in 1961, as reported in "Private Trucking at 32% of Total." *New York Times*, October 28, 1962, p. F11.

[2] Data obtained by the "establishment approach" is represented by surveys of the Bureau of Labor Statistics and the Agricultural Marketing Service. These data are based on reports from employers. This is different from the "population approach" represented by the Census of Population and the Population Surveys of the Bureau of the Census.

[3] Does Distribution Cost Too Much? (New York: *The Twentieth Century Fund*, 1939), p. 10, and Harold Barger, Distribution's Place in the American Economy Since 1869 (Princeton, N. J.: Princeton University Press, 1955), pp. 4–6.

*Exhibit 1. Method for Estimating
Employment in Freight Transportation
by Highway, 1950*

This method consists of the construction of a table of the number of people engaged in freight transportation activities in the United States based on the detailed occupations of people included in the Decennial Census of Population for 1950.

approximately 7.9% of the total employed labor force in 1930. Barger's study used a figure of 8.5% for the same measure in 1950, compared with 9.3% in 1930. However, a comparison of transportation labor to the total labor force probably understates the importance of transportation in terms of national activity, as measured by income. Income earned by the labor, capital, rent, management, and government factors in transportation, expressed as revenue per employee, is likely to result in an average figure greater than that for most industries. Large amounts of capital investment in equipment, per man, in freight transportation plus the large amount of transportation activity carried out by farmers and other persons not employed wholly in transportation make this likely.

The most complete and accurate estimates of transportation, materials handling, and traffic management costs currently available are those prepared for recent years by the Transportation Association of America.[4] The T.A.A. approach is based primarily on the expenditure or cost method of estimating transportation costs in relation to gross national product. This method involves the construction of an estimate by adding the proportion of freight transportation costs in personal consumption expenditures and government purchases of goods and services. It places primary emphasis on the cost of obtaining service, particularly in its estimates of intercity and local truck, international water, inland waterways, and Great Lakes transportation activity falling outside the economic regulation of the I.C.C.

The T.A.A. methods of estimate eliminate the

negative bias present in most other comparative statistics of transportation costs. They allow a most detailed break-down of costs of transportation provided by types of carriers. As such, they were used both as a check on certain estimates derived by the methods used in this study and as an actual model for extending other estimates backward in time.[5]

Estimates of This Study. An alternate estimate of the costs of rail and highway freight movement in the economy, for purposes of this study, was constructed with primary emphasis on the value added, or input, approach. Basically, this relies upon an estimate of the sum of employment by mode multiplied by an imputed revenue per employee for each mode.

To illustrate the method employed, the detailed occupational information generated by the Decennial Census of Population provided the basis for estimating actual employment in several of the modes of transportation. A comparison of total employment to employment statistics reported by regulated[6] carriers indicated the importance of non-regulated transportation by each mode. Where this was significant, particularly in highway transportation, factors were developed to expand annually reported statistics to account for revenues generated by persons engaged in both regulated and non-regulated transportation. Assumptions inherent in the method are presented in Exhibit 1.

Estimates of movement costs, as a proportion of gross national product[7] are shown for the years 1950 through 1960 in Figure 1.

It is important to note the contrast between

[4] This information is prepared in the form of a packet of information sheets entitled "Transportation Facts and Trends," published by the Transportation Association of America, 1710 H Street, N. W., Washington, D. C.

[5] The writer is indebted to Mr. Frank A. Smith, Director of Research, Transportation Association of America, for making available the methods by which T.A.A. estimates were derived.

[6] The terms, "regulated and non-regulated" will be used to indicate those carriers or transportation activities falling within and without, respectively, the economic regulation of the I.C.C.

[7] Gross national product is defined by the Department of Commerce, Bureau of the Census as "the total national output of goods and services at market price. It measures this output in terms of the expenditures by which the goods and services are acquired. The expenditures comprise the purchases of goods and services by consumers and government, gross private domestic investment, and net exports of goods and services." Source: *Statistical Abstract of the United States, 1962* (Washington, D. C.: U. S. Department of Commerce, 1962), p. 310.

estimates of movement costs by the Department of Commerce, Office of Business Economics, the T.A.A., and this study. Reasons for the divergence of the trend lines for the former as opposed to the latter two have been suggested. Differences between the latter two largely appear to arise from the assessment of non-regulated highway transportation. The T.A.A. approach estimates a cost per ton-mile for non-regulated intercity highway transport about 1c below that for regulated transportation. Costs for local truck transportation are derived on a vehicle mile basis. It is not entirely clear whether these costs include elements for management expense and contributions to profit or whether they resemble more closely out-of-pocket operating costs. If the latter, much of the difference between T.A.A. and current estimates would be accounted for.

Inventory Carrying Costs

Inventory carrying costs as a proportion of average value of inventory on hand have been estimated generally at 25%.[8] There is some argument over how this figure should be compartmentalized. One oft-quoted allocation has been made as follows:[9] storage facilities, .25%; insurance, .25%; taxes, .50%; transportation, .50%; handling and distribution, 2.50%; depreciation, 5.00%; interest, 6.00%; obsolescence, 10.00%; for a total of 25.00%.

In order to avoid double counting of expenses between transportation and inventory carrying costs, transportation (if assumed to be expended for transfer movements between storage points) and handling and distribution (to avoid inclusion of local transportation and warehouse shipping and receiving) were excluded from the estimates. These exclusions, ½% for transportation and 2½% for handling and distribution, reduced estimated inventory carrying costs to 22% of the average value of inventory on hand in the United States over the period of a given year.

[8] For the results of one informal study which indicates values in use ranging from 12% to 35%, see John B. Holbrook, "A Simple Tabular Method for Determining Economic Order Quantities," in *Managing the Materials Function, AMA Management Report No. 35* (New York: American Management Association 1959), p. 66.

[9] See L. P. Alford and John R. Bangs, *Production Handbook* (New York: The Ronald Press Company, 1955), pp. 396–397.

Information regarding macroeconomic inventory levels is compiled on a monthly and annual basis by the Departments of Agriculture and Commerce. Annual average inventory levels, adapted from year-end levels reported by these agencies. In addition to inventories of the Commodity Credit Corporation (farm products), retailers, wholesalers, and manufacturers, farmers' inventories of stored crops and livestock were included in this figure.

The adjusted cost of carrying inventory as a proportion of its average value, 22% was applied to annual average inventory values. The result, an annual national cost of carrying inventory as a proportion of gross national product, is shown in Figure 2.

Non-Carrier Management Costs

Amounts paid for talent to manage the considerable expenses of transportation and inventory holding in the economy are made difficult to assess by the problem of identifying the wide variety of functional executives who actually manage these activities. As a result, what is likely to be a very conservative estimate was used for this study. It included the amount of salaries paid to estimated numbers of traffic managers and shipping and receiving clerks over the period of time under consideration.

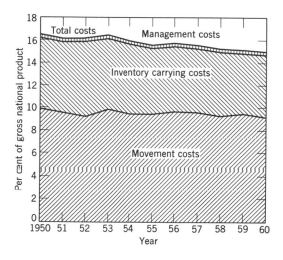

FIG. 2. Trends in inventory carrying costs for retailers, wholesalers, manufacturers, and agricultural enterprises, as a percentage of gross national product.

Limitations

Certain limitations are inherent in the methods used in this study. They include major assumptions employed in estimates for highway freight and international water freight transportation, and omissions in estimates for: (1) transportation by wire, (2) freight carried in private automobiles, (3) certain government expenditures for transportation services and facilities, and (4) non-carrier management costs.

Highway Freight Transportation

Important factors used to estimate employment in transportation activities not falling under the economic regulation of the I.C.C. were developed from a measurement of one time period, that of the 1950 Census of Population. A check on the validity of the factors can be made only when benchmark data in the form of detailed occupation statistics from the 1960 Census of Population become available in the spring of 1963.

The less data available, the greater the number of assumptions required for estimates. And although assumptions used in the computations for this study are indicated in the exhibits, it is important to mention those that are likely to have had the greatest effect on the outcome of the estimates. Highway freight transportation is by far the most important element in value added by transportation. These assumptions are three in number:

1. That the "operating personnel—clerical personnel" ratio does not vary significantly between different modes of transportation, and between regulated and non-regulated transportation and materials handling operations.

2. That "revenue per employed person" is approximately 11% less for trucking performed regulated vs. non-regulated carriers.

3. That employment levels and revenues per employed person in private and exempt highway freight transportation increased in direct proportion to those of Class I and II common and contract carriers between 1950 and 1960.

The first assumptions, if all facts were known, is likely to be valid. The lack of identification of administrative costs associated with private and exempt highway operations is common knowledge. And even the absence of billing and payments in these legal forms of transportation is offset in large measure by increased problems of accounting for costs of operation.

Revenue per person in common and contract highway transportation is a return not only on labor, but on the other factors of production as well (rent, capital, management, and government). Conflicting factors are present in the per capita revenue comparison of regulated and non-regulated highway operations. On the one hand, firms utilizing private equipment in over-the-road operations probably obtain a high imputed per capita revenue (including an increment for profit) compared to common and contract carriage. This is the result of more intensive utilization of manpower and equipment. On the other hand, a great portion of non-regulated transportation activities is carried out on a local basis with equipment of smaller capacity and revenue-generating power. It stands to reason that revenue per capita in these types of operations is somewhat below that of common and contract carriers. A consideration of these conflicting factors, and of available statistics, resulted in the estimated relationship shown in the second assumption above.

The third major assumption is based primarily on "economic common sense." If the revenue generated per person in non-regulated trucking declined in proportion to that for regulated trucking, one would expect non-regulated trucking to become less attractive, assuming a constant relationship between wages paid to labor in both segments. We know, at least in intercity motor truck movement, that the proportion of goods moving in non-regulated equipment has varied little in the post-war years.[10] This has been substantiated by the announcement of the preliminary findings of a recent major study of private and unregulated transportation.[11]

[10] The actual range in the proportion of volume of intercity movements carried by non-regulated motor carriers was a low of 61.6% in 1951 to a high of 67.1% in 1958. The figure for 1960 was estimated to be 64.9%, based on figures published in *American Trucking Trends,* 1961 (Washington, D. C.: American Trucking Association, Inc., 1961), pp. 8–9.

[11] One preliminary finding of the study conducted by the Transportation Center at Northwestern University indicated that the growth rates of regulated and non-regulated highway transportation have been "roughly comparable" during the period 1939–1959, as reported in "Private Trucking at 32% of Total," *New York Times,* October 28, 1962, p. F11.

International Water Freight Transportation

In estimating the revenues from freight transportation in international trade, some arbitrary rule had to be followed to avoid a double counting of revenues in relation to gross national product. The latter includes only the net surplus of export values over import values. In this case, the total cost of moving exports by water was used to the exclusion of any consideration of import costs. One might argue that costs of moving imports used as raw materials and components of products subsequently produced in the United States were rightly a component of movement costs. But more logically they are counted by the vendor country as transportation costs on its products.

Possible Omissions

Movement of electrical energy by wire, to the extent that it competes with the transportation of commodities such as coal by other modes, well might have been included in estimates of value added by transportation. Traditionally, such estimates have been excluded from consideration. In addition, problems of appraising value added by the transmission of electrical energy from the point of manufacture to consumption prevented any rational basis for including it.

It was impossible to assess the extent, in terms of cost or "displaced" revenue, to which the private automobile was used as a freight-carrying device. The total volume, even though measured in minute individual "shipments," may have been of considerable size, confined primarily to the transportation of non-durable goods from retail outlets to the home. Expense per unit volume of this type of transportation activity was likely very high.

Government expenditures for freight transportation, at first glance, might appear to be excluded from the above estimates. Purchases of services from other carriers, however, were appraised. And the contributions of carriers, in the form of taxes, for the use of physical facilities were also included in the estimates. Where government expenditures exceeded allocated user charges, of course, omissions developed. In addition, no consideration was given the bill of physical distribution costs arising from transportation and inventory management activities carried on by the government itself.

Costs of maintaining non-carrier organizations to manage physical distribution activities were only partially accounted for by the assessment of salaries paid to management and supervisory personnel. However, the "revenue per employee" estimates for transportation activities carried on outside the economic regulation of the I.C.C. included administrative costs of operating private equipment. In spite of these inclusions, administrative costs probably were not accounted for totally.

The net effect of assumptions and omissions on the total estimate is likely to have been small in quantity, with the possible exception of freight movement carried out by ultimate consumers. There is little reason to believe that costs trend would have been greatly different had some attempt been made to include one or more of the omitted categories. In total, they introduced a conservative element into the estimates.

Conclusions

Annual estimates of gross national product contributed by physical distribution activities for 1950 through 1960 are shown in Figure 3.

Trends

The information shown in Figure 3 indicates that, contrary to popular belief, transportation as well as inventory carrying costs have decreased in proportion to gross national product. The former has declined from 9.8% of the total product in 1950 to 9.2% in 1960. While not

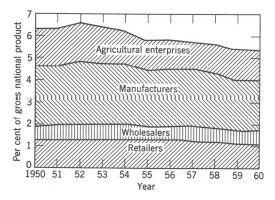

FIG. 3. Trends in estimated movement, inventory carrying, and physical distribution management costs as a percentage of gross national product.

dramatic in percentage comparisons, the magnitude of this decline can be appreciated by the fact that it represents a relative cut of over $3 billion in the nation's annual freight transportation bill between 1950 and 1960. When added to reductions in the relative annual costs of carrying inventory between the same two years, the resulting annual deduction exceeds $7½ billion. In total, physical distribution accounted for an estimated 16.4% of gross national product in 1950 as opposed to 14.9% in 1960. What are possible explanations for this trend?

Interpretation

Available evidence indicates that transportation rates may not have risen quite as rapidly as other costs of doing business. Average revenues per ton-mile of all carriers reporting to the Interstate Commerce Commission rose less than 13% between 1950 and 1960.[12] In comparison, the wholesale price index rose 19%, the cost of living index, 23% during these same eleven years.[13]

Carrier and non-carrier managements have been responsible for improved methods and new concepts in freight transportation. However, estimates arrived at in this study should not be interpreted necessarily as an indication of trends only in the efficiency of the nation's physical distribution system. Long-run shifts in the development and size of market areas and location of industries in relation to raw material sources and markets could affect physical distribution cost trends as much as internal technological and managerial changes in the physical distribution system itself. Changes in the nature of commodities shipped, particularly finished goods, also serve to mitigate any absolute indications of increased efficiency for the system.

A possible counter-trend from the use of systems of physical distribution utilizing more costly methods of transportation, even though glamorous to talk about, has not been large enough to produce a significant influence on total figures.

Both transportation and inventory carrying

cost trends have probably benefitted from the development of greater "mass" in the major markets of this country. This has likely led to a more concentrated use of available facilities for the movement of goods. Expanded sales volume generally fosters an increased turnover of inventory in the individual firm. The same principle may apply to a limited extent in the economy, although no significant trends are apparent in the inventory turnover ratios of any one segment of the nation's economy.

Increases in speed and dependability of all modes of transportation, in response to the demand for them, undoubtedly have contributed to a general decline in average inventories on hand in relation to sales. Attempts to reduce inventories often require more rapid and dependable intercity or local transportation if customer service is to be maintained. The most significant improvement in speed and dependability probably has been made by the rail and highway carriers which account for such a large proportion of transportation activity.

In addition, of course, total inventory levels are affected by such other factors as the general price outlook and the stage of the economic cycle, among others. These obscure somewhat the effects of developments in physical distribution upon inventory levels.

Comparison With Other Costs

Estimates have been made of the relative importance of production (or formation) and distribution (promotion and physical distribution) costs in the economy.[14] A combination of these estimates with those developed in this paper indicates the relative importance of formation, promotion, and physical distribution activities in the economy, to the extent that they can be identified. The relationship is shown in Table 1.

Although physical distribution ranks third in costs among the core business activities in the United States, its importance is much greater than that with which it has been regarded by many businessmen and scholars in the past.

---

[12] Based on information reported in the *Annual Report, Interstate Commerce Commission,* for appropriate years.

[13] Department of Labor statistics, reported in "Economic Indicators," prepared for the Joint Economic Committee by the Council of Economic Advisers, for appropriate years.

[14] One estimate of distribution costs in 1939 placed the proportion at 59% (Does Distribution Cost Too Much? pp. 117–119). Another for 1948 placed the proportion at 42% but included merchandising arctivities of producers or distributors of unfinished goods with production, and not with distribution (Distribution's Place in the American Economy Since 1869, p. 63).

Table 1. Estimate of the Relative Contribution of Major Activities to Gross National Product of The United States Economy

Activity	Per Cent of G.N.P.
Formation (Production)[a]	45%
Promotion[b]	40
Physical Distribution[c]	15

[a] Including farm production, all value added to natural resources by mining, fishing, and petroleum development, and value added to raw materials by manufacturing.

[b] Including all sales promotion such as sales, advertising, merchandising and marketing research conducted by producers, processors, manufacturers, service institutions, wholesalers, and retailers.

[c] Including all transportation, storage, materials handling, and inventory holding conducted by producers, processors, manufacturers, service institutions, wholesalers and retailers.

In summary, physical distribution cost components can no more be considered separately in our national economy than in an individual firm. If one is reduced at the expense of others, no net improvement results. Where a reduction in one component results also in a net reduction in others, savings are compounded. While results of this study indicate a rather marked reduction in national costs of physical distribution relative to gross national product, further strides undoubtedly can be taken by carrier and non-carrier management to contribute to an extension of the current trend.

Sources

Sources of information on which the estimates were based are listed below. For the sake of simplicity in the explanation of methods, each source will be referred to in the text by encasing the appropriate number on the list below in brackets immediately succeeding the description of procedures which used information from one of these sources:

1. "Detailed Occupation of Employed Persons by Sex; 1950," *Statistical Abstract of the United States*, 1959, 80th Annual Edition, U.S. Department of Commerce, Bureau of the Census (Washington, D.C.: U.S. Government Printing Office, 1959), pp. 220–223.

2. *Yearbook of Railroad Information*, 1951 Edition, (Washington: Eastern Railroad President's Conference, 1958), pp. 44 and 62.

3. "Average Employees Per Carrier, 1944–1957," *American Trucking Trends*, 1959 Edition (Washington, D.C.: American Trucking Associations, Inc., 1959), p. 19.

Method

From employment statistics presented in (1), a compilation of all persons employed in jobs associated with freight transportation and materials handling by rail, water and highway was made, and is shown in Table 2. The compilation of railroad, water, and air employment (included in Table 3) was made to provide a statistical tie between known and unknown statistics for highway freight transportation. Not all job categories could be attributed immediately to one form of transportation. These had to be allocated in later steps.

Several job groupings were completely excluded from consideration in this procedure because of the impossibility of estimating accurately that portion of the total number employed working in transportation activities. These job classifications included all types of engineers, lawyers, machinists, cranemen, derrickmen and hoistmen, and boilermakers. Exclusion of these job classifications contributed to the conservative nature of the estimate.

An attempt was made to allocate those job types not associated with one mode of transportation among the three modes under consideration, rail, highway and water. Two types of allocations were considered: (1) allocation of non-classifiable transportation employment among modes, and (2) allocation of non-classifiable general employment, such as secretarial, to the modal categories.

Allocation of Non-Classifiable Transportation Employment Among Modes

Transportation jobs of a type difficult to classify were assigned to modes on the basis of the number of classifiable personnel in each mode. This somewhat arbitrary assignment was made on a prorata basis, using a four-step procedure, based upon differences in the nature of the job classifications.

First 99,000 salesmen were assigned to rail, highway and water carriers on the basis of the

Table 2.   *U. S. Employment in Jobs Associated with Freight Transportation by Rail, Water, and Highway, 1950*

Job Category	Numbers Employed (to nearest hundred)	
Employment Classifiable by Mode		
RAIL		
Express messengers and railway mail clerks	18,700	
Foremen (n.e.c.)—railroads and railway express service	53,900	
Inspectors (n.e.c.)—railroads	36,800	
Locomotive engineers	72,800	
Locomotive firemen	54,100	
Mechanics, railroad and car shop	47,500	
Brakemen	78,400	
Switchmen, railroad	61,300	
Operatives, railroads and railway express service	90,900	
Laborers, railroads	262,900	
Motormen, mine, factory	23,800	
Sub-Total	801,100	
WATER		
Officers, ship	38,100	
Boatmen	8,100	
Sailors	40,300	
Longshoremen	62,700	
Sub-Total	149,200	
HIGHWAY		
Transportation managers, officials and proprietors (n.e.c.)—self-employed	51,300	
Dispatchers	30,800	
Deliverymen and routemen	238,600	
Motor vehicle maintenance	162,600	
Truck and tractor drivers	1,329,200	
Sub-Total	1,812,500	
Total, All Modes		2,762,800
Non-Classifiable Transportation; Employment to be Allocated to Rail, Highway, and Water		
Transportation managers, officials and proprietors (n.e.c.)—salaried	95,800	
Salesmen (other than manufacturing, wholesale trade, retail trade, and other special classifications)	99,000	
Total		184,800
Non-Classifiable Transportation; Employment to be Allocated to Highway and Water		
Foremen, transportation, except railroad	19,800	
Inspectors, transportation, except railroad	12,400	
Operatives, transportation, except railroad	34,300	
Laborers, transportation, except railroad	104,300	
Total		170,800

Table 2. U. S. Employment in Jobs Associated with Freight Transportation by Rail, Water, and Highway, 1950 (continued)

Job Category	Numbers Employed (to nearest hundred)
Non-Classifiable General Employment	
Accountants and auditors	376,500
Personnel and labor relations workers	52,100
Purchasing agents or buyers	63,000
Bookkeepers	721,000
Office machine operators	142,100
Stenographers, typists, and secretaries	1,589,500
Other clerical (n.e.c.)	2,929,700
Total	5,875,900

existing numbers of classifiable employment, as reported by the Eastern Railroad President's Conference for rail, (2), by the American Trucking Association for Class I common carriers,[15] (2), and as estimated in this paper for water. On this basis, 68,000 salesmen were assigned to

[15] Nearly all highway carrier salesmen are believed to be employed by Class I common carriers. Therefore, the assignment of sales personnel excluded highway statistics for private and local transportation.

rail transportation, 19,000 to highway common carriage, and 12,000 to water carriers.

Next, 95,800 managers were allocated to rail, highway, and water on the basis of total employment figures built in this discussion. These figures included all types of transportation, including air and non-rail passenger transportation, which is compiled from Bureau of Census statistics (1) and shown in Table 2.

Third, all non-classifiable transportation employment to be allocated highway, water, air and non-rail passenger transportation was ap-

Table 3. Results of Calculations, Allocation of Transportation Employment, 1950

Mode of Transport		1st Allocation	2nd Allocation	3rd Allocation	4th Allocation	Total Employment
Rail						
Passenger	88,000					
All other	801,100					
Total	889,100	68,000	25,800		113,300	1,096,200
Highways and private trans.	1,812,500	19,000	49,400	120,400	230,600	2,231,900
Water	149,200	12,000	4,300	10,600	20,700	196,800
Air and non-rail pass.[a]	605,900		16,300	39,800	76,400	738,400
Total	3,456,700	99,000	95,800	170,800	441,000	4,263,300

[a] This figure was compiled from the following job classifications: pilots, 13,700; baggagemen, non-rail, 3,900; ticket agents, non-rail, 40,000; airplane mechanics, 70,700; bus drivers, 155,000; conductors, local transportation, 11,300; motormen, street railway, 26,500; and taxi drivers, 202,100. The figure also includes an allocation of 15,400 for non-classifiable highway transportation for buses and taxis (1).

portioned on a prorata basis to these three groups.

Allocation of Non-Classifiable General Employment Among Modes

Finally, all non-classifiable general employment was apportioned to the four major groups under consideration. To do this, the total clerical employment, 5,873,900 was subtracted from the national total of non-farm employment, 44,738,000. The difference, 38,864,000, when divided into non-clerical transportation employment, 3,822,-300, provided a factor of .0985 which, when multiplied by the total of applicable clerical employment, yielded a figure of 441,000 for transportation clerical employment. This was then allocated on a prorata basis to the four major classifications of transportation employment. The results of the calculations in these steps are shown in Table 2.

3. *Physical Distribution, Military Logistics, and Marketing Management**

Among business costs perhaps the most neglected, until recently, has been that of physical distribution. The irony of this neglect is suggested by Table 1, which shows estimated physical distribution cost for the American economy in 1963.

Although man created distribution problems when he first developed crops in anticipation of future consumption, the birth of modern physical distribution management may be dated as recently as the start of World War II and the advent of computer technology. Pertinent research, initially designed to fulfill military logistical requirements, quickly interested businessmen. Linear programming in solving problems with simultaneous multiple variables, and subsequently a repertoire of largely quantitative methods of the "operations research" type, evolved.

* Reprinted by permission from *The University of Houston Business Review,* Winter, 1964/65.
† Michigan State University.

The development of model-building techniques especially concerned physical distribution management. Simulation permits a wide range of quantifiable considerations and operating circumstances involving production runs, inventories, transportation, etc. In effect, simulation provides the analytical techniques of an empirical science whereby optimum solutions are possible regardless of present operations.

However, budgetary constraints of military logisticians and of business administrators do not completely coincide. Whereas military budgets depend upon political appropriation, private-enterprise budgets are based upon markets and competition. Military budgets are implemented by sanctioned authority; private enterprise budgets are founded upon sales revenue. Military logisticians may enjoy *ad hoc* budgetary increases; a businessman's budget is largely restricted by his satisfaction of customer requirements. Briefly stated, the success of military logistics is founded upon authoritarianism;

Table 1. *Estimated Cost of Physical Distribution—1963*[a]

Cost Item	Total Dollars Billions of Dollars	Estimated Physical Distribution Cost	
		Per Cent	Billions of Dollars
1. Transportation (freight only)	45	100	45
2. Packaging	20	50	10
3. Inventory	25	50	12.5
4. Handling	NA	—	—
5. Communications and Order Processing	NA	—	—
TOTALS			67.5

[a] Author's estimates.

the success of physical distribution in private enterprise depends upon market competition and customer good will.

Marketing Management and Physical Distribution

The marketing concept, a scientific expression of "the consumer is king," rose concurrently with modern computer technology, military logistics, and physical distribution management. Historically, so long as scarcity ruled the market, producers had been certain of satisfactory sales. But since the advent of a buyer's market, business that is primarily production-oriented has failed to maintain its relative position. Mainly because of the shift from an economy of relative scarcity to one of abundance, and because of an apparent absence of consumer loyalty, major emphasis in business concepts has moved from production to marketing.

The "four *p*'s" of marketing—*p*roduct, *p*rice, *p*romotion, and *p*hysical distribution—identify the major foundations of effective marketing practice. Application of the four *p*'s within the marketing concept implies tailoring and balancing to maximize impact in the market.

Product

Product design, founded upon customer satisfaction, leads to a widening of product lines through differentiation of consumer needs and wants. The Chevrolet Division of General Motors, for instance, may produce in one model year as many as 2,000,000 unique cars. The relationship of physical distribution to product design is associated with the impact of product differentiation on total distribution cost; consequently, an extensive widening of the line will increase distribution cost through excessive inventory requirements. Indeed a doubling of product line may more than double the inventory necessary to serve market demand. Historically, the era of "any color you want so long as it's black" reduced not only production costs but also distribution expense. In terms of product design, physical distribution principles can lead to achieving product diversity while maintaining inventories within manageable limits.

For example, magic numbers in the food business include 24 or 48 units of a product in a single-case lot. But the average retail grocery store moves 90 per cent of all items at the rate of one case or less per week. Thus the selection of case size influences product turnover. Combining several products in a single case, the quantities of which are adjusted to consumer-demand patterns, may substantially increase inventory turnover. Although not extremely common today, such practices apparently exist and are increasing.

Price

Pricing in today's market revolves around the continuing cost-price squeeze. And, factually, whereas virtually every important economic ratio shows an increasing trend, the level of business profit in the post-war period has remained in splendid and virtually isolated stagnation. Following the 1948 postwar adjustments, after-tax profits of American business were about twenty billion dollars. Having hovered around that level since then, they stood in 1963 at 28 billion dollars. While prices increased somewhat, profit levels apparently could not be generally improved to keep pace with other economic sectors by means of across-the-board price increases.

Marketing management provides the framework within which a more sophisticated approach to selective pricing can improve profit positions and market shares. The extension of the price line to complement product line extensions is apparent in the automobile industry. In the past pricing tended toward few classes in this industry. Today, however, many price options are available to meet market needs. Nowhere is the pressure toward more astute pricing more clearly evident than in the auto industry's response to foreign small-car competition.

Physical distribution relates to pricing on the cost side of the market equation. Through distribution cost reductions, greater variations in pricing are possible. Again in the auto industry, the tri-level car in the United States has permitted pricing adjustments through cost savings that measure in the hundreds of millions of dollars. If the average transport costs of a car were $800 before the tri-level car, and industry reports of 50 per cent reductions on transport cost are reasonably correct, then for Chevrolet alone these savings could be about $300,000,000. That large a saving permits quite substantial pricing variations without affecting profit adversely.

Promotion

As in the other three *p*'s, the marketing concept indicates use of precise tools to enhance maximum impact on tailored markets. In the din of advertising and promotion today, impact depends on selection and identification of markets, which then have specialized promotion and advertising programs aimed at them.

Physical distribution relates to timely promotion. In a national soap advertising campaign, sales may increase by 40 per cent above normal. Stocks must be strategically located in order to ensure product availability at the optimum moment during the campaign. Production runs must be carefully fitted to ensure logistical support to advertising expenditures.

Alternatively, promotion may be carefully timed in a sequence of markets. The advantage in this approach is its effect on leveling production runs with attendant economies. Again, careful scheduling of inventory locations and patterns must precede implementation of promotional plans.

Physical Distribution

The fourth and most recently introduced of the four *p*'s, physical distribution, provides the necessary support of markets by assuring the right quantity of goods placed at the right point at the right time. Thus, while marketing has its four *p*'s, physical distribution has its three *r*'s.

The two constraints of physical distribution are cost and service. Each of the three *r*'s contains these two elements. Thus, in terms of right quantity, service considerations dictate large supplies, but cost requires small quantities in the interest of reduced inventory costs. Right-point considerations, in terms of service, require numerous stock points located adjacent to customers. But cost constraints dictate reducing the number of points in the interest of reduced warehousing costs. Right time requires scheduling accomplished, for example, through the use of air freight. But transport costs dictate use of slower modes of transportation, such as rail and motor carrier.

Proper application of physical distribution principles, therefore, requires a constant balance between the needs of revenue-producing policies, as reflected in customer service requirements, and cost-reducing aspects which adversely affect service. In the interest of economic opportunities based on cost criteria, physical distribution points to larger shipment sizes, smaller inventory levels, and fewer stocking points. Service considerations point to smaller shipment sizes to fit customer orders, larger inventory levels, and many warehousing points.

Evidently the careful balancing of these diverse considerations depends on the particular marketing plan followed by a specific firm in a designated industry. Often two firms in the same industry follow what appear to be diametrically opposed physical distribution programs. While these differences may be partly explained by differences in managerial skills, it seems that the more dominant forces are marketing plans of the firms involved.

Market Analysis

In order to develop a sound physical distribution system, market analyses must be made. Of special interst to the physical distribution analyst are the geographic and product dimensions of the market. Present methods of reporting data satisfy the needs of political units outside the firm or management groups that have no special interest in a sophisticated geographic reporting system.

Accounting largely is centered in the production process and has few geographic considerations built into it. Selling, while broken down into territories, almost exclusively relates territorial considerations to sales balance by territories and salesmen. Production is the clearest nongeographically-oriented group.

Of additional interest to the physical distribution specialist is the measure of activity by product. It seems a natural law that a small percentage of a population accounts for a majority of a group by some selected criterion. The best known example of this phenomenon is that a relatively small percentage of the population accounts for a surprisingly large percentage of income produced. A small percentage of all the states accounts for a relatively large percentage of the population, and so on. The illustrations of this phenomenon apparently are endless.

Precisely the same phenomenon applies to economic activity by products. A rank array of sales volume by items universally shows that a small percentage of the items available for sales accounts for a large percentage of the revenues. This fact enables the physical distribution analyst to isolate much of his problem. For example, such a study may show that 20 per cent of the items account for 80 per cent of the sales volume. In that case, focusing attention on these items generally yields much higher rewards than indiscriminately planning an across-the-board attack. Invariably a firm which approaches its physical distribution problems from this perspective finds immediate and substantial rewards.

In the same way markets may also be arranged by size. This sorting provides useful information relative to such important problems as retail-store and distribution-center location.

Transportation

Transportation influences physical distribution decisions by its impact on transit stocks, transport costs, handling expense, and packaging cost.

Reduction in transit stocks via shorter transit periods may lead to rather surprising cost economy. For example, if average daily transit stocks are $1,000,000 and average transit time is ten days, then average transit inventories are $10,000,000. When one reduces transit time to five days via faster transportation, average transit stocks are only $5,000,000. This becomes a capital recovery item of $5,000,000 initially and also a permanent reduction in operating expense due to reduced inventory levels.

The major force which influences a decision in favor of shortened transit periods is value of the product. Generally the higher the unit value, the higher the inventory value and the greater its carrying cost.

Since reduced transit times are associated with higher transportation costs, the trade-offs involve changes in inventory levels against changes in transport expense. The value-of-service concept in transport pricing, therefore, is closely related to the effect of transit on inventory costs. Consequently much finer adjustments of transport rate determination are possible. Apparently this implies that for very low-valued products, transport costs dominate distribution decisions, whereas for very high-valued commodities, inventory considerations predominate.

The stages and incidental delays of handling affect a product's ultimate cost. Water transportation delay costs at terminal point may reach 50 per cent of the total transportation bill. Concerning motor carriers, the best estimate shows about 25 per cent of transport costs embedded in terminal-type operations. Recent studies have shown that reductions in handling cost and terminal expense affect demand for a specific form of transportation much more than does the actual rate.

A few recent examples demonstrate the point. Before the all-door boxcar was introduced, virtually no lumber moved by rail in the South. The main reason was that side-loading of boxcars virtually required loading by one stick at a time. Motor carriers, since they could be end-loaded, economized the handling expense of lumber. In fact, for this reason alone, rail rates had to show a 75 per cent advantage over motor carriers just to break even on shippers' total cost. Since lumber rates already rested at depressed levels, such rate reductions were impossible.

With the introduction of the all-door boxcar, handling costs dropped for rail shipments to such a degree that total costs favored rail over motor carrier. In fact, rail rates could have been raised somewhat with still an advantage to the shipper, based on his total cost. The important point here is that the transport purchase decision was made on the basis of handling-cost differential and not mere rate comparisons.

Packaging costs account for a surprising 20 billion dollars in the United States. While much packaging relates to marketing, advertising, and production, it also affects distribution decisions. Transport media have different characteristics which affect packaging requirements.

Just a few years ago it would have been safe to assert that protective packaging in transportation would show highest costs via rail shipment. This statement no longer contains its former validity. While rail shipments generally require more protective packaging than do other modes, as reflected by insurance rates, numerous exceptions must now be made. With the increase in damage-free cars, sliding sills, collapsible dunnage, etc., damage ratios for rail shipments have recently declined.

More sophisticated aspects of packaging relate to unitized loading. Loading 3,000 croquet sets by hand from a vehicle to a warehouse results in substantially greater costs than unloading the same quantity in 50 palletized and unitized loads. Package design engineers invest much time in package design to fit an integrated distribution and transportation system. As an example, choosing the least efficient package design in a palletized truck-rail movement can result in a 30 per cent loss of over-all efficiency in cube utilization. With transport rate structures increasingly moving to a cost-based system, such inefficiencies simply cannot be permitted.

Organization

Organization of the physical distribution function frequently requires a reassessment of present organizational charts. The diversity of elements affecting physical distribution creates difficulty in their proper managerial assignment.

Inventory control may fall to purchasing, manufacturing, or sales, each with equally valid grounds for such a structure. Transportation must be responsive to purchasing for inbound materials and sales for finished goods. Materials handling, like packaging, also crosses many functional lines.

In short, any attempt to consolidate all functions related to physical distribution requires such a broad definition of authority as to foreclose real potentials inherent in its application. The general organization pattern seems to follow the particular causal factors which demonstrate distribution requirements. This results in diverse organizational structures difficult to classify. In one company critical production processes require that distribution be subordinate to manufacturing. In another, high value of finished goods force a sales or marketing orientation. In a third, heavy transport expenses create a transportation orientation.

The organizational question clearly relates to the orientation of goals and objectives. Physical distribution management principles merely provide an outlook which permits more appropriate construction of corporate effort to reach predetermined goals. Of course, the most important of its influences requires orientation to the market place and, ultimately, the efficient satisfaction of consumer needs and wants.

Some Case Illustrations

The foregoing observations may be delineated by case illustrations in physical distribution.

UNIMARKET

One interesting application of physical distribution is the UNIMARKET concept of Raytheon. It is especially interesting since it seems to violate many traditional rules in business.

The UNIMARKET concept provides a conceptual framework for implementing a rather advanced marketing program. Essentially UNIMARKET, as the name implies, results in considering a market as a unified whole. A central control center provides the means of implementation.

Raytheon concentrated its marketing and distribution activities at this center, which was physically located in Massachusetts. All messages, communications, and orders filtered through the center, thus ensuring that all activities were known at one point. Inventories were consolidated by eliminating field warehouse stocks. Time responsiveness of the system to market demands was achieved by combining an electronic communications system to an airfreight distribution system.

Initial results showed a 50 per cent reduction in inventory investment and a quarter of a million dollars reduction in direct, fixed expense —by any measure an outstanding achievement.

Inventory reduction usually results from distribution studies. Such reduction profoundly affects the balance sheet and profit and loss statement. For example, when one reduces inventory from $10,000,000 to $5,000,000, as in the Raytheon case, the immediate balance sheet effect is a release of $5,000,000 of previously committed capital. This may be picked up as an addition to cash or as support of capital expenditure previously grounded for lack of funds.

Pillsbury Company

Pillsbury Company shows the forces necessitating a system of field distribution centers to gain distribution efficiencies. With several plants scattered about the country, each producing a relatively narrow band of the product line, some centralizing function must provide the appropriate product mix to customers.

The marketing institution which provides this function is the distribution center. Receipt of carload shipments of single products occurs at the distribution center. In turn, carload lots move to customers in a product mix suited to their needs. Thus, the distribution center provides the proper marketing mix by combining products from diverse sources of supply. At the same time it provides large-volume shipments for maximum transport economies.

The entire operation is geared to a unified communications system which permits ready identification of inventories at plant, distribution center, and in transit. The instantaneously available information permits a highly responsive system by production assignments to plants and customer order assignments to distribution centers.

A Photocopy-Paper Manufacturer

The critical element in photocopy paper is shelf life. Once sensitized, paper maintains its quality for a relatively short period. Thus, stock turnover and short production runs seem to be a natural condition of the market. Combining six grades of paper, eight different run-sizes, twenty basic shapes, and special order items results in 960 stock items with no shelf life exceeding 90 days. In addition, strict control over temperature and humidity must be maintained. All these correlations lead directly to a most complex distribution problem. All stock items are carried at numerous stocking points.

Careful evaluation may help identify those markets of sufficient volume to justify changes in stock practices, resulting in more favorable operating costs and improved customer service. In this case the six grades were sent to a stock point in only eight basic sizes, reducing stock items from 960 to only 48. Inventory levels and the discard rate of over-age stock substantially decreased.

A product-activity analysis showed that ten per cent of the items accounted for 60 per cent of the business in the specified market area. These items were produced for stock, increasing the total inventory items to 144 (48 + 96). This still meant that items carried in stock dropped by almost 80 per cent. Obviously inventory investment dropped substantially to serve the same sales level.

The remaining 90 per cent of the items were cut to order only, further reducing the amount of each master type and size.

Olin Mathieson

An interesting application of physical distribution involves geographic accounting. Those costs which are geographically variable are identified by type of account and degree of geographic variability. The most obvious of these is transportation cost.

In the case of Olin Mathieson, marketing and distribution costs began at the end of the production line. In effect, marketing and sales acted as purchasers of their own company products.

The usual assignment of costs to products was done. Account analysis for profitability was also undertaken. In addition, however, a separate analysis of geographically variable costs showed that market profitability depended on geographically variable costs. Traditional sales-account analysis without such adjustment could result in a completely erroneous picture of profit sources. While $10,000 might fall at the lower limit of profitability with standard accounting practices, introduction of geographic variability would show a range of, say, $500 to $50,000, depending on location.

The analysis caused a revamping of marketing effort to cultivate those accounts and areas which showed greatest potential. After the changes indicated by the analysis, sales increased by five per cent while profits rose by 95 per cent. These startling results of a pilot project caused considerable alteration of marketing thought and distribution practices among trade sources.

4. For Good or Ill, Users Influence Transportation*

E. GROSVENOR PLOWMAN†

ABSTRACT: A few decades ago, common-carrier enterprises dominated the American transportation scene; today, though vital and indispensable, they are losing their position of relative importance. Transportation has become a buyer's market; users dominate and influence transportation, for good or ill, whether they choose their transportation randomly or on the basis of comparative cost. There currently exists an ill-defined boundary between legitimate use and unauthorized use of privately owned, not for-hire means of transportation. A developing concept of business logistics influences shippers in their analysis and choice of transportation in relation to other aspects of making a product and getting it to the market. Logistical thinking, in the past, has generally fostered the use of company-operated private carriage, but there is no inherent reason why common carriers cannot offer comparable or even greater logistical advantages to users. From mergers, as they are necessary, common carriers can gain increased ability to compete with private carriage. Also, common carriers can and should adjust their services to the needs of available freight, not vice versa. In transportation, common carriers are everybody's stand-by service. Adjustments by common carriers to meet user requirements and over-all equitable regulation among the various modes and types of transportation are indicated for the benefit of users and carriers alike.

Increasingly, the growing population of the United States is causing utilization conditions in transportation that are noted and criticized by users. The solution to such a problem involves creating a transportation-availability response

* Reprinted by permission from *The Annals of the American Academy of Political and Social Science,* January, 1963, James C. Charlesworth, President.

† Vice-president, United States Steel Corporation.

which will avoid still more "grief for ourselves" by using all transport more efficiently. By definition, what transportation students call "common carriage" can be and generally is the most efficient kind. This is because there usually is relatively better balancing of the load factor in both directions. Common carriage has many virtues. Common carriage deserves its place as the backbone of each of the modern power-driven means of transportation. But it has many ills, so many that users have become concerned over the ability of some important common carriers to survive.

Users are constantly voting for or against particular carriers or means of transport. They vote each time they decide to go somewhere or to make a shipment. They vote frequently. Each use of transportation counts as one vote.

When users decide not to use a particular carrier, they are casting a negative vote. There is a political saying that "poor government is created by good voters who don't vote." Similarly, costly and poor transportation is created by former users who have ceased to be patrons. This may be stated also as a positive choice. When users turn to newer or better transportation, they may be driving the older and poor transportation out of existence. The carrier formerly patronized is left with excess because of unused capacity. This may result in bankruptcy. In any case, the "deserted" carrier has been financially hurt. It will be less able to adjust itself to new needs and new conditions.

Some transportation is in short supply at all times and at most places. Yet, concurrently, most carriers will be in a state of chronic over-capacity. Reasonable balancing of demand by users and supply by carriers is rarely attained. This lack of balance may be observed either in individual situations or in transportation viewed as a whole. To achieve improvement in balance between equipment supply and the demand for transportation sometimes becomes a major reason for development of private carriage.

Usage Pattern

Most users choose their transportation in the form of a repeatable and repeated pattern. People travel from the same home to the same workplace and back, again and again. Property moves as freight, first as raw material, then as salable product, and a portion will move as scrap. Freight moves between predetermined points in predetermined and, therefore, predictable quantities. The need for this patterned transportation is relatively inelastic, insofar as normal requirements are concerned. Of course, this "normal" is only an average. Each year it seems to be becoming more erratic, farther above or below the average. This is because the actual shipments are determined by the impact of business-cycle variations and by long-time trends, such as population growth. There will be seasonal and weekly and daily ups and downs. Although the normal or average pattern is an example of inelastic demand, the actual use of transportation will vary because of the factors just cited and because of users' choosing. Important user choices are made for reasons separate from those that create the normal pattern.

Randomness in Choosing

If a young child is offered his choice of one piece of candy from among five that look exactly alike, he is most likely to pick the nearest one. He will make a random, haphazard decision because he has no guide, no basis for judgment. Choice between kinds of transportation, and especially between like kinds of carriers such as railroads or truck lines, may resemble this accidental sort of choosing. That is why carriers stress the importance of "friendly companionship" as a selling device. Solicitors who are pleasant luncheon or golf companions often can tip the balance toward choice of their carrier. This means that, to the user, the different carriers look like.

Cost Factors

The real significance of user choosing is that the different carriers and different kinds of transportation do not look alike when cost is considered and compared. In fact, most choices are

made only after analysis of all the costs. By "costs" are meant all the disadvantages. These may be tangible or intangible, that is, may or may not be measurable in money. Examples of intangible costs are the convenience of having one's own automobile or the inconvenience of having to maintain an inventory in the wrong place. The user naturally tries to maximize the convenience advantage, minimize the money costs, and also minimize the inconveniences.

Common Carriers' Losing Position

For good or ill, users do influence transportation. We in America would not have it otherwise. People have acquired personal mobility—a kind of personal freedom they will not readily or willingly give up. Freight also has acquired a kind of mobility. It can be shifted from one kind of carrier to another, as users seek and find an advantageous combination of all factors, including transportation. Despite their valiant efforts, common carriers have not held their own. Most of the passenger transportation is now performed by privately owned and operated automobiles. Nearly half of the freight transportation is furnished by other than the fully regulated common carriers. Much of the contract carriage and all of the private transportation in the owner's truck or barge or vessel is exempt from all government controls other than safety. Railroads and other common carriers, submitting each major action to slow moving regulatory agencies for approval, correctly protest that they compete with unregulated carriers in spite of the handcuffs they must wear.

The Transportation Association of America (TAA) annually measures the gradual loss of position of the common carriers. Their estimate for 1961 is that, of about $53 billion spent for passenger transportation, 87 per cent went for purchase, maintenance, and operation of private automobiles and nearly 2 per cent for private aircraft. The remaining 11 per cent, or about $6 billion, was the share of common carriers. The railroads earned about $700 million by carrying intercity and commuter passengers. This was 1.3 per cent of the total and about one ninth of the portion going to all the common carriers.

The estimate for 1961 freight transportation, exclusive of international movements, is that it cost American users about $43 billion. A liberal estimate is that less than $10 billion, or about 23 per cent, was spent for rail transportation, including costs borne by the user in loading and unloading freight cars and also assuming that most of the express and forwarder transportation was by rail. This compares with the estimated $19 billion, or about 44 per cent, received as freight revenue by intercity trucks, both fully and partially regulated.

These freight data also show that the common carriers fully regulated by the Interstate Commerce Commission or the Civil Aeronautics Board—rail, truck, barge, coastwise, pipeline, express, forwarder, and air, other than international—received in 1961 about $19 billion, or about 44 per cent of the total freight costs paid by users. The regulated common carriers of all modes earned less than half of the total freight payments. Of this $19 billion spent for fully regulated freight service, intercity trucks received 38 per cent and railroad gross revenue accounted for 43 per cent.

These are huge amounts of money. TAA comments that the estimates show that transportation of passengers and freight equals about one fifth of the gross national product. The total is about twice the nation's annual expenditure for military defense, a startling fact.

Vital Future for Common Carriers

In the nineteenth century, industrial progress was made possible by the invention and establishment of steam-powered navigation, rail service, and pipelines. Construction and subsequent maintenance, particularly of the constantly expanding rail network, acted as further stimulus by providing an enormous market for materials and a need for workers.

In the twentieth century, as the estimates just cited show, the importance of the common carrier kind of transportation has been declining in a relative sense. In 1887, when the Interstate Commerce Commission became the prototype of all regulatory agencies, it surveyed an America whose economic progress was almost completely dependent on the common-carrier steam railroads. Today the same regulatory agency hears the clamor of many voices urging deregulation. The argument runs that common carriers now must compete, that former monopolistic facts or tendencies that justified regulation are now gone. There is no general point of view among users as to whether regulation can or should be abandoned. But users are aware of the fact that the continued expansion of private carriage of pas-

sengers has already threatened the survival of passenger-carrying by rail. Similarly, users cannot close their eyes to the fact that further and substantial expansion of private carriage of freight will weaken some of the common carriers and perhaps destroy them.

Despite loss of position, the common carriers are essential. They have a vital role today and in the future. In fact, users cannot do without them. Common carriers, as they exist in America today, are everybody's stand-by service. The government in time of war or natural disaster, large and small manufacturers, wholesale and retail enterprises, and the public in general all expect common-carrier service to be available from anywhere to anywhere, at fair and openly published rates or charge, and in equipment adapted to the particular need. No system of contract carriage or private carriage, or both, can be a substitute. By definition, both contract and private carriage are for the benefit of selected users, not for everyone.

There is growing awareness that some of the loss of position of common carriers has been due to overliberal interpretation of the proper role of private carriage. Some existing private carriage, as well as some of the so-called "exempt" contract carriage, has, in fact, been unauthorized or even illegal. User awareness of this situation has been increasing. With better understanding has come greater ability to avoid "stepping over the line" between private or "exempt" and regulated carriage. The Interstate Commerce Commission has, in recent years, issued a number of decisions helpful both to users and carriers because they more clearly identify the boundary line.

Urban Transportation

A good example of the necessity of common carriage, from the user standpoint, is urban transportation. It is obvious that the relatively well to do have moved into more and more distant suburbs. They want and insist on expensive limited-access highways so they can commute in their own automobiles. But there remains in the area close to the central part of the city a mixture of relatively poor persons—who cannot move to the suburbs—and well-to-do persons who have returned from the suburbs to become apartment dwellers. These want and insist on urban transportation of common-carrier type, not private automobiles. In response to this demand, the federal government has become interested in the co-ordination of planning for new suburban-to-downtown urban highways either with the existing or with an improved transit system.

Users are often heard to say that they do not favor government operation of urban mass transportation; at the same time, they tend to cause its development. Lack of patronage, because of users' choosing to drive their own cars to and from work, turns the normal "stand-by" situation into the red-ink condition of excess capacity. And some users or former users then seem to look with complacency or even favor upon demands that the government bolster the mass transportation urban common carriers, weakened by this loss of patronage, with financial support. Hence, to a degree, users talk in one way but act in another way.

Logistics In Freight Movement

User appraisal of "total costs," both monetary and nonmonetary, in a chosen personal journey or shipment of property has been becoming more important. Hence, new terms have come into use to describe this change in emphasis. Logistics, a word borrowed from military language, is the broadest of the new terms. Business logistics describes the new emphasis both as a management procedure and as changed organizational arrangements.

As a management procedure, the logistical concept is that the bringing together or "assembly" at a factory of every needed tangible item, such as the raw materials and the replacement tools or machine parts, involves transportation and many other kinds of choice. These choices are interrelated in the sense that, if a decision as to inventory is made, this will determine what transportation alternatives there are to choose from. Similarly, after a finished product has been made and is ready for sale there are numerous choices, in addition to transportation. Again, these non-transportation choices such as the location of warehouses are interrelated and determine what transportation alternatives there are to choose from. Viewing the factory as the central point or dividing line, there is inbound assembly of materials and outbound physical distribution of salable products. Because the management procedures are the same, that is, co-ordinating the various possible choices so as to select the best combination, the broad term

"business logistics" applies to both inbound assembly and outbound distribution.

Organizational Aspects of Business Logistics

In addition to the basic tasks of making and selling, business enterprises have many staff or facilitative activities. These include purchasing, inventory control, transportation, production scheduling, and warehousing. Each of them is itself a grouping of specialized tasks or activities. The term "recentralize" is used to identify the organization process of rearranging a group of staff activities and establishing their top executive at a higher level in the management structure.

There is controversy and discussion today as to whether recentralization of staff activities now separate is needed in order to accomplish the business-logistics objective of making optimum inbound assembly and outbound distribution choices. Those who advocate recentralization say it is necessary to place all activities related to this choosing activity under a major executive who will rank with the production manager and the sales manager. Those who deny the need for such reorganization argue that the new computer techniques will accomplish the same result—that drastic changes in management structure are unnecessary. The important point is not who is right but that there is acceptance of the need for relating the transportation choice to all the other assembly or distribution factors. This recognition has broader-than-company value. To the extent that distribution costs are thereby reduced, the domestic customer benefits—and more foreign customers will be able to buy American-made products.

Private Carriage Fostered

One of the reasons for continued development of private carriage of freight, at least up to the present time, has been the increasing use of logistical thinking in making a transportation choice. The logistics point of view is to seek the optimum or most advantageous combination of all the elements entering into inbound assembly or outbound distribution. Very often this can only be achieved by using transportation that adjusts itself, in providing service, to the greatest "advantaging" of other factors such as inventory or warehouse costs. Sometimes higher cost but faster and more reliable transportation make possible the optimum combination. Up to the present time, these needs have quite often best been met by development of one's own private carriage.

Common Carriers' Advantages

There is no inherent reason or disability that prevents a common carrier from providing its customers with required services at the cost competitive with private carriage. True, the common carrier cannot give one customer either service or freight rate that is not equally available to other similarly situated users of transportation. This is not a disadvantage. Rather, it opens the way to weaning the others away from private carriage also.

At least one large railroad is sending its own team of specialists into the plants and warehouses of important customers. The team makes a survey or audit of transportation in its relation to the other elements of assembly or distribution logistics. The team determines what it believes is the best arrangement of factors that will minimize total costs and maximize advantages. The common carrier then makes its suggestions and recommendations. In this way, it is meeting the competition of private carriage on its own ground. This exemplifies the logistical approach to the marketing of their services by common carriers who are on their toes.

Common-Carrier Mergers

President Kennedy's 1962 Message on Transportation discussed the merger problem. The message stated that the soundness of a railroad or airline merger should be determined not in the abstract but by applying appropriate criteria. The message stated that the federal interagency committee or task force should include in its study of each pending merger consideration of three criteria, together with others they may develop.

(1) Effective competition should be maintained among alternative forms of transportation and, where traffic volume permits, between competing firms in the same mode of transportation.

(2) The goals of economical, efficient, and adequate service to the public—and reduction in any public subsidies—should be secured by the realization of genuine economies.

(3) Affected workers should be given the assistance to make any necessary adjustments caused by the merger.

These criteria, from the point of view of the government as regulator and planner, deal with the situation to be anticipated or planned for after the merger has been approved and effectuated. It may be assumed that the pressure toward merger of certain common-carrier airlines, railroads, highway common carriers, and ocean fixed-route enterprises is due to seemingly permanent loss or diminution of their earning power. Usually, this is due to diversion of traffic to other kinds of transportation. It may be due to dilution of traffic among too many carriers. Hence, a fourth criteria may be suggested: An aim should be concentration of the available traffic so as to permit optimum use of facilities and equipment. Concentration of the remaining traffic will encourage modernization, innovation, and, where justified, automation. It will be an energizing factor, a "shot in the arm."

Adjustment to the Freight

During the one and one-half centuries since steam power was first used for mechanizing means of transport, much has changed. At first, freight had to adjust itself to the power-driven transportation that was available. Today, the means of transport are so varied and the possible choices so numerous as to reverse this situation.

As common carriers must survive, they have the task of adjusting themselves to the freight. Transportation, in other words, can now be chosen by users so as to provide the optimum conditions from the standpoint of their desire to maximize facilitation of production and sale.

Assume that in 1910 a baker of a specialty product, such as Germantype pumpernickel bread, found that his local market had been saturated. His horse-drawn delivery wagons could not reach stores located more than about fifteen miles from the factory. Beyond this fifteen-mile circle, his distribution was limited by several factors.

(1) He could not find many retail outlets willing and able to send their own wagons to the railroad station several times a week. This was necessary to pick up a few loaves of bread constituting each less-than-carload shipment.

(2) Each small shipment moved slowly in a

freight car from one local station to the next. Therefore, his marketing area was further limited by the slowness of the rail delivery service. Beyond a certain number of days in transit, the bread spoiled.

This same baker today will use his own trucks instead of his own horse-drawn wagons. This change to mechanized local and intercity delivery will have greatly extended his range.

A Buyer's Market

Both passengers and freight shippers have been choosing their transportation in a manner that reduces the relative importance and, in many cases, the earnings of the common carriers, especially the railroads. Being in a "buyer's market," users can exert pressure on "sellers," that is, on common carriers, by making adverse choices. As has been shown, this leverage may be at its peak. Common carriers are needed today and in the future in order to increase and insure our ability as a nation to expand our economic posture. Users are friendly toward their efforts to survive, even when making adverse

choices, due to their own logistical considerations.

On the hopeful side, it is evident that common carriers of all kinds have been learning how to join in and make themselves part of the logistics of the user. Also, by appropriate merger, carriers have increased their ability to compete with private carriage. Railroads, truck lines, and barge operators have designed and improved their equipment so that it fits the needs of the freight. Government agencies are helping, too, by becoming more vigorous in combating "borderline" or so-called "unauthorized" transportation by noncommon carriers.

The efforts of the common carriers to plan, adjust, and compete more effectively are encouraged by most users. The common carriers will be deprived of the needed traffic and earning power only if excessive regulation prevents them from meeting our requirements. Thus, we need not fear nationalization of common carriers because of shipper demands. Assuming equitable regulation among the various modes and types of transportation, the future will be bright and the path will be easier for both users and common carriers.

5. By Barge—River Transportation's Confluence*

Yates Catlin†

ABSTRACT: The United States is drawing a new transportation map, abandoning routes and canceling out transport services. On this new map, there will be more miles of inland waterways but fewer miles of railroads. All freight carriers are curtailing common-carrier services. The navigable rivers and canals played a principal role in settling America, were a factor in the industrial revolution, and helped decentralize industry after World War II. River-rail and river-truck transshipping facilities have multiplied manyfold as thousands of mass-production industries and mass-distribution agencies have moved to the inland navigation channels. Common-carrier barge lines are losing business to the contract and private carriers and have organized their own association to make common cause with the railroads and the common-carrier truck lines. Divided into two camps, the barge and towing vessel industry seems to be losing the battle against federal tolls on the river freight traffic, a battle which divides the South and Middle West against the East and Far West. Many great corporations—oil, steel, coal, electric power, farm co-operatives, cement, chemicals, building materials, aluminum, paper—have a stake in this coming legislative debate in the nation's capital. River men see more traffic in the future but no more revolutionary changes.

Elements within America's transportation system would like nothing better than the right to erase from the transport map their own portions of the total system that they might remap their routes and be more selective in their choice of services to be offered the shipping and traveling public. The railroads, for example, have abandoned more than 32,000 miles of rail line since 1926 and will abandon many more miles of right of way as plans to merge the larger systems are consummated. The extent to which the railroads have withdrawn from the less-than-carload freight business can be measured by the countless freight stations boarded up. All of the common carriers of freight are in trouble and are pressuring the government for relief.

As a matter of fact, the transportation map is being redrawn to create, many years from now, the ideal of an integrated and realistic system engineered to meet the needs of the shipper, consumer, and traveler, to serve the nation's hopes for economic expansion, to provide efficient transportation at the lowest cost, to provide carriers tailormade for each type of cargo, and to assure solvency for the carriers.

Inland waterway channel mileage will be greater by hundreds of miles on this map of tomorrow than on the present map showing a system of 28,999 miles. Navigation is being extended on such rivers as the Missouri, Columbia, Snake, and Trinity (Texas) rivers, and new canals are projected, such as the Tennessee-Tombigbee, Trans-Florida, Lake Erie-Ohio River.

The inland waterways, including the Great Lakes, and the pipelines are the last two domestic freight carriers in the low-cost category; therefore, they would furnish the basic systems on the new map. Both are prime movers of freight.

The inland waterways are meeting a vital economic need of the nation by contributing to the growth of the gross national product as well as to economic stabilization at a time when, paradoxically, government agencies seem more concerned with the problems of the carriers than with those of the shippers.

* Reprinted by permission from the *Annals of the American Academy of Political and Social Science,* January, 1963, James C. Charlesworth, President.

† Public Relation Consultant Specializing in Transportation.

Rivers Carried First Settlers

The United States was first settled where there was water for transportation. The Erie Canal was built to open a trade route to the West. Early settlers were rafted down the Allegheny, Ohio, and Mississippi rivers. Canals were built to bring Pennsylvania coal to seaboard markets. Packet boats were an important factor in the settlement of the Middle West and Northwest.

Navigation channels were a prime factor in the early industrial revolution—witness Boston, New York City, Philadelphia, Baltimore, Buffalo, Detroit, Chicago, Pittsburgh, and St. Louis.

Decentralization and expansion of industry on a gigantic scale followed World War II with the bulk of the development along the navigable rivers and port channels. During the period 1951–1957, more than 3,000 multimillion-dollar mills, factories, plants, and distribution centers were built where low-cost movement of bulk cargo was available by barge and scow.

Low-cost electric power produced from coal or oil delivered to generating stations by barge at significant savings in transportation costs was a prime factor in postwar plant location.

Approximately 10 per cent of the nation's total intercity freight load is now being carried on the improved rivers and canals, and another 7 per cent is moving on the Great Lakes. The share of the inland waterways was only 3.6 per cent in 1940, although that of the Great Lakes was 15.8 per cent twenty-two years ago. The ton-miles of freight carried by the railroads dropped from 61.7 per cent in 1940 to 43.3 per cent in 1961. During the same period, the motor trucks increased their share of the total freight load from 8.4 to 22.6 per cent while the pipelines upped their percentage from 10.5 to 17.7.[1]

In 1961 the inland waterways handled 396 million tons of freight, the Great Lakes handled 137 million tons, and the coastwise vessels handled 212 million tons, making a total of 745 million tons of domestic water-borne commerce, compared with 331 million tons in foreign trade.

Barges were moving only 262 million tons of freight on the rivers and canals at the end of World War II.

All consumers—every family—share in transportation-cost savings effected by barge freight-ing, because barge cargo is essentially fuel, raw materials, semifinished products, and the goods basic to manufacture and processing. Petroleum, petroleum products, coal, building materials, chemicals, iron and steel, aluminum, grain, scrap iron, and paper constitute the bulk of barge cargo. All of these commodities are in the living-costs structure of every American family.

Diversification of farming in the cotton states of the South by adding livestock and poultry was made possible by a price cut for feed equivalent to the savings in transportation costs on grain barged from farms in the upper Mississippi and Missouri valleys.

Cargo-Handling Costs a Factor

Mass-production industry measures the economy of water transportation not only in low rates but in major savings in cargo-handling costs. A 1,000-ton hopper barge or one-million-gallon tank barge can be loaded or unloaded in but a fraction of the time required to load or unload the equivalent capacity in fifty-ton or 8,500-gallon railroad cars.

Designers and manufacturers of equipment for handling cargo have made important contributions to economic transportation. Belt conveyors load a 2,000-ton barge in a few minutes from a coal mine beyond a hill ten miles away. Marine legs have revolutionized the handling of bulk grain at river terminals. Electric generating stations burning up to four million tons of coal annually have found cranes and shovels equal to the gigantic job.

Operating on the 29,000 miles of navigable rivers and canals are more than 4,100 towboats and 16,600 barges. The total capacity of the barges is about 16,300,000 tons. The aggregate capacity of all freight cars of American railroads is under 90 million tons.[2]

There are 250 rivers and canals in the United States reporting barge and scow traffic of 50,000 or more tons. The upper bay of New York Harbor leads them all with more than 133 million tons. There are an equal number of ports handling more than 100,000 tons of waterborne commerce and serving all but eight states in the continental United States.[3]

[1] Eastern Railroad Presidents Conference, *Yearbook of Railroad Information, 1962.*

[2] U. S. Army Corps of Engineers, Statistical Division, Board of Engineers for Rivers and Harbors.

[3] Yates Catlin, *New Dimensions in Transportation* (Washington, D. C.: The American Waterways Operators, Inc., 1956).

There are 2,000 facilities for loading and unloading barges on the Mississippi River system of inland waterways and the Gulf Intracoastal Waterway.[4]

River traffic was handicapped during World War II and during the first few years following the end of the war by a system-wide deficiency in port facilities. Some municipal wharves and terminals had been long in disuse, and, on most reaches of the rivers, the docks and piers were privately owned. Expansion of industry along the barge routes during the last twelve years has necessitated the addition of hundreds of new terminals, wharves, piers, docks, and harbors for the handling of grain, coal, oil, chemicals, iron, steel, scrap iron, cement, bauxite, aluminum, sand, gravel, oyster shell, paper, molasses for livestock feed, sulfur, coke, fertilizer, motor vehicles, and pulpwood. It was during this same period that river towns and cities rediscovered the economic value of the new river traffic and began building wharves, terminals, harbors, and industrial districts.

River Traffic Is Increasing

Traffic on the navigable rivers and canals is increasing at a healthy rate, and all signs point to a continuing flood tide for the foreseeable future. The United States Army Corps of Engineers, which builds and maintains the inland waterways, is optimistic to the degree that each year it recommends to the Congress of the United States huge appropriations for the improvement of more rivers for navigation, for doubling the chamber sizes of old locks, and for the lengthening of the navigation pools through the construction of higher dams and locks with higher lifts.

Army engineers visualize traffic on the 981-mile-long Ohio River requiring, within a very few years, a new system of locks with chambers 1,200 feet long and pools between the locks fifty-two miles long instead of the present average of twenty-one miles. The standard locks are 600 feet or less in length. Each of the new 1,200-foot chambers on the Ohio River will have an auxiliary lock 600 feet long. Each will be 110 feet wide. Traffic on the Illinois Waterway linking the Mississippi River with Lake Michigan at Chicago already justifies the dual locking of that channel of high-density coal, oil, and chemical traffic.

[4] U. S. Army Corps of Engineers.

Our economy in the 1960's is one characterized by mass production and mass distribution, calling for freight carriers of equal proportions. The inherent advantage of inland-waterway transportation is the capacity for moving bulk and heavy commodities long distances, in vast quantities, and at the lowest cost. Storage rather than time is a factor here.

Americans clung to their Mark Twain packet-boat fixation until, in the late 1950's, there was publication throughout the United States of composite photographs showing the length of a typical Ohio-Mississippi River freight tow to be several hundred feet longer than the longest ocean liner.

Common Carriers Hurt

Shippers on the inland waterways, as the magnitude of their shipments increases, are turning from the common-carrier service to contract-carrier service. Contract rates are far below commercial carrier or regulated rates because the contract shipment fills the several barges of a tow whereas the common-carrier tow consists of single barge loads of as many as forty shippers. Contract carriers barge petroleum and petroleum products for as little as 2 mills per ton-mile. Some has moved for only 1.9 mills.

Common-carrier traffic on the inland waterways has been declining for several years at a rate which the operators have found sufficiently alarming to justify the formation of their own association—the Inland Waterways Common Carriers Association—with a membership of eight barge lines. The association makes common cause with the railroads and the common-carrier truck lines on such legislative matters as the extension of government regulation to all freight carriers and to all types of cargo.

Loss of business has forced the common-carrier barge lines to increase their efficiency in terms of ton-mile cost of operation by replacing small towboats with a smaller number of modern boats of greater horsepower and, therefore, more push power, which is translated into more barges per tow. These economies too often result in impaired service to the shipper, because deliveries are reduced in number and turnaround time is lengthened by more port calls per tow.

Formation of the Inland Waterways Common Carriers Association was followed by the organization of another splinter group, the contract carriers, who outnumber the common carriers by several hundred. This association is opposed to the extension of regulation to its type of service.

A third type of operator on the inland waterways is the private carrier who moves his own fuels, raw materials, and products in his own barges and by his own towboats. Numbered among these fleet owners are the larger oil companies, the steel manufacturers, farm co-operatives, chemical producers, the sand, gravel, and oyster shell companies, members of the grain trade, the cement makers, paper and pulp manufacturers, coal-mining companies, and electric companies.

Private carriers expanded their fleets and contract carriers largely benefited during the industrial boom in the Ohio Valley which saw $15 billion invested in ten years in new plant construction and plant expansion along its navigation channels. This was also true along the Mississippi River, Gulf Intracoastal Waterway, and the Illinois Waterway.

Barge Industry Weakened

Before the common-carrier barge lines made common cause with the railroads, the barge and towing-vessel industry seemed to have had little to fear in the area of federal legislation. Legislation detrimental to the industry never came out of committee. Few now remember that the President's Committee on Water Resources Policy recommended tolls on the improved rivers.

Division of the industry into warring splinter groups seems to have weakened its defenses in the nation's capital. Two national administrations have recommended either a toll or a special tax on river traffic. A Special Study Group on Transportation Policies has proposed such tolls. The present administration proposes removal of the dry-bulk cargo exemption from regulation, a regulatory device greatly prized by the contract carriers. The Kennedy Administration wants more competition between the several types of carriers with greater competitive freedom—in which the barge operators see disaster for themselves. Policies of the present and preceding administrations in the national capital encourage common ownership of the several modes of transportation, an eventuality much feared by the river-transportation industry.

Many voices have been speaking for the barge and towing-vessel industry since it broke up into several splinter organizations in 1957 to fight an internecine war triggered by the fear of the common carriers that they were losing control of the industry. For thirteen years, the industry

had spoken with one voice and had enjoyed prestige, security, growth, and prosperity. This is the industry's hour of greatest peril.

Signs of industry-wide weakness in the fight to preserve low freight rates on the waterways are as obvious as the changing mood of the government. For example, a recent conference in Washington, D. C. to marshal the forces opposed to river tolls failed to assemble more than a corporal's guard of powerful shippers. Less than twenty shippers were represented by staff members, and all but two of them own their own river fleets. Otherwise, representation of industry and commerce was by Washington representatives of trade associations.

The outcome of the river-tolls controversy will be determined largely by the amount of pressure exerted on Congress by the lobbyists for the major industries now using barge transportation to hold down one of the costs going into their price structures. Collectively, big steel, big oil, chemicals, farm co-operatives, coal, electric power, and the rivertown Chambers of Commerce can influence the votes of many congressmen. It is highly unlikely that the United States Steel Corporation, which operates two barge lines, barges its own coal, and builds barges in its American Bridge Division, will sit still for an assessment of millions of dollars against its own customers. The first chairman of the National Waterways Conference is board chairman of the Ashland Oil and Refining Company, which owns towboats, barges, and pipelines.

Tolls Fight Will Divide Nation

The coming fight over river tolls will divide the South against the East and West with the Middle West joining forces with the South. The inland-waterway system is largely a southern system.

Freight movement on the inland waterways in the South has jumped in twelve years from 180 million tons to 330 million tons, an impressive jump which the South will defend to the last ton. There is the making of a long filibuster in these figures—the South is very proud of its rising standard of living bolstered by low-cost barge transportation and water-compelled railroad freight rates.

After the Civil War, the federal government exchanged public lands for railroads to develop and settle the West. Since World War I, the federal government has employed river improvements as its principal instrument for the economic development and expansion of depressed areas. The key is low-cost transportation.

When and if the Congress votes on the question of tolls for the use of federally built and maintained waterways, it will weigh the complaint of the railroads that they maintain their own rights of way although the barges operate without cost in navigation channels built and maintained by the government against the fact that low barge rates are expanding markets, developing depressed areas, expanding the national economy, increasing the gross national product, and pouring into the federal treasury more billions in additional taxes than it is pouring into river improvements. Congress must decide between fairness to the railroads and what is good for the nation's economy.

Naval architects do not foresee revolutionary changes in towboat and barge design in the next decade or two. Towboats seem to have reached the ultimate in horsepower, and the draft of barges is limited to the standard nine-foot channel. Special requirements of the chemical industry have called for tank barges capable of transporting such commodities as molten sulfur and highly corrosive and heavy chemicals.

Rivermen never expect to witness a revolution on the rivers equal to that sparked by the introduction of diesel power and the propeller on towboats on the western rivers.

6. *New Developments and Brisk Sales Keeping Inventories Low**

PHILIP SHABECOFF

Inventory Ratio Shows a Decline

Like Old Mother Hubbard, American business and industry has been keeping its inventory cupboard bare in recent months—at least in relative terms.

The ratio of inventory to sales in the first quarter stood at about 1.48 ($1.48 worth of inventory was maintained for every $1 in sales) for all manufacturing and trade in the United States. This ratio is as low as it has been for any time in the last decade.

Inventory accumulation in the first quarter amounted to $2 billion, at an annual rate, compared with $3.2 billion in the last quarter of 1963 and an average accumulation of $4.7 billion for all of 1963.

While inventories are high in absolute terms—$105 billion at the end of March, according to the Department of Commerce—their growth has been slow for a period of economic prosperity.

Boom Indicated

In simple—perhaps oversimple—terms, these figures indicate that what has long been regarded as a key economic indicator points to a continuation of the prolonged economic boom in the United States.

Inventories are basically stock waiting on a shelf for sale or shipment. Iron ore in a stockpile, an unsold automobile or an assembly line, a washing machine in a manufacturer's warehouse or a department store stockroom are all items in inventory.

Declining inventory ratios historically have signaled a period of economic expansion. Manufacturers and retailers draw from their inventories to meet rapidly increasing orders and sales. Thus, more capital expenditures and work hours are generated.

Conversely, rising inventories have been regarded as a major indicator of a recession. When sales drop off after inventories have been built up to meet growing orders or to hedge against rising prices, manufacturers, and retailers will sell from their overloaded stocks rather than buy new merchandise.

A rising inventory-to-sales ratio is looked at as a red flag warning that a downswing is on.

Situation Good

Right now, the general inventory situation is "very good," according to William B. Franklin, manager of the business conditions department of the National Industrial Conference Board. Mr. Franklin sees little imbalance in current stocks. He said:

"Where stocks are unusually high, sales are also very high."

He attributes the relatively low level of inventories to several factors. One is the price stability of most commodities and products in recent years. Because prices have not been climbing, manufacturers and retailers have not had to do any hedge buying of products.

For example, in a period of rising prices a textile manufacturer might stock up on cotton to protect himself against new increases. With cotton prices stable, or even falling, the manufacturer could invest in new textile machinery to increase his production, rather than build his inventory of raw material.

Another factor cited by Mr. Franklin is that many industries, such as steel, are operating well under capacity and are therefore under no pressure to build inventories to meet sales levels.

* Reprinted by permission from *New York Times,* June 7, 1964.

Steel makers have been able to meet new orders largely from production.

Another explanation for the current level of inventories was suggested by the Federal Reserve Bank of San Francisco in its monthly report for April.

The bank noted that there has been a gradual shift in the components that make up this country's total production of goods and services. The importance of durable goods, such as washing machines, refrigerators and drill presses, has been receding, while nondurable areas, such as food and liquor, services and construction, have had a growing percentage of the nation's output.

Since durable goods traditionally have maintained the heaviest inventories, their reduced role in the economy has meant a slackening in the overall accumulation of inventories.

The inventory situation differs, of course, from industry to industry. In the first quarter, the sharpest reduction in inventories was made by manufacturers of textiles and apparel, according to the Department of Commerce.

In recent years the inventory-to-sales ratio of the textile industry has been steady at 1.9 to 2.1. In past cycles it has swung more sharply, reaching 2.7 in 1957, for example.

Peter H. Conze, group vice president of fibers for the Celanese Corporation of America, which produces man-made fibers, noted that "inventories have been declining since the beginning of the year, with market demand continuing to exceed plant capacities."

However, another textile official noted that "from a financial point of view, inventories are always too high."

Steel inventories are starting to build up again after reaching a low of 15.3 million finished tons in December 1963, according to one steel producer. Inventories now stand at around 16.4 million tons and are expected to reach 17.2 million tons by the end of the first half.

New Orders Cited

One observer said that the inventory buildup in steel, unlike the buildup last spring, when there was a great deal of strike hedge buying, is directly attributable to new orders.

"I think these orders will be maintained," the observer said. "Building our inventories at this stage is not borrowing from future production."

Inventories of automobiles are quite high, but so are auto sales. Meanwhile, the Chrysler Cor-

poration noted that its inventories of raw materials are lower than at any time since 1958 and are as much as one-third lower than in comparable boom periods such as 1955 or 1957.

At about $461 million, railroad inventories of materials and supplies are about half what they were 10 years ago. Further cuts are planned. The Pennsylvania Railroad said it is working toward another 10 per cent cut in its stock.

The Grocery Manufacturers Association has reported that food stocks on the shelves of retailers are 6 per cent higher than a year ago. On the other hand, the General Foods Corporation said it was operating with a smaller inventory of raw materials than in previous postwar upturns. It expects no significant changes in the near future.

Inventories of cigarette tobacco leaf are slightly lower than in previous booms, partially because people have been smoking fewer cigarettes since the Surgeon General's report linking smoking with disease.

Oil Products Up

Inventories of oil products are higher than a year ago, but they are not considered excessive, since crude oil production is controlled by most states and imports are regulated by the United States in keeping with the demand for oil products.

Because the coal industry is operating well below capacity and has greatly increased its efficiency, there is no problem of inventories. Inventories are kept at working levels at mineheads and these levels are now normal.

Electrical equipment makers, according to one observer, have no inventory problems. Heavy equipment, such as generators, circuit breakers and transformers, are never kept in inventory but are produced on order. The chief problem for this industry is meeting its backlog of orders.

This, then, is the present inventory situation. But it is not the whole story. There are broad indications that influences other than classic economic factors are operating on inventory levels.

The inventory-sales ratio, for example, is well below where it stood in the last major upswing in 1957. One must go all the way back to the post-World War II and the Korean War periods, when there was a chronic shortage of goods for sale, to find a lower index.

A number of economists and businessmen have begun to argue that inventories may not be, at this point, the reliable economic indicator they have traditionally been. The economists say that "secular" influences (mechanical processes unrelated to traditional economic events) have tended to keep inventories at lower levels.

These secular influences include the use of computers for inventory control, more rapid communications and transportation, and a growing business concern with inventory control.

Probably the most significant new development is the use of computers in the stock room. Archie J. McGill, industry marketing manager for distributing industries of the International Business Machine Corporation, noted that counting inventories was one of the earliest applications for computers.

With the application of mathematical techniques to inventory control in recent years, however, computers have taken a much more sophisticated role in inventory management, Mr. McGill asserted.

Computers now are programmed not only to tell a manufacturer how much stock he has on his shelves, but also to assist him in deciding when and how much stock to buy.

With this tool, Mr. McGill explained, companies can cut down on the time it takes to keep inventories at the optimum level and can maintain a higher level of service from inventory. That is, a higher level of orders can be filled directly from their shelves.

The J. C. Penney Co., a large general merchandise chain, has made a number of computer applications in inventory control. Stanley Kritzik, manager of engineering and systems, explained how computers were used for inventory management in the chain's retail operations.

Working Levels

Penney store managers, Mr. Kritzik said, establish working stock levels for all staple merchandise such as women's hosiery. Each packet of three pairs of stockings has a punch ticket attached to it.

When the packet is sold, the punch ticket is immediately forwarded to Penney's data center where it is fed directly into a computer. The computer records the item sold, the place of sale and the amount sold and automatically writes a repurchase order, which is forwarded to the hosiery manufacturer.

"The goals we are seeking with our computers

are lower inventories, better in-stock positions and less expensive manpower costs," Mr. Kritzik explained. "We have not achieved all that yet but we are moving in the right direction."

Industry also is making rapid strides in getting orders and shipments from manufacturer to warehouse to retailer through the use of telecommunications, jet airfreight, bulk piggyback rail shipments and increasingly mechanized warehouses.

The last word in the use of telecommunications and computers in inventory control, for the moment at least, is represented by the Pittsburgh Tele-Computer Center of the Westinghouse Electric Corporation.

One of the functions of the center is to link 53 Westinghouse warehouses holding industrial electrical products with company sales offices.

2-Minute Process

Every order that is placed at a sales office is transmitted by teletype writer to the Pittsburgh center, run through a Univac 490 computer, where the order is processed, shipping orders are prepared automatically and sent by teletypewriter to the nearest warehouse to be filled. The entire process, from the time the order is made at the sales office to the time shipping instructions are received in the warehouse, takes about two minutes, according to George Maxton, manager of teletype writer order processing for Westinghouse.

The computer also maintains in its "memory," the level of each item in inventory and determines at what point reorders should be made to replenish stocks, based on a wide variety of variables.

"The Tele-Computer center means we do not need as many stocking locations, because we can get higher volume out of fewer warehouses," Mr. Maxton said. "It also means that we have been able to lower our shelf stock from $33 million to $18 million."

"Since the cost of carrying inventory is about 20 cents for each dollar of merchandise, this has been a major benefit. The biggest benefit, however, is that we have been able to provide better customer service."

Does the use of computers, teletypewriter communications, air freight and other methods to keep inventories tightly under control mean that inventories will have a new meaning as an economic indicator? Some economist and businessmen are saying yes.

Effect Minimized

But others tend to minimize the effect of these innovations. "We use computers, but we can't rely on them," declared M. H. Westrich, merchandise controller of Sears, Roebuck & Co. "You can't compute ahead of judgment."

Mr. Franklin acknowledged that the use of computers and air freight have helped keep inventories down. But he argued that these secular factors have been offset by other factors.

One such factor, he said, was the need for manufacturers to keep a much broader stock of models on hand, as modern tastes dictate increased variety. He noted that auto manufacturers are adding more models to their lines.

Another factor is the growing demand by customers for more speed in delivery. Tighter inventory control is needed just to meet this demand, he said.

In sum, there is growing disagreement over the present use of inventories as an economic indicator. It is an argument that probably will not be resolved very soon.

Section II.   Customer Service and Facility Location

Customer service is not totally dependent upon plant and warehouse location decisions, but it can take many forms. This paraphrase, based on Bud Reese's article, "Boosting Sales Through Customer Service," serves to bring out the central theme of the articles appearing in this section. However, the bounds of the economically practicable, when setting standards for most types of customer service, are circumscribed by the geographical positioning of plant, warehouse, and other distribution facilities of the firm in relation to the communications, movement, and other services that firm commands.

Customer service should not be considered as the antithesis of facility location, nor should it be thought of as the handmaiden of promotion. Rather customer service, facility location, and promotion must act in concert with one another to the end that the *optimum* solution is achieved.

Total Distribution in the Age of the Computer by L. O. Browne, supplies a generalized view of the practicality of using machine rather than manual methods for attacking problems related to achieving savings in costs, simultaneously with improving customer service, as well as other facets of the physical distribution function.

7. *Boosting Sales Through Customer Service**

Bud Reese†

Sounds to me as though IMC is some kind of an altruistic management consulting firm. . . . Of course, it makes a little money on the side selling agricultural chemicals.

This bit of waggery came from a Chicago adman after he heard Anthony E. Cascino, marketing vice-president of International Minerals & Chemical Corp., Skokie, Ill., tell a local ad club about the customer services offered by his company's Agricultural Chemicals Division.

The fact of the matter is that the wag wasn't far wrong about the management consulting; for the past three and one-half years the IMC division has been offering its customers a vast array of services, including counsel on just about every aspect of their business, from training salesmen to buying insurance.

As for making "a little money on the side": Since the division announced its customer service program in mid-1958, annual sales have increased more than 20%. And according to IMC's 1959–60 annual report (the most recent available as of this writing), "The increase in net earnings from these operations was *the major* contributor to total corporate earnings" (corporate earnings for that fiscal year were up 21% to $7.5 million, on sales of $124 million).

And IMC marketing men, including president Thomas M. Ware, give much of the credit for the division's success to its customer service program. Their attitude is that the program gives the division a distinct competitive advantage.

Supply and Demand

The reason for the division's customer service program, which it has dubbed, "full orbit," dates

* Reprinted by permission from *Industrial Marketing,* November, 1961.
† Associate Editor, *Industrial Marketing.*

back to about the mid-1950's. At that time, existing seller's market was beginning to shift to a buyer's market, and IMC management realized that a more intensive marketing-sales effort would soon be required to hold on to the division's customers,—400–500 fertilizer manufacturers.

But, the division's products (phosphate minerals, phosphate chemicals and potash) offered little in the way of a strong competitive advantage upon which to hang a sales pitch; the products were nearly identical, in quality and price, to those of major competitors.

In addition, IMC felt that the division's fertilizer manufacturer customers were not likely to be impressed with fancy sales pitches and elaborate promotional material. The typical customer company was, and still is, relatively small, serving dealers and farmers within a 50-mile radius; and the president of the average customer company is one-third of the sales force—along with being plant manager, traffic manager, advertising manager, etc. With all these jobs to do, he doesn't want to spend much time with lengthy sales talks or promotional copy.

IMC marketing management decided, therefore, to turn to customer service, on the theory that although products may be standardized, suppliers need not be.

Full Orbit Announced

The first phase of the division's customer service program was announced to the sales force in May, 1958, at a meeting in Chicago. At that time president Ware told the salesmen, "This is a new corporate way of life for IMC; all of our energies, talents and services are to be oriented to the benefit of the customer."

The salesmen were also told: "This full orbit program is a group of services specifically designed to assist the fertilizer manufacturer in the profitable execution of day-to-day operations. They cover a wide range of activities—market research, advertising and sales promotion, process development, technical service, sales management, transportation, and many others. They are free; this assistance doesn't cost a cent, or obligate the customer or prospect in any way."

Then, Phase I of full orbit was outlined and explained; it consisted primarily of:

1. *More management consultation.* Because of their small size, few of the division's customers could afford to hire specialists in, say, advertising and sales training; and occasionally a customer would write to the respective IMC department head for advice. But IMC had not promoted this service; and as a result, many customers did not know of its availability.

Now, as part of full orbit, the division's salesmen were told to explain that IMC's specialized knowledge was "free for the asking." The division wanted all of its customers and prospects to know it had "experts" on all aspects of running a business—advertising, sales management, traffic, production, accounting, purchasing, etc. —and that these specialists would help them with their problems. Most of the problems were to be answered by mail; or if the customer wished, he could arrange to visit IMC's specialists in Skokie; or, when necessary, IMC's "experts" would travel to the customer.

2. *Better organized technical service.* The division had technical service men in the field long before May, 1958; but, these men were usually called in only in emergencies—on a "fire fighting" basis.

Now, under full orbit, the technical service staff would, if permitted by the customer, make regularly scheduled visits to the customer plant, locating potential trouble spots and making suggestions to head off expensive and irritating breakdowns. The division's salesmen were told to urge customers to take advantage of this service.

Along this same line, the technical service staff published a preventive maintenance checklist, covering 103 potential trouble spots.

In addition the technical staff was ready and willing to help with formulation problems, process development, plant reorganization, plant design, product development and training of personnel in new processes.

3. *Expanded transportation service.* About one-third of the average fertilizer manufacturer's selling cost is transportation. The IMC division's salesmen were told to explain to customers that IMC transportation experts were willing to help in these areas:

Routing assistance, advice on loading and transportation techniques, freight rate negotiation with carriers for the customer, plant and warehouse location studies, and handling of formal and informal complaints (if the carrier is at fault, IMC will file the claim for the customer; and very often, allow the customer credit, thus freeing his money).

In one ad on its transportation service, IMC stated that its traffic men represent customers in legislative discussions; carry their cases to legal bodies; and work for better rates and regulations.

4. *Full orbit library.* Also at the May, 1958, meeting, the salesmen were shown copies of six manuals, covering (1) advertising, (2) dealer meetings, (3) market analysis, (4) sales management, (5) technical service, and (6) transportation.

The latter two outline the expanded services available in their respective areas; the other four manuals were of the how-to type, covering the basic information a customer would need to advertise effectively; plan dealer sales meetings, etc.

The advertising manual, for example, covered the fundamentals of budgeting, selecting media, and planning ad strategy. This 88-page manual also contained information on the mechanics of preparing and placing advertisements, and a glossary of the most common advertising terms.

The manual on market analysis told the customer how to determine his total market and share of market, current sales trends by fertilizer grades, competitors' sales, his sales potential and sales goals. It also outlined and described the various sources of market information, i.e., government consumption reports and census data.

Customers Leery

The idea, at that time, was for the salesmen to devote the next call on each customer to explaining the over-all service program. Succeeding calls would be devoted to each of the six subjects, on a planned basis.

That didn't work. Few of the customers

wanted the planned program, primarily, IMC frankly admits, because they were skeptical of the program's worth. They doubted that IMC personnel would be willing to spend enough time on any one of their problems to come up with any real assistance. They realized that the division, because of its size, had the specialized know-how, but they couldn't see any company taking any large amount of time to help customers without the usual strings attached.

IMC feels, however, that Phase I of the full orbit program was a success. Most of the customers were willing to accept some help in one or two of the areas covered by the program; and the manuals were, in general, well received. More important, Phase I laid the necessary groundwork for Phase II.

It "Clicks"

The second phase of full orbit began in January, 1959. During this phase IMC introduced the customer service which IMC feels "sold" the services already offered, and those still to come.

That service was sales training. In January and February of 1959, the Agricultural Chemicals Div. held 10 sales training clinics in as many cities around the country. About 350 customer salesmen (many of the 350 were salesmen-presidents of customer companies) attended the two-day meetings, at which IMC sales and sales training men explained the basics of selling.

All of the most up-to-date training aids were used—slides, movies, skits, role playing, etc. And little mention was made of IMC products.

Reaction, says IMC, was swift and gratifying. Many letters praising the clinics were received from customers—along with requests for more of the same. The result was a second series of clinics in the fall of 1959. This series drew almost 500 customer salesmen; and again, many were top executives.

Now the division's prospects and customers were beginning to be convinced that IMC was trying to help them with "the profitable execution of day to day operations." The division's salesmen received more requests for the full orbit manuals, and for information not covered in the manuals.

In response to the latter, the division made up loose-leaf binders, each containing 200 pages, for its salesmen. The binders contained abstracts of papers on some 50 fertilizer manufacturing and

marketing topics. Copies of the papers were available upon request.

Two New Manuals

Also during Phase II, two new booklets were added to the orbit library, one on credit and collections, the other on insurance and safety.

Credit and Collections

This manual described the screening of credit risks, building prospect credit files, making credit decisions, collection practices and terms, etc.

Insurance and Safety

This 12-page booklet outlined and explained the dozen or so types of insurance of interest to a fertilizer manufacturer, and told him how to set up an effective safety program.

Both booklets also reminded customers and prospects that the IMC personnel in charge of these functions would be glad to answer any and all questions.

Planalyzer

Another important facet of full orbit was introduced at this time: The Planalyzer. This was a series of large wall calendars, each of which dealt with an important aspect of manufacturing or marketing fertilizer.

The purpose of the Planalyzer was to help the customer plan his year. For example, if the customer decided to have his advertising appear in early spring, before the planting season, the calendar would be filled out to tell him when to budget, when to begin planning the ads, when to contact media, etc.

The sales management calendar was filled out to remind the customer when to review his sales manpower requirements, hold sales meetings, hold dealers meetings, etc.

Production calendars, when completed, reminded the customer when to set cost standards, review labor requirements, order raw materials, schedule bagging operations, etc.

The Planalyzer calendars induced the customers to be more sophisticated in their planning and operation; and this, in turn, resulted in more requests for advice and assistance.

Educating IMC Sales

At this time, approximately June of 1959, full orbit hit a snag.

The complete service "package" was widely accepted, and IMC salesmen were being asked an increasing number and variety of questions. The "snag": the salesmen didn't know enough of the answers, and were becoming bogged down with correspondence with home office "specialists."

Part of this problem resulted from the fact that, up until this time, the division's sales force was organized by products, namely, phosphate minerals, phosphate chemicals and potash. The phosphate salesmen didn't know enough about potash, and vice versa.

Also, some customers were being called upon by three different salesmen; and this, naturally, created confusion and duplications. Customers were willing to accept the complete customer service program, on a planned basis; but they wanted to work through one salesman, not two or three.

To solve this problem the IMC division's management began, on July 1, 1959, to call in the salesmen on a rotating basis. The salesmen were given more extensive training on the various aspects of making and selling fertilizer, and on the lines they had not previously handled. Sales territories were also realigned.

In addition, in September of 1959, the potash salesmen were sent to IMC's phosphate mines and chemical processing plants in Bartow, Fla., where they underwent a week of instruction by technical men and phosphate salesmen on the fine points of the phosphate products. Later, the potash salesmen went through a similar course at Carlsbad, N.M., where the company's potash mine and refinery are located.

With this and additional training (through sales bulletins) the salesman became both liaison men and counselors. In some cases the salesman was able to provide all the help the customer needed, i.e., in putting on dealer sales meetings. In other cases the salesman performed the liaison function between customer and divisional specialists.

Phase IV

The fourth phase of the full orbit program, started in January of 1960, added two more services to those already offered. The two are IMC's traveling traffic team and its management seminars.

Traffic Team

During January, February and March of 1960 an eight-man traffic team, headed by Eugene Landis, IMC director of transportation, made the rounds of customer and prospect plants and asked "What's your traffic problem? How can we help?"

Mr. Landis explained that, in many instances, "faulty rates and faulty service have resulted simply because local freight agents were unfamiliar with certain commodity rates, volume rates, intermediate scheduling and other factors. Carriers want to charge the correct rate and offer the best service, but sometimes the smaller company hasn't the time or the personnel to call its problem to the attention of the carrier."

As a result of the traveling traffic team's efforts, IMC's customers and prospects have saved thousands of dollars.

This transportation service is still being offered on a limited basis, as requests for it come in from regional offices.

And to coincide with the program, the traffic department publishes a "transportation newsletter," containing information developed at rate hearings and industry meetings and from trade publications, boiled down and aimed specifically toward the plant food industry.

Management Seminars

In July of 1960 the IMC division held its first "fertilizer management seminar."

Top executives of customer and prospect companies were invited to Skokie for a three-day program whch included instructions on organizational structure, financial management, profit planning, credit and collections, personnel development, public and community relations, industry trends, etc. Approximately 60 customer executives attended the seminar.

Textbook for the three-day school was a 454-page, hard-cover book titled, "Managing for Profit." The book, edited by IMC's marketing division, contained all of the material covered in the eight already-mentioned full-orbit manuals, plus that of a new manual on accounting.

The new accounting manual, published about the same time as "Managing for Profit," covered "planned profits through accounting;" "making a profit plan;" "checking results against objectives;" and "reporting results against the profit plan."

Included were examples of the charts and statements needed to obtain decision-assisting information from accounting records.

"Managing for Profit" also contained a case history, described as follows in the textbook's preface; "Here is a complete portfolio of specific management information set forth in solutions to a typical fertilizer management situation . . . The approaches are worked out in a way that enables ready and easy application of the principles and methods to one's own particular problems. It contains step-by-step procedures, together with sample forms and visual examples . . . It demonstrates how you may analyze your own company."

One customer who attended the seminar described it as "Years of top management experience packed into three priceless days."

Additional proof of the acceptance of the seminar is the fact that 70 more customers and prospect executives showed up for the management seminar held in July of this year, and IMC expects to hold another seminar in '62.

Another Manual in '61

IMC introduced still another manual in time for the 1961 management seminar. The manual, titled "Purchasing for Profit," contains 44 pages of information on purchasing practices, administration, selecting supplers, buying plant equipment, forms and record-keeping, and other purchasing topics.

And in addition to publishing this new manual, IMC has updated and expanded the information it provides on sales training and farmer meetings. It has increased the number of its sales management and training films to 16, and has revamped its Planalyzer to a more elaborate and useful "action calendar."

Results

Obviously, a customer service program of this magnitude is expensive. Has it been worth the cost?

The division's sales and profit figures have already been covered. Still more proof of the program's success is afforded by this quote from the 1959–60 annual report:

"Four out of ten customers for IMC fertilizer ingredients now buy the company's full line. A year ago only one customer in ten bought all these products from IMC. . .

"Looking to the future, the corporation is planning additional production facilities for high-concentrate phosphates. Meanwhile, IMC has entered into an agreement with Electric Reduction, Ltd., of Toronto, Canada, which will provide additional high-concentrate products . . .

"Sales volume of potash ran ahead of last year and despite record production it was necessary to buy substantial tonnage from other sources to meet our customers' needs . . ."

The "other sources" referred to in the preceding paragraph are, of course, competitors—and this in a buyer's market.

8. *Total Distribution in the Age of the Computer**

L. O. BROWNE†

In early 1961 the financial vice president of Burroughs Corporation raised a provocative question within the management group. "Where," he asked, "can we best use our know-how to save the most money within our operations without adversely affecting service to our field branches and customers?"

Analysis revealed that one major area where significant economies could be made—while at the same time improving customer services—was in the specific area of physical distribution of products.

A comprehensive study was undertaken of existing inventory and distribution practices within the company. This study by an outside consultant disclosed that physical distribution functions were widely scattered throughout the corporate organization. Marketing, manufacturing, and finance were each involved in various aspects of the total physical distribution function. Overlapping and lack of complete coordination and efficiency were an inevitable consequence of this splintered operation.

Out of this comprehensive study came a recommendation to the Corporate Operating Committee to consolidate all distribution functions under the control of a single department. In August, 1961, the Distribution Services Department was created by executive order of Burroughs' president, Ray R. Eppert, answerable to Ken T. Bement, vice president of Equipment and Systems Marketing Division.

Today, Distribution Services provides all of the machines and data processing systems, service parts and service tools, together with sales and service promotional and technical literature used by the 136 domestic branches of the E & S Marketing Division.

* Reprinted by permission from *Distribution Age,* July, 1964.
† Burroughs Corporation.

In addition, the Distribution Center provides to the International Division all finished machines and data processing systems not produced by the International Division's overseas factories, as well as a substantial portion of the service parts, service tools and literature required by the International Division's overseas branches and subsidiaries.

After just two-and-a-half years, Distribution Services is presently saving the Corporation in excess of $2 million annually while distributing some $200 million worth of Burroughs products. At the same time, service to field branches and customers has been measurably improved through streamlined operating procedures.

How to Add $2 Million to Profits

Let's take a quick look at the major accomplishments of central distribution at Burroughs Corporation thus far in terms of direct increases to corporate profit:

• The number of finished machines in inventory has been reduced by over 40% during the past two years. This can be converted into a net annual savings of over $1 million in inventory-carrying costs.
• All eight former company regional warehouses in the United States were closed, with net savings in rent and personnel costs in excess of $200,000 each year.
• Central distribution of service parts and tools has reduced former space requirements by over 65%, while order-filling efficiency has been increased more than four-fold. The results of these improvements have added more than $300,000 in annual savings.
• Transportation savings from pooling of shipments to branches and direct shipments to customers has trimmed over $175,000 from the annual transportation bill.

• Reduction in personal property taxes last year exceeded $400,000 on inventories. This savings was due both to the reduction of inventory and the storing of idle inventory in tax-exempt locations.

• Savings from a new universal stand to support accounting machines will save another $150,000 annually. This universal stand was engineered under the guidance of Distribution Services to simplify an inventory stocking and distribution problem.

The Accent is on "Service"

While these major savings have been rather spectacular, they do not begin to tell the story of overall improvement in service to field branches and customers. The basic operating philosophy of Distribution Services *starts with service*—and we never lose sight of its importance.

We recognize that our responsibility to field branches is *primarily that of providing the right product at the right time to the right location.* Our people are trained to be *responsive* to field needs for our services. At the same time, great care has been taken to provide these services at the lowest possible cost to the corporation consistent with good business practice.

Distribution Center Never Closes

In order to provide continuous service to the field branches, the Distribution Center is open 24 hours each day, seven days a week. A skeleton force is on duty at night and weekends, providing the vital link to the field and the customer which is so important in the age of computers.

For example, a Burroughs' field engineer at a customer site may be performing preventive maintenance on the customer's computer installation in the evening after-hours, when he detects a need to replace a vital part which may not be available in local branch stock. A call to Distribution Services in Dearborn, Mich., brings a welcome reply that they have the vital part in stock and will have it on the way by air express within the hour. As an added service, the Distribution Center will even call the field engineer back to tell him the flight number and the time to expect delivery of the requested part at the airport.

Planning is Key to Success

There is quite a bit more involved in saving $2 million annually for the corporation in distribution costs than the mere decision to centralize the overall distribution costs.

Considerable advance planning was devoted to the physical layout of the various distribution functions before the move of the first personnel into our central facility, a one-story building containing some 85,000 sq. ft. of space. In this facility are located all of the basic functions for which Distribution Services is responsible.

Advance planning included work simplification techniques, material handling studies, together with paper flow diagrams and communications engineering and control.

At Distribution Services we started with a clear statement of objectives, responsibilities and authority. Of even greater importance was the careful selection of key personnel for the major functional responsibilities together with determining the organization to meet the basic objectives.

Organized on Functional Lines

The organizational planning for Distribution Services was all completed prior to the transfer of the first functional group to the new operation. The wisdom of this advance planning has been demonstrated many times. The organization chart (*see chart*) indicates that Distribution Services is organized on a straight functional basis covering the following major areas:

1. Inventory and Production Scheduling function;
2. Sales Order Processing function;
3. Service Distribution function.

A good example of the use of clear-cut organization and responsibility lines of authority can be seen in the successful reduction of finished machines in inventory. One of the initial target objectives of Distribution Services was to reduce finished machine inventory by approximately 25% over a two-year period.

In order to reach this 25% reduction objective, Distribution Services combined the responsibility for both Production Scheduling and Inventory Control under the same manager.

On the one hand, he had the responsibility to

Burroughs' Distribution Services Department

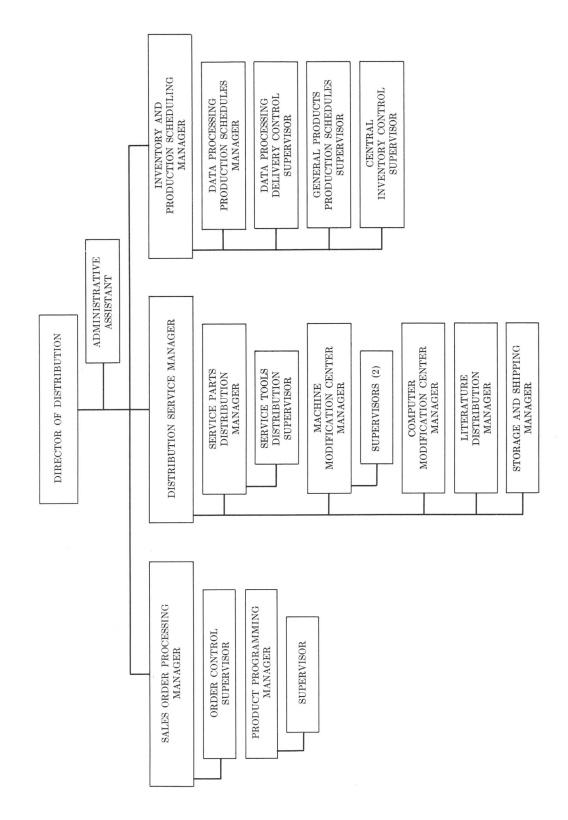

develop required production schedules for the manufacturing plants, to produce necessary finished machines to meet current sales forecasts. On the other hand, this same manager had the responsibility to trim the total field and central warehouse inventories by at least 25%.

Responsibility to trim inventories without authority to control the rate of new production output would have been an impossible assignment, and so these two basic functions were placed under the same manager.

Concurrence on Operating Methods

One of the key reasons for the success of this plan was the complete understanding and agreement by Manufacturing management, as well as by Marketing management at the home office and all 136 district and branch offices. Working inventories of machines for individual branches were carefully re-established by branch management and controlled by the supervisor of Inventory Control.

Because of the inter-relationship between production schedules, sales results and available inventories, computer programs were developed to simulate any desired combination of possibilities. In this way it was possible to examine a number of different daily production rates for various styles of machines depending upon the simulated changes in sales for various machines during the period under consideration.

Because of the speed of the Burroughs B280 computer, it was easy to simulate a number of different situations involving various inventory levels and required rates of daily production. The production rates which were actually established for a particular production period were generally those which gave Manufacturing the optimum level rate, and which also provided Marketing with adequate inventory to meet anticipated sales and required working inventory levels in the individual branches.

In monitoring operating results, actual sales each month are fed into the computer which has been programmed to produce management reports, plus visual display graphs including sales, production and resulting inventory levels by products. This ability to monitor results against the overall master plan has been of great assistance in moving continuously toward the planned inventory objective. The use of the computer as a planning tool for management, and then as a means of monitoring results, is a complete story in itself.

Inventories Reduced Over 40%

Suffice it to say, the results of this program far exceeded the original 25% reduction objective, actually producing a net reduction of just *over 40%*. As a result of careful planning, this was accomplished without any serious problems of inventory shortages or stockouts.

Another key to the success of this program and its continued effectiveness today is the role played by Central Inventory Control. This group was planned and organized to have available at a central point at all times the up-to-date location records of every finished machine, whether in the field or in warehouse inventory. The location and availability of this inventory is literally under constant change . . . machines are being applied on orders or transferred to other locations continuously. It is obvious that central control and current information are a necessity for smooth and efficient use of this precious inventory asset.

Back to Central Warehousing

It is significant to point out that the substantial reduction in finished machines inventory gave added weight to the wisdom of closing the original eight regional warehouses. These warehouses were opened following the close of World War II. The reasoning at that time was primarily one of improved service to branches and customers. Experience indicated some improvement in customer service, but even with eight warehouses it was not always possible to have the right style machine at the right location at the right time.

In fact, today we are able to come much closer to supplying the exact equipment needed from the central warehouse stock. If delivery is urgent, today's jet air freight service makes it possible to deliver merchandise to almost any major marketing area in the United States within 24 hours. The $1 million annual savings that have been achieved in inventory-carrying costs fully justify the occasional use of premium transportation to meet a specific need for quick delivery.

Another clear-cut responsibility in the Distribution Services Department is the Sales Order Processing function. This department has responsibility for processing all sales orders for machines which cannot be delivered from local branch inventory. It further maintains necessary liaison with the interested branch until the order is filled.

The importance of maintaining liaison with the local branch until the order is filled cannot be over-emphasized. All inquiries and communications regarding the status of an order flow into the Sales Order Processing department. The field branches have learned that they can depend upon Sales Order Processing to supply them with prompt and dependable information regarding their various unfilled orders for equipment. Of equal importance is the ability of Sales Order Processing to perform apparent miracles of deliveries on short notice to meet urgent customer requirements.

Prior to the establishment of Distribution Services, orders were channeled to the manufacturing plant which had production responsibility. This arrangement left much to be desired in terms of service to the field, since manufacturing was primarily interested in producing machines, not in processing sales orders.

Four Routes to Order Filling

Today, Sales Order Processing has a choice of several alternatives to fill a specific order. The urgency for delivery and the type of machine are governing factors, but in general Sales Order Processing may select any one of the following routes to fill a specific order:

1. Supply a machine direct from central warehouse stock.
2. Authorize the transfer of a new machine with the required features from a neighboring branch.
3. Take a machine from the central warehouse stock and have it modified in the Machine Modification Center to fit the requirements of the specific order.
4. Schedule for production a machine with all customer-required options at the proper manufacturing plant and follow through to insure shipment on the promised date.

A Product Programming group is also included as an integral part of the Order Processing function. By working directly with the field branch, this specially trained group provides the necessary technical support to pro-gram more involved accounting machine operations to meet specific customer requirements.

Order Processing: Vital Function

As a result of this direct approach to processing and finalizing sales orders, Sales Order Processing provides a vital function in the total distribution operation. Its entire function is geared to provide all required order-filling services to field branches in the U. S. and overseas. In providing these services, it strives constantly to operate with the lowest possible inventory levels, while at the same time providing maximum service to field branches and customers.

Service Parts Distribution

The third major functional area of Distribution Services includes several key departments under the direction of the Distribution Service manager. The objectives and responsibilities of these individual departments are also clear cut and together they round out the total Distribution Services' operation.

The Service Parts department is a good case to illustrate the savings which have accrued to the corporation by centralizing this function and by applying work simplification techniques to the parts ordering, stocking and distribution procedures.

Prior to centralization, field branches were required to place orders for replenishment of their local stock of service parts by transmitting such orders to one of three manufacturing plants, depending on the type of parts involved. However, if a shortage for any particular part existed in the manufacturing plant, production supervisors were inclined to use available parts in new machine production, rather than fill service parts orders from the field branch, occasionally creating poor customer relations in the field.

In addition to this basic conflict, the manufacturing plants were also not geared for a rapid service-parts order-filling operation. Their entire operation was oriented toward manufacturing new machines according to production schedules. Parts, for example, were usually located in several different stock rooms in various areas of the plants for the convenience of the manufacturing operation, certainly not for efficient and rapid filling of service parts orders from field branches.

Detailed Planning for Parts Stocking

In setting up the Service Parts Distribution function within Distribution Services, careful planning was given to the physical layout of the operation as well as the paper flow from receipt of order to the final shipment of parts to the field branch.

Considerable investigation was even given to such details as the selection of steel shelving and the size of boxes to house the individual service parts to be stocked in the department. The boxes are of two lengths (12″ and 24″) and include three different widths (4″, 8″ and 10″). This selection permits stocking the individual shelf items in the size carton which is adequate for the normal amount of inventory carried in stock, and at the same time conserves shelf space where a smaller box will suffice.

Very small items, including items where the quantity is extremely limited, are carried in modular drawers. One set of these drawers occupies space equivalent to three feet of shelving and accommodates parts that would be spread for approximately 57 ft. of shelving, if carried in even the smallest size box.

Large items, or where the normal amount of inventory carried in stock requires larger storage facilities, are carried in baskets approximately 2 ft. high and 3 ft. square. These baskets form the bulk storage area for the larger items and are stacked four high in rows.

This carefully planned approach toward space saving has enabled Distribution Services to set up the entire Service Parts Distribution facility —with over 30,000 different part symbols— in approximately one-third of the area formerly devoted to this function by the manufacturing plants.

Efficiency Increased by Over 400%

Aside from the space-saving aspect, this improved arrangement has made it possible to concentrate the order-picking assignments to individual parts-pickers on a zone basis. The system actually works so efficiently that the individual parts-pickers average one step of physical travel to the filling of each four orders. In other words, in taking 10 steps in her assigned area, the parts-picker would normally fill 40 service parts orders from shelf stock.

The order-filling efficiency of individual parts-pickers has been increased by more than 400% as compared to the previous operation at the manufacturing plants due to the concentration of inventory stock and the streamlining of order-filling procedures.

The orders to be filled by the parts-pickers— now averaging 12,000 each week—are automatically sorted to the parts areas before being assigned to the picker. The individual parts-picker utilizes a traveling work station, similar to a push cart in a supermarket, as an aid to her actual parts-picking run. This traveling work station contains all necessary equipment to facilitate filling orders with the least amount of wasted motion. Included in the traveling work station are envelopes in which the parts for each order may be placed as filled; a stapler to staple the order to the envelope; a file for retaining a copy of the filled order; and a carton to hold the envelopes of individual filled orders.

Parts Shortages Almost Non-existent

It is quite significant that the streamlining of procedures in the Service Parts operation, along with the space-saving techniques, has contributed to an annual savings of more than $300,000 over the former operation. In addition to this, service to the field branches has been dramatically improved. Shortages of parts are all but non-existent. A service parts expeditor swings into action when any particular part requires expedited handling from the manufacturing plant to meet a temporary shortage of stock in the Service Parts department.

The distribution of service tools and test equipment has also come in for careful scrutiny. Here the most significant savings have resulted from trimming of on-hand inventory by more than one-third without any compromise in service to field branches and customers. The service tools function is an integral part of the Service Parts department and functions in the same basic manner.

Another area in which Distribution Services has been able to reduce expenses and inventory-carrying costs for the corporation has been in its Machine Modification Centers. Here the Distribution Center has set up special groups to modify existing new equipment to meet the requirements of a customer's order where quick delivery is desirable. The Modification Centers have the technical know-how, plus the availability of required service parts and features from the central Parts Distribution departments, to make any reasonable and economic modification to a new machine or system from the central warehouse stock. Obviously these groups hold one of the very important keys to operating with fewer total finished machines in stock and yet making it possible to deliver the required machine to the customer at the right time to meet a quick delivery request.

Modification Originates Savings

To take advantage of highly skilled specialists, the Distribution Center has two separate modification centers. One of these is devoted entirely to computers and data processing equipment, while the other is responsible for handling basic accounting and figuring machines. In both instances, the primary objectives are identical, and the savings from these two groups contribute significantly to the overall annual savings by the Distribution Center.

The centralized stocking and distribution of sales and service literature, including technical and training manuals, has also come in for considerable streamlining with greatly increased efficiency. The Literature Distribution department provides a truly vital service in the company's total communications program. Not only is this group concerned with stocking and distributing promotional material and training manuals, but it is also the department through which almost all day-to-day printed communications flow to the field organization.

A high percentage of these day-to-day communications require collating and gathering operations, which are performed in this same department before they can be distributed. Because of its key role for addressing and distributing such communications to the field and the home office, this function takes on added importance in meeting deadlines for various group mailing schedules.

From a cost-reduction standpoint, this department has planned the distribution of literature on a routine basis wherever possible to effect maximum savings in postage. The gathering, addressing and packing of this material, when urgent delivery is not required, provides an excellent opportunity for pooling literature with other shipments of machines, service parts and service tools to the same branch on the same bill of lading. The net savings in parcel post and freight and the use of only one shipping document contributes substantially to the total annual savings effected by Distribution Services.

One of the unique procedures employed by the Distribution Center involves the sorting to local branch destinations of service parts orders which have been picked and filled earlier by the Service Parts department. The collection of several parts orders destined for any particular branch is accomplished by sorting to branch numbers rather than branch city names. The increased speed and accuracy of sorting by numbers has cut in half the distribution time formerly required, and it almost completely eliminates the problem of mis-sorts to such locations as Portland, Maine, instead of Portland, Oregon; or Columbus, Ohio, instead of Columbus, Georgia.

Branch gathering boxes, located on flow-through racks, are adjacent to the Central Packing department. Routine shipments of service tools are packed and shipped once each week with shipments to 20% of the branches each day (Monday through Friday). Emergency shipments are packed and shipped immediately to meet the field branch requirement.

The Pooling department, as its name implies, is concerned simply with pooling together all shipments to a single branch on the designated branch shipping day. Such pooled shipments include service parts, service tools, literature, machines and machine stands. Prior to the establishment of Distribution Services, each of the above items would have been shipped to the individual branch from separate locations on individual shipment documents.

Wherever the individual shipment was less than the minimum shipping weight, the company paid for minimum weights which resulted in increased overall transportation costs to the corporation. The net savings in total transportation to the company have been a significant contribution by the Distribution Center during the past two-and-a-half years.

Standardizing for Efficiency

One of the underlying reasons for the outstanding success of the Distribution Center has been the management philosophy of constantly challenging each procedure from the standpoint of "Is there a better and more efficient way of handling this routine?"

One tangible example showing the potential savings of this philosophy can be illustrated in connection with the distribution of machine stands, or support units. Prior to the establishment of the Distribution Center, five different styles of stands were used with the numerous models of accounting machines. All these stands performed the same basic function; yet they presented a complicated inventory problem because the different style stands were not interchangeable, and it was extremely difficult to forecast the specific requirements of individual branches in advance.

With the help of Product Planning and Engineering, a universal stand was developed which replaced all five of the former styles. This new stand enabled us to reduce the inventory of stands from six months' to three months' supply. Because of improvements in the design of the universal stand and the elimination of unnecessary frills, the acquisition cost of the new style unit will save the company $75,000 annually. In addition, the new stand was designed to be delivered as a completely welded unit, requiring no set-up time in the branch. The former units required considerable set-up time by branch personnel, which was a hidden cost.

The total savings of the new universal stand to Burroughs Corporation including acquisition cost, freight savings because of lighter weight, and reduction in inventory investment exceed $150,000 annually.

Although the accomplishments of the Distribution Center to date have been highly gratifying, we are most enthusiastic about the future possibilities for further savings and even greater service to the field branches and customers. Immediately ahead lies the completion of our computerization programs. When completed, every distribution routine will have maximum computerized efficiency.

How the President Sees It

Perhaps the spirit and the future of the Burroughs Distribution Center are best expressed in the words of Burroughs' President Ray R. Eppert, when he last toured the Distribution Center and stated: "The decision in 1961 to centralize distribution functions has proved to be one of the most significant and profitable organizational moves of the company in recent years. Improvement of service to our customers and field branches has been extremely gratifying. The direct expense savings and contribution to corporate profits have far exceeded all original estimates."

9. *Physical Distribution the Neglected Marketing Function**

Bud Reese†

He read the company's ads and talked to its salesman. He liked what he read and heard; and placed a trial order, to be delivered in six weeks.

That was seven weeks ago—and still no sign of the shipment. He has decided to wait another three days before canceling; *and he has decided to stick with his regular supplier.*

A lot of promotion and sales effort has gone down the drain, whether the shipment arrives in the three days or not. The cause of the waste is faulty physical distribution—not having the product at the right place at the right time.

Not Unusual

This situation is hypothetical, but similar situations are by no means unusual in industry today, say the nation's physical distribution specialists. These experts on the movement of finished goods to customers and distributors all seem to agree that:

Sales are being lost and advertising claims are falling on deaf ears because of faulty physical distribution; and marketing men are primarily to blame for permitting this situation to exist.

They say that marketing men have sadly neglected this important facet of their job—despite the fact that in the area of physical distribution there exists industry's finest opportunity to improve customer service *and reduce costs.*

They say that the movement of goods is over-managed, under-managed and mis-managed—at one and the same time. The purpose of this article is to examine the reasoning behind this

rather unanimous belief, and to answer these basic questions:

1. Should marketing men concern themselves with the physical distribution of their company's products?

2. If physical distribution is a function of marketing, are industrial marketing men neglecting it?

3. What needs to be done to improve physical distribution? And what part do marketers have to play in this movement?

Why Concern Yourself?

"For the average firm, physical distribution consumes between 25% and 33% of each sales dollar [that is, the cost of warehousing, transportation, etc., make up from 25% to 33% of the total cost of products delivered at the customer's location]. A firm's longevity may well depend upon reducing this third highest cost of doing business [after labor and materials]."

That statement was made by Dr. Donald J. Bowersox, assistant director of business development for REA Express, New York, at a June meeting of the American Marketing Association.

And at an American Management Association conference, Paul A. Wassmansdorf, marketing administration consultant for General Electric Co., New York, said, "There is a growing belief that the costs of physical distribution which are not readily apparent are perhaps as great as the obvious ones. These are the costs that result from not having the right goods at the right place at the right time.

"The first, and possibly the largest of these costs is the cost of lost sales. Unfortunately, a great deal of work remains to be done in computing the cost of sales as a result of an unbalanced flow of goods. The preliminary work that has been done, however, indicates that the

* Reprinted by permission from *Industrial Marketing,* October, 1961.
† Associate Editor, *Industrial Marketing.*

cost of lost sales is substantially larger than any-one has suspected . . . many sales are lost without the seller's knowing it."

A check with physical distribution executives and consultants brought out two more immediate reasons for marketing men to take a new, long look at the way their companies move their goods to customers and distributors. The two are closely related.

1. *The Cost-Service Struggle*. Marketing and sales management are caught in the middle, between the field sales force asking for faster delivery and top management demanding cost reductions.

Field sales wants inventories maintained in each customer's backyard; but, maintaining many localized field inventories is an expensive habit.

2. *Less Stocking by Distributors*. And yet, the majority of the experts contacted by IM admit that industrial companies are being forced into adding more warehouses because an increasing number of industrial distributors are shirking their stocking function.

The manager of a newly established branch warehouse in Chicago said, "My company hated to create my job, but they had no choice. Distributors are becoming brokers, refusing to carry adequate stock. Our competitors face the same problem, and are establishing more branch warehouses; we have to go along."

The "Bottomless Cup"

Speaking at an American Management Association meeting, Jerome P. Shuchter, market research director of Federal Pacific Electric Co., Newark, N.J., told why his company's marketing and sales management decided to devote more attention to the problem of physical distribution:

"We backed into our general warehousing policy some ten years ago. With sales expanding rapidly and freight costs mounting, we had to reach an understanding about the function of warehouses. Two different concepts were under consideration:

1. "The 'emergency stock' theory. Were warehouses to be used only to provide local emergency stocks to our distributors? Under this theory, bulk shipments would normally be made

directly from our central warehouse in Newark.

2. "The 'bottomless cup' theory. Were warehouses to be a full-dress distribution channel, with large stocks available locally? Under this theory, our distributors could stock lightly and be assured of an unlimited secondary source of supply.

"On the table were surveys backing the emergency-stock viewpoint. They showed the tremendous inventory saving that could be achieved through this approach. They showed conclusively that direct LCL [less than car load] shipments to customers were more economical than through use of the warehouse as a dog-leg station.

"We reached an easy decision that day—and had to toss it out the next month! The pace of industrial and corporate growth almost passed us by. There was no way in the world we could hold to the emergency-stock concept if even one of our major competitors took the road to all-out customer service through large local backup stocks. And many of our competitors did take that road. The bottomless-cup theory carried the day."

Judging from what has been said and written on the subject, Federal Pacific Electric is just one of many industrial companies to be forced into bottomless-cup physical distribution. The function of having the product at the right place at the right time, of meeting customer service demands, has become an important determinant of sales effectiveness. But . . .

"Most Neglected"

In his AMA speech Dr. Bowersox said, "Among the many problems consuming the time and talents of marketing executives, those most neglected relate to physical distribution."

At the same meeting, Philip F. Cannon, vice-president of Barrington Associates, New York, stated, "I don't want to be so trite as to say— as other speakers over the years have said— that there is no more promising field for improvement than physical distribution; but that is really the way I feel. Allow me, if you will, to say at least this much: I think that in physical distribution there is a great potential for improving customer service and reducing costs. And, this potential stands relatively unexploited. This is virgin territory."

Why do these men feel that physical distribution is being "neglected" by marketing men?

Mr. Cannon explained it this way. "The fact that physical distribution, as something other than a cost factor, has received very little attention suggests that perhaps there is something peculiar or particularly difficult about this function.

"The fact is, however, that the technical, procedural and operational aspects of physical distribution do not pose any more difficult problems than are found in manufacturing or selling. The real reason for the neglect of physical distribution, I believe, is that it is usually not organized very well. Too many physical distribution functions are left to fall between the chairs, creating many 'grey areas' where objectives, policies and organizational lines are at best fragmentary, if they exist at all. Most commonly, the functions of distribution are split haphazardly between manufacturing and sales . . .

"Not infrequently, in discussing job responsibilities with senior marketing executives, we have had them wryly add, 'Oh yes, another part of my job includes liaison with the plant shipping department.' "

Who Does What?

In his book, "Modern Marketing Management," Ferdinand F. Mauser, marketing professor at Wayne State University, wrote, "All too often . . . inter- and intra-plant flow of goods are under traffic, and the control of regional warehouses and inventories are under the jurisdiction of the sales department."

The manager of a warehouse on the outskirts of Chicago said that in his company, traffic, finished goods inventory control and order processing are directed by the controller; planning of warehouse space is done by the planning manager; order status inquiry is headed by the sales manager; and the factory manager controls finished goods materials handling and warehouse management.

Mr. Shuchter of Federal Pacific Electric said that before his company woke up to the importance of physical distribution, "We had no . . . really consistent concept of the distribution function. True, we did have a traffic manager; someone did schedule shipments; someone did back the process with production schedules; someone did modernize and lay out new warehouses; and someone from the marketing department did bird-dog the activity, policing warehouse expenses and counting inventories. But, all these activities were carried on in differ-ent departments, with insufficient common direction and policy."

The physical distributions specialists say that because of this hodge-podge of authority, customers receive incorrect answers to their order status inquiries; orders are not processed with dispatch; and, in general, customer service suffers severely.

What's the Answer?

What is the answer to the Hydra-headed distribution problem. Centralization of physical distribution planning, obviously—but under whom? And just what would this person administer?

Here, again, the experts seem to agree. They say that the man for the job is the marketing manager. But, they are quick to qualify their suggestion. They realize that the man with the marketing manager title in many companies is really the sales manager, given the title to pay lip service to the "marketing concept."

In such cases, the experts suggest that a new marketing title be established, as is being done by an increasing number of companies; the title being that of physical distribution manager.

The Only Way

Why couldn't the job simply be given to the sales manager, or the production manager, or the controller?

Mr. Shuchter answered this question bluntly: "There has never been a sales manager who thought he had too much inventory—or a finance manager who thought he had too little. There has never been a production manager who thought production runs were long enough—or a sales manager who didn't prefer smaller, more frequent runs."

Mr. Cannon was more specific as to what happens to physical distribution when it is under sales or manufacturing:

First, here are some things that he said can happen when distribution is sales-directed:

1. "Sales is naturally inclined to provide customer service at any cost, i.e., it might well overinvest in branch warehouse inventories [Mr. D. Bowersox said that for a typical warehouse it takes about 75% more inventory to satisfy 95% of customer sales from stock than it does to satisfy 80%], incur excessive LCL or LTL shipping costs, and so forth.

2. "The traffic department is called upon to serve other divisions or functions of the business, such as manufacturing and purchasing; its position under sales may limit its ability to render corporate service.

3. "Branch warehouses tend to be located automatically with branch sales offices, even though the organization and location of selling functions in a territory bear no relationship to the economics of warehouse location.

[John T. Thompson, general manager of distributor products, Raytheon Co., Westwood, Mass., has stated that field warehouses frequently create availability problems rather than solve them, and sometimes they inject a communications delay point.]

4. "Sales executives get saddled with an operating function for which they may have little training, and less understanding—physical distribution economics."

[Mr. Mauser wrote that, "Out of habit, sales departments often promise deliveries on the 1st and 15th. The distribution executive who creates an awareness of the importance of staggering promised delivery dates induces a smoother and less costly outgoing merchandise flow. The sales department should be checked to determine what the lag time is between the customer's placing the order and its actually arriving in the shipping department. Such a check may reveal delays which often mean the difference between high and low transportation costs and between prompt deliveries and less satisfactory ones. It is often surprising to discover the extent of internal delay to which an order is subjected."]

Now, here's what Mr. Cannon said might happen when distribution is directed by manufacturing:

1. "Operations are restricted under the dominance of the manufacturing point of view, which generally tends to be introverted and which cannot evaluate objectively the needs of marketing for physical distribution support.

2. "Distribution is treated as a subordinate and secondary function that does not merit first-rate, top-drawer attention from manufacturing executives."

Qualifications

What would be the qualifications of this physical distribution manager? Would he be a traffic manager with planning authority?

Most physical distribution specialists say "no" to the idea of a glorified traffic manager. They say that the traffic manager's preoccupation with detail and with activity that is massively routine usually disqualifies him for the job of physical distribution manager. The right man for the job would be:

Appreciative of the fundamental nature and importance of physical distribution in corporate planning.

Familiar with distribution costing. "On a national average," says Dr. Bowersox, "transportation services account for less than 25% of the total cost incurred in marketing logistics [physical distribution]. A total cost perspective provides the analytical framework necessary for a penetrating evaluation of alternative distribution systems. It is interesting to note that astute distribution planning will often lead to higher transportation cost . . . total cost is the fundamental concept."

Appreciative of the need for exacting research to support distribution planning, in place of crude approximations, fictitious averages and intuitive guesses, distribution planning must be the result of effectively utilizing electronic data processing and quantitative techniques.

Dr. Bowersox explained that many advancements in this area of quantitative techniques have mushroomed under the catch-all label of operations research, including a technique commonly called linear programming. He said, "While much criticism can be voiced on the relative sterility of OR in providing significant pay-offs to date, if quantitative techniques do hold the promise of significant pay-offs, it is reasonably certain they will be realized first among logistics problems.

"The foundations for this prediction are simple: many elements of total cost distribution are quantifiable and can be approximated by near linear relationships. . . . It is safe to generalize that better than 90% of historical distribution planning lacked the benefits of system logic, mathematical structure and, in many cases, even advanced statistical analysis. The history of distribution planning represents an era of stagnant check-lists and static formulas."

Centralize What?

So much for the man; now for his job. Here's what the majority of the experts contacted by

IM say should be administered by the physical distribution manager:

1. *Transportation and traffic.* The movement of inbound materials to the factory, and the movement of finished goods from the factory to final customers, branch warehouses and regional distribution centers, another factory, freight forwarding or classifying points.

2. *Finished goods inventory control.* The method of a company's data processing system may dictate the assignment of the responsibility for actual maintenance of the inventory records elsewhere; but where circumstances warrant, it may be logical for distribution to maintain these records, particularly where branch warehouse inventories are concerned.

Sales and finance would, of course, have the major voices in determining levels of inventory; but, finished goods are the immediate physical responsibility of distribution, which serves as the connecting link between sales and manufacturing.

3. *Location of branch warehouses.* First, sales would define service, in terms of number of days between the date of an order from the customer and the date of its delivery to the customer. Then it would be the distribution manager's responsibility to maintain at least this level of service. As was pointed out earlier, the organization and location of selling functions in a territory bear no relationship to the economics of warehouse location.

4. *Operation of branch warehouses.* Sales management skills and energies are best devoted to selling, not in handling the routines of warehouse operation.

5. *Order processing and administration.* This would include: (1) acknowledgment, done under policies issued by sales; (2) credit review, done under policies, procedures and current credit ratings issued by the treasurer's office; (3) pricing, done under strict formulae and price lists issued by sales; (4) order editing, done as specified by the controller and by sales; (5) invoice preparation and mailing, as prescribed by the controller; (6) reorder from production—inventory replenishment according to formulae emanating from manufacturing, as well as from distribution.

Many physical distribution specialists claim that order processing time can be cut from a third to a half through organization of the various facets under one man.

6. *Customer service.* Distribution should also be concerned with answering inquiries on order status from salesmen and customers. Distribution would not, of course, be responsible for technical service.

7. *Materials handling.* Manufacturing has historically been responsible for this function, say the experts. They point out, however, that in-process materials handling methods are not readily applicable to finished goods handling.

8. *Package design.* Merchandising and sales aspects of package design are not the concern of physical distribution. However, package design as it affects the handling and transporting of merchandise are his concern.

Improvement

Are the physical distribution specialists correct in suggesting that planning of the movement of finished goods to customers and distributors be centralized? Compare the improvements in customer service and the reduction of marketing costs possible through proper physical distribution management with the distribution system of the early growth days of Federal Pacific Electric, as described by Mr. Shuchter:

"Sam O'Toole was the 1949 version of Ramac. He guided the destiny of our stock from its source for many years. With orders and memos tucked in every pocket, he charged through each day as though it were the decisive moment in human history.

"Emergency! The ABC Distributing Co. placed an order for 12 400-amp, three-pole, solid neutral switch devices three months ago. The order, it seems, has been misplaced and now the salesman, Sam's buddy, is on the phone crying his heart out: He faces cancellation of the $600 order and other reprisals too terrible to mention. The card inventory shows zero.

"Enter Sam O'Toole. From the dark recesses of the stockroom he drags out three of the precious devices. His friend, Jake the foreman, will convert two from similar units. Up in the factory Sam has spotted five almost-complete assemblies coming down the line. He drags the plant manager (no lesser mortal will do) to the spot and stands panting as the foreman is ordered to stop all work until the devices are complete.

"That's ten down and two to go. In a flash Sam has wired the people at the St. Louis warehouse that the switch they will receive today is to be air-freighted back to Newark. And finally Sam calls a Paterson distributor who is sure to help him out by returning a switch he has in stock. His task complete, Sam calls the salesman to promise shipment of eight switches today and four tomorrow, and knows in his heart that this was a job well done. (Sam, by the way, was also the best pitcher our softball team ever had.)"

1965

As for the future, in an American Management Association report on physical distribution, A. W. Greene, editor of *Distribution Age*, Philadelphia, wrote:

"In 1965 there will be many physical distribution managers. They will come from traffic and transportation, from warehousing, from industrial engineering, from production, marketing and sales. Each will have greater scope and greater breadth of vision than the present pioneers of distribution management.

"I see such a man at his desk. It's a clean desk, except for rows of push-buttons, intercoms and other executive gadgets. Behind him, and on all sides, there are live charts and graphs, pulsating with electronic recordings of up-to-the-moment inventories at all distribution points. There are direct wire communication lines to all points.

"As the distribution manager of 1965 sits in his white tower of control, his telephone rings. An angry voice is heard: 'Nine weeks ago I sent you an order for three sizes of your model X-5 components. You promised seven-week delivery. As of now, I haven't received a single unit. If I don't get this shipment by the end of the week, cancel the order!'

"Well, . . . maybe in 1966 . . .' "

10. New Reasoning in Choosing a Warehouse Location*

IRVIN R. WHITEMAN†

Problems of outer space make headlines every day; but problems of space on earth constitute the day-to-day challenges.

Consider, for example, the decisions faced by the Milford Company of California, a wholesale liquor distributor which holds exclusives with a number of leading distilleries. Its growth over the years has been a steady one. In 1961 the sales volume was approximately $22,000,000 per year. Having already exhausted any further expansion possibilities at existing facilities in Beverly Hills, management was confronted with the familiar problem of selecting a new site.

A study covering the selection of warehouse sites in the time period 1965 to 1975 was conducted; both single and multiple warehouse arrangements were considered. As a result of the study, a site was selected and ground broken on a plot of 4.3 acres. The building, completed in July 1962, covers 71,400 square feet, of which 60,000 is occupied by the warehouse and the remainder by offices. Sufficient land is available to expand the facilities by 50%.

The Study

The selection of a site, typical of problems of management, is one clouded with uncertainties. In problems of time-phasing, there is real ambiguity in deciding dollar costs. Business is not executed in a single instant of time; it is built up over a number of years and is expected to have a continuous existence in the future.

What are the costs of using facilities which are already in use, and what will be the salvage

value in future years of any expenditures made this year? If something new is being procured or developed, no real experience upon which to base cost estimates may exist. It is surprising, in practice, how inaccurate even careful estimates of future costs have proved to be. Careless estimates tend to be "out of this world."

Of the expenses borne by the company, some are applicable to the selection of a warehouse site, whereas others are not. Clearly, wherever the warehouse is located, the internal arrangement and the operation of the warehouse must be conducted efficiently; this is true regardless of location. Also essentially independent of the location is the type of warehouse, provided sufficient acreage is available.

Those costs deemed applicable to the selection of the warehouse site were broken down into the following three primary categories:

1. Distribution costs
2. Real estate costs
3. Processing costs—differential additional data processing costs between a multiwarehouse complex and a single warehouse.

Distribution Costs

Preliminary investigations showed that of the three primary expenses—(1) distribution, (2) real estate, and (3) processing—those of distribution were major.

Costs such as inventory, internal warehouse operation, and type of warehouse were omitted from consideration, inasmuch as they remain essentially independent of the ultimate warehouse location.

To obtain that warehouse site associated with minimal distribution costs, the cost of distribution associated with a warehouse located in each of the 44 existing sales districts was determined. A comparison of all possible locations showed

* Reprinted by permission from *Journal of Marketing*, National Quarterly Publication of the American Marketing Association, January 1964.

† Director of Operations Research, Computer Concepts, Inc.

that area associated with minimal distribution costs.

For pictorial purposes, topographical maps were prepared for the 1960 and 1970 time periods. These maps—see Figures 1 through 4—consist of a Los Angeles background upon which contour lines of equal distribution cost have been superimposed.

The areas of minimal cost are fairly large and flat, with relatively little change in shape between the two time periods. This indicates that the warehouse location is not dramatically affected by the expected changes of population growth and sales posture in the next decade. The variation of distribution costs in the minimal area is very slight and, hence, other considerations—such as real estate costs, railroad sidings and zone limitations—prove to be overriding.

Procedure

The distribution cost of any given warehouse location was computed as follows:

1. Locations of sales districts were laid out on a large oversized map, geographical centers of each district estimated, and aerial distances between centers determined.

2. Since aerial distances understate ground traveling distances, a sample of ground mileage distance was taken and found to differ from aerial distance by a factor of approximately 0.3. All aerial mileage was converted to ground mileage by multiplying by 1.3. To obtain a round-trip distance, a multiplier of 2 was subsequently used.

3. To obtain the number of truck trips necessary to serve any given sales district, the annual sales total for each district was converted to cases of liquor. Dividing this number by the average truck-load capacity provided the annual number of truck trips necessary to supply the district.

4. The cost of servicing a given district was obtained as the product of the number of trips per year, the length of trip, and the average mileage cost of truck operation.

5. The cost of warehouse operation in any given district is the summation of distribution costs to every other district.

1970 Estimates

Essential to the selection of a suitable warehouse site was a prediction of sales for Milford

Liquor in the decade ahead, around 1970. The predictions were based upon the premises that sales volume is closely correlated with population and that newly-formed sales districts grow faster than old, well-established districts.

1. Estimates on population growth rates were formulated from Census data for the year 1950 and 1960, complemented by estimates of the Los Angeles City Planning Commission. Based upon the expected growth rate in each sales district and upon whether the district was new or well established, the district sales volumes for the year 1970 were adjusted by factors of 1.5, 2, or 3. Study of sales growth indicated that these factors were reasonable.

2. Some of the recently created sales districts were adjusted by factors of 2 or 3. With intensified sales effort, it is reasonable to believe that these districts should, on the whole, increase at a greater rate than the older, already well-established districts. Those new districts, located in areas which were expected to experience a high population growth, were given the higher rating.

3. Based upon expected 1970 sales, distribution costs were obtained as before.

Real Estate Costs

The figures on transportation costs for the years 1960 and 1970 indicate that the area of minimal distribution cost is large and relatively shallow. Since the differences in distribution costs within this area are slight and not significant in the face of future uncertainties, the specific location was determined by the additional considerations of real estate costs, taxes, railroad sidings, and zoning. That area which best met the requirements of minimal cost was found to be the City of Commerce.

Real estate costs were based upon a lease-back arrangement. That is, Milford would purchase the property, sell it to an interested financial party, and then lease the building from this party. The yearly lease-back price was assumed to be 10% of the original cost of the property. The cost of the warehouse was not included as a consideration, because this cost would remain essentially invariant with respect to location.

Warehouse Considerations

The cost associated with a two-warehouse policy was examined. Two considerations are of

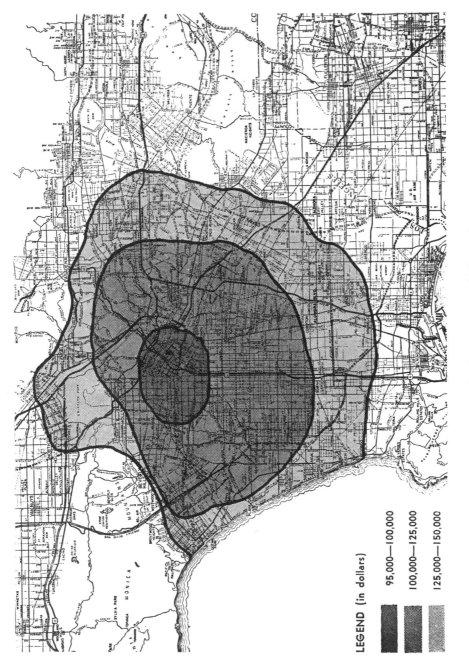

FIG. 1. Distribution costs—1960 single warehouse.

LEGEND (in dollars)

95,000—100,000

100,000—125,000

125,000—150,000

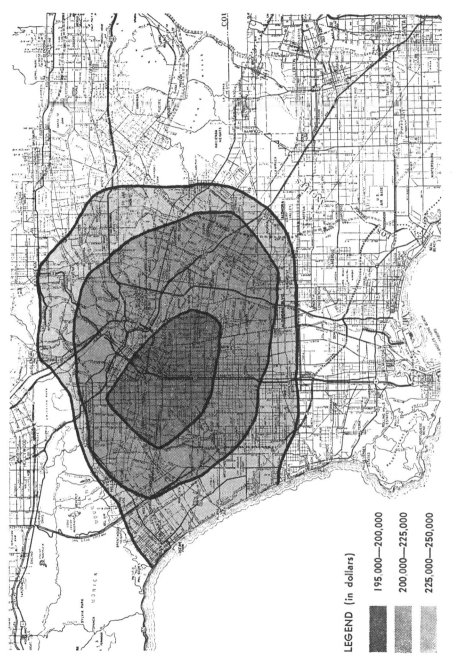

FIG. 2. Distribution costs—1970 single warehouse.

LEGEND (in dollars)

195,000—200,000

200,000—225,000

225,000—250,000

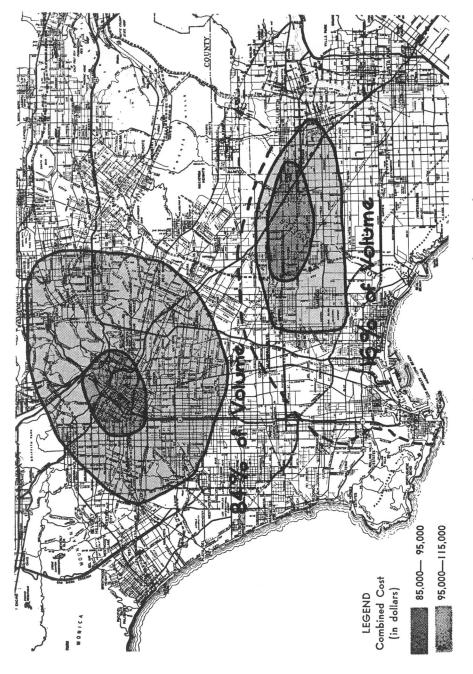

FIG. 3.   Distribution costs—1960 two-warehouse complex.

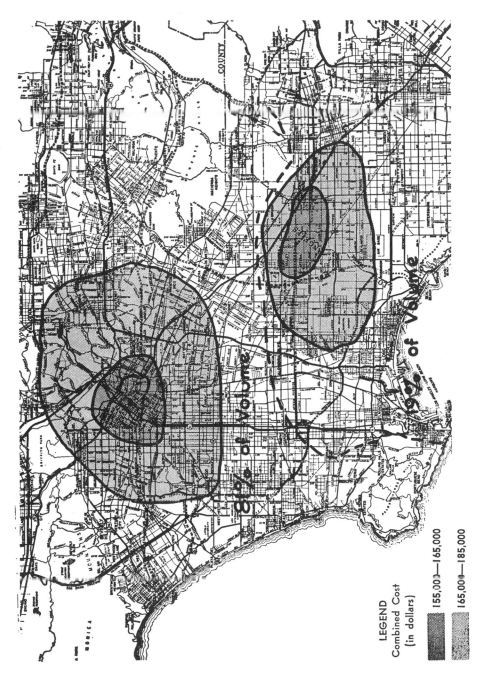

FIG. 4. Distribution costs—1970 two-warehouse complex.

LEGEND
Combined Cost
(in dollars)

155,000—165,000

165,000—185,000

prime importance: (1) the location of the respective warehouses; and (2) the amount of volume each should share.

As to the location of the warehouses, it is possible, in terms of the Milford area sales distribution, to consider the Los Angeles area in terms of an ellipse extending from San Fernando Valley to Orange County. Clearly the two warehouses should be located in the proximity of the major axis.

In examining the actual sales breakdown, the lowest cost was found to be one in which the main warehouse carries approximately 80% of the load, and the second warehouse approximately 20%.

Splitting the Los Angeles environs into two separate areas decreases the sensitivity of warehouse location to transportation costs. Each warehouse has less overall area to cover.

Hence, the specific location of each warehouse is not quite so critical in that the effects of the longest trips have been eliminated. Referring to Figures 3 and 4, it can be seen that the individual contours are very "shallow" and that a great deal of flexibility exists with respect to warehouse location in these areas. Within the proximity of these areas, other overriding features predominate.

Comparison of a Single Warehouse with a Two-Warehouse Complex

Single warehouse costs were calculated for different locations for the years 1960 and 1970. These costs are shown in Tables 1 and 2.

Comparisons of several selected two-warehouse combinations for the years 1960 and 1970 are shown in Tables 3 and 4.

For both time periods, it is seen that the com-

Table 1. Distribution and Total Operating Costs, Single Warehouse, 1960

Location	Distribution costs	Real estate costs	Total
Los Angeles	$ 94,733	$55,000	$149,733
City of Commerce	*103,659*	*6,250*	*109,909*
Vernon	97,137	40,000	137,137
South Gate	103,535	20,000	123,535
Huntington Park	96,170	32,500	128,670

Table 2. Distribution and Total Operating Costs, Single Warehouse, 1970

Location	Distribution costs	Real estate costs	Total
Los Angeles	$193,760	$55,000	$248,760
City of Commerce	*200,083*	*6,250*	*206,333*
Vernon	196,452	40,000	236,452
South Gate	203,300	20,000	223,300
Huntington Park	195,395	32,500	227,895

bination 1—City of Commerce and Buena Park —show a savings of $1,162 and $16,472 respectively annually. As indicated previously, a great deal of latitude exists in the actual combinations of locations chosen with respect to distribution costs; hence, the combinations chosen reflect realistic considerations.

Based upon the optimum volume distribution, real estate acreage was apportioned between the two warehouse locations. In the single-warehouse case, real estate costs were based upon a lot size of five acres. In the two-warehouse case, it was felt that an apportionment of 20% to 80% (1 acre to 4 acres) was not entirely realistic because, even though the warehouse might be proportionately reduced, the surrounding land requirements would not.

As a basis for real estate costs, a minimum of 2.5 acres was chosen for the smaller warehouse, and the figure of 4 acres for the larger. The assessment of these costs is shown in the columns of the tabular breakdown. One item of interest is the column entitled "Communication Costs." Clearly there is a major difference between the single warehouse and the two-warehouse complex in the processing of invoices.

Two possible situations exist. First, each of the two different warehouses may function as autonomous units. Second, one warehouse may act as the "master" warehouse, in which all administrative functions are performed, and the other as a "satellite."

Each of these possibilities poses some cost penalty. In the case of two separate independent units, those savings which accrue by being able to warrant a large single central processing unit are lost. In the second case, in which the master warehouse processes all invoices and transmits this information to the satellite warehouse via

Table 3.   Distribution and Total Operating Costs, Two-Warehouse Case, 1960

Locations of warehouse combination	Distribution costs —each warehouse	Total distribution costs	Optimum volume division	Real estate costs— each plant	Total real estate costs	Communication costs	Total operating costs	Gain over one warehouse in optimum location
1. City of Commerce	$81,411		84%	$ 5,000				
		$95,897			$ 9,250	$3,600	$108,747	$ 1,162
Buena Park	14,486		16%	4,250				
2. Los Angeles	59,834		81%	44,000				
		70,110			48,250	3,000	130,903	−21,004
Buena Park	19,230		19%	4,250				
3. Vernon	63,659		80%	24,000				
		84,599			28,250	3,600	116,449	−6,540
Buena Park	20,940		20%	4,250				

some data link, there is the additional cost of communication.

However, the master-satellite combination appeared to be less costly—approximately $300 per month. This cost was taken to be additive to the cost of the two-warehouse operation.

Again, even with this additional cost, the savings intrinsic in the lowering of distribution costs result in an overall lower total operating cost; that is, the cost of operating two warehouses is less than the cost of operating one warehouse.

It is difficult to tell whether these savings are real, in that they are based on predictions of business and community growth in the next 10 years. Regardless of whether a single-warehouse or a two-warehouse policy is chosen, however, the location of the main warehouse should be near the "centroid" of the Los Angeles area, that is, the City of Commerce.

As shown in the two-warehouse case, a fair amount of flexibility exists with respect to the actual locations; no penalty is associated with keeping the main warehouse in the City of Commerce. This is based upon the knowledge that if a warehouse is to be self-sustaining, it should be located in the heart of the area it serves.

Action Taken

Since the location of the main warehouse is essentially independent of whether it is the sole warehouse or a master warehouse supporting a satellite, a step-by-step expansion was advocated. It was recommended that a single warehouse be established in the environs of the City of Commerce, and that within the next five years or so a decision based upon sales figures of that date be made as to the establishment of a warehouse in the heart of the new area.

Table 4.   Distribution and Total Operating Costs Two-Warehouse Cases, 1970

Locations of warehouse combination	Distribution costs —each warehouse	Total distribution costs	Optimum volume division	Real estate costs— each plant	Total real estate costs	Communication costs	Total operating costs	Gain over one warehouse in optimum location
1. City of Commerce	$133,918		81%	$ 5,000				
		$175,611			$ 9,250	$5,000	$189,861	$16,472
Buena Park	41,693		19%	4,250				
2. Los Angeles	106,238		75%	44,000				
		153,496			48,250	5,000	206,746	−413
Buena Park	47,258		25%	4,250				
3. Vernon	117,075		77%	24,000				
		160,924			28,250	5,000	194,174	12,159
Buena Park	43,849		23%	4,250				

11. *A Model for Scale of Operations**

Edward H. Bowman and John B. Stewart†

Implications of Scale of Operations

The president of a well-established New England company recently asked one of those infrequent but important questions—"Should we add some warehouses to our existing distribution system?" The answer proved to be a dual one: a *no* to the specific problem he had in mind; and a *yes* to one not suspected. Fortunately, the method of solution employed helped provide answers for both problems. Anticipated savings from the first problem alone were 10 per cent of net annual profits.

The usefulness of this method is significant in two respects. First, companies with similar problems may find some of the ideas directly applicable to their situations. Second, the general method employed is illustrative of a way of thinking that has broad potential application to business problems. Some similar methods have been receiving increasing management interest under the name of "operations research."

For instance, the same general procedure could be used to determine the best size for salesmen's territories, the best number of branch production facilities, or other issues which are fundamentally problems in the scale of operations.

The Problem

Optimum Warehouse Territory

This New England company had acquired more than a dozen warehouses in the five states served from its manufacturing plant. Warehouses had been added in some areas and discontinued in others as changing conditions seemed to dictate. These decisions had been

made on a "common sense basis," and often had proved advantageous to warehouse operations in one area but at too great a cost in reduced operating efficiency in adjoining areas. The problem was further complicated by the fact that two basic delivery methods are used. One type of distribution involves semi-trailer delivery from plant to warehouse, unload and storage, and then individual deliveries to market, while in the manufacturing plant area, individual or direct delivery to market is the rule.

The general manager recently raised the question of what was the optimum size of a warehouse territory. Some executives believed drivers making deliveries directly from the plant warehouse were spending too much time getting to and from cities located about an hour's drive from the plant.

The problem as restated by the analysts was, "How large a territory should be served by a warehouse to result in a minimum total cost for warehousing, trucking between plant and warehouses, and delivery from warehouse to customers?" It was imperative that this question be answered from an over-all standpoint—covering the company's complete physical distribution system—rather than on an individual territory basis.

Criteria for Optimum Territory

The real and useful objective of the whole project first had to be determined. Profits would be a good place to start. However, sales for this particular problem were fixed, so to maximize profits was equivalent in this case to seeking minimum costs. The "measure of effectiveness" chosen, after examination of warehouse operations, was cost (within the warehouse district) per dollar's worth of goods distributed. It was this cost which should be minimized. Initially, minimum cost per warehouse sounds good. However, this would yield a legion of very small warehouses which when totaled would give an inefficient total operation.

* Reprinted by permission from *The Journal of Marketing,* National Quarterly Publication of the American Marketing Association, January, 1956.
† Massachusetts Institute of Technology.

Determinants of Cost

Available data were obtained from the company's records. Examination of these data revealed that the cost of material handled in each warehouse district appeared to be primarily dependent upon two opposing factors: the volume of business passing through the warehouse and the area served by the warehouse. The greater the volume handled, the smaller would be the cost per dollar's worth of goods distributed. However, the greater the area served, the greater would be the cost per dollar's worth of goods distributed.

Finding this relationship was, of course, no surprise. The crucial job was to establish the precise relationship between these factors; that is, their relative importance and the rate at which their variation affected the over-all economy of the system. To be satisfactory, the analysis would have to handle both factors simultaneously. This done, it would be possible to predict the cost of distributing goods as the area served by and the volume handled in each warehouse changed. More importantly, the systems could be so arranged that total cost would be minimized.

The analysts recognized that many other variables in this situation could affect the measure of effectiveness. For instance, the price paid for gasoline in each warehouse area would affect the cost of operations in the area and undoubtedly varies throughout the New England states. The particular design of the warehouse, for example, whether the loading platform was at tailgate level of trucks or on the ground, might also affect these costs. However, it was desirable to keep the analysis fairly simple and so only the two factors considered most important were included.

The Warehouse District Model

Objectives and Limitations

Because of the great complexity of the "real world," models of aspects of situations are often built as aids to analysis and understanding. These models may be physical replicas, electrical analogues, blue prints, charts and graphs, and so forth. The most abstract and probably the most universal type of model is the mathematical one. It has been widely used in the physical sciences, in some of the social sciences, and in engineering. It is well to keep in mind that none of these models *are* the real world. They are at best *useful* simplified representations or abstractions of it. Mathematical models were chosen for this particular real world because of the precision with which they could portray the relationships involved and with which they could reveal minimum-cost solutions.

Elements of the Warehouse District Model

To build the mathematical model, it was necessary to understand the economics of the problem. Warehousing costs per dollar of goods handled tend to decrease with increasing volume: costs of supervision and other overhead are spread over more units, labor can usually be used with a lower proportion of the idle time, etc. Since distance traveled would be the main factor determining costs associated with area, it followed that this cost would tend to vary approximately with the square root of the area. (Radius and diameter vary with the square root of the area of a circle.) As concentric rings of equal area are added, rings rapidly become narrower, that is, *additional* distance traveled becomes smaller.

Mathematical Expression

To summarize, it had been determined that for the problem at issue here, the cost per dollar's worth of goods distributed (the warehouse efficiency) was equal to certain costs which vary inversely with the volume plus certain costs which vary directly with the square root of the area plus certain costs which were affected by neither of these variables. Putting this last factor first, these same variables arranged as a mathematical expression are as follows:

(1) $$C = a + \frac{b}{V} + c\sqrt{A}$$

Notation: C = cost (within the warehouse district) per dollar's worth of goods distributed—the measure of effectiveness.

V = volume of goods in dollars handled by the warehouse per unit of time.

A = area in square miles served by the warehouse.

a = cost per dollar's worth of goods distributed independent of either the warehouse's volume handled or area served.

b = "fixed" costs for the warehouse per unit of time, which divided by the volume will yield the appropriate cost per dollar's worth distributed.

c = the cost of the distribution which varies with the square root of the area; that is, costs associated with miles covered within the warehouse district such as gasoline, truck repairs, driver hours, etc.

Method for Solution

The company had over a dozen warehouses and it was possible to determine for each the cost per dollar's worth of goods distributed (C), the volume of goods handled by the warehouse (V), and the area served by the warehouse (A). Then, by the statistical method of least-squares multiple regression, it was possible to use this warehousing experience and to determine mathematically the values of the coefficients or parameters a, b, and c, which will make the model the closest predictor of the actual cost for all present warehouses using the individual volume and area figures.[1]

[1] This method minimizes the sum of the squares of the differences between the actual cost and the predicted cost. An expression for this is as follows:

Minimize:

$$\sum_{i=1}^{i=N}\left[C_i-\left(a+\frac{b}{V_i}+c\sqrt{A_i}\right)\right]^2$$

where C_i, V_i, and A_i indicate actual values in a given (the ith) branch warehouse operation and the $\sum$ indicates a sum total of all (N) warehouses. Actually a set of three simultaneous equations are solved for a, b, and c.

$$\frac{\partial\sum_1^N\left[C_i-\left(a+\frac{b}{V_i}+c\sqrt{A_i}\right)\right]^2}{\partial a}=0$$

$$\frac{\partial\sum_1^N\left[C_i-\left(a+\frac{b}{V_i}+c\sqrt{A_i}\right)\right]^2}{\partial b}=0$$

$$\frac{\partial\sum_1^N\left[C_i-\left(a+\frac{b}{V_i}+c\sqrt{A_i}\right)\right]^2}{\partial c}=0$$

These equations establish what the statistician calls the normal equations.

How Good Was the Warehouse District Model?

In order to confirm the accuracy of this model, a Cost (C) was computed for each warehouse using the determined values of a, b, and c from the multiple regression calculation and the warehouse's specific figures for V and A. By comparing these computed costs with the actual warehousing costs, the correlation coefficient was found to be .89, indicating a fairly high degree of correlation.

Minimization With the Warehouse District Model

Conversion of the Model

Developing this model is only the first step making it possible to predict costs. What is desired is cost minimization. However, in this case, it was necessary to convert a part of the model mathematically in order to minimize it. The object was to express cost as a function of only one unknown (area). A relationship was found between volume and area for each section of New England. This sales density (K), expressed in dollar volume per square mile of area, is

$$(2)\qquad K=\frac{V}{A}$$

Therefore, $V=KA$, and it is possible to substitute this expression for V in the original model, giving

$$(3)\qquad C=a+\frac{b}{KA}+c\sqrt{A}$$

where a, b, and c are now specific figures determined from the multiple regression calculation.

Cost Minimization With Respect to Area

What is desired now is an expression for A which will make this cost model a minimum. It is possible to do this by differentiation which gives[2]

$$(4)\qquad A=\left(\frac{2b}{cK}\right)^{2/3}$$

[2] The expression for differentiation is

$$\frac{dC}{dA}=-\frac{b}{kA^2}+\frac{c}{2\sqrt{A}}=0$$

This expression for the area A indicates that area which would yield a minimum cost and is a function of b and c (costs calculated from the empirical data) and K (the sales density of the area in question).

The cost which is minimized is the explicit cost within the warehouse district. The implicit cost, interest on investment in inventory and equipment, was analyzed and demonstrated to be insignificant for the purposes of this study. The costs also did not include the cost of loading semi-trailer trucks at the plant and transporting them to the branch warehouses, since—as long as goods are handled from a branch warehouse —these costs will be incurred and will not be affected by volume handled or area served by each branch warehouse.

Branch Warehouse Findings

The company's actual branch warehouse areas ranged from about 95 to 150 per cent of the individually computed optimum areas. This disclosed an answer to a question not originally framed, namely, that most of the branch warehouse areas were too large and that, therefore,

$$\frac{2T_oP_d + T_f + T_dH_d}{P_h(H_d - 2P_dH_m - F_t)} = \frac{S_l + B_e + 2S_oD_p + S_f + 2S_dH_mD_p + I_w}{P_s} + \frac{2T_oD_b + T_f + T_dH_d}{P_h(H_d - 2D_bH_m - F_t)}$$

there were not enough warehouses in outlying districts.

The Plant District Model

Cost Relationships

The problem of the area to be served from the plant warehouse was distinct from the branch warehouse problem since goods which are distributed directly from the plant do not have to be loaded into semi-trailer trucks and transported to the branch warehouses and then unloaded, supervised, and stored in that warehouse. Therefore, as this area served from the plant is increased, these costs are saved. However, increasing this area makes it more expensive to serve the increasingly distant perimeter areas from the plant because more of the delivery driver's time and the truck's miles are spent in unproductive time driving to and from the delivery area.

Marginal Model

The type of model set up for this problem was a marginal model. The plant warehouse area should be expanded out to the point where the cost of serving the marginal area (the last addition) from the plant is equal to the cost of serving it from an optimally placed branch warehouse. Reducing the plant warehouse area from this line would mean that intervening customers served by a branch could be served more cheaply from the plant. Expanding the plant warehouse area beyond these points of marginal equality would mean that the additional customers then served from the plant could be served more cheaply from branch warehouses.

Elements of the Marginal Model

This model of marginal equality, the cost of handling one piece of goods for the marginal area, follows:

Plant direct delivery cost per piece = branch delivery cost per piece (that is, plant to branch plus branch to customer).

Notation:
T_o = Truck operation cost per mile
P_d = Plant delivery miles
T_f = Truck fixed costs per day (amortization type charge)
T_d = Truck driver costs per hour
F_t = Fixed driver time per day (check in, check out, coffee break, etc.)
D_b = Miles from branch to delivery
S_l = Semi load and unload costs
B_e = Branch expense per semi
S_o = Semi-operating costs per mile
D_p = Miles from plant to the branch
S_f = Semi fixed costs per day (amortization type charge)
S_d = Semi driver costs per hour
I_w = Inventory costs per semi per week
H_d = Hours per day
H_m = Hours per mile
P_h = Pieces per hour
P_s = Pieces per semi

Both sides of the equation ultimately resolve to expressions of cost per piece. The distance D_b to the marginal district from the optimally placed branch warehouse is determined from the general model, that is:

$$A = \left(\frac{2b}{cK}\right)^{2/3}$$

From this expression for optimum area may be computed an approximation of the optimum radius ($A = \pi r^2$) which is the figure used in the model for D_b. The fixed branch expense per semi, B_e, was determined from the value for b in the general model. The figure 2 in each case represents a round trip.

Plant Delivery Findings

Most of the cost expressions in the plant district model could be determined directly from the company's internal records. Several of the costs such as a truck fixed cost per day or cost per mile were checked also from outside sources. After all the specific values were inserted in the model, it could be solved for P_d, the distance from the plant to the farthest district within the plant warehouse area.[3]

Solving the model above for the problem posed indicates that the marginal boundary of the plant warehouse area should be extended out to approximately two and one fourth times the present area radius and that the area to be served from the plant warehouse is thereby increased to five times the original size. Thus, the initial question is answered with an emphatic *no*; that, far from decreasing the plant delivery radius, the company can best be served by increasing that radius.

Summary

Generalization of the Method

As many business problems will yield to similar methods of analysis, the particular approach found useful here may be generalized as a sequence of steps as follows:

1. Following a study to determine the economics of the problem, a measure of effectiveness was selected.
2. A mathematical model of the problem was

---

[3] The equation was an implicit expression for P_d. This resulted in a quadratic form, which was then solved for P_d.

built around this measure of effectiveness and included those variables which most appeared to influence the measure of effectiveness.

3. The coefficients in the model were chosen by mathematical manipulation (multiple regression) to make it as accurate a symbolic description as possible.
4. The model was "tested" by statistical means (correlation coefficient).
5. Again by a mathematical manipulation (differentiation) the model was minimized with respect to the factor to be used in the decision rule. That is, an expression for area was determined, which should give the minimum warehousing cost per dollar's worth of goods distributed in each particular area.
6. In the special case of the plant warehouse area, an equation of marginal analysis was employed to establish the optimum radius to be served directly from the plant.

Variations Within the Method

Some variations within the same general framework of analysis might be considered.

(a) The measure of effectiveness might have been cost per pound of goods distributed or some other similar criterion.
(b) The model might have included more variables such as warehouse design, etc.
(c) The coefficients in the model might have been determined from an engineering or cost accounting type of approach. From a chart of accounts and past records and budgets, a, b, c, etc., might have been determined. This type of approach is more common in business today. However, by definition (the statistician's), these values could have been no better and might have been poorer.
(d) A tabular or graphical comparison of costs "predicted" by the model to actual warehouse costs might have been used rather than the correlation coefficient.
(e) A tabular, graphical, or trial and error method might have been used to determine the A (area) which minimized the cost expression. However, this would vary with K—the sales density—and, therefore, it would have been necessary to repeat this procedure for selected values of K.
(f) Rather than set up an equation for marginal analysis in the special case of the plant warehouse, it would again have been possible to tabulate, graph, or try many radius dis-

tances with their associated costs to determine the best one.

Implications of the Method

The length of time necessary and the accuracy of results for these different methods of analysis would probably vary with the person using them. It is suspected that the more conventional approach would have been substantially more time consuming and probably less precise. Possibly the best advice is: if the more elegant shoe fits, wear it.

12. *Determining Optimum Distribution Points for Economical Warehousing and Transportation**

ARTHUR W. NAPOLITAN†

Certainly there is no question that the purchasing of materials and the forecasting, planning, and control of production are major materials management responsibilities. In our concern with these basic functions, however, it would be well to bear in mind that the job of materials management does not end at the factory shipping-room door. Though they do not always receive the management attention they deserve, warehousing and transportation are also vital functions which, if properly managed, can be the source of significant savings.

In Coats & Clark, as in most industrial enterprises today, warehousing and transportation costs are absorbing an ever-increasing proportion of the sales dollar. Our mills have been subjected to pressure for cost reduction in recent years, and, as the result of an extensive modernization program, our processing costs have been drastically reduced. We have recently built the most modern wet-processing and finishing mill in the South. Clearly, further cost reduction must be accomplished in other areas, including warehousing and transportation.

In this paper, I shall describe the system we use for identifying those distribution points which will result in the most economcal warehousing and transportation. First, however, to place our distribution problems in proper perspective, a few words about our company, our product, and our management would be useful.

About Coats & Clark

Our parent company began operations in Paisley, Scotland, in 1812. In 1818 or there-

abouts, Clark's sewing thread was introduced to the women of America by the captains of British sailing vessels. By 1840, both the Clarks and the Coatses had agents in New York City. In 1864, George and William Clark, grandsons of one of the original Clark brothers, opened a cotton mill in Newark, New Jersey. Five years later, Coats purchased an interest in a mill in Pawtucket, Rhode Island. Near the turn of the century, the Coats and Clark businesses were consolidated.

Our major product line is still cotton sewing thread for the retail trade. We also produce embroidery, crochet, and woolen knitting yarns, zippers, and other allied products. We distribute our products directly to retail stores and to some wholesalers, and warehouse them accordingly. In addition to our retail sales business, a substantial portion of our production is in long-length put-ups for the clothing, textile, and luggage trades—indeed, for all users of thread and zippers.

J. & P. Coats, Limited, of Glasgow, Scotland, is the parent company of the present American companies, which are Coats & Clark, Inc. (the manufacturing unit) and Coats & Clark's Sales Corporation (the selling unit). Operating control of the American companies is vested in the Executive Committee, which consists of the heads of the Manufacturing, Sales, and Finance Divisions. The chairman of the committee is Mr. John B. Clark, who actively directs the business and represents the fifth generation of threadmaking Clarks. Pride in quality and resourcefulness in adapting to the times continue to inspire the activities carried on under these famous names. We remain the largest manufacturers of home sewing threads in the United States.

Our branch location study, which will be described in this paper, was authorized by the

* Reprinted by permission from *Managing the Materials Function*, American Management Association, Report 35, 1959.

† Manager, Procedures and Computer Operations, Coats and Clark, Inc.

Executive Committee and was, in fact, instituted by that committee. We believe that it was this strong backing by management, more than any other factor, that was responsible for the success of our study. Since certain details of the study are still classified, I am not at liberty to disclose either the final solution to the problem or all of the essential facts involved. Some of the exhibits accompanying this paper, for example, have been distorted deliberately to avoid disclosure of certain information. The discussion should prove no less interesting or useful, however, for I shall describe in some detail our method of approach to the problem of determining optimum distribution points for economical warehousing and transportation.

The Nature of the Problem

Basically, our warehousing and transportation problem is not unlike that faced by most companies engaged in the national distribution of a consumer product. In simplest terms, it can be stated as follows:

1. How many branches should we have?
2. Where should the branches be located?
3. What area should each branch serve?

This is not a new problem to us. We have been faced with these same questions on many occasions in the past, and we have always managed to do something about them. During the past 25 years, for example, we have closed five branches in certain cities and opened five branches in other cities. These actions of the past would certainly seem to indicate that the thinking of our management has not been static: It did not hesitate to move a branch when changing population concentrations or other considerations indicated the wisdom of such action. It should be pointed out, however, that decisions to close a branch and/or to open another in a different location were made by our management in the past without the benefit of complete factual information regarding the effects of such actions on profits. Furthermore, to our knowledge, the subject was never studied as a whole, on a nation-wide basis, but only piecemeal, one branch at a time.

We knew that, in recent years, a large, nationally known company had made certain nation-wide studies of potential store locations. Our management had been kept fully informed of developments in this area, and it came as no surprise when I was asked by the Executive Committee to determine whether these new techniques could, in fact, be applied to develop an over-all solution to our branch location problem. Except for the stipulation that the locations of our finishing mills and of our central warehouse in Atlanta were to be considered fixed, our management imposed no restrictions of any kind. In other words, the object of the study was to find the *optimum* solution to our problem. Our management did, of course, reserve the right to determine the degree to which the final results of the study would be implemented.

At the time we began our study we knew that certain large companies had already organized operations research staffs to help solve some of their management problems. Since we had no such organization, and did not wish to establish one, it was apparent that we would have to recruit technical assistance from the outside to obtain the scientific know-how required for the solution of our problem. To this end, we contracted with a well-known management consulting firm to provide us with qualified statisticians and mathematicians. A team was organized, consisting of Coats & Clark staff members and technicians from the consulting firm. As it turned out, this team approach worked very well for us.

Reports of the team's progress were made periodically to our management: altogether, seven such reports were made, all of them in person. At each of these meetings, continuation of our studies into the next phase was approved.

Although our branch location problem is certainly not unique, it involves certain special considerations which tend to make it more difficult than most. For example, we ship directly to thousands of independent notion and department stores, chain variety stores, and other outlets. Although we do ship to some wholesalers, this accounts for a comparatively small proportion of our total sales. Because the retail stores with which we deal are located in cities and towns of almost every size, and because of the small unit value of our product, our average invoice amounts to something less than $100. We therefore make a tremendous number of small individual shipments to many customers located all over the country. In view of the almost infinite number of possible branch locations, the task of determining comparative transportation costs from each of the various possible branch locations to our customers is truly staggering.

Exhibit 1. Location of central warehouse branches

- ◎ Branch
- ▨ Warehouse

Exhibit 1 shows the location of our central warehouse and branches at the start of the study. Our finishing mills producing goods for the retail trade are concentrated in Georgia, except for a zipper finishing mill in Newport News, Virginia. Because of this, our central warehouse is located in Atlanta, Georgia. As mentioned previously, we had ten branches at the time our study was initiated: one in Atlanta (in the same building as our central warehouse), and the other nine in Baltimore, Maryland; New York City; Pawtucket, Rhode Island; Cleveland, Ohio; Skokie, Illinois (a suburb of Chicago); St. Louis, Missouri; Dallas, Texas; Los Angeles, California; and Portland, Oregon. Each of these branches served customers in the surrounding area.

A Mathematical Statement of the Problem

As stated previously, our problem was to determine the optimum number of branches, the optimum location of these branches, and the optimum area to be serviced by each branch. We made the following mathematical statement of all the factors that had to be considered to arrive at a decision.

$$f(X) = C_1X_1 + C_2X_2 + C_3X_3 + C_4X_4,$$

where C_1X_1 = cost attributable to sales lost because of distance from branches (customer service),

C_2X_2 = cost of operating branches (branch model),

C_3X_3 = transportation costs from central warehouse(s) to branches (transportation in),

C_4X_4 = transportation costs from branches to customers (transportation out), and

$f(X)$ = total costs under consideration.

The "customer service" factor represents the additional profit attributable to sales gained because of proximity to branches where a branch is to be established in a county currently without a Coats & Clark branch. The "branch model" factor is the cost of setting up or maintaining a branch—that is, a branch model. The "transportation in" factor is the cost of transportation from our Atlanta warehouse to the potential branch. The "transportation out" factor is the cost of transportation from the potential branch to the customer. Obviously, the many combinations possible would result in varying values for each factor. One combination, for example, might indicate the lowest "transportation in" cost, another the lowest "transportation out" cost.

The values of the individual factors were not, however, significant in themselves. What we were aiming for was the lowest *aggregate* cost of the four factors in each instance, so that we would arrive at the optimum solution.

Any departure from the optimum solution could, of course, be made at the discretion of management, and measurement of the cost of such a departure could be based on the formula given above, since it includes all the measurable costs involved in the problem. We recognized that management would have to take other factors into consideration in making a decision, but we hoped to be in a position to supply it with figures which would show the cost to the company of each deviation from the optimum solution.

Finding Factor Values

Once we had stated the cost relationship mathematically, we proceeded to calculate the value of each factor of the formula. Our first step was to establish the cost of customer service. As we stated previously, our company had had some experience in opening and closing branches. We proceeded to determine what (if any) impact these changes had had on our sales volume.

Exhibit 2 indicates the effect on our sales to a county of the opening of a typical branch in that county. We charted per capita sales for four years prior to and four years subsequent to the opening. Note that when the branch was opened, the per capita sales in the county increased somewhat over the sales trend projected from previous years.

Exhibit 3 indicates the effect on our sales to a county of the closing of a typical branch in that county. Note that when the branch was closed there was a decrease in per capita sales from the trend line.

Exhibit 4 indicates the movement of per capita county sales for a typical branch which remained in existence over a ten-year period.

Exhibit 3.   Effect of branch closing on per capita county sales* (Location D)

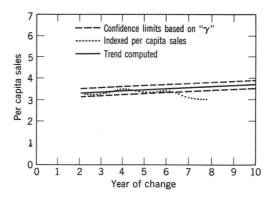

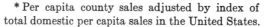

* Per capita county sales adjusted by index of total domestic per capita sales in the United States.

Note that per capita sales followed the trend line very closely. Our objective in preparing this graph was to establish a control. (In each of these three graphs, as the footnotes indicate, per capita county sales were adjusted to account for the national sales trend in the year in question.)

What did these three graphs indicate to us? We could only conclude that, when we opened a new branch in a county, the per capita sales for that county would increase—at least for a period of time—and that, when we closed a branch in a county, the per capita sales would decrease. To have a branch in every one of the

Exhibit 2.   Effect of branch opening on per capita county sales* (Location C)

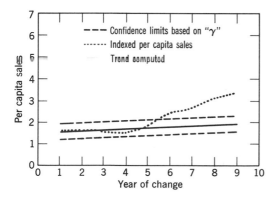

* Per capita county sales adjusted by index of total domestic per capita sales in the United States.

Exhibit 4.   Effect of continuous branch operation on per capita county sales* (Location A)

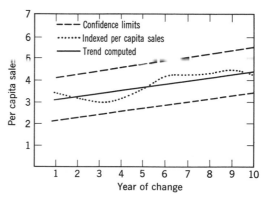

* Per capita county sales adjusted by index of total domestic per capita sales in the United States.

Exhibit 5. *Percentage distribution of counties with respect to servicing interval*

Servicing Interval	% of Counties
A	1
B	21
C	28
D	24
E	18
F	8
	100%

more than 3,000 counties in the continental United States, however, would obviously be economically unfeasible, and in any case, the cost of customer service was merely one factor in our formula. We therefore proceeded to determine the service currently rendered all our customers. For the purpose of this study, we defined customer service as the elapsed time from the moment a customer mailed his order to the time he received the merchandise. To eliminate a non-significant factor, an average branch processing time was used for all our branches. Exhibit 5 shows the distribution of counties with respect to servicing interval.

The figures compiled in Exhibit 5 were interesting, but we did not consider them conclusive. To achieve a more meaningful comparison, we prepared a graph to show the percentage distribution of dollar sales and of population by branch and servicing interval. The exhibit indicated there is no correlation between our sales and customer service. Indeed, in some instances, the percentage distribution of dollar sales to

certain counties receiving a given level of service was actually greater than sales to certain counties receiving better service.

This information might appear to contradict that given in Exhibits 2 and 3; however, we did not consider this to be the case. Our product was being distributed to each of the 3,000-odd counties in the United States, not just to the ten in which our branches were located. We believed it fair to assume that our customers habitually adjusted their inventories and re-ordering practices to the service they normally received from us. Also, although the impact of closing and opening branches did have some (at least temporary) effect on sales, there was no discernible effect upon our total sales. This fact is further demonstrated in Exhibit 6. Our per capita sales for servicing interval *D*, for example, were actually higher than our per capita sales for servicing intervals *A*, *B*, and *C*, which represents better service.

Thus, on the basis of measurable factors alone, any relocation of our branches involving a minor reshuffling of customer service should not affect our total dollar sales. We concluded, therefore, that the value of the first factor in the formula (effect of sales lost because of distance from branches) was nil, as long as no significant deterioration of customer service was proposed—a contingency which proved to be purely academic. I should like to emphasize at this point that our findings with respect to

Exhibit 7. *Total branch operating costs in relation to sales volume ("Standard" branches)*

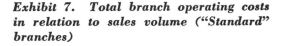

Exhibit 6. *Per capita sales of counties grouped by servicing intervals*

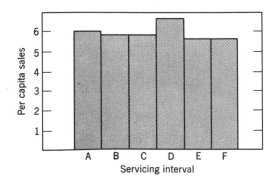

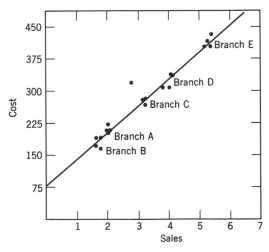

customer service apply only to our particular business, and not necessarily to any other.

The second factor in the formula, the cost of maintaining a branch, was determined by plotting the total operating cost of each existing branch against that branch's sales (Exhibit 7). As shown in the exhibit, it is possible, by drawing a mean line, to determine the cost of maintaining a branch of any size. Unusual local factors, such as the levels of rents, wages, and taxes, were considered in arriving at the cost of setting up a new branch in any location. The cost of investment in and maintenance of inventories was included in the branch model.

The third factor, "transportation in" costs, was easy to calculate because of the carload-size shipments involved.

The fourth factor, "transportation out" costs presented major problems because of the volume of individual shipments and the numerous possibilities for originating points. Although extensive use was made of the latest sampling techniques, this was the most time-consuming part of the study. I cannot go into complete detail concerning the solution of this phase of the problem. Suffice it to say that large samples do not insure accuracy; small samples, if truly representative of the whole, can be much more accurate. Success therefore lies in developing small but representative samples. The matrix of the transportation costs from the various potential

branch locations to representative customer destinations is illustrated by example in Exhibit 8.

Testing the Formula and Solving the Problem

At this point, we were ready to test the formula to prove its adaptability. To do so, we chose the West Coast area, which is particularly amenable to studies of this nature in view of its geography, freight rate schedules and other factors. A list of potential branch sites was developed by application of certain criteria established by our management—minimal requirements with respect to rail, trucking, and postal services, for example. By applying these criteria, we gradually narrowed down the potential branch locations to a workable number.

With the value of the four factors in the formula known for all possible combinations, the problem of the West Coast branch locations was solved by minimization, using combinatorial programming techniques originated by the OR team for the solution of this problem. The same methods were then used to solve the problem in the area east of the Rockies. In both cases, the results were summarized in such a manner that the cost of deviations from the optimum could be measured for use by management in making a decision.

Because the solution we arrived at through

Exhibit 8. Matrix of "transportation out" costs (test area)

Trading Area	Potential Origins						
	A	B	C	D	E	F	G
1	$ 470	$ 409	$ 318	$ 577	$ 274	$ 485	$ 376
2	1,182	1,182	742	1,471	955	894	633
3	61	76	76	46	77	61	73
4	1,863	2,136	2,150	2,289	2,061	2,788	2,376
5	3,847	7,726	14,558	8,167	15,378	12,725	16,389
6	727	1,013	1,893	486	1,880	1,273	1,997
7	3,742	2,833	1,423	5,167	2,105	4,106	2,663
8	864	651	787	1,304	984	1,424	1,073
9	758	712	1,181	1,349	1,256	1,136	1,421
10	1,818	1,606	1,241	1,834	1,455	970	1,270
11	1,364	1,379	2,090	1,743	2,364	803	1,977
12	3,818	2,606	6,347	5,955	6,803	7,332	7,405
13	3,620	2,924	1,575	4,910	1,319	3,969	2,194
14	1,985	1,636	998	2,789	1,092	1,863	906
	$26,119	$26,891	$35,379	$38,087	$38,003	$39,829	$40,753

the approach described above is classified information, it cannot be revealed here. In any event, since it is optimal only for Coats & Clark's operations, it would not be generally applicable to other businesses. What is significant, however, is not so much the particular solution we arrived at but the approach we took, and it is this approach that we believe will prove useful to others.

The findings of our study were accepted by our management as accurate and reliable, even though some of them came as a distinct surprise. Of the changes indicated by the study, some have already been made, others will be made in the future. It would obviously be foolish to attempt to make wholesale changes of this nature at one time.

In general, the study is paying off hand-somely for Coats & Clark. Although it took almost two years to complete, this was largely owing to the circumstance that much of the work had to be performed by our own operating people, in between their current work assignments. We did not utilize an electronic computer for the computations involved in finding the optimum solution to our problem, although we did use a service bureau's computer to generate a special random-number table which we used in our sampling. Had it been economically feasible to do so, we certainly would not have hesitated to use an electronic computer.

Since the completion of the initial study in 1958, we have made three supplementary studies by manipulating more recent data in the same basic formula.

13. *A Warehouse-Location Problem**

WILLIAM J. BAUMOL AND PHILIP WOLFE†

This paper describes a method for determining a more profitable geographic location pattern for the warehouses that are employed by a firm in delivering known quantities of its finished product to its customers, where the number of warehouses is also permitted to vary. It is shown that this can normally be expected to be a concave minimization problem. Unfortunately, there are usually no practical computational methods for determining the values of the variables that correspond to the absolute minimum of a concave cost function. However, a local optimum can be determined by a method described in the article. The method involves a sequence of transportation computations that are shown to converge to the solution. An illustrative small scale computation is included. An appendix explains in intuitive terms the nature of the computational difficulties that arise in a concave programming problem.

A division of a large corporation asked us to investigate the number and location of its warehouses. Its inventory is kept in public warehouses. Since none of these installations is owned by the company, the division can, with relative ease, move all or part of its operations to other warehouses or change the number of warehouses it employs.

It was assumed in the investigation that sales volume at each geographic customer location is given, and is not affected by the choice of warehouse through which shipments to that destination are routed. (This is probably not strictly true because the distance of a warehouse from the market can affect the speed with which a retailer who has exhausted his stock of the product can replenish his inventory, and the warehouse location can, therefore, influence the volume of sales.

Programming Formulation of the Problem

In principle this would appear to be an example of the difficult *location problem* because the set of possible warehouse locations constitutes a two-dimensional continuum. But in practice a crucial simplification was made possible by the fact that the company rents space in public warehouses, and that the number of places† in this country at which are located warehouses possessing the requisite physical characteristics (including loading facilities, etc.) is relatively small, apparently of the order of magnitude of one to two hundred.

This permitted formulation of the problem as the following (nonlinear) program, which is very closely related to the transportation problem: Let

X_{ijk} be the quantity shipped from factory i ($i = 1, 2, \cdots, m$) via warehouse j ($j = 1, \cdots, n$), to retailer location k ($k = 1, \cdots, q$),
$C_{ijk}(X_{ijk})$ be the cost of this shipment including the relevant inventory cost,
Q_i be the quantity shipped from plant i,
R_j be the capacity of warehouse j,
S_k be the quantity required at destination k.

The problem is to minimize the total delivery

* Reprinted by permission from *Operations Research*, March–April 1958.
† Princeton University & The Rand Corporation. This is a report on a project undertaken by the management consulting firm of Alderson and Sessions in Philadelphia.

† For our purposes a 'place' or 'location' can designate an entire city, so that all the warehouses in the New York metropolitan area are taken to occupy a single location. This is, of course, the explanation of the small number of relevant warehouse locations.

cost, i.e., to minimize

$$\sum_{i,j,k} C_{ijk}(X_{ijk}), \qquad (1)$$

subject to $\qquad \sum_{j,k} X_{ijk} = Q_i \qquad (2)$

(all goods must be shipped out of the factory),

$$\sum_{i,k} A_{ijk}(X_{ijk}) \leqq R_j \qquad (3)$$

(no warehouse capacity can be exceeded), and

$$\sum_{i,j} X_{ijk} = S_k \qquad (4)$$

(all customer demands must be met), where all $X_{ijk} \geqq 0$. The expression $A_{ijk}(X_{ijk})$ in (3) represents the amount of inventory that will be held as a result of the flow X_{ijk}.

The resemblance to the standard transportation problem is obvious. There are only three differences: (*a*) the possible nonlinearity of the cost function (1); (*b*) the presence of the warehouse-capacity constraints (3); and (*c*) the need for a three subscript rather than a two subscript notation for the variables X_{ijk} arising out of the necessity of routing each flow through a warehouse. Of course, a nonlinear objective function is not necessarily ruled out for the transportation problem, and in fact nonlinearities in the objective function do sometimes occur in practice. Moreover, for practical purposes it transpires that the warehouse capacity limitations in our problem can be ignored because the firm never ends up renting more than a small fraction of the public warehouse space available at any location. This fact eliminates difference (*b*) between this and the standard transportation problem.

The Effects of Linearity

Assume, to begin with, that our objective function (1) is linear, so that difference (*a*) from the transportation problem also disappears. Then elimination of difference (*c*), i.e., of the three subscript notation, becomes a trivial matter. For we have the following rule: *An optimal (least cost) solution will involve shipment of all goods that go from factory i^* to destination k^* via that (those) warehouse(s) j^* for which*†

$$C_{i^*j^*k^*} = \text{Min}_j \, C_{i^*jk^*}. \qquad (5)$$

† Proof by *reductio ad absurdum:* Suppose there is an optimal solution, *S*, which violates condition (5). This means that there are values i^*, j^*, j' and k^* of i, j and k, such that $X_{i^*j'k^*} = A > 0$ and $X_{i^*j^*k^*} = B \geqq 0$ where j' is a warehouse for which

$$C_{i^*j'k^*} - C_{i^*j^*k^*} = D > 0;$$

In other words, it will always pay to make any shipment via the warehouse that offers the lowest delivery cost.

The solution of the linear program is now very simple. For each factory, destination combination, i^*, k^*, select a value j^* of j for which (4) is satisfied. That can be done by simple inspection of the C_{ijk} data. This will eliminate all but one of the n possible warehouse locations that can be used to service goods en route from factory i^* to destination k^*. We can now revise our notation, writing $X_{i^*j^*k^*} = X'_{i^*k^*}$, $C_{i^*j^*k^*} = C'_{i^*k^*}$ (since in an optimal solution all other $X_{i^*jk^*}$'s will be equal to zero). Substituting this notation in (1), (2), and (4) obviously leaves us with a standard transportation problem, the optimum values of whose variables can be found by the standard methods.

This solution has a remarkable property that deserves emphasis. It is likely to involve the employment of many more warehouses than one might a priori expect to be optimal. To take an extreme example, suppose one case is to be shipped from factory i' to customer k'. If there is a warehouse j' which would otherwise not be used by the company, but which offers minimum costs for regular large scale shipments from i' to k', then the linear programming solution requires arrangements to be made to have warehouse j' handle this one case shipment.

This may strike the reader as unusual because we have come to expect the solution of a linear program often to be biased toward a small (in economic terms) number of nonzero elements. This view appears to be in line with the basic theorem of linear programming which states that in a (nondegenerate) linear program there always exists an optimal solution in which the number of variables whose values are positive is no greater than the number of constraints in the problem. For example, if a factory has nine machines of limited capacity and

---

i.e., warehouse j' is not on the cheapest route from i^* to k^*. Now consider the alternative solution, *T*, which differs from *S* only in that in *T* we have $X_{i^*j'k^*} = 0$, $X_{i^*j^*k^*} = A + B$ (i.e., elimination of shipments from i^* to k^* via warehouse j' and a compensating increase in shipments via warehouse j^*). The solution *T* is feasible since the totals in (2) and (4) are unaffected by the change, and inequalities (3) have been dropped. Moreover, by (1), costs will have fallen by $AD > 0$, contradicting the hypothesis that *S* is optimal. It is clear that if two warehouse locations offer the same minimum cost it makes no difference which is chosen.

no other bottleneck problems, a linear program will always indicate that the firm can maximize its profits by offering a product line that contains no more than nine items![†]

The Nature of the Nonlinearities

It is clear that the nonlinearities in the system do not occur in contraints (2) and (4). However, they may be expected to appear in the objective function (1), and in the warehouse capacity contraints (3) if they are relevant. An obvious type of nonlinearity will arise out of the transportation rate structure since any shipment so small that it necessarily involves less than carload lots will move at higher rates. Some of the warehousing contracts also involve similar rate structure changes. Both of these nonlinearities help to increase the cost incurred in using a larger number of warehouses to handle a given sales volume because this must cut the average volume per warehouse, and small shipments through any one warehouse will be charged for at higher rates.

Two other nonlinearities work in the same direction. The use of additional warehouses increases negotiation, bookkeeping, and administration costs. In addition, there are usually economies of large scale in the amount of inventory that should be kept against the flow of shipments through a warehouse. In fact, standard inventory analysis suggests that optimally, important inventory components will vary approximately as the square root of the volume of shipments going through the warehouse.[‡] All of this suggests that the cost (objective) function can be approximated by the nonlinear expression

$$\sum_{i,j,k} K_{ijk} X_{ijk} + \sum_j W_j (\sum_{i,k} X_{ijk})^q + \sum_j V_j i_j,$$
$$(0 < q < i)$$

where K_{ijk} is the cost of transportation and handling per unit of X_{ijk}, W_j is the cost of storage per case per period (including taxes, interest on investment, pilferage, etc.), and

[†] The reason for both types of bias is discussed in the Appendix. Actually, there it is seen that the basic theorem, in making an optimal number of nonzero activities largely independent of the parameters of the linear objective function, is involved in both types of bias.

[‡] Cf. T. M. Whitin, *The Theory of Inventory Management*, Princeton University Press, 1953, pp. 33 and 48.

$r_j = 1$ if $\sum_{i,k} X_{ijk} > 0$, and $r_j = 0$ otherwise, i.e., $\sum r_j$ is the number of warehouses used, and V is the administrative cost to the renting firm per warehouse employed.

This is unfortunately, a 'concave' program. No general method has been developed for computing the optimum values of the variables of such a problem.[†] However, it is possible to find a *local* optimum by methods that are described below.

We now describe a computing procedure for dealing with some of the nonlinear aspects of the Warehouse Location Problem. Although no practical computing method is known for obtaining the general solution to this problem, the procedure to be described will yield a solution that probably cannot be improved except by prohibitively expensive computation for large-scale problems. This procedure has the additional advantage that it relies almost entirely on the well-known procedure for the ordinary transportation problem.[‡]

In the next section we give the mathematical description and justification of the method; in the third section a flow diagram for programming the computation is given; and the last section follows through the calculation of a small-scale example.

Mathematical Description of the Computational Procedure

It is convenient at this point to divide our problem into two separate transportation problems: (*a*) from the factory to the warehouse, and (*b*) from the warehouse to the customer location. For this reason the notation employed here diverges slightly from that used earlier in this article. Let c_{ij} be the unit cost of transportation from factory i to warehouse j, and let d_{jk} be the unit cost of transportation from warehouse j to retailer k. Then $c_{ij} + d_{jk}$ is the C_{ijk} above. Let $Z_j = \sum_{i,k} X_{ijk}$ be the total flow through warehouse j, where X_{ijk} represents the flow from factory i through warehouse j to retailer k. Supposing the home office administrative costs for the jth warehouse (if used) to be V_j, the total administrative cost for a given

[†] For the definition of a concave problem and an indication of the natural of the computational difficulties, see the appendix below.

[‡] The most powerful method to date for solving transportation problems is that due to L. R. Ford and D. R. Fulkerson, "Solving the Transportation Problem," *Management Sci.* **3**, 24–32 (1956).

transportation schedule will be the sum of terms $V_j r(Z_j)$, where

$$r(Z_j) = 0 \quad \text{if} \quad Z_j = 0,$$
$$r(Z_j) = 1 \quad \text{if} \quad Z_j > 0.$$

The total cost of the transportation schedule X_{ijk} will then be

$$f(X_{ijk}) = \sum_{i,j,k}(c_{ij} + d_{jk})X_{ijk}$$
$$+ \sum_j W_j(Z_j)^q + \sum_j V_j r(Z_j).$$

The computing procedure can be outlined mathematically in a recursive fashion as follows, where the initial calculation (zeroth) and the nth calculation are given.

0th Calculation

For each pair i, k of factory and retailer, find the least cost of shipment, ignoring the warehouse loading charges and administration costs:

$$C_{ik}^0 = \text{Min}_j \,(c_{ij} + d_{jk}) = (c_{ij_{ik}}^0 + d_{j_{ik}k}^0),$$

where j_{ik} denotes the warehouse routing selected by this criterion.

Using these costs C_{ik}^0, solve the ordinary transportation problem of shipping from the factories with known availabilities to the retailers with known demands so as to minimize the cost function $\sum_{i,k}C_{ik}^0 X_{ik}$; and denote the solution of this transportation problem by $\{X_{ik}^0\}$.

nth Calculation

For each pair i, k, let X_{ik}^{n-1} represent the solution of the transportation problem solved in the $(n-1)$th calculation, and determine the warehouse loadings involved in that solution:

$$Z_j^{n-1} = \sum\{\text{all } i,k \text{ such that } j_{ik}^{n-1} = j\} X_{ik}^{n-1},$$

where j_{ik}^{n-1} denotes the warehouse selected for shipment from factory i to retailer k in the $(n-1)$th calculation.

Now define new transportation costs by

$$C_{ik}^n = \text{Min}_j \,[c_{ij} + d_{jk} + W_j q(Z_j^{n-1})^{q-1}]$$

letting j_{ik}^n denote the warehouse for which the Min_j above is assumed.

Using the costs C_{ik}^n, find the solution $\{X_{ik}^n\}$ of the transportation problem with these costs.

Test for Stopping

Compare the quantities Z_j^{n-1} with the quantities Z_j^n. If they are the same, stop. If different continue.

Proofs

We now show that this procedure will reduce the total cost $f(X_{ijk})$ in each step.

The objective function $f(X_{ijk})$ of the original problem is a *concave* function. To prove this, we use the definition that a function is concave if extrapolation by means of the derivative does not underestimate it:

That is, the function g is concave if, for any x and y,

$$g(y) \le g(x) + g'(x)(y - x).$$

The linear part of f is, of course, concave. That the terms which are raised to the qth power are also, follows from Taylor's theorem, which states that

$$y^q = X^q + qX^{q-1}(y - X)$$
$$+ \tfrac{1}{2}q(q - 1)\xi^{q-2}(Y - X)^2$$

where ξ is some number between Y and X. Since, by hypothesis, $q < 1$, the last of these terms is negative or zero so that

$$Y^q \le X^q + qX^{q-1}(Y - X),$$

as required for concavity.

The terms $V_j r(Z_j)$ are shown to be concave by virtue of the fact that the derivative in question is 0 if $Z_j > 0$ and infinite if $Z_j = 0$. Finally, multiplying by nonnegative numbers preserves the concavity of the terms, and the sum of concave functions is concave.

It follows that if, given any transportation schedule $\{X_{ijk}^{n-1}\}$, we compute the derivatives of the cost function $\partial f(X_{ijk}^{n-1})/\partial X_{ijk}$, and use these as costs to obtain a solution $\{X_{ijk}^n\}$ of the transportation problem

$$\text{Min} \sum_{i,j,k}[\partial f(X_{ijk}^{n-1})/\partial X_{ijk}]X_{ijk},$$

we will have

$$f(X_{ijk}^n) \le f(X_{ijk}^{n-1});$$

and further, that if there has been a change in the quantities under the exponent sign, we will have an actual improvement in the cost.

Finally, the transportation problem just indicated can be replaced by the transportation problem of the 'nth calculation' above: For, as was shown in the footnote on p. 84, the solution

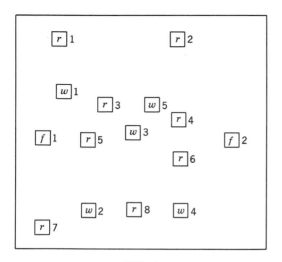

FIG. 1.

of the $\{X_{ijk}\}$ problem with *fixed* warehousing costs just sends the flow from factory i to retailer k through the cheapest route j, which is exactly what is selected in the nth calculation.

Since

$$f(X_{ijk}) = \sum_{i,j,k} c_{ij} X_{ijk} + \sum_{i,j,k} d_{jk} X_{ijk}$$
$$+ \sum_j W_j ([\sum_{i,k} X_{ijk}])^q$$
$$+ \sum_j V_j r (\sum_{i,k} X_{ijk}),$$

we have indeed*

$$\partial f(X_{ijk}) / \partial X_{ijk} = c_{ij} + d_{jk} + W_j q (Z_j)^{q-1}.$$

† It should be noted that at an interior point the derivative of the warehouse administration cost term $\Sigma V r$ will be zero, so that it does not enter into the next expression. But at a corner point the derivative is not defined (or rather, it is either zero or infinite) and for this reason the computing method does not fully take into account these administration costs, since the program will have an optimal corner solution. In practical terms this means that it may be possible to effect some further savings by eliminating a few warehouses from the computed optimum. But since these administrative costs apparently run to less than $500 per year per warehouse the total savings that can be effected in this way are negligible.

Illustrative Small-Scale Computation

Below we trace through the complete solution (by hand) of a problem involving two factories, five warehouses, and eight retailers. The transportation costs were taken to be the distances between locations on a map which is approximately represented in Fig. 1; in this figure, factories are designated by f, warehouses by w, and retailers by r.

The factory-warehouse distances are given in the distance (transportation cost) matrix

$i = $	$j = 1$	2	3	4	5
1	7	7	8	12	11
2	14	12	9	6	8

and the warehouse-retailer transportation costs in the matrix

$j = $	$k = 1$	2	3	4	5	6	7	8
1	5	11	3	8	5	10	11	11
2	14	16	8	9	4	7	4	4
3	10	11	3	5	2	5	9	5
4	15	13	9	6	7	2	10	2
5	9	7	3	2	6	5	12	8

The availabilities at the factories are taken to be, in units,

$i = 1$	40
2	50

The retailer's demands are taken to be, in units,

$r = 1$	2	3	4	5	6	7	8
10	10	10	15	5	15	10	15

The warehousing costs are taken to be

$$\| \ 75\sqrt{Z_1} \ \ 80\sqrt{Z_2} \ \ 75\sqrt{Z_3} \ \ 80\sqrt{Z_4} \ \ 70\sqrt{Z_5} \ \|,$$

so that $q = \frac{1}{2}$. (The warehousing costs have deliberately been taken to be rather large in this example. This is because such a small transportation problem is relatively insensitive to changes in external costs—i.e., is quite stable in its solutions, and thus might not reflect the effect of the warehousing costs in the computation if they were small.) The bookkeeping costs have, for simplicity, been neglected in this example.

Initial Cycle

Minimal transportation costs C_{ik}^0

$i = $	$k = 1$	2	3	4	5	6	7	8
1	12	18	10	13	10	13	11	11
2	17	15	11	10	11	8	16	8

Warehouse for minimal route: j_{ik}^0

$k = 1$	2	3	4	5	6	7	8
1	5	1	5	3	3	2	2
5	5	5	5	3	4	4	4

Solution of initial transportation problem: Load   Costs
X_{ik}^0 (transp. cost 935) Z^0

$i = 1$	10	0	10	0	5	0	10	5		Whs. 1	20		336
2	0	10	0	15	0	15	0	10		2	15		310
										3	5		168
										4	25		400
										5	25		350

Warehousing cost   1564
Transportation cost   935

Total cost   2499

Cycle $n = 1$

Warehouse marginal costs $W_j(2\sqrt{Z_j^0})^{-1}$, rounded to integers:

$$w = 1 \quad 2 \quad 3 \quad 4 \quad 5$$
$$\| \ 8 \quad 10 \quad 17 \quad 8 \quad 7 \ \|.$$

Factory warehouse transportation costs + marginal warehouse costs: $_{ij}$

$$j = 1 \quad 2 \quad 3 \quad 4 \quad 5$$

$i = 1$	15	17	25	20	18
2	22	22	26	14	15

Minimal costs C_{ik}^1 Warehouses for min: j_{ik}^1

$k = 1$	2	3	4	5	6	7	8		$k = 1$	2	3	4	5	6	7	8
$i = 1$	20	25	18	20	20	22	21	21		1	5	1	5	1	4	2	2
2	24	22	18	17	21	16	24	16		5	5	5	5	4	4	4	4

Warehouse loads and costs

Solution of transportation problem: Load   Cost
X_{ik}^1 Z_j^1

$i = 1$	10	0	10	5	5	0	10	0		Whs. 1	25		375
2	0	10	0	10	0	15	0	15		2	10		253
										3	0		0
										4	30		439
										5	25		350

Warehousing cost   1417
Transportation cost   840

Total cost   2257

Note: The computing process does not use the actual costs of transportation. These must be figured from the separate $f - w$ and $w - d$ costs. In this cycle, the $f - w$ and $w - d$ parts of the solution are

$$j = 1 \quad 2 \quad 3 \quad 4 \quad 5$$

$i = 1$	25	10	0	0	5		Cost 535,
2	0	0	0	30	20		

$$k = 1 \quad 2 \quad 3 \quad 4 \quad 5 \quad 6 \quad 7 \quad 8$$

$j = 1$	10	0	10	0	5	0	0	0	
2	0	0	0	0	0	0	10	0	
3	0	0	0	0	0	0	0	0	Cost 305,
4	0	0	0	0	0	15	0	15	
5	0	10	0	15	0	0	0	0	

yielding a total cost of transportation of 840.

Cycle $n = 2$

Warehouse marginal costs $w_j(2\sqrt{Z_j{}^1})^{-1}$

$$
\begin{array}{c|ccccc}
w = & 1 & 2 & 3 & 4 & 5 \\
\hline
\| & 8 & 13 & \infty & 7 & 7 \| \\
\end{array}
$$

Factory-warehouse transportation costs + marginal warehouse costs: e_{ij}

$$
\begin{array}{c|ccccc}
j = & 1 & 2 & 3 & 4 & 5 \\
\hline
i = 1 & \| \; 15 & 20 & \infty & 19 & 18 \; \| \\
2 & \| \; 22 & 25 & \infty & 13 & 15 \; \| \\
\end{array}
$$

	Minimal costs C_{ik}^2										Warehouses for min$_i$ j_{ik}^1							
$k = 1$	2	3	4	5	6	7	8			$k = 1$	2	3	4	5	6	7	8
$i = 1$ $\| \; 20$	25	18	20	20	21	24	$21 \; \|$			$\| \; 1$	5	1	5	1	4	2	$4 \; \|$
2 $\| \; 24$	22	18	17	20	15	23	$15 \; \|$			$\| \; 5$	5	5	5	4	4	4	$4 \; \|$

Solution of transportation problem: X_{ik}^2

$$
\begin{array}{cc}
i = 1 & \| \; 10 \quad 0 \quad 10 \quad 5 \quad 5 \quad 0 \quad 10 \quad 0 \; \| \\
2 & \| \; 0 \quad 10 \quad 0 \quad 10 \quad 0 \quad 15 \quad 0 \quad 15 \; \| \\
\end{array}
$$

Warehouse loads $Z_j{}^2$

Whs. 1	25
2	10
3	0
4	30
5	25

Since the warehouse loads $Z_j{}^2 = Z_j{}^1$, the problem is finished (indeed, in this case the $X_{ik}^2 = X_{ik}^1$). The total cost of the schedule found by this method is 2257.

Appendix. The Bias of Nonlinear Programs

We noted above that the linear programming approximation to a nonlinear program often calls for a number of activities smaller than that required for a true optimum and that the reverse holds in our present warehouse location problem. In Figs. 2 and 3 we give two types of nonlinear programming problems, both having the same constraint set of feasible programs—the shaded region of the horizontal plane, bounded by two coordinate axes and the line labelled AB in Fig. 3. In each case the graph of the cost function for the problem is given, and below that graph, in the horizontal plane, are sketched contour lines—isoquants— of the function.

The cost function of Fig. 2 is convex (the chord between any two points of its graph lies above its graph). The associated programming problem, that of finding the point in the constraint, yet yielding least cost, thus commonly has a *middling* solution, like C of Fig. 2 in which a large number of activities enter at nonzero levels.

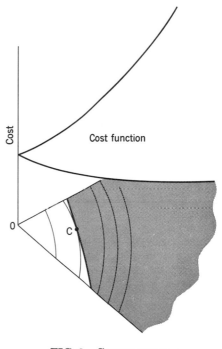

FIG. 2. Convex program.

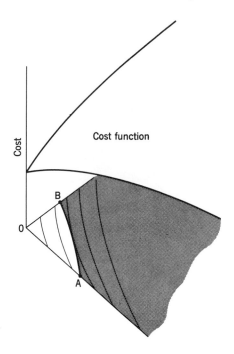

FIG. 3.   Concave program.

The cost function of Fig. 3, on the other hand, is concave (the chord between two points of its graph lying below its graph). Here it is clear that the solution is forced toward extreme values, such as either *A* or *B* of Fig. 3, containing as few nonzero activities as possible, as would a linear-programming problem.

How is this related to our warehousing problem? Here there are costs to adding another warehouse: paperwork costs, costs involved in less than proportionate reductions in the stocks per warehouse as the number of shipments per warehouse decreases. Thus as we leave the axis (when a warehouse is introduced) costs will rise sharply, and the warehousing problem will strongly exhibit its bias toward having many activities at zero levels—perhaps even more than if it were linear.

We can also see now why the convex nonlinear problem is not too difficult computationally. If we start at a nonoptimal point, so long as we continue to move downhill we can be sure we will eventually get to the one lowest point, *C*, of the cost function. This is very helpful because in nonlinear computations we are like nearsighted men descending a mountain. We cannot see the bottom, but we can always be sure whether we are going uphill or downhill. But in a concave program, if we start from a nonoptimal point, going downhill may take us to the bottom of a ravine (a local optimum point like *A*) and not to the true lowest point *B*; but, even so, this procedure can lead to substantial improvement.

14. *A Heuristic Program for Locating Warehouses**

ALFRED A. KUEHN AND MICHAEL J. HAMBURGER†

The linear programing algorithms available for optimizing the routing of shipments in multi-plant, multi-destination systems cannot, in the current state of knowledge, be applied directly to the more general problem of determining the number and location of regional warehouses in large-scale distribution networks.

This paper outlines a heuristic computer program for locating warehouses and compares it with recently published efforts at solving the problem either by means of simulation or as a variant of linear programing. The heuristic approach outlined in this paper appears to offer significant advantages in the solution of this class of problems in that it (1) provides considerable flexibility in the specification (modeling) of the problem to be solved, (2) can be used to study large-scale problems, that is, complexes with several hundred potential warehouse sites and several thousand shipment destinations, and (3) is economical of computer time. The results obtained in applying the program to small scale problems have been equal to or better than those provided by the alternative methods considered.

The Warehouse Location Problem

Regional warehouses may perform a variety of functions in the distribution of a manufacturer's products. These include: (1) the reduction of transportation costs relative to direct shipment to customers by permitting bulk or quantity shipments from factory to warehouse; (2) the reduction of delivery costs by combining products manufactured at several factories into single shipments to individual customers; and (3) the improvement of customer relations by decreasing delivery time relative to direct factory shipment, thereby permitting customers to re-duce their inventories. There are, however, substantial costs associated with the operation of a regional warehouse system.

The problem at issue may therefore be phrased as follows: determine the geographical pattern of warehouse locations which will be most profitable to the company by equating the marginal cost of warehouse operation with the transportation cost savings and incremental profits resulting from more rapid delivery. A heuristic computer program which appears to be capable of generating reasonably good solutions to this class of problems will be described in the following sections, after a brief discussion of the heuristic approach to problem solving. A mathematical formulation of the warehouse location problem is given in Appendix I. A comparison of the heuristic program with several alternative approaches to the problem is contained in Appendix II.

The Heuristic Approach to Problem Solving

Simon [27] has referred to heuristics as rules of thumb selected on the basis that they will

* Received February 1962. The research upon which this article is based has been supported to varying degrees by the Graduate School of Industrial Administration and IBM and Ford Foundation Fellowships. While a number of individuals have offered valuable comments in reviews of earlier drafts of this paper, the authors particularly acknowledge the suggestions and encouragement of W. W. Cooper and Ralph L. Day of Carnegie Institute of Technology.

† Carnegie Institute of Technology, Pittsburgh, Pennsylvania.

91

aid in problem solving. In an earlier paper, Simon, in collaboration with Newell and Shaw, used the term "heuristic" to denote "any principle or device that contributes to the reduction in the average search to a solution" [21], p. 22. Making use of the latter definition, a heuristic program can be defined (after Tonge [29]) as a problem-solving program organized around such principles or devices. Simon [27] has distinguished between such programs and algorithms on the basis that *only* the latter guarantee solution of the problem to a desired degree of accuracy. We do not believe that this is the most appropriate way to characterize heuristic programs. There are many solution procedures referred to as algorithms which do not guarantee solutions to a desired degree of accuracy, but rather, as is possible with the heuristic warehouse location program, provide only upper and lower bounds to the solution (for example, the fictitious play method for solving matrix games [17]). Furthermore the definition of algorithm generally used by mathematicians (for example, Courant and Robbins [8], p. 44) is "a systematic method for computation." Such a definition would include all computer programs.

We prefer to look at heuristic programing as an approach to problem solving where the emphasis is on working towards *optimum solution procedures* rather than *optimum solutions*. This is not to say that we ever expect to obtain an optimum solution procedure. The requirement of optimality would, in fact, be contradictory to the concept of using heuristic techniques. Heuristic techniques are most often used when the goal is to solve a problem whose solution can be described in terms of acceptability characteristics rather than by optimizing rules (Tonge [29], p. 232).[1] The traditional operations research approach has been to search for optimum solutions. The heuristic approach differs in the following ways:

1. Explicit consideration is given to a number of factors (for example, computer storage capacity and solution time) in addition to the quality of the solution produced.
2. The evaluation of heuristic techniques is usually done by inductive rather than deductive

procedures. That is, specific heuristics are justified not because they attain an analytically derived solution (for example, an optimum) but rather because experimentation has proved that they are useful in practice ([27], p. 11).

Recent interest in the heuristic approach to problem solving has led to the development of computer programs designed to: compose music [15], play checkers [24], play chess [5, 18, 20], discover proofs for theorems in logic and geometry [22, 12], design electric motors and transformers [13], and balance assembly lines [28].

A Heuristic Program for Locating Warehouses

The heuristic program which we propose for locating warehouses consists of two parts: (1) *the main program,* which locates warehouses one at a time until no additional warehouses can be added to the distribution network without increasing total costs, and (2) *the bump and shift routine,* entered after processing in the main program is complete, which attempts to modify solutions arrived at in the main program by evaluating the profit implications of dropping individual warehouses or of shifting them from one location to another. The three principal heuristics used in the main program are:

1. *Most geographical locations are not promising sites for a regional warehouse; locations with promise will be at or near concentrations of demand.*[2]

The use of this heuristic in searching for and screening potential warehouse locations permits us to concentrate upon substantially less than 1/100 of 1 per cent of the United States and thereby eliminate mountains, marshes, deserts, and other desolate areas from consideration. To be sure, the program may as a result miss a good location. In general, however, computer time is put to much better use in screening and evaluating a finite number of concentrations of demand than in searching blindly for a possible profitable desolate location. (If management or the program operator is interested in evaluating

[1] These points have been discussed in more detail elsewhere in the context of a theory of human problem solving and choice (see for example, Simon [26], pp. 196–207 and pp. 241–74, March and Simon [19], chaps. vi and vii, and Cyert, Dill, and March [9]).

[2] Baumol and Wolfe [4] also consider only a limited number of places at which to obtain warehouse space. However, their problem considers only the leasing of warehouse space and consequently the number of available locations is already limited and no heuristic is required to restrict the alternatives to be considered.

any specific locations of this type, they can be entered as alternatives.)

2. *Near optimum warehousing systems can be developed by locating warehouses one at a time, adding at each stage of the analysis that warehouse which produces the greatest cost savings for the entire system.*

The use of this heuristic reduces the time and effort expended in evaluating patterns of warehouse sites. Thus, if there are M possible warehouse locations, the above heuristic would reduce the number of cost evaluations necessary from 2^m to approximately $N(M' + 1) < NM$ where N is the size of the intermediate buffer, discussed further below, and M' is the number of warehouses located. One can think of several classes of examples in which this heuristic would not work very well. However, such situations appear to occur only rarely in practice.

3. *Only a small subset of all possible warehouse locations need be evaluated in detail at each stage of the analysis to determine the next warehouse site to be added.*

To insure adding that warehouse location producing the greatest cost savings we could evaluate completely each of the remaining potential warehouse sites. The time required by such an approach can, however, be reduced very substantially with the addition of only slight risk with a good, easily computed method of screening potential sites. The heuristic used for screening calls for N of the M potential warehouse locations $(M > N > 1)$ to be evaluated in detail at each stage (see step 3, Figure 1, Flow Diagram). The N potential warehouse sites chosen at each stage are those which, considering only local demand, would result in the greatest cost savings (or smallest increase in costs) if serviced by a local warehouse rather than by the system existing in the previous stage (see step 2, Flow Diagram). In other words, it is assumed that at any stage we can do reasonably well by locating the next warehouse in one of the N areas chosen on the basis of local demand and related warehousing and transportation costs.

In the detailed evaluation of each of the N locations placed in the buffer at each stage, the program either eliminates the site from further consideration, assigns a warehouse to that location, or returns the location to the list of potential warehouse sites for reconsideration at later stages in the program (steps 4, 6 and 7, respectively, in the Flow Diagram). Any site whose

addition would not reduce total distribution costs is eliminated from further analysis in the main program. Of those sites which reduce total costs, that location which affords the greatest savings is assigned a warehouse; all others are returned to the list of potential warehouse sites. When the list of potential warehouses is depleted, all sites having been either eliminated or assigned a warehouse, the program enters the Bump and Shift Routine.

The Bump and Shift Routine is designed to modify solutions reached in the main program in two ways. It first eliminates (bumps) any warehouse which is no longer economical because some of the customers originally assigned to it are now serviced by warehouses located subsequently. Then, to insure the servicing of each of the territories established above from a single warehouse within each territory in the most economical manner, the program considers shifting each warehouse from its currently assigned location to the other potential sites (original list) within its territory. It should be noted that this routine does not guarantee that each territory will in fact be serviced in the most economical manner (this deficiency is illustrated below with reference to several sample problems).

The basic steps in the heuristic program are summarized in the Flow Diagram, Figure 1. Before going on to examine the results obtained in applying this program to several sample problems, let us discuss briefly the heuristics used in handling the shipping cost data (see step 1d, Flow Diagram). The inclusion of lists of actual transportation costs and delay times (or distance) between all potential shipping points as data might appear to be unwieldy relative to the Shycon-Maffei approach [25] outlined in Appendix II, since locating M customers and warehouses by longitude and latitude takes only M computer locations whereas up to $M^2/2$ locations are required for recording all shipping costs. In practice the problem is not nearly so unwieldy and produces some compensations. For example, in many cases *a priori* judgments can be made that customers in certain geographical regions will not be serviced from potential warehouses in other regions. Thus, in one of the sample problems discussed below, we do not consider shipping from warehouses in Eastern cities to the West Coast since the factory is located in Indianapolis. In addition, customers can frequently be aggregated into concentrations of demand (for example,

Flow Diagram

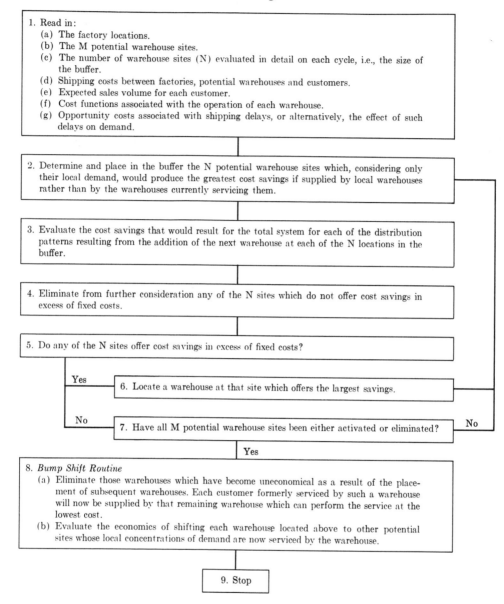

1. Read in:
   (a) The factory locations.
   (b) The M potential warehouse sites.
   (c) The number of warehouse sites (N) evaluated in detail on each cycle, i.e., the size of the buffer.
   (d) Shipping costs between factories, potential warehouses and customers.
   (e) Expected sales volume for each customer.
   (f) Cost functions associated with the operation of each warehouse.
   (g) Opportunity costs associated with shipping delays, or alternatively, the effect of such delays on demand.

2. Determine and place in the buffer the N potential warehouse sites which, considering only their local demand, would produce the greatest cost savings if supplied by local warehouses rather than by the warehouses currently servicing them.

3. Evaluate the cost savings that would result for the total system for each of the distribution patterns resulting from the addition of the next warehouse at each of the N locations in the buffer.

4. Eliminate from further consideration any of the N sites which do not offer cost savings in excess of fixed costs.

5. Do any of the N sites offer cost savings in excess of fixed costs?

   Yes
   6. Locate a warehouse at that site which offers the largest savings.

   No
   7. Have all M potential warehouse sites been either activated or eliminated?   No

   Yes

8. *Bump Shift Routine*
   (a) Eliminate those warehouses which have become uneconomical as a result of the placement of subsequent warehouses. Each customer formerly serviced by such a warehouse will now be supplied by that remaining warehouse which can perform the service at the lowest cost.
   (b) Evaluate the economics of shifting each warehouse located above to other potential sites whose local concentrations of demand are now serviced by the warehouse.

9. Stop

FIG. 1. Flow diagram.

metropolitan chain grocery and wholesaler warehouses) because of close geographical proximity. The program also automatically eliminates from the search list potential warehouse sites and warehouse-customer combinations that no longer offer promise of cost reduction. As a result, by the time that the program has located two or three warehouses, the list being searched is frequently reduced by 90 per cent. The reduction in list size continues as more warehouses are added, speeding up the analysis on each cycle. These heuristics make the use of actual costs computationally efficient (computation times for 12 sample problems are outlined in the following section). They also permit us to: (1) avoid the errors associated with the use of air miles as a basis for approximating shipping costs; and (2) solve large-scale problems, involving, for example, several factories, 10 products, at least 200 potential warehouse sites,

Table 1. Heuristic Solutions to Sample Problems   Factory Location: Indianapolis

	Fixed Costs of Warehouses						
$7,500		$12,500		$17,500		$25,000	
Warehouse Located at Each Stage	Cost of System at Each Stage	Warehouse Located at Each Stage	Cost of System at Each Stage	Warehouse Located at Each Stage	Cost of System at Each Stage	Warehouse Located at Each Stage	Cost of System at Each Stage
Main Program		*Main Program*		*Main Program*		*Main Program*	
No warehouses	$1,248,688	No warehouses	$1,248,688	No warehouses	$1,248,688	No warehouses	$1,248,688
Philadelphia	1,075,120	Philadelphia	1,080,120	Philadelphia	1,085,120	Philadelphia	1,092,620
Los Angeles	910,514	Los Angeles	920,514	Los Angeles	930,514	Los Angeles	945,514
Seattle	876,429	Seattle	891,429	Seattle	906,429	Seattle	928,929
San Francisco	861,967	San Francisco	881,967	San Francisco	901,967		
Houston	850,645	Houston	875,645	Houston	900,645		
Chicago	839,853	Chicago	869,853	Chicago	899,853		
New York	830,424	New York	865,424				
Detroit	824,721	Detroit	864,721				
Denver	819,073	Kansas City	860,484				
Pittsburgh	815,818	Atlanta	859,125				
Washington, D.C.	813,321	Cleveland	858,764				
Kansas City	809,827						
Boston	808,203						
Atlanta	801,845						
Bump-Shift Routine		*Bump-Shift Routine*		*Bump-Shift Routine*		*Bump-Shift Routine*	
Drop Denver	$801,748	Drop Detroit	$857,725	Replace Houston with Dallas	$896,864	No change	$928,929
		Replace Phila. with Wash.	856,257				
Improvements not Found by the Heuristic Program		*Improvements not Found by the Heuristic Program*		*Improvements not Found by the Heuristic Program*		*Improvements not Found by the Heuristic Program*	
Replace Houston with Dallas	$800,163	Replace Houston with Dallas	$854,672	None known		None known	

Table 2. *Heuristic Solutions to Sample Problems   Factory Location: Jacksonville*

	Fixed Costs of Warehouses						
	$7,500		$12,500		$17,500		$25,000	
	Warehouse Located at Each Stage	Cost of System at Each Stage	Warehouse Located at Each Stage	Cost of System at Each Stage	Warehouse Located at Each Stage	Cost of System at Each Stage	Warehouse Located at Each Stage	Cost of System at Each Stage
Main Program								
	No warehouses	$1,832,861	No warehouses	$1,832,861	No warehouses	$1,832,861	No warehouses	$1,832,861
	New York	1,602,504	New York	1,607,504	New York	1,612,504	New York	1,620,004
	Los Angeles	1,376,900	Los Angeles	1,386,900	Los Angeles	1,396,900	Los Angeles	1,411,900
	Chicago	1,239,864	Chicago	1,254,864	Chicago	1,269,864	Chicago	1,292,364
	Seattle	1,211,687	Seattle	1,231,687	Seattle	1,251,687	Seattle	1,281,687
	Washington, D.C.	1,169,916	Washington, D.C.	1,194,916	Washington, D.C.	1,219,916	Washington, D.C.	1,257,416
	St. Louis	1,143,998	St. Louis	1,173,998	St. Louis	1,203,998	St. Louis	1,248,998
	Cincinnati	1,123,224	Cincinnati	1,158,224	Cincinnati	1,193,224	Cincinnati	1,245,724
	Houston	1,106,239	Houston	1,146,239	Houston	1,186,239		
	San Francisco	1,098,949	San Francisco	1,143,949				
	Denver	1,096,245						
	Detroit	1,093,780						
	Pittsburgh	1,092,163						
	Atlanta	1,091,374						
Bump-Shift Routine								
	No change	$1,091,374	No change	$1,143,949	No change	$1,186,239	No change	$1,245,724
Improvements not Found by the Heuristic Program								
	None known		None known		None known		None known	

Table 3. Heuristic Solutions to Sample Problems   Factory Locations: Baltimore and Indianapolis

	Fixed Costs of Warehouses							
	$7,500		$12,500		$17,500		$25,000	
	Warehouse Located at Each Stage	Cost of System at Each Stage	Warehouse Located at Each Stage	Cost of System at Each Stage	Warehouse Located at Each Stage	Cost of System at Each Stage	Warehouse Located at Each Stage	Cost of System at Each Stage
Main Program								
	No warehouses	$899,770	No warehouses	$899,770	No warehouses	$899,770	No warehouses	$899,770
	Los Angeles	735,164	Los Angeles	740,164	Los Angeles	745,164	Los Angeles	752,664
	Seattle	701,079	Seattle	711,079	Seattle	721,079	Seattle	736,079
	New York	672,666	New York	687,666	New York	702,666	New York	725,166
	San Francisco	658,205	San Francisco	678,205	San Francisco	698,205		
	Houston	646,882	Houston	671,882	Dallas	691,772		
	Chicago	636,091	Chicago	666,091	Chicago	690,980		
	Denver	630,442	Kansas City	661,853				
	Detroit	626,481						
	Kansas City	623,114						
Bump–Shift Routine								
	Cleveland	620,405	No change	$661,853	No change	$690,980	No change	$725,166
	Atlanta	617,337						
	Drop Denver	$617,116						
Improvements not Found by the Heuristic Program								
	Replace Houston with Dallas	$615,531	Replace Houston with Dallas	$660,268	None known		None known	

97

Table 4. Sales Potential of Concentrations of Demand Used in Sample Problems (population in 1000's)

Concentrations of Demand	Sales Potential	Concentrations of Demand	Sales Potential
Albuquerque, N. Mex.	146	Knoxville, Tenn.	337
Amarillo, Tex.	87	Los Angeles, Calif.*	4368
Atlanta, Ga.*	672	Louisville, Ky.	577
Baltimore, Md.	1337	Memphis, Tenn.*	482
Billings, Mont.	31	Miami, Fla.*	495
Birmingham, Ala.	559	Mobile, Ala.	231
Boston, Mass.*	2370	Nashville, Tenn.	322
Buffalo, N. Y.*	1089	New Orleans, La.*	685
Butte, Mont.	33	New York, N. Y.*	12912
Cheyenne, Wyo.	32	Oklahoma City, Okla.	325
Chicago, Ill.*	5495	Omaha, Nebr.	366
Cincinnati, Ohio*	904	Philadelphia, Pa.*	3671
Cleveland, Ohio*	1466	Pittsburgh, Pa.*	2213
Columbia, S. C.	143	Portland, Oreg.	705
Dallas, Tex.*	615	Richmond, Va.	328
Denver, Colo.*	564	St. Louis, Mo.*	1681
Des Moines, Iowa	226	St. Paul, Minn.	1117
Detroit, Mich.*	3016	Salt Lake City, Utah*	275
Duluth, Minn.	253	San Antonio, Tex.	500
El Paso, Tex.	195	San Francisco, Calif.*	2241
Fargo, N. Dak.	38	Seattle, Wash.*	733
Houston, Tex.*	807	Spokane, Wash.	222
Indianapolis, Ind.	551	Tucson, Ariz.	49
Jacksonville, Fla.	304	Washington, D. C.*	1464
Kansas City, Mo.*	814	Wichita, Kansas	222

* Potential warehouse sites.

Source: *The World Almanac*, 1960; New York World-Telegram and the Sun, New York, 1960.

and more than a thousand concentrations of demand.

Sample Problems

The operation of the program will be illustrated with reference to 12 sample problems. The problems represent all combinations of three sets of factory locations—(1) Indianapolis, (2) Jacksonville, Florida, (3) Indianapolis and Baltimore—and four levels of fixed warehouse costs—$7,500, $12,500, $17,500, $25,000—for each warehouse in the system. Each of the sample problems considers only a single product. Transportation costs and costs associated with shipping delays are assumed to be proportional to the railroad distance between shipping points.[3] For purposes of illustration, bulk ship-

ping rates from the factory to warehouses are evaluated at $0.0125 per mile per unit, whereas the sum of the shipping and delay costs from warehouses to customers is considered to be $0.0250 per mile per unit. To further simplify the 12 distribution problems analyzed in this paper, the variable costs of operating the warehouses are assumed to be linear with respect to the volume of goods processed.[4] Consequently,

---

[3] Railroad distances between cities were obtained from the *Rand McNally-Cosmopolitan*

World Atlas (Chicago: Rand McNally & Co., 1951), p. 193. It should be noted that the simplifying assumption of linearity of transportation and delay costs with respect to railroad mileage is strictly a matter of convenience in making the cost data available to the reader. In practice, actual shipping costs and delay times would generally be read into the computer.

[4] The 12 sample problems were not specified so as to fully test the generality of the program. The simplification of linear warehousing cost functions was incorporated in the test problems so that the

these costs do not affect the optimal warehouse system and need not be further considered in the sample problems.[5] The size of the buffer (N) was equal to five in each of the 12 sample problems.

The market structure considered in the sample problems consists of 50 concentrations of demand scattered throughout the United States. Twenty-four of these centers of demand are treated as potential warehouse sites. The metropolitan population of each of these areas was used to represent sales potential, a population of 1,000 representing one unit of demand (see Table 4).

The results obtained for each of the 12 cases are shown in Tables 1 through 3. These tables summarize:

1. The warehouse locations selected by the main program, in the order of selection.
2. The modifications introduced into the main program solution by the bump-shift routine.
3. Alterations to the heuristic warehouse network which are known to lower total distribution costs.
4. The total distribution costs at each stage of the heuristic solution and for the warehouse network which incorporates subsequent improvements.[6]

---

heuristic solutions obtained might subsequently be compared with optimal solutions developed by the application of integer programing. Such a comparison has not yet been made since we are not aware of the existence of an integer programing routine capable of solving a problem of this size.

[5] It should be noted that the heuristic program, in addition to being able to treat the case where both shipping costs and the variable and fixed costs of warehousing vary throughout the country, can determine which of several different types of warehouses (some of which might include packaging facilities) and transportation systems should be used to service each concentration of demand. The program can also be employed to locate regional factories, choosing among alternative factory sites for which production costs are specified.

[6] The improvements upon the heuristic solutions tabulated for four of the 12 problems have been found by evaluating the modifications in the heuristic distribution network which, upon inspection, appeared most likely to result in lower distribution costs. Approximately 25 types of modifications were tested, but only one resulted in a minor improvement in four of the problems. To determine the optimal system by complete enumeration

In each of the four cases in which an improvement upon the heuristic solution was discovered, the improvement consisted of replacing a warehouse in Houston with a warehouse in Dallas. This improvement was not found by the shift portion of the bump-shift routine since Dallas was not being serviced from the Houston warehouse. The shift routine as currently programed considers as alternatives only those warehouse sites which are located within the territory served by the warehouse under examination. The rationale for limiting the alternatives considered in this fashion was (1) it provided a convenient method of identifying most of the nearby unactivated warehouse sites, and (2) computation time would be minimized by not considering the realignment of regions at this point in the program.

The shift routine as specified above cannot be applied directly to multiple product systems in which different mixes of products might be shipped to the customer from different warehouses since the regions for the different product mixes will not necessarily be identical. A simple heuristic now being programed to treat the multiple product problem considers shifting the warehouses located by the main program to all sites specified in the input as "neighboring warehouse sites." That is, the neighboring warehouse sites of each potential warehouse location are specified in the input to the program and are evaluated as alternatives in the shift routine. Since this routine does not make use of

---

would require the evaluation of the 2^{24} possible ways of locating up to 24 warehouses. With an IBM-704, which could perform approximately one such evaluation per second, this operation would take more than six months of continuous operation per problem. Testing all combinations of three and four warehouses, which would probably be sufficient to insure finding the optimal network for any one of the two least interesting cases (those problems in which, because of high fixed warehousing costs, the heuristic program locates only three warehouses) would require approximately four computer hours. The use of integer programing offers more promise. Once such a computer program is available, it should be feasible to test the sample problem solutions we have found for optimality in one iteration by using the heuristic solutions as the initial basis for the integer program. This points to another possible application for heuristic programing. Insofar as heuristics can be used to develop an advanced starting basis for an integer programing problem, a substantial reduction in the total computation time required to reach an optimum may be possible.

Table 5. Frequency Distribution of Warehouses Selected for Activation from Each Position in the Buffer

Position in the Buffer	Number of Warehouses Located from Each Position	Percentage of Total Warehouses Located from Each Position
		%
1	48	49.0
2	15	15.3
3	15	15.3
4	10	10.2
5	10	10.2

the concept of warehouse territories, it will also correct errors of the Dallas-Houston variety when applied to problems involving only a single product. (This routine will increase computation time in most cases.) It will not, however, correct for less-localized deviations of the main program solution from the optimal warehouse network.

In considering the development of new or more elaborate bump-shift routines (or, the inclusion of such devices in the main program to be performed after the addition of each warehouse) it is desirable to determine the improvements which might be expected. In the 12 sample problems discussed above, the improvements upon the main program solution developed in the bump-shift routine and through subsequent analysis never amounted to more than 0.5 per cent. If future research indicates that the main program solution is generally near-optimal, it would give strong support to the use of the three basic heuristics in the main program and limit the gain to be expected in searching for corrective routines.

Some support for the heuristic which selects warehouse sites to be placed in the buffer is obtained by reference to the frequency distribution of warehouses selected for activation in the 12 sample problems from each of the positions in the five-place buffer used in the analysis. This distribution is tabulated in Table 5, the buffer positions representing the rank of the potential warehouse sites in terms of their cost savings considering only local demand (Step 2, Figure 1, Flow Diagram).

Computation Time

The time required to reach a solution for the 12 sample problems in the main program totaled 72 minutes on an IBM-650 with RAMAC disc

storage. The individual problems required an average of 2 minutes setup time and 30 seconds per warehouse located. Experimentation with and analysis of the heuristic program indicates that computation time increases at a much slower rate with increases in problem size than is the case with linear programing algorithms designed to handle fixed cost elements. It appears that the problem setup time increases linearly with the product of the number of warehouses, the number of products, and the number of customers (concentrations of demand). The time required for locating warehouses increases approximately linearly with the size of the buffer (N), the number of products, and the number of customers, but almost negligibly with the number of potential warehouse sites. The effect of multiple factories on setup time is at most linear; if capacity constraints are not operative the effect is substantially less than linear. Surprisingly, increasing the number of factories actually tends to decrease the total warehouse location time since there is no effect upon the time required to locate individual warehouses and the total number of warehouses located will generally be reduced.

Accurate time estimates for the bump-shift routine are not available since only an inefficient routine was operating when the IBM-650 at Carnegie Tech was replaced. Processing the 12 sample problems with this version of the bump-shift routine required a total of one hour. We would expect an efficient computer routine to perform this operation in 10 to 15 minutes since comparable reductions in computer time were achieved in the revision of the main program.

Extensions and Applications

Improved heuristics in terms of reduced computation time and/or more nearly optimum solutions of the warehouse location problem will probably be forthcoming. The six-minute solution time on an IBM-650 in itself probably suggests to the reader that additional check and bump-shift routines might be interspersed between the location of individual warehouses; after all, the difference in cost between six minutes and even six hours of computation time on an IBM-650 is negligible relative to the cost savings that might be achieved in the sample warehouse network problems studied. It is not clear, however, that such approaches will on the average improve upon the solutions generated by the existing heuristic program if at least four warehouses are located. Care must also be taken to avoid the chase for optimal solutions to simple problems and thereby miss the actual problem of business—the solution of large-scale problems containing many customers buying various mixes of a full product line, many potential warehouse sites, alternate warehouse types with different cost structures, several factories and, perhaps, a number of potential factory sites.[7]

Two warehouse network problems containing many of the above complexities are now being examined, one representing the distribution of a

[7] It should be noted that the distribution of order-shipment mixes of products can be treated by considering each geographical concentration of demand as several concentrations at the same location, each concentration representing a given mix of products of a given total size. Insofar as discrete distributions can be used to approximate the empirical distributions, the specification of the problem can be greatly simplified. The number of computer locations required to store each of these mixes would then be reduced substantially from that which would be required if each of the mixes were treated as the demand at an individual geographical location. An interesting aspect of this treatment of the problem is that the total warehouse network would be established with full recognition of the fact that customers will not necessarily receive all of their shipments from a single warehouse if all factories do not produce all products. An order of packaged detergents and toilet bar soap, for example, might be received from one warehouse if it consists largely of detergent and from another if the order is primarily composed of bar soaps. Similarly, not all products will necessarily be stocked at all warehouses. In the distribution of appliances, for example, yellow refrigerators, for which there is a relatively small demand, might be stocked in only the larger warehouses.

variety of grocery-drug type consumer products, the other a line of consumer appliances. In both cases the problem is of such magnitude that the solution time could easily come to several hours on an IBM-7090 computer unless the problem is simplified beyond the level now thought to be desirable. Furthermore, in view of some uncertainty as to the actual nature of warehousing costs, it appears prudent to make several runs with different warehousing cost functions to determine the sensitivity of the heuristic warehouse solutions to the cost functions. It is in this context that the advantages of improved solutions to test problems must be evaluated relative to increased computer time requirements. Additional check or bump-shift heuristics increasing computer time on test problems from six minutes to six hours would increase the IBM-7090 time per run from 3–6 hours to 180–360 hours, time which might well be better spent in testing the sensitivity of the solutions to variations in warehouse cost structures and in providing an improved model of demand through greater detail in the description of the product mix and size of customer orders.

It has been suggested that the heuristics might be applied by eliminating warehouses rather than adding them. That is, a warehouse is assumed to be operating at each potential site at the start of the program. Warehouses would then be eliminated one by one on the basis of cost savings. It is not clear how the quality of solutions produced in this manner would compare with those developed from the heuristic program outlined in this paper. In terms of computation time, however, it seems likely that the current program would be the more efficient when the number of warehouses located is less than half the number of potential sites being considered. This seems to be generally the case in industry although situations could, no doubt, be found where this is not true (for example, the firm which is interested only in considering the possibility of closing existing warehouses).

Once we know the optimal solutions to the test problems (through the application of integer programing, using the heuristic solution as a starting basis), we will be in a better position to evaluate the potential gains possible through the use of improved heuristics. In addition, knowledge of the optimal solution should provide sound direction as to the types of heuristics which offer most promise in correcting the deviations inherent in the current program.

Summary

A heuristic program was developed and applied to several warehouse location problems. The results suggest that a heuristic approach to this class of problems may be quite profitable in practice, producing near-optimal solutions within acceptable limits of computer time.

The use of heuristics in solving these problems has two prime advantages relative to the currently available linear programming formulations and solution procedures: (1) computational simplicity, which results in substantial reductions in solution times and permits the treatment of large-scale problems, and (2) flexibility with respect to the underlying cost functions, eliminating the need for restrictive assumptions. It also represents an important extension to the simulation approach to locating warehouses in that it incorporates a systematic procedure designed to generate at least one near-optimal distribution system without reducing flexibility in the modeling of the problem.

The proposed heuristic program permits fast screening and evaluation of alternative types of warehouses, transportation systems, and warehouse locations. It should, however, be emphasized that this program is not the end of the road. It may some day become practical to solve large-scale warehouse location problems with optimizing algorithms given continued development of computer hardware and linear programing techniques. Heuristic programing, too, is capable of improvement and such developments will probably be forthcoming as a result of the large amount of research on heuristic models and computer programing now being carried on at the RAND Corporation, Carnegie Tech, and elsewhere.

Appendix 1. Mathematical Formulation of the Warehouse Location Problem

The problem can be expressed mathematically as follows:

$X_{h,i,j,k}$ = the quantity of good h ($h = 1, \cdots, p$) shipped from factory i ($i = 1, \cdots, q$) via warehouse j ($j = 1, \cdots, r$) to customer k ($k - 1, \cdots, s$).

$A_{h,i,j}$ = the per unit transportation cost of shipping good h from factory i to warehouse j.

$B_{h,j,k}$ = the per unit transportation cost of shipping good h from warehouse j to customer k.

$C_{h,j}(\sum_{i,k} X_{h,i,j,k})$ = total cost of warehouse operation associated with processing good h at warehouse j. Without loss of generality we may express this function as the sum of $S_{h,j}$ and F_j defined below.

$D_{h,k}(T_{h,k})$ = explicit or imputed cost due to a delay of T time units in delivery of good h to customer k. when the customer imposes a maximum delivery time (constraint), D becomes infinite whenever the indicated time limit is reached.[8]

F_j = fixed cost per time period of operating warehouse j. Note that this is a planned fixed cost to be incurred and not a sunk cost.

$S_{h,j}(\sum_{i,k} X_{h,i,j,k})$ = semivariable cost of operating warehouse j per unit of good h processed, including variable handling and administrative costs, storage costs, taxes, interest on investment, pilferage, and so on (the homogeneous portion of the very general function $C_{h,j}$).

$Q_{h,k}$ = quantity of good h demanded by customer k.

W_j = capacity of warehouse j.

$Y_{h,i}$ = capacity of factory i to produce good h.

Z_j = 1 if $\sum_{h,i,k} X_{h,i,j,k} > 0$ and zero otherwise (that is, $\sum Z_j$ = the number of warehouses used).

The problem then becomes one of minimizing total distribution costs, an objective function

---

[8] The effect of delay in supplying customers has been treated above as an "opportunity cost" since this simplifies the notation and is consistent with current research practice. However, an alternative formulation which reflects management's view of the problem more accurately is to have delivery times affect demand.

of the form

$$f(X) = \sum_{h,i,j,k}(A_{h,i,j} + B_{h,j,k})X_{h,i,j,k}$$
$$+ \sum_j F_j Z_j + \sum_{h,j}S_{h,j}(\sum_{i,k}X_{h,i,j,k})$$
$$+ \sum_{h,k}D_{h,k}(T_{h,k}),$$

subject to constraints of the following form:

$$\sum_{i,j}X_{h,i,j,k} = Q_{h,k}$$

(customer k's demand for product h must be supplied),

$$\sum_{j,k}X_{h,i,j,k} \leq V_{h,i}$$

(factory i's capacity limit on good h cannot be exceeded),

$$I_j(\sum_{h,i,k}X_{h,i,j,k}) \leq W_j$$

(the capacity of warehouse j cannot be exceeded), where $I_j(\sum_{h,i,j}X_{h,i,j,k})$ is a function which denotes the maximum inventory level associated with the flow of all goods from all factories to all customers serviced through warehouse j.

Appendix 2. A Comparative Study of Alternative Approaches to the Warehouse Location Problem

Linear Programing

In theory, a linear programing approach (for example, using Gomory's integer algorithm [14] or other variations) could be used to solve the problem. In practice, however, the size and nonlinearities involved in many problems are such that application is not currently feasible.[9]

The most important types of nonlinearities generally encountered stem from the fixed costs associated with the operation of warehouses and variable warehousing and delivery costs which are nonlinear. Two types of warehousing and delivery cost functions have been suggested in the literature, strictly concave functions and piecewise linear functions. Figure 2 describes the strictly concave cost function proposed by Baumol and Wolfe [4]. Figure 3 represents the piecewise linear function which, apart from the fixed cost element, is equivalent to that illus-

[9] The difficulties that have been encountered in applying linear programing directly to the warehouse location problem are similar to those encountered in the application of these algorithms to production scheduling problems. See for example, C. C. Holt, F. Modigliani, J. F. Muth, and H. A. Simon [16], chap. xx.

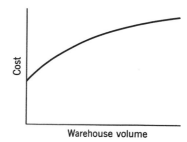

FIG. 2. A strictly concave function.

trated by Balinski and Mills [2]. The fixed cost element is incorporated in Figure 3 for purposes of generality.[10]

Both of the above functions describe essentially the same types of cost structures, that is, cost structures where the transportation rates and the marginal cost of operating a warehouse decrease as the quantity of goods handled by the warehouse increases. The different functions reflect slightly different views of the total problem, Baumol and Wolfe focusing primarily upon the warehouse operating costs which, in a sample problem, they approximate by square root functions (see [4] p. 255) and Balinski and Mills concentrating upon freight and storage rates specified in terms of the volume of goods handled.

Let us now examine several other approaches to the warehouse location problem discussed in the literature, paying particular attention to the treatment of those aspects of the problem not handled adequately by linear programing in its current state of development.

[10] In the previous formulation of the warehouse location problem the warehouse operating costs and the cost of delivering goods to warehouses were separated. However, these two types of costs may be combined into one function without any loss of generality.

FIG. 3. A piecewise linear function.

The Baumol-Wolfe Marginal Cost Approach

Baumol and Wolfe [3, 4] pose the problem as minimizing total distribution costs which, utilizing the symbols defined above, may be stated as follows:

$$\text{Min. } f(X) = \text{Min. } \sum_{i,j,k}(A_{i,j} + B_{j,k})X_{i,j,k} + \sum_j S_j(\sum_{i,k}X_{i,j,k}) + \sum_j F_j Z_j$$

subject to

$$I_j(\sum_{i,k}X_{i,j,k}) \leqq W_j$$

(the warehouse capacity constraint), and

$$\sum_{i,j}X_{i,j,k} = Q_k$$

(customer demand constraint, that is, all demands must be satisfied).

The effects of delay in delivery times are not incorporated into the Baumol-Wolfe treatment of the problem although it is apparent that opportunity costs associated with such delays could be added to the shipping costs. It should also be noted that the above symbolic representation of the problem requires only three subscripts. The reason for this is that the Baumol and Wolfe method deals with only one product or, perhaps, a composite product (that is, a constant product mix). It is possible that the method can be extended to deal with the multiproduct case although Baumol and Wolfe do not indicate how this might be done.

The Baumol-Wolfe algorithm consists of an iterative procedure which requires the solution of an ordinary transportation problem at each stage. The steps involved in this procedure are as follows:

1. *The Initial Stage.* For each pair, i, k of factory and retailer, find the least cost of shipment considering only the transportation costs:

$$C_{i,k}^0 = \text{Min.}_j (A_{i,j} + B_{j,k}) - (A_{i,j_{i,k}}^0 + B_{j_{i,k},k}^0)$$

where $j_{i,k}$ denotes the routing between factory i and customer k via warehouse j as selected by this criterion. The superscripts refer to the stage in the solution process. Thus, $C_{i,k}^0$ is the lowest unit cost of shipping the product from factory i to customer k considered over all warehouse possibilities at the initial stage. These $C_{i,k}^0$ are then used to solve an ordinary transportation problem[11] involving shipments from factories

[11] Many efficient computing methods for solving this special form of linear programing are available [10, 6, 11].

with known availabilities to retailers with known demands so as to minimize the cost function $\sum_{i,k}C_{i,k}^0 x_{i,k}$.

2. *The nth Stage.* Thus starting at stage 0, the iterations are continued until a stage, say $n-1$, is reached. From the warehouse loadings computed at stage $n-1$, $(\sum_{i,k}X_{i,j,k}^{n-1})$, the marginal warehousing costs are computed by means of the expression

$$\frac{dS_j(\sum_{i,k}X_{i,j,k}^{n-1})}{d(\sum_{i,k}X_{i,j,k}^{n-1})},$$

the derivative of the operating costs of warehouse j.

The new set of transportation costs to be used in the transportation problem at this stage is defined as

$$C_{i,k}^n = \text{Min.}_j A_{i,j} + B_{j,k} + \frac{dS_j(\sum_{i,k}X_{i,j,k}^{n-1})}{d(\sum_{i,k}X_{i,j,k}^{n-1})}$$

3. *Test for Stopping.* Compare the warehouse loadings of the nth stage with those of the previous stage. If the same stop, if different continue by returning to step 2.

The justification for this approach is contained in a set of proofs which Baumol and Wolfe present in their paper. They do not claim that the method will produce an optimal solution but rather that:

(a) "this procedure will reduce the total cost . . . in each step."[12]

(b) "the procedure . . . will yield a solution that probably cannot be improved except by prohibitively expensive computation for large-scale problems."[13] that is, the method determines a local optimum.[14]

The Baumol-Wolfe method may be satisfactory for solving certain special types of warehouse location problems. However as a general approach to this class of problems the method appears to be unsatisfactory. First, although the formulation of the problem permits fixed costs associated with the operation of warehouses, there appears to be no mechanism within the solution procedure itself designed to handle this aspect of the problem. That is, both the differential calculus as used in adjusting the transportation costs and the transportation model

[12] Baumol and Wolfe [4], p. 257.
[13] *Ibid.*, p. 256.
[14] Baumol [3], p. 413, and Baumol and Wolfe [4], p. 252.

Table 6

Method of Solution	Warehouses Used	Cost
Baumol-Wolfe[a]	1, 2, 4, 5	$2,362
Heuristic program	3	$2,047
Arbitrary choice of single warehouses	1	$2,452
	2	$2,379
	4	$2,194
	5	$2,070

[a] Baumol and Wolfe [4] calculated the total cost associated with their warehouse network solution as $2,257, which is $105 less than that tabulated above. This difference is due to an error in the computation of factory to warehouse costs. It should be noted, however, that this error does not in any way influence the Baumol-Wolfe solution with respect to warehouse locations or loadings.

are not well designed to handle fixed cost elements. Furthermore, even if fixed costs are neglected, the solutions to concave programing problems[15] produced by the Baumol-Wolfe method will frequently not be satisfactory. The quality of the solutions produced will in general depend on the degree of concavity of the cost function. To illustrate the impact which a concave cost function can have upon the solution to even a simple problem, let us consider the example used by Baumol and Wolfe to demonstrate their procedure.

The Baumol-Wolfe sample problem involves two factories, five potential warehouse sites and eight retailers. The problem involves no fixed costs in the operation of warehouses, warehousing costs being regarded as square root functions of warehouse volume. Table 6 shows the solutions derived by several procedures. The table shows that the Baumol-Wolfe warehouse location procedure has a strong bias in the direction of locating more than the optimal number of warehouses. Baumol and Wolfe recognized the existence of such a bias ([4], p. 262), but did not, in their paper, concern themselves with the extent of its impact. In fact, the Baumol-Wolfe solution is not even a local optimum in terms of changes in warehouse location patterns; a reduction in total costs can be accom-

[15] That is, problems in which the cost function possesses the property that $dC(x)/dx < C(x)/x$. For a more precise definition see Charnes and Cooper [7], p. 284.

plished by eliminating any one of the four warehouses in the solution set.[16] The heuristic solution, obtained through application of the program discussed in this paper, has since been proven to be the optimal solution.

Balinski-Mills Average Cost Method

The Balinski-Mills approach to the warehouse location problem is similar to that of Baumol and Wolfe in that it requires the problem to be cast in the framework of the linear programing transportation model [2]. However, that is as far as the similarity goes. Baumol and Wolfe viewed the cost of delivering goods to warehouses and storing them as being described by a concave function whereas Balinski and Mills treated these costs as a piecewise linear function. Furthermore, Balinski and Mills specifically restrict their solution procedure to the case of a single factory (or vendor) and a single product.

In terms of the symbols defined above, Balinski and Mills pose the following problem:

Minimize $\sum_i C_i(\sum_k X_{j,k}) + \sum_{j,k} B_{j,k} X_{j,k}$

(total distribution costs)

subject to $I_j(\sum_k X_{j,k}) \leqq W_j$

(the warehouse capacity constraint), and

$$\sum_j X_{j,k} = Q_k$$

(the customer demand constraint), where the variable portion of $C_j(\sum_k X_{j,k})$ is a piecewise linear function (see Figure 3.)

In principle, an optimal solution to this problem can be found by using integer programming. However as Balinski and Mills point out ([2] p. 6) even small sample problems often involve as many variables and constraints that they cannot now be handled on existing computing equipment. As a result of these restrictions on

[16] The Baumol-Wolfe solution is a local optimum in the sense that no individual unit of product can be shipped by an alternate route without increasing total distribution costs. Costs can be reduced, however, by transferring the total demand of a retailer (or a major portion thereof) from one warehouse to another or, as indicated above, by eliminating individual warehouses. Baumol [3] did apparently believe that his solution was a local optimum in the latter sense when he wrote, "No *minor* changes from this computed set of warehouse locations could yield any reduction in costs (the result was sure to be a local optimum)."

the current use of integer programing, they develop an approximation technique which they report has proven to be highly successful in certain cases.[17] This technique consists of approximating

$$C_j(\textstyle\sum_k X_{j,k}) \text{ by } C_j(a_j)/a_j,$$

where $a_j = \min (W_j\sum_{j,k}X_{j,k})$. That is, the warehousing cost function for each warehouse is approximated by the average unit cost of operating that warehouse at some high level, such as the warehouse capacity (W_j) or the total flow of goods passing through the system during the year.

By using the above approximation of the warehousing cost function all nonlinearities are eliminated from the problem. As a result the problem is cast into the framework of a simple transportation problem. The solution to this transportation problem yields a distribution network which minimizes the objective function

$$f(X) = \textstyle\sum_{j,k}(B_{j,k} + C_j(a_j)/a_j)X_{j,k}$$

subject to the constraints listed above. The value of this solution, denoted by λ_*, represents a lower bound to the cost of the optimal solution to the original problem. The $X_{j,k}$ shipment routings arrived at through the use of this algorithm are regarded as the solution to the original problem. The value (cost) of this solution to the original problem designated by λ^* can then be calculated by substituting these $X_{j,k}$ into the original cost functions. Balinski and Mills prove ([2] p. 8) that the cost of the actual optimal solution to the original problem (denoted by λ^0) must lie between these two values, that is $\lambda_* < \lambda^0 < \lambda^*$.

Thus we see that the Balinski-Mills method possesses the very desirable property of providing a lower bound to the optimal solution λ^0 to help evaluate the quality of the solution λ^*. Such a property is desirable since it cautions one against accepting a poor solution as a good one. A large spread between λ_* and λ^* does not, however, necessarily indicate that λ^* is a poor solution. To be sure, the worst that can happen if λ^* is near-optimal and the spread between λ^* and λ_* is substantial is that one might continue to look for better solutions. More important, however, is the question of whether the technique does in fact produce near-optimal solutions.

Extensive examination of the Balinski-Mills

[17] Balinski and Mills [2], p. 6.

method suggests that it is not well designed to handle the decreasing marginal cost functions generally postulated for the warehouse location problem. This can be illustrated by applying the method to the sample problem posed by Baumol and Wolfe. The Balinski-Mills solution calls for the use of all five warehouses at a cost of $2,499 which is 22 per cent above the optimal solution of $2,047.

The lower bound (λ_*) to the solution of any problem provided by the Balinski-Mills method depends upon the quality of the solution used as a basis for calculation. The lower bound calculated on the basis of the Balinski-Mills solution to the Baumol-Wolfe problem is $1,655, some 19 per cent below the optimal solution. In contrast, the lower bound that would be calculated if the optimal warehouse network (namely, using only warehouse 3) had been identified is $2,047, identical with the distribution cost of the warehouse network used as the basis for computing this value of the lower bound. Such an equality would insure that the optimal had indeed been attained. This pleasant state of affairs is not, however, guaranteed by the Balinski-Mills lower bound. In general the lower bound will be equal to the optimal solution only when each warehouse entering the solution is used to some predetermined capacity or alternatively, when the optimal solution consists of using only a single warehouse (that is, each warehouse in the optimal solution handles the volume a_j).

Mills, in personal communication, has stated that the Baumol-Wolfe problem violates one of the conditions set forth in the Balinski-Mills paper, namely, that the warehouse cost functions is "piecewise linear but not concave"([2], p. 3).[18] However, application of the method to such a problem does not seem inappropriate since the concave functions used in the Baumol-Wolfe problem can be closely approximated by piecewise linear functions containing the essential elements of the problem.

In comparing the Balinski-Mills and Baumol-Wolfe methods it should also be noted that the former permits the treatment of fixed costs

[18] The piecework linear function illustrated by Balinski and Mills ([2], p. 4) is similar to the cost function in Figure 3. This function, with or without a fixed cost element, is concave (even strictly concave) over suitably specified regions. (For definitions of concavity, convexity, and the related extreme-point optimization properties, see Charnes and Cooper [7], pp. 284–87.)

whereas the latter appears to be unable to handle such cost elements. Comparing the two methods on a problem which does not contain fixed costs does not, therefore, fully test the Balinski-Mills method. However the difficulty with the method appears to stem from its inability to cope with functions which deviate significantly from simple linear functions. Thus, adding fixed costs might appear to aggravate the situation. For example, if there were fixed costs associated with operating warehouses in the Baumol-Wolfe sample problem, and if these costs were equal for each warehouse, the Balinski-Mills solution would be independent of the level of fixed costs. In contrast, we might logically expect to make use of fewer warehouses in a distribution system if the fixed costs per warehouse were increased. Consequently, the existence of fixed costs tends to increase the deviation of the Balinski-Mills solution from optimality.

Balinski [1] has applied this same average cost approximation technique to what he calls the fixed cost transportation problem. His results seem to show that the method, although not guaranteeing optimality, works fairly well in solving such problems. This problem is not the same, however, as the warehouse location problem. The essence of the difference between the two problems is that in the fixed cost transportation problem the function describing the fixed cost elements is a separable one. That is, the fixed cost associated with using any route (that is, any path from a source of supply to a point of demand) is independent of the other routes used. In the warehouse location problem, shipping and handling costs may take this form but, in addition, a fixed cost may be associated with the use of each warehouse. This cost is incurred if a warehouse is used, but is independent of the number of routes passing through that warehouse.

Simulation of a Distribution System

The use of simulation techniques in the modeling of warehouse networks has been proposed by Shycon and Maffei [25] as a means of avoiding the approximations in problem specification required by the techniques outlined above.

The value of a simulation approach to solving the warehouse location problem, much as with the use of any other technique, depends upon how well the model describes the essence of the system being studied and the time required in

computation. As with the other approaches, some balance must be reached in terms of model detail and costs of computation. Once a model has been constructed containing the basic characteristics of the distribution system under study, it is used to evaluate the distribution costs associated with alternative sets of warehouse sites and customer ordering rates. The problem that remains is to devise an algorithm which can be used to generate at least one near-optimal warehouse system.

Shycon and Maffei do not outline a computational method for determining the sets of warehouse sites to be evaluated. Their approach requires that management or a consultant specify the warehouse systems (number of warehouses and their locations) to be evaluated. Maffei has stated that new warehouse systems can be generated from any given distribution network by moving individual warehouses fixed or random distances in random directions, but such a procedure does not appear to be an efficient method for searching for near-optimal warehouse location patterns.[19]

One other aspect of the Shycon-Maffei approach differs with respect to the other methods outlined in this appendix and the heuristic program itself. To save computer storage space they locate factories, warehouses, and customers in terms of longitude and latitude and subsequently approximate shipping costs between all of these points in terms of the computed air miles. The other methods outlined in this article would in general use actual costs, although a similar estimation technique could be used if actual data were not readily available. The use of air mile distances as approximations for shipping costs is an interesting approach to the problem and should be studied in more detail to determine the magnitude of error likely to result in cost data generated in this manner. If the error is within acceptable limits, it affords a means of reducing the time required in collecting and analyzing the cost data.

In its most detailed application, a simulation approach to the warehouse problem would permit the processing of actual customer orders through the alternative warehouse distribution systems being analyzed and imputing costs to the various phases of the operation. This would be a desirable approach, particularly for seasonal products, since it would permit incorporation of

---

[19] Marketing Theory Seminar, University of Vermont, August, 1960.

the dynamic elements of warehousing and inventory costs. The Shycon-Maffei approach, like the other methods discussed in this paper, does not simulate the distribution system in that degree of detail but rather estimates the warehousing and inventory costs as functions of the total volume of each product routed through any given warehouse. (In the heuristic program, since the number of products considered can be increased with less than a linear effect on computation time, it is possible to describe customer demand in terms of discrete distributions of product mix and order size such that the program treats each order-size, product-mix combination as a separate product, except insofar as it influences inventory levels.)

In summary, the linear programing approaches to the warehouse location problem outlined in this section have as a desirable feature a systematic routine for generating alternative warehouse systems for evaluation. However, they are inferior to the simulation approach in that there is less flexibility available in the modeling of the distribution system. The computer program described in this paper combines most of the desirable features of simulation with a set of heuristics designed to generate near-optimal warehouse systems.

References

1. Balinski, M. L., "Fixed-Cost Transportation Problems," *Naval Research Logistics Quarterly*, Vol. 8 (March 1961), pp. 41–54.
2. ———, and H. Mills, "A Warehouse Problem," prepared for: Veterans Administration; Mathematics, Princeton, New Jersey, April 1960.
3. Baumol, W. J., *Economic Theory and Operations Analysis*, pp. 410–413, Prentice-Hall, 1961.
4. ———, and P. Wolfe, "A Warehouse Location Problem," *Operations Research*, Vol. 6 (March–April 1958), pp. 252–263.
5. Bernstein, A., M. de V. Roberts, T. Arbuckle and M. H. Belsky, "A Chess-Playing Program for the IBM 704," *Proc. of the 1958 Western Joint Computer Conference*, pp. 157–159.
6. Charnes, A., and W. W. Cooper, "The Stepping Stone Method of Explaining Linear Programming Calculations in Transportation Problems," *Management Science*, Vol. 1 (October 1954), pp. 49–69.
7. ———, and ———, *Management Models and Industrial Applications of Linear Programing*, John Wiley & Sons, 1961.
8. Courant, R., and H. Robbins, *What Is Mathematics*, Oxford University Press, 1941.
9. Cyert, R. M., W. R. Dill, and J. G. March, "The Role of Expectations in Business Decision Making," *Administrative Science Quarterly*, December 1958.
10. Dantzig, G. B., "Application of the Simplex Method to a Transportation Problem." Chapter 23 of *Activity Analysis of Production and Allocation*, T. C. Koopmans (Ed.), Cowles Commission Monograph No. 13, John Wiley and Sons, 1951.
11. Ford, L. R., and D. R. Fulkerson, "Solving the Transportation Problem," *Management Science*, Vol. 3 (1956), pp. 24–32.
12. Gelernter, M., and N. Rochester, "Intelligent Behavior in Problem-Solving Machines," *IBM J. of Research and Development*, Vol. 2 (October 1958), pp. 336–345.
13. Gomory, R. E., "An Algorithm for Integer Solutions to Linear Programs," Princeton-IBM Mathematics Research Project, Technical Report No. 1, Princeton University.
14. Goodwin, G. H., "Digital Computers Tap Out Designs for Large Motors Fast," *Power* (April 1958).
15. Hiller, L. A., and L. M. Isaacson, *Experimental Music*, McGraw-Hill, 1959.
16. Holt, C. C., F. Modigliani, J. F. Muth, and H. A. Simon, *Planning Production, Inventories, and Work Force*, Prentice-Hall, 1960.
17. Kemeny, J. G., and G. L. Thompson, "The Modified Fictitious Play Method," *Dartmouth Mathematics Project Report*, 1958.
18. Kister, J., P. Stein, S. Ulam, W. Walden and M. Wells, "Experiments in Chess," *Jour. of the Association for Computing Machinery*, Vol. 4 (April, 1957), pp. 174–177.
19. March, J. G., and H. A. Simon, *Organizations*, John Wiley & Sons, 1958.
20. Newell, A., J. C. Shaw and H. A. Simon, "Chess Playing Programs and the Problem of Complexity," *IMB J. of Research and Development*, Vol. 2 (October, 1958), pp. 320–335.
21. ———, ———, and ———, "The Processes of Creative Thinking," The RAND Corporation Paper, P-1320, August, 1958.
22. ———, and H. A. Simon, "The Logic Theory Machine," *IRE Trans. on Information Theory*, IT-2 (September, 1956), pp. 61–79.
23. *Rand-McNally—Cosmopolitan World Atlas*, Rand-McNally & Co., Chicago, 1951.
24. Samuel, A. L., "Some Studies in Machine Learning Using the Game of Checkers," *IBM J. of Research and Development*, Vol. 3 (July, 1959), pp. 210–229.
25. Shycon, H. N., and R. B. Maffei, "Simulation—Tool for Better Distribution," *Harvard Business Review* (Nov.–Dec., 1960), pp. 65–75.
26. Simon, H. A., *Models of Man*, John Wiley & Sons, 1957.

27. ———, "Modeling Human Mental Processes," *Proc. of the 1961 Western Joint Computer Conference.*

28. Tonge, F. M., *A Heuristic Program for an Assembly Line Balancing Problem,* Prentice-Hall, 1961.

29. ———, "The Use of Heuristic Programming in Management Science," *Management Science,* Vol. 7 (April, 1961), pp. 231–237.

30. *The World Almanac,* 1960, New York World-Telegram and the Sun, New York, 1960.

Section III.   Information Flows

Information systems, by themselves, provide no profit for the firm: they provide no concrete and immediate sales, they create no product. And yet no firm exists without information systems of one sort or another. If no formal systems exist, informal ones arise; if overt systems are condemned, surreptitious ones are created.

Although information systems certainly are ubiquitous, Professor Dearden holds the view that no one system or set of systems will serve in all firms. Professor Dearden in his article, "How to Organize Information Systems," concludes that the total systems approach is leading the discipline in precisely the wrong direction. He suggests that a different approach is required if management is to realize the potential of modern information systems.

Robert Ivie presents a more descriptive, traditional article, thus enabling the reader to grasp the important aspects of information systems in the business logistics concept.

15. How to Organize Information Systems*

JOHN DEARDEN†

Many companies today are faced with serious problems in utilizing the capabilities of computers. Computers are not being used effectively in providing management with the best information available for decision making; they are not being used efficiently in terms of properly integrating the various information systems. Moreover, the situation appears to be getting worse rather than better. From observing this situation in business, I have come to the following conclusions:

The problem of organizing for effective management information systems will become progressively more severe in most companies as computer applications are extended.

Present concepts for organizing the systems and data-processing activities have fallen far short of providing a real solution. In fact, the favorite current approach—total systems is leading us in precisely the wrong direction.

A new and different approach to the organization of systems responsibility is necessary if business is to begin to tap the potential of the modern digital computer and the related data-processing and transmission equipment.

The purpose of this article is to suggest an approach to systems organization which will help business to take advantage of future developments in modern data-processing equipment and techniques.

The Wrong Direction

About ten years ago, when computers first began to be acquired by business, the computer was used to automate a few independent systems. Typically, the first system to be automated was the payroll, followed by such applications as customer billing and stockholder records. When these applications were safely digested, the company might next consider automating the general accounting system and perhaps the inventory records.

At this point, redundancy of input, processing, and output began to appear. It became evident that developing and maintaining a series of independent, automated information systems was not an efficient way to utilize the computer. With many companies reaching this stage at about the same time (five to seven years ago), a new term came into wide use—"integrated data processing" (IDP). IDP was used to indicate the need to integrate the various automated information systems. The term soon was replaced by another phrase—"total systems."

Ambiguity and Illusion

For at least four years, the term "total systems" has appeared with monotonous regularity in the literature about computers and systems. The term has been used so much by so many people to mean so many different things that, as far as I can see, it has become completely meaningless. For example, take two recent definitions:

"The total systems concept came about several years ago in view of the complexity of business systems. Simply interpreted, it calls for an over-all study of all systems in a company before making major revisions in any one system."[1]

"The goal of this management effort and investment of funds is often called the 'total systems concept.' This is nothing less than the

* Reprinted by permission from *Harvard Business Review*, March/April, 1965.
† Harvard University.

[1] John W. Field, "A New Brand of Data Processing Manager—Part II," *Computers and Data Processing*, September 1, 1964, p. 40.

complete monitoring of the business enterprise by a computer, or group of interconnected computers; the automatic control of machine by inventories, production scheduling, shipping, accounting, and all other operations that can be reduced to mathematical representation; and the limiting of human control to such functions as setting over-all objectives and reacting to such totally unexpected situations as earthquakes or wars."[2]

In other words, total systems can mean anything from our old friend "integrated data processing" to the ultimate automated business. The problem with the term, however, is not only its lack of precise meaning but also the implications it has for most systems people. The term implies to them that there is a single information system for a company and that this information system should be considered in total.

If the total systems concept assumes a single information system for a company, I have two objections to it. First, the entire information system of a company is just too large and all-encompassing to be a meaningful and useful classification. Second, the development of an information system requires such different kinds of skills that the term has little use in helping management approach the problem of organizing for the development of effective management information systems. In fact, the concept of a single information system implies a central control of the system effort, and this is where I believe that the total systems concept (regardless of how it is defined) is leading us in the wrong direction.

More Useful Approach

I believe that a more useful way to approach the organization of the systems effort is to break down the systems and data-processing activities both horizontally and vertically. Horizontally, the systems activities can be classified by the type of work performed; vertically, the systems activities can be classified by the kind of information handled. Let us examine these classifications and see how management can use them in organizing a company's systems and data-processing activities.

[2] Herbert E. Klein, "The Office: Management's Billion Dollar System," *Dun's Review and Modern Industry*, September 1964, p. 134A.

Horizontal Classification

The development of an information system is a more or less continuous process from the time that it is first conceived until it is in operation. Each phase tends to blend into the following phrase so that there is rarely a clear cut-off point where one phase ends and another phase starts. Consequently, the development of an information system is frequently considered to be a relatively homogeneous operation. The result of this is a tendency to classify certain people as "information systems specialists" and certain organization components as "systems departments," and then to consider these people and departments as specialists in the entire continuum of the development of an information system.

Stages of Development

I believe it is incorrect to treat systems development as a homogeneous operation. It appears to me that there are three stages in the development of an automated information system which are distinctly different and which, consequently, should be treated differently (even though the points where one stage stops and another starts will always overlap, since the exact divisions are somewhat arbitrary). These stages are as follows:

Stage 1: Systems Specification. Systems specification includes the design of all of the aspects of a management information system that are important *to the users*. It includes principally the basic decisions as to what information should be provided by the system. In many systems the timing of the information, the output, and the input format will be defined in this stage. For example, in a budgetary control system, the format of the budget proposals, the procedure for approval, and the format and timing of the budget performance reports would all be specified because they are important to the users. On the other hand, the specifications for an automated inventory control system might not include the format of the replenishment order to the supplier; as long as the order is intelligible, it makes no difference to the warehouse manager what the order format looks like.

Stage 2: Data-Processing Implementation. Data-processing implementation is concerned

Classification of Vertical Systems

• There are three major information systems in the typical company. Each of these systems is different with respect to the type of information handled. One concerns the flow of monetary information; one concerns the flow of personnel information; and one concerns the flow of physical goods.

• Although these three systems have interfaces they can be treated separately for organization purposes. In most companies at the present time, the financial and personnel information systems are already organizationally separate.

• The three major information systems are similar in that they are concerned almost exclusively with historical, recurring, internal information. These systems together account for most of this kind of data in the typical company

• There are, however, many other minor information systems. Many of these systems use little or none of the information developed by the three major systems.

---

with those things that are important *to the processing of the data.* The purpose in this stage is to design a data-processing system that will most efficiently implement the systems specified in Stage 1.

Stage 3: Programming. Programming generally starts with the systems flow charts and ends when the program is running on the computer.

The foregoing stages of systems development are, of course, interrelated. The systems specification must take into account the restraints inherent in the data-processing function; the data-processing stage must take into account the capability of the equipment available and, to some extent, the abilities of the programmers. The important point is that the person responsible for data processing can restrict the systems requirements only as a result of the data-processing capabilities; *he is in no way responsible for deciding what kind of information should be generated by the system.* The same is true of the programmer. He develops as efficient a program as possible to provide the specified data-processing system. This system would be modified only because of equipment requirements.

Distinguishing Characteristics

One of the principal reasons why these three stages are often confused in business is that different systems go through different stages. Some systems will go through only the specification stage. For example, a system for accumulating personnel information on top executives might be handled exclusively at that stage, for the data processing, being relatively trivial in

nature, could be managed as part of the design of the system.

Other systems go through only Stages 2 or 3. There are two major reasons for this:

1. Many systems are well established. Their specifications are already defined when they come up for management decisions; the only problem is to automate them. This is often true, for example, when accounting systems are automated.

2. Many systems require no system design at all of the Stage 1 type. The requirements are prescribed by the nature of the task, as, for example, in payroll or customer billing.

What are the distinguishing characteristics of the stages? Let us look at each in turn.

Systems Specification. From an organization point of view, the most important characteristic of systems specification is that, as a general rule, it should be *decentralized to operating management;* that is, it should be controlled by the people who are to use the system. I conclude this for the following reasons:

The operating manager is responsible for the effectiveness of his information system. He cannot delegate this responsibility to a staff group outside of his control. In many areas, developments in new information techniques make it vital that a continuing program of keeping up to date be maintained. It is likely that this process will become more important in these areas. Already here the seat-of-the-pants operating manager is a thing of the past. The operating manager must now accept the responsibility for adopting new, improved information techniques or be replaced by someone who will. But he cannot be held properly responsible for the adequacy of his information system if the function is performed by an independent staff group.

In general, systems responsibility has proved to be less successful in actual business situations when it has been centralized than when it has been decentralized. In a study he made of the systems activities of several companies, Philip H. Thurston observes:

"It seems to me that the specialist should *not* dominate, and that companies would do well to give more responsibility to operating managers."[3]

A somewhat similar opinion was reached by John T. Garrity in his study of computer effectiveness in 27 companies.[4] He concludes that the factors which marked the difference between those companies that used computers effectively and those that did not were the involvement of operating management in the selection of computer projects, the manning of these projects, and the responsibility for the progress of these projects.

My own experience completely supports these findings.

The design of different types of systems requires different types of skills and knowledge— and frequently there is little overlap. For example, the skills required to design a manufacturing expense-budget system are quite different from the skills required to design a production-scheduling system. In other words, the task of specifying those things that are important to the user varies from function to function and company to company, a fact which argues for decentralization.

In designing an information system for management, an intimate knowledge of the problems in the particular field is necessary. Often this requires spending a not inconsiderable amount of time working directly with users and in installations. For example, it would usually be necessary for a man to work in budgetary control for some time before he would be qualified to design a budgetary control system. On the other hand, it would be quite easy for a budget man to gain a knowledge of computers sufficient to enable him

to understand how they could improve the budgetary control system.

Many information systems use new communication devices other than the computer. For example, James Bright listed 20 such devices used in production scheduling and control (e.g., closed-circuit television and two-way radios) in a paper presented at the international conference of the American Institute of Industrial Engineers in September 1963. These devices tend to be different for different kinds of information systems. The staff systems specialist will, therefore, usually be less well informed about them than about machines like the computer which are standardized.

In summary, the systems specification function should be decentralized because management cannot delegate this responsibility to a staff group, because the work does not usually progress well when done by a staff group, and because the knowledge and capabilities required to perform these jobs are not usually found in staff systems specialists.

Data-Processing Implementation. As contrasted to systems specification, the data-processing activity *can and should be centralized.* I conclude this for the following reasons:

1. Integration of the information systems of a company is desirable from an economic point of view. Information once captured and recorded on punched cards, magnetic tape, or a disk file may be used in several different systems. Also, the storing, updating, and processing of the data can usually be accomplished more efficiently with one integrated system. Finally, integration of the data-processing *requirements* of a company can be accomplished best where the responsibility for data processing is centralized.

2. Many companies are moving toward developing a companywide (or, in large, decentralized companies, divisionwide) data base. This consists of storing in one place all the data that will be used in the various automated systems. This not only helps achieve the economics of integration just mentioned, but frequently makes it possible to provide management with information that otherwise would not be practicable to obtain.

3. The development of data-processing systems can be handled best by staff specialists because knowledge of equipment and data-processing techniques is the primary requirement. When automated information-systems development reaches the data-processing stage, there is a

[3] "Who Should Control Information Systems?" HBR November–December 1962, p. 135.

[4] "Top Management and Computer Profits" (Thinking Ahead), HBR July–August 1963, p. 6.

great deal of similarity among systems. Consequently, data-processing development tends to be a homogeneous type of activity, not significantly different for different kinds of business information systems.

4. There is no reason why operating management should not delegate to a staff group the responsibility for implementing the information system *once this system has been specified.*

In summary, therefore, I believe that the work of implementing a new data-processing system should be centralized because it provides economies through the integration of information systems, because it can best be handled by staff specialists, and because it is the type of activity that operating management can delegate to a staff function.

Programming. As might be expected, of all of the three stages programming lends itself best to centralization. The reasons are:

1. Programming is more economically accomplished on a centralized basis.

2. Writing business programs requires a special knowledge of equipment and programming languages, and there is practically no difference in the skills required to program the different systems.

3. Management must delegate the task of programming to someone, and it makes little difference whether it is a staff unit or a department reporting directly to the manager.

Vertical Classification

I believe that there are three major information systems in a typical company, and a varying and indefinite number of minor systems. A major system is one that affects the entire structure of an organization. A minor system is one that is confined to a limited part of the organization. Let us look at the major systems first.

Financial Information

Every company has a financial information system of some kind. The basis of this system is the flow of dollars through the organization.[5] The financial system is largely concerned with internal and historical information, although in

budgeting or capital investment analysis the system does provide future projections.

The financial information system frequently involves handling huge amounts of data. To this extent, therefore, computers and related data-processing equipment can be very useful. The computer's main purpose, however, is to reduce the cost of data handling. In most instances the quality of the data will not be significantly changed.

The financial system is used principally for management control; honor speed of data in terms of minutes (or even days) is not generally important. It is important that deadlines be met, once established; but deadlines are not likely to be such that information must be transmitted as soon as it is known. For example, it is important to meet a payroll date, but you have considerable flexibility in setting this date. It is not imperative that you pay your people as soon as possible after they complete their work.

The financial system is perhaps the most important single management information system in any company. It is also, probably, the oldest and best developed. The custom has been for management to give the controller the responsibility for administering this system, but management cannot delegate the responsibility for the *adequacy* of the system. Top executives have the continuing responsibility for evaluating how well the controller is performing his functions and for replacing him when this performance is not adequate.

Personnel Data

The personnel information system is concerned with the flow of information about people working in an organization. Almost every company maintains records of its personnel. In the smaller companies these records may be quite sketchy. In the larger companies they can be very elaborate and, in some instances, maintained on random-access equipment.

A personnel information system has many uses to management. It provides a systematic way for accumulating data that can be used to make promotional decisions by every level of management. It is a means of knowing what talents are available to fill specific jobs. A good personnel information system will ensure that a company is not firing people in one plant while hiring people with the same skills in another plant.

The data in a personnel-information system

[5] For a visual portrayal of this flow, see James W. Culliton, "Diagram of Management Control," HBR March–April 1960, p. 144.

are exclusively concerned with people. The information is largely internal and historical, although some information is obtained from outside sources. As in the financial information system, timing in terms of minutes or hours is usually not critical.

Computers and related equipment may be used in a personnel information system. The main use of such equipment is information storage and retrieval. Consequently, the size of a company and the amount of data maintained for each employee will determine whether computers, or even punched-card equipment, are economically feasible. Computers can increase the efficiency of storing and retrieving data, but I do not see that they can make any substantial improvement in the *quality* of the data available to management.

The responsibility for the personnel information system is usually assigned to the industrial relations officer. Here, also, management is responsible for evaluating the adequacy of the system.

Logistics Information

The logistics system is concerned with information about the physical flow of goods through an organization. It covers procurement, production, and distribution. As with the other two systems, it uses mostly internal and historical data; but, unlike them, it is largely concerned with operating control, not management control. Thus it includes such activities as inventory control, production planning and control, scheduling, and transportation.

In this type of system, timing is very important. Moreover, huge amounts of data must be handled and manipulated. Consequently, the logistics system offers the greatest potential for using the new communication equipment—in particular, the computer and related information-processing and transmission devices.

There can be several separate logistics systems in any one company. Where separate product lines are manufactured in separate facilities, each product line could have a more or less independent information system.

The assignment of the responsibility for the logistics information system is not nearly so well developed and thought out in the typical company as the other two systems are. For one thing, being an operating control system, it has not required the degree of top-management involvement which is characteristic of the other two systems. The main concern of top management is that production schedules are being met. (If they are not, this condition is reflected in the financial information.) A second factor is that the responsibility for coordinating a logistics system is frequently not assigned to a particular executive. As a result, the system in many companies is relatively uncoordinated and far from optimum in development. In fact, much of the total systems activity has been started because of the problems in the logistics field. If you examine carefully the description of a typical total system, you will find that it is concerned almost exclusively with the logistics system.

Other Systems

The financial, personnel, and logistics information systems have several characteristics in common: they exist in nearly all companies; they affect almost all parts of the business; they usually involve handling large amounts of data; and they are principally concerned with internal and historical data.

But what about other information systems? Some of them can be integrated to some extent with the three main ones just mentioned; others may be completely separate. I shall describe a few of them briefly:

Marketing Information. One of the most important information systems to many businesses is marketing information. The characteristics of this kind of system will differ widely among companies. For example, some systems maintain a great deal of data about such things as competitive actions, customer profiles, and advertising effectiveness; other systems maintain only information about sales records. A marketing information system tends to be handled completely within the marketing function and usually presents no problem of coordination with the other systems.

Research and Development. Many companies have systems for exchanging information on the results of research findings. Other companies set up systems to examine and store the literature on relevant research.

Strategic Planning. The three main information systems in my classification are largely concerned with historical, *internal* data. The two minor ones just described are largely concerned with historical, *external* data. A strategic planning system deals with still another aspect: future projections. Many companies have formal systems for long-range planning. Although a strategic planning system will use information developed for other systems, it will tend to use it in a different manner, i.e., as a basis for projecting the future. Also, because of the confidential nature of much strategic planning, this group tends to be separated organizationally, and the information developed is carefully guarded.

Executive Observation. Much important management information comes from the personal observations of company executives or discussions with outside people at clubs and meetings. These sources comprise a system (if it can be called a system) which is concerned with *non-documentary* information; yet it can be of primary importance to top management. In fact, some companies would miss this information more than they would miss the monthly financial statements!

Proposed Organization

I would now like to propose an organization structure based on the vertical and horizontal classifications just described.

The principal features of this proposal organization are as follows:

1. The systems-specification function (the first stage) is organized by type of system.
2. The responsibility for systems specification is decentralized to the managers who are responsible for using the data.
3. The data-processing function (second stage) is centralized to the extent that it encompasses the responsibility for implementing the data processing of all systems using the same base of facts, figures, and other data.
4. Information systems not using the data base generally control their own data-processing implementation.
5. The programming (third stage) is centralized for reasons stated earlier in the article.

Changes in Management

The effect on the typical company of changing to an organization similar to that proposed in the preceding section may not be so great as might be supposed at first glance. For one thing, most companies have organized their financial information system and their personnel information system in a manner very simi-

lar to that proposed. To the extent that this is true, only four major changes are necessary.

1. *A group must be established (probably under the manufacturing vice president) with responsibility for developing and maintaining the logistics information system.* This group would do for the logistics information system what the controllership function does for the financial information system.

The establishment of such a group would be the biggest change that most companies would have to make. Notice, however, that it is frequently the logistics function that has created many of the problems in utilizing computers effectively, and these problems will never be solved until an effective organization to solve them is established.

2. *The data-processing function would have to be removed from the controllership function.* It is not necessary to remove data processing from the supervision of the controller; it should, however, be properly identified as a separate service function for all information systems using the data base.

3. *The systems-specification functions would have to be removed from the data-processing function.* For example, operations research personnel working in the data-processing group would properly be assigned to logistics information specification.

4. *Management must assign the responsibility for developing and maintaining a data base to a central data-processing group.* The extent of this group's responsibilities and authority should be precisely and explicitly stated.

Conclusion

At the present time, many companies tend to mix data-processing functions with the task of designing logistics information systems. A symptom of this condition is the development of an inventory control system by a data-processing group which reports, say, to the corporate controller. I believe that this condition has led to severe problems in the effective utilization of the computer.

Coordination is necessary among the people responsible for the various stages in the development of an information system and among the various types of information systems. The need to coordinate, however, is no reason to combine unlike activities and differing levels of responsibility into a single group responsible for all information systems.

If the data-processing function is to be reasonably effective in integrating the data requirements of the various systems using the same main reservoir of data, it will be necessary for it to coordinate carefully with the people responsible for systems specification concerning future plans. This, also, is no reason for combining two types of different activities.

As for the proposed organization plan, it does not preclude the "team" approach to systems development. In fact, this will always be a useful approach, particularly when a company is undertaking a considerable amount of new systems work. The important point is that the responsibility for a team that is developing systems specifications should be with the operating management.

Nor does the proposed organization preclude the use of staff specialists. These specialists, however, should perform as an advisory function and, when working directly on a systems specification project, report to the operating manager who is to use the system.

In the new scheme of things the data base does not constitute a "total system" by any means. It includes only the information common to the participating systems that can be stored economically and maintained centrally. It will be largely historical, internal information. There is a great deal more information than this that management will need. In fact, the higher up in the managerial hierarchy we go, the more important becomes external and projected information that may be no part of the data base.

There appears to be a fad developing for storing as much data as possible on random-access equipment. This is all right if it is more economical to do so or if the availability of the information is sufficiently vital to warrant the extra cost. It appears to me, however, that much management information is not meaningful, nor is it necessary to obtain it on an instantaneous basis. Management should, in my opinion, question the unbridled use of random-access equipment and be sure that the added expense is offset by added benefits.

Perspective on Progress

It will never be possible to have a perfectly integrated data-processing system. Nevertheless,

it is vital to have adequate management information. Consequently, care should be taken not to delay the installation of an information system merely because it does not fit conveniently into an integrated plan. Executives may be losing some important advantages of developing an information system earlier in order to save a few dollars in data-processing costs. Sometimes, too, delay is a cover-up for inadequate performance on the part of data-processing personnel. They argue that they are giving up benefits now for the large future benefits of having a total system, when in fact, the delays are the result of poor implementation.

The important thing is to have effective management information systems. Any organization that will accomplish this objective is satisfactory. If, for example, the controller is the only one in an organization who is able and willing to develop logistics information systems, he must be the one to do it. (But in such a case it should be recognized that the step is taken for purposes of expediency, not because it is the best way to operate.)

At some time in the future, the dream may materialize of having *all* of the information relevant to the management of a particular company stored on random-access equipment in one place; of having this information continuously updated; of having any information management wants immediately available on request; of having all information systems controlled by a group of high-level experts. At the present time, however, I believe that this dream is not possible, practicable, or even desirable. We do not have the equipment or the techniques. Indeed, at present the typical company does not have people with anywhere near the ability to develop such systems even if they were practicable. In fact, most companies have trouble obtaining people who can perform the much less demanding tasks that are required by the organization scheme described in this article.

We should not be sacrificing today the real gains from practical computer applications for the sake of this will-o'-the-wisp concept of "total systems." We can realize these gains only by organizing in a realistic manner, using the resources we have and meeting the needs we can understand.

16. *Information Systems for Logistics Management**

ROBERT M. IVIE†

Introduction

Before discussing business logistics information systems it is important to define the business logistics concept. By re-assembling and re-arranging many elements, techniques and problems of management studied in other functional areas of business, and by adding certain additional concepts to these elements, an entirely new approach is possible for the study of a subject that runs like a connecting thread through all other functions of business: logistics.

Recent recognition of the elements of business logistics as components of a single entity or area of management might lead one to overlook the fact that the elements themselves have been previously identified, studied and developed.

The military, as it has with so many other management concepts, provides a likely origin for the term "logistics." Logistics has long been considered as one of the three major functions of the military mission, along with tactics and strategics. In the business enterprise the strategists are those who plan manufacturing methods, designate products to be included in the product line and decide on the amounts of supplies needed to fulfill manufacturing requirements. The tacticians are those who purchase necessary supplies and carry out the job of transforming them into usable finished products if this is necessary. The logistician is responsible for managing the physical placement of goods at the point and time that they are needed by the strategist and tactician.

There are important differences between logistics in the military and business sense. Military logistics can be described as the transport, quartering, and supply of troops and their materiel. The military logistician can and does set up priorities for demand that constantly exceeds supply.[1] Customer "control" is possible in the military but virtually impossible in business. This control or lack of control over the customer (user of goods) can be considered the major difference between military and business logistics.

Exhibit 1 illustrates how the various managerial and operational functions of business logistics are grouped or aligned within the firm. Demand-supply coordination includes order processing, information flow, inventory management, scheduling and allocation. Movement control includes warehousing and traffic and transportation; those activities concerned with the physical movement of the product.

No matter who manages or performs activities of physical supply and physical distibution within an individual organization, a set of activities exists which undeniably belong within the same scope of managerial activity. It is in this sense that "business logistics" is defined as *the management of all activities which facilitate movement and the coordination of supply and demand in the creation of time and place utility in goods.*

In discussing logistic information systems we are concerned with that phase of demand-supply coordination which pertains to the processing of orders and the flow of logistics information inside and outside the firm. The fact that this paper deals almost exclusively with the physical distribution aspect of logistics management should not be construed as a de-emphasis of the physical supply element of business logis-

* Reprinted by permission from *Transportation Research Forum*.
† President, Guild Wine Company.

[1] For an interesting discussion of a recently implemented military system, for the purpose of comparisons, see N. D. Chetlin, "The Navy's New Supply Priorities System," *National Defense Transportation Journal*, July–August 1960, pp. 38–39 ff.

Exhibit 1.   The Business Logistics Concept

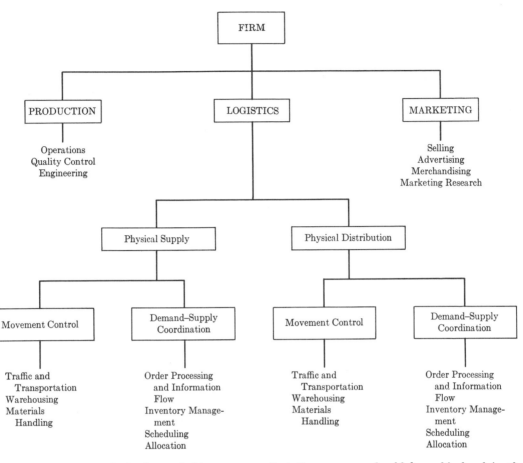

tics. Time and space limitations of this paper make it necessary to restrict the discussion to physical distribution, that phase of business logistics with which managers and educators are most familiar.

The "Need to Know" Concept

Information is valuable to a manager only if he "needs to know" about a particular aspect of the firm, its market, or the techniques that can be employed to improve the operations for which he is responsible. He may be curious about many phases of business activity with which he is not concerned, but he is probably well advised to become involved only with that information which is required for operation of his department, essential to effective communication with other departments within the firm, or necesssary to maintain sound relations with customers and suppliers. This is not to suggest

that the manager should bury his head in the sand of his own operational problems but it does suggest that he determine what he "needs to know" about the firm and its market, and what other parts of the firm "need to know" from him. For example, the logistics manager may be curious about special "deals" made with specific customers, the reasons for sales declines even with maintenance of standard customer service levels, or why production has so much scrap at the end of production line. None of these are his problem. Investigation of them (no matter how slight) can create managerial conflict and waste managerial time.

As an introduction to the detailed discussion of external and internal information systems it is important to document the nature and type of information that flows between the firm and its customer (external) and between the logistics department and other functional departments. The information that the functional managers "need to know" and must communicate to the customer is included in Exhibit 2. Exhibit 3 illustrates the type of information that flows, or should flow, between logistics and other functional departments within the firm. In this latter exhibit it should be noted that to cover the entire scope of information flow within a firm it would be necessary to diagram the types of information that move between each of the functional areas. These diagrams of information flow provide a general overview which will vary materially among firms as the relative importance of one or more functions is changed.

Before beginning the discussion of external and internal logistics information it is important to note the importance of personal communication between manager, supervisor and worker. The fact that organizations operate with people cannot be over-emphasized. People communicate more information than all of the forms and reports combined. Forms and reports do not provide any indication of the extent to which communication or information flow may be accomplished verbally in the conference room, on the telephone, or by other means. It is not my intention to discuss the psychology of personal communications except to emphasize that personal contact, and a proper attitude toward it, is perhaps the most important element of a sound information system.

External and Internal Information Systems

External information flow refers to the communication of information between the firm and its customers and suppliers. Internal information flow systems provide for the exchange of information between functional departments within the firm. With respect to external information flow, this discussion will deal primarily with communication of information between the logistician and the customer. The fact that a similar information system must be maintained with suppliers should not be overlooked because we consider in this discussion only the communications system between the logistician and the customer. The discussion of internal information systems will be concerned primarily with the methods of processing customer orders.

External Information Systems

The customer has a variety of demands all of which tend to improve the profitability of his operations. The customer will "demand the moon" if he believes that there is any chance that his supplier will arrange to send it to him. The determination of the level of customer service is a matter for which the sales manager is responsible. It is the function of the logistics manager to determine how the firm's and its customers' logistics systems can be made more compatible without changing the established standard of customer service.

Two of the keys to success in establishing a sound external logistics information system with customers are: (1) the ability to enlist the cooperation of customers, and (2) the degree to which proper information is provided for the advance planning, operation, and control of logistics activities. Their accomplishment requires coordination both outside and inside the organization. The necessary flow of information for planning and control of logistics and other functions of management is covered in the "need to know" diagrams referred to above. Types of customer cooperation, and ways in which they can be enlisted, are the subject of the following section.

Customer Coordination

Various steps can be taken, with the customer's cooperation, which make it easier for a supplier to meet predetermined customer service levels, particularly from the standpoint of logistics. They include adjustment of customer: (1) order patterns, (2) materials handling systems, (3) reorder point on stock, and (4) order procedures. In this regard, the logistics manager must rely heavily upon marketing's "eyes" and "ears," the salesman, and work with and through him. The logistics manager can review reports from sales representatives to obtain much valuable information about customer service performance and specialized requirements of customers but this method of communication has its limitations. For example, the sales representative may not be adequately qualified to determine how the firm can meet the specialized customer service requirements. In many firms the number or location of customers may make it impractical for the logistics manager or members of his staff to visit customer facilities to develop improved methods of customer service. However, when it is feasible, this type of inquiry can provide a completeness of information that is difficult if not impossible to obtain by other means. It is not reasonable to assume that

Exhibit 2. External Information Flow

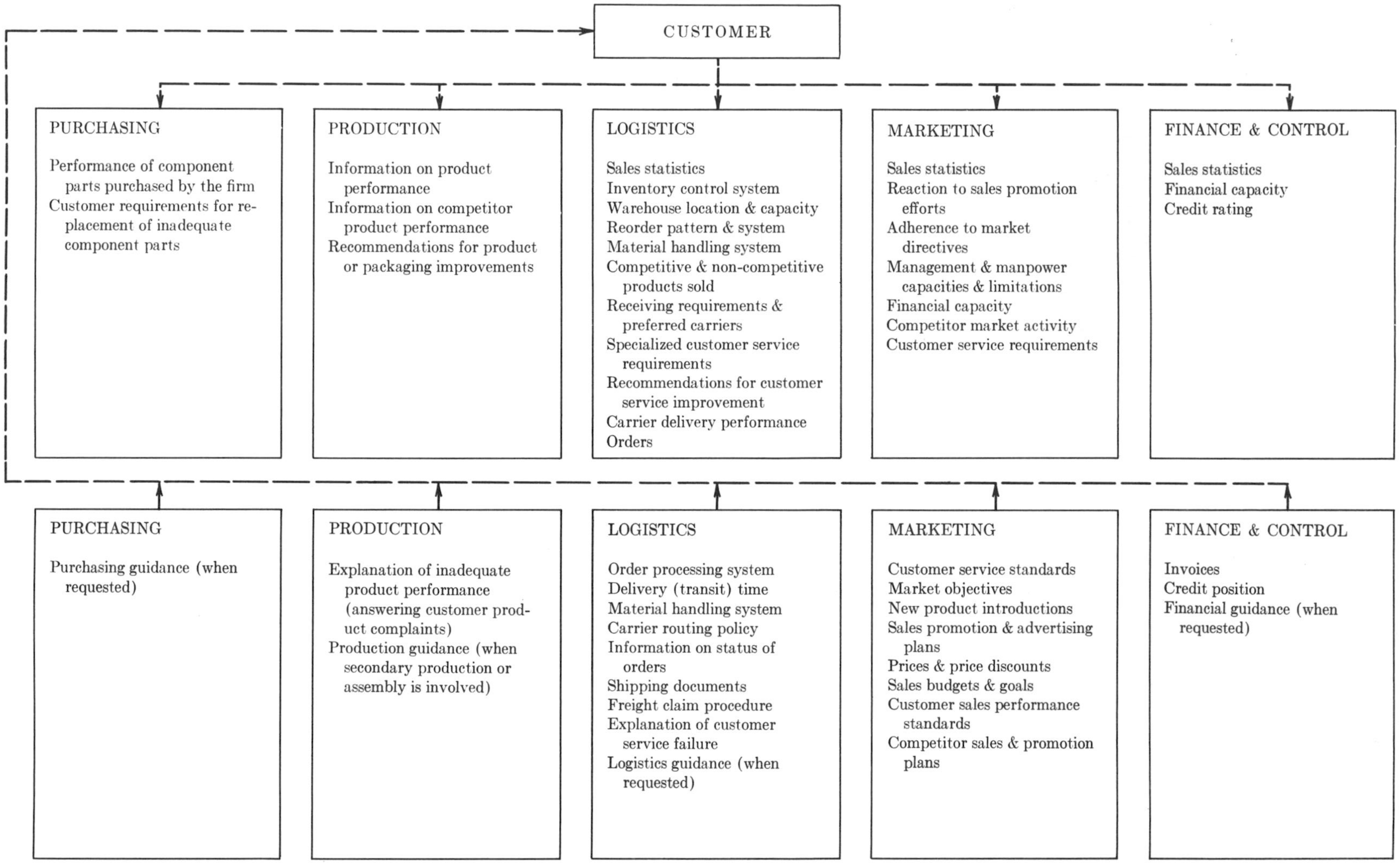

CUSTOMER

PURCHASING

Performance of component parts purchased by the firm
Customer requirements for re-placement of inadequate component parts

PRODUCTION

Information on product performance
Information on competitor product performance
Recommendations for product or packaging improvements

LOGISTICS

Sales statistics
Inventory control system
Warehouse location & capacity
Reorder pattern & system
Material handling system
Competitive & non-competitive products sold
Receiving requirements & preferred carriers
Specialized customer service requirements
Recommendations for customer service improvement
Carrier delivery performance
Orders

MARKETING

Sales statistics
Reaction to sales promotion efforts
Adherence to market directives
Management & manpower capacities & limitations
Financial capacity
Competitor market activity
Customer service requirements

FINANCE & CONTROL

Sales statistics
Financial capacity
Credit rating

PURCHASING

Purchasing guidance (when requested)

PRODUCTION

Explanation of inadequate product performance (answering customer prod-uct complaints)
Production guidance (when secondary production or assembly is involved)

LOGISTICS

Order processing system
Delivery (transit) time
Material handling system
Carrier routing policy
Information on status of orders
Shipping documents
Freight claim procedure
Explanation of customer service failure
Logistics guidance (when requested)

MARKETING

Customer service standards
Market objectives
New product introductions
Sales promotion & advertising plans
Prices & price discounts
Sales budgets & goals
Customer sales performance standards
Competitor sales & promotion plans

FINANCE & CONTROL

Invoices
Credit position
Financial guidance (when requested)

the logistics manager can sit at his desk and determine what the optimum system will be for any customer or group of customers without direct contact with them. It goes without saying that this can only be accomplished with the support and cooperation of the marketing function.

Customer Order Patterns

The timing of customer orders can affect the costs and speed required to serve them. If obtained concurrently, orders from adjacent customers can be consolidated to move in the same shipment, thereby reducing the transportation cost per unit required to serve each. Because vehicle-load shipments generally move faster than those of smaller quantity, consolidation of orders into a vehicle-load shipment can result in better transportation service at lower cost to the shipper. This may require the customer to adjust his procedures. If he has carefully planned his reorder pattern to comply with an individual inventory control system, adjustment may be a difficult, if not impossible, task for the logistician and sales representative to accomplish. When previous orders have not been placed according to a formalized plan, a customer may be unwilling to conform in any way to supplier suggestions without a price incentive to do so.

In the case of one company supplying many wholesale outlets over a multi-state region, the firm was able to obtain customer cooperation in ordering every two weeks (on a staggered basis for various territories) by reducing prices 5% under the new system. Unfortunately, all customers must either comply with the new order pattern, or those not complying must be given the discount uniformly with cooperating distributors. This is necessary to avoid a Robinson-Patman Act stipulation [Section 2(a)] prohibiting discrimination in price between different purchasers for commodities of like grade and quality, and in like quantity.

Materials Handling Systems

Compatibility of materials handling and movement systems between supplier and customer can result in substantial savings. For example, palletization of product at a supplier's storage point, and in transportation equipment, is of no advantage to the customer not equipped to handle pallets in his warehouse. In such cases, supplier financing may be necessary to encourage the customer to adjust his system.

In a recent situation involving a West Coast processor of convenience grocery items and one of its distributors, the distributor was encouraged to move its main warehouse out of its traditional location and into the center of its major market area in order to obtain savings on subsequent delivery costs. The logistics manager of the supplying firm assisted the distributor in relocating his warehouse on a rail siding to obtain savings possible from receiving shipments at lower rates by rail rather than truck. Situations such as this point up the fact that a supplier, whether he be manufacturer or wholesaler, usually has more resources which he can bring to bear on problems of customer service involving logistics.

Stock Reorder Levels

Customer stock reorder levels are considered in terms of the number of days of inventory (given anticipated sales) in stock at the time of reorder. Stockout situations (emergency customer logistics service problems) arise when the reorder cycle exceeds the customer stock reorder level in length of time. For example, a reorder cycle of four days would make a customer vulnerable to a stock-out where products are supplied on a five-day reorder period. A customer stock reorder cycle can be any quantity, positive or negative. The customer who, for one reason or another, allows his stock to run out for seven days before reordering actually has a reorder level of minus seven days. A four-day reorder cycle for a supplier, when added to the customer's reorder cycle, would result in an eleven-day stock-out period.

Several types of techniques can be employed to avert the situation described above. First, a major part of the selling effort (which often comes under the category of sales service) often involves the appraisal of inventory and the stocking of shelves in retail and wholesale customer facilities. In addition to insuring the acceptable appearance of the product, such effort also makes certain that the customer realizes his stock situation and anticipates possible stock-outs. The logistician must place heavy reliance on the sales representative to accomplish results that can ease his problems.

In some situations, pre-punched data cards are enclosed with the supplier's shipments. These cards provide a rapid feedback of information on the proficiency of the logistics system in maintaining customer service standards and provide partial information on inventory levels at various wholesale or retail points. This type of system has several pitfalls. It relies upon: (1) the conscientiousness with which the wholesaler or retailer removes and mails the pre-punched data cards, and (2) the effectiveness of sales representatives in encouraging the customer to carry out the manufacturer's wishes. Because of human reluctance to cooperate or neglect to do so, information derived from these systems generally has to be adjusted to reflect the number of unreturned cards.

Order Procedures

This is an area of external customer coordination most common to many firms. Implicit in a customer's agreement to adhere to a standard or uniform ordering procedure proposed by a supplier is a hope for better service.

In the past, uniformity in the physical nature of customer orders was achieved by: (1) assigning supplier salesmen the responsibility for personally filling out the orders, and (2) placing a supply of standard reorder forms in the hands of customers. Uniformity of order size and location of pertinent information has saved suppliers a great deal of clerical effort in the processing of incoming orders.

Many suppliers, particularly of industrial goods, are attempting to establish punched-card ordering processes with their customers. In this type of system, a customer need only select a pre-punched card supplied him previously and mail it to his supplier's order processing point. Here it is used to create the necessary order information on either paper or tape for subsequent processing. Makers of aircraft parts and the various airline users are believed to be the first to have created a uniform ordering system such as this on an industry-wide basis. Because of the desirability of complete customer cooperation, this type of system appears more feasible for suppliers of industrial than ultimate consumer goods.

Principles of Successful External Information Systems

The several elements of a successful adjustment of customer order patterns, materials handling systems, stock reorder levels, or order

procedures have been implied in the previous discussion. Stated more explicitly, they are:

1. Adjustment should be undertaken to make customer-supplier procedures more compatible.
2. Any plan suggested should provide a mutual increase in the profitability of operation for customer and supplier if it is to be acceptable to both.
3. The sales representative is ultimately responsible for external coordination with customers; it is he who must enlist a customer's cooperation in procedural change. The logistician is likely to play the role of technical or expert adviser to his company's sales representatives and customers in these matters.
4. New ideas for changes in the supply procedures do not necessarily all come from the supplier; in fact, it may be necessary for the logistician to consult with larger customers (usually in the presence of his company's sales representative) in order to detect opportunities for change leading to a higher degree of customer-supplier system compatibility.

Internal Information Systems

Exhibit 3 illustrates the major forms of information which must be communicated between logistics and other functional areas of management. The customer order is the single document of physical distribution on which an overwhelming portion of internal information flow is based. The same relationship holds for the purchase order and physical supply activities. As indicated previously, this paper is necessarily limited to the discussion of the physical distribution aspect of business logistics.

The order that a customer sends to his supplier may appear to be only a piece of paper with a name, address, and series of digits written on it. Where the order came from, what it contains, and when it demands servicing structures and sets the entire logistics system in motion. When the customer order is properly anticipated and its demands are met, the logistics system is likely to function properly. When the order is not anticipated, or when it is over-anticipated, the logistics system moves out of phase. When it is not anticipated, customer service performance fails; when it is over-anticipated, logistics costs become excessive. For this reason, the order and the processing of it must be considered in relation to the over-all system

Exhibit 3. Internal Information Flow

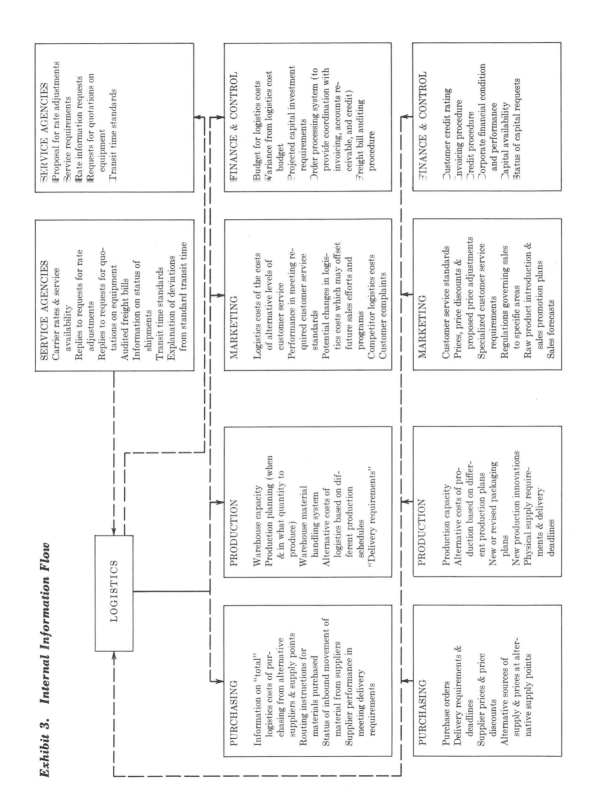

SERVICE AGENCIES
Proposal for rate adjustments
Service requirements
Rate information requests
Requests for quotations on equipment
Transit time standards

SERVICE AGENCIES
Carrier rates & service availability
Replies to requests for rate adjustments
Replies to requests for quotations on equipment
Audited freight bills
Information on status of shipments
Transit time standards
Explanation of deviations from standard transit time

LOGISTICS

PRODUCTION
Warehouse capacity
Production planning (when & in what quantity to produce)
Warehouse material handling system
Alternative costs of logistics based on different production schedules
"Delivery requirements"

PURCHASING
Information on "total" logistics costs of purchasing from alternative suppliers & supply points
Routing instructions for materials purchased
Status of inbound movement of material from suppliers
Supplier performance in meeting delivery requirements

FINANCE & CONTROL
Budget for logistics costs
Variance from logistics cost budget
Projected capital investment requirements
Order processing system (to provide coordination with invoicing, accounts receivable, and credit)
Freight bill auditing procedure

MARKETING
Logistics costs of the costs of alternative levels of customer service
Performance in meeting required customer service standards
Potential changes in logistics costs which may offset future sales efforts and programs
Competitor logistics costs
Customer complaints

FINANCE & CONTROL
Customer credit rating
Invoicing procedure
Credit procedure
Corporate financial condition and performance
Capital availability
Status of capital requests

MARKETING
Customer service standards
Prices, price discounts & proposed price adjustments
Specialized customer service requirements
Regulations governing sales to specific areas
Raw product introduction & sales promotion plans
Sales forecasts

PRODUCTION
Production capacity
Alternative costs of production based on different production plans
New or revised packaging plans
New production innovations
Physical supply requirements & delivery deadlines

PURCHASING
Purchase orders
Delivery requirements & deadlines
Supplier prices & price discounts
Alternative sources of supply & prices at alternative supply points

for information flow which exists formally or informally in any firm.

The purposes of the following discussion are: (1) to define the elements of order processing, (2) to consider alternative methods of order processing, and (3) to assess the importance of the speed and accuracy with which orders are processed.

Elements of Order Processing Systems

The "order cycle" is the period between the time of placement of a customer order and time of arrival of the order at the customer's place of business. The cycle is made up of order transmittal, processing, and shipment components. It is the second of these components, order processing, with which this discussion is mainly concerned.

Order processing can be designed as a routine activity, or it can be complicated by failure to systematize it. Common functions of order processing are to: (1) complete order forms and/or check customer or purchase orders for error, (2) keep customers, salesmen and/or manufacturing and purchasing executives informed of the status of orders in process, (3) make the order or copies of it available to promotion, finance, accounting, and purchasing for the extraction of necessary information from it, (4) coordinate with the credit department on the clearance of orders from customers with doubtful credit ratings, (5) communicate the order to the appropriate shipping point with a minimum of delay, and (6) up-date inventory control records and manufacturing or purchasing schedules.

Order Collection

Problems of order collection primarily concern control over the manner in which orders are placed. Adherence to a pre-set form in the placement of orders is a necessity if a mechanized order processing facility is to operate at peak efficiency; it is highly desirable for the manual system. Problems of internal control over the placement of orders by purchasing or manufacturing arise much less frequently than those placed by customers external to a firm's organization.

Control over the form in which customer orders are placed may take many forms. Included among these are the provision of a supply of

standard company order forms, offering a list of pre-printed items opposite which only quantities need to be entered. This might be termed the "laundry list" approach. A derivation of this technique made desirable by the adoption of electronic equipment or order processing is that of the pre-punched order card. Even standard order quantities, customer addresses and special instruction for processing may be punched into the cards, supplied in quantity to the customer.

A classic method of controlling the collection and completion of orders is to charge the sales representative with the job. It is a technique that has not been made obsolete by more modern methods because of the influence that personal contact may have on the size of the order when it is being made up.

Order discrepancies can be limited by reducing the number of transcriptions of information from one document to another. Where customers are allowed to use their own purchase order form, the supplier must transcribe the information to a form in which he can use it, thereby opening the door for error. In addition to the time (and cost) saved by eliminating order transcription, the order processing activity can be absolved of any responsibility for order errors if the customer is responsible for preparing the order form used throughout the processing system.

Status Reporting

If the logistics system performs consistently (that is, consistently complies with customer service standards), the necessity of keeping others informed of the status of orders will be decreased. A customer, for example, might indicate on his order: "confirm order on receipt, advise car number and route on date shipped, trace and expedite shipment, and advise any delays—please communicate by wire." As calculated in Table 1, the cost to the supplier to meet this type of customer request could reach serious proportions. Consistent performance would eliminate the necessity for much reporting activity.

Internal Order Transmission

Sales records, credit status reports, billing schedules, manufacturing and purchasing schedules, and many other types of records are derived from the order form. A basic question is that of the function with greatest priority for

Table 1. Costs to Provide Order Status Reports: An Example

	Cost to Supplier
Confirmation of receipt of order (wire)	$1.50
Car number & route on date of shipment (wire)	1.50
Tracing & expediting: 4 local phone calls @ 10c	.40
Manpower: 10 minutes per call @ $2.50/hr.	1.67
TOTAL without an order delay	$5.07
Report of delay (wire)	1.50
TOTAL with delay	$6.57

handling this much-demanded document first. Order processing systems which allow the inexpensive and accurate duplication of completed order forms allow all demands to be satisfied concurrently. Where the system either does not provide for duplicate documents or they are not thought necessary, it is likely that the most expeditious route for a customer order form to take is logistics to finance to accounting to sales to manufacturing or purchasing. All other operations and record up-dating can then be performed while the order is being readied for shipment. In the case of purchase orders (physical supply), a possible corresponding sequence is logistics to manufacturing to purchasing to accounting and/or to finance, to sales (for processing of reciprocal sales information). In either of these cases, the exact order may be debated. The question leading to the determination of a proper sequence to meet any situation is: "Which sequence least interrupts the flow of information resulting in a minimum order cycle?"

Credit Checking

Credit clearance is another order processing activity which can be routinized or complicated, depending on the attention given to it. Credit problems are handled best between the credit manager and the local sales representative. With prompt communication between them, the credit status of an order need not be a problem involving logistics. No orders would be received unless they were "credit cleared." Frequently, this is not the case. A sales representative often is interested in obtaining orders irrespective of credit status. In some cases he may even act contrary to credit policy and try to "get an

order through" even when there is a known credit problem. In the absence of field credit control, credit clearance must be obtained quickly upon receipt of customer orders to prevent order processing delays, and credit "holds" must be resolved one way or the other without delay.

Internal Order Communication

Internal order communication time can be as short as the 30-second period for the order to pass through an air chute from the order processing desk to the warehouse to as long as three or four days to mail an order from the order processing center to a distant warehouse facility. Efficient order transmittal and documentation can be negated by an ineffective internal communication system. The longer an order "rests" at any point in the order processing cycle the greater the opportunity the customer has to amend his order. These amendments may be the result of variations in customers' forecast sales patterns or errors by the customer in preparing his order. Changes in orders are expensive to the supplier because of the duplication of work and the increase in error possibility. Rapid internal communication is necessary to "keep the order moving." Each time an order comes to rest in a pile of orders, it means that it must be re-examined to determine its status and analyzed again to determine its relative priority.

There is no substitute for speed in internal order communication. The faster an order is processed, the more quickly things which depend upon order processing will occur. For the warehouse which has an optimum inventory (i.e., all items in stock in quantities necessary to meet demand) the receipt of the order triggers the shipment. The only warehouse delay would be the interval between the receipt of the order and the placing of the transportation vehicle at the shipper's loading dock. To a warehouse which has something less than optimum inventory (i.e., a stock-out situation) rapid communication of the order permits early recognition of an out-of-stock situation and may provide time for stock replenishment without delaying the shipment. The possibility of timely inventory replenishment or adjustment diminishes as the speed of the order system decreases.

Firms which manufacture to order (job shop operations) frequently maintain order backlogs. The question might be asked: If the order just goes into the order backlog file why is there a need for order system speed? The answer is that managers need to know their position relative to capacity and the demand placed upon that capacity. With prompt information on orders the production manager can schedule or reschedule production to make optimum use of machine time or can communicate material requirements in time to allow purchases in optimum quantities.

Rapid order communication may appear to be an expensive operation, but it is incorrect to regard it as expensive without comparing the cost of improvement with the effect that it will have on the entire logistics system.

Alternative Order Processing Systems

Manual Systems

It is most likely that no two firms process orders in the same way. In most firms, orders are processed manually, that is, without the aid of modern data processing equipment. Assuming a manual system of order processing, the most effective device for reducing order processing effort and cost is to use one form, with multiple copies for different purposes. The multi-copy order form reduces errors (by limiting the number of times that order information must be transcribed from one document to another) and manpower requirements (by reducing the number of transcriptions).

Little value would be obtained from a discussion of various types of manual order processing systems. Suffice it to say that they vary greatly. The design of order forms to be easily integrated into the system is a major task in the use of manual order processing procedures.

Mechanical Systems[2]

The primary attribute of the mechanical system of order processing is its ability to routinize the creation of accurate records which stem from the customer order. In the absence of a mechanical system much duplication or repetition of the work related to a customer's order must be done by clerical workers.

[2] The material in this article relies heavily upon the work of John Peter McNerney, *Installing and Using an Automatic Data Processing System* (Boston: Division of Research, Harvard University Graduate School of Business, 1961).

A mechanical data processing system is not inherently "faster" or "better" than manual systems. In some cases, mechanical systems of order processing may be completely impractical because of a limited volume of sales, orders, or items.

A basic problem connected with all mechanical data processing systems is the tendency to concentrate on making the machine work correctly rather than effectively and accurately designing the system. As illustrated by McNerney, there is also a tendency to attribute system improvement to the mechanical equipment rather than the design of the system:

In an attempt to justify office machinery, whether it be punched card equipment or a computer, gains or improvement which are really due to the *design* of the system are often attributed to the equipment. In many cases, these same gains or improvements could be achieved with much less expense by modifying the existing system. One of the real needs in evaluating data processing proposals and equipment is to ascertain whether various operations can be performed only by the use of certain equipment, and to consider alternative (and less expensive) ways of handling the same operations.[3]

When the operations involved in order processing are subject to many exceptions, manual methods may be preferable. According to McNerney:

Clerks are extremely flexible; where many exceptions and special situations must be handled, manual methods may be quite desirable. Where operations are completely internal and highly routine, as they tend to be in accounting or payroll operations, punched card equipment can be quite satisfactory. But if mechanical means are used, many of the exceptions and special situations that are processed with no difficulty by the clerks cannot be handled by machine. In types of operations where more variations and exceptions occur, provision must still be made to handle these situations clerically. Clerks are more versatile and more flexible data processors than tabulating equipment; handling exceptions and varying situations by mechanical means is so inefficient and expensive that the

[3] *Ibid.,* p. 64.

variation must either be eliminated or handled by extra clerks.[4]

The fact that more separate steps may be required in the mechanical system should not, however, be interpreted as an indication of its comparative speed and cost. These elements must be separately computed, based on the characteristics of an individual situation.

Logistics, in common with other functions of the firm sometimes suffers from the fact that electronic data processing equipment for use in record-keeping and in analytical work is usually controlled within one function, most often that of accounting. Where they have been used most effectively, computers are considered as a company-wide resource which benefits all functions.

One of the most elaborate and sophisticated mechanical order processing systems in current use is that devised by the Westinghouse Electric Corporation for its apparatus products group. Orders are processed between the Company's 90 sales offices, 265 plants, and 85 warehouses within an average time span of 30 minutes.[5] The 30-minute order processing cycle starts when an order is sent by the regional sales offices to the Company's "Information Center" near Pittsburgh, Pennsylvania. As such, the 30-minute interval does not cover the time required for the transmittal of the order from the firm's 15,000 customers to a regional sales office. This could, of course, be as short as one minute for an order phoned in by the customer to a day or more when a salesman takes a written order and mails it into the regional sales office.

Using a Univac 490 as the core of the system, orders are teletyped from the sales office telecomputing center. The computer locates the stock which is in the most appropriate location to move to the customer, prepares the invoices, and up-dates the inventory records. According to a report on the system:

The speed of this operation—sales order to computer to warehouse—means immediate information on all inventory balances. It enables the company to have a report on the most active items on each salesman's desk every Monday morning, telling him how many of what products are in stock and where.[6]

This firm has reported a reduction of inventory costs on its apparatus products group by $2.3 million per year as a result of reducing its average order processing time from 6 days to 30 minutes.

Principles of Successful Internal Information Systems

In the design of an internal logistics information system the following principles have been stressed:

1. Speed is the single most important element in obtaining market information through the flow of orders from customers.
2. The customer order is the document which triggers the subsequent flow of much internal information in an organization.
3. Where necessary, a priority on information availability must be established.
4. Priorities in the planning of an internal information system should be established on the basis of that priority ranking which least delays actions based on the information.
5. External and internal coordination is the key to the successful exchange of information necessary to meet performance objectives in the processing of customer orders.

[4] *Ibid.*, pp. 64–65.
[5] For more complete discussions of this order processing system, see Joseph S. Coyle, "Comuter Speeds Distribution," *Traffic Management*, January, 1962, pp. 51–52, and "At Westinghouse," *Traffic & Distribution Management*, November 1961, pp. 8–13.

[6] Joseph S. Coyle, "Computer Speeds Distribution," *Traffic Management*, January 1962, pp. 51–52.

Section IV. Packaging, Materials Handling, and Storage

In this section, as in most of the others, some selections included are not narrowly oriented to the specific aspects of the subject category under which they have been placed. For example, the article by Smykay and Mossman, "What the DM Should Know About Product Flow," covers far more territory than packaging, materials handling, and storage. However, each of the component parts of this section have had an abundance of books, monographs and articles written on the subject. Quite certainly the parts are intertwined, with each function impinging heavily on the other.

The interactions which can and do occur between materials handling and storage are equally as important as the interfunctional exchanges described in earlier sections of this book. Trade-offs between these three interrelated functions can do much to enable the firm to operate at its optimum. As Charles Zusi puts it,

> Since packages are for the purpose of protecting their contents while they are being moved from the maker to the consumer, it is apparent that changes in shipping and handling methods affecting the hazards to which the containers are subjected will be reflected in corresponding changes in box designs.[1]

The change in one aspect has an important bearing on the *status quo* of the other to the end that any proposed change in one must be considered in its impact on the total.

[1] See Charles Zusi's article, "An Industrial Packaging Transformation," Article 18.

17. *What the DM Should Know About Product Flow**

EDWARD W. SMYKAY AND FRANK H. MOSSMAN†

The distribution manager, to perform efficiently as a top-level planner, must understand the structure within which physical distribution operates.

Marketing of commodities takes place in a framework which can be divided into two interdependent parts. The first consists of those marketing institutions which create demand and perform the break-bulk functions. The second is the transportation network which moves commodities from producer to consumer.

In discussing demand factors, my principal emphasis is on the manufacturer of consumer goods. This is because demand for consumer goods determines the demand for industrial goods. The same principles set forth are applicable to the manufacturer of either. There is some tendency, however, for the average size of shipment to be larger in the industrial market.

The industrial goods market, as contrasted to the consumer goods market, generally possesses the following characteristics:

Larger average size of purchase.
A derived and more widely fluctuating demand.
A more limited number of customers.
A more rational basis of purchase.
More technical selling.
More reciprocity.
More direct distribution from manufacturer to consumer or user.

Example of Product Flow

The petroleum industry applies physical distribution principles to its movement problems. The main elements of this industry are a number of scattered well sites, a system of collection and storage of crude petroleum, a main trunk pipeline, a refining facility, wholesale and retail outlets, and the consumer.[1]

The design of the entire system connecting the origin of the movement to its ultimate destination must be consistent with sound engineering and economic principles.

That design is best which meets market requirements at minimum costs. The simplest part is the main line. Once total demand is estimated, then that size pipe will be chosen which makes it possible to maintain regularity of flow. This will maximize utilization of pipeline investment.[2]

Then sub-systems for crude oil collections and gasoline deliveries must be designed. Wells will be located in a certain pattern within the producing territory. After a study of these patterns, the wells will be grouped into a series of self-contained producing units.

Some wells probably will be located at considerable distance from the collection and storage point at the end of the pipeline. Those which can be grouped into self-contained units and which are in an area of relatively dense well populations ordinarily are connected together into a gathering system for that particular group. This gathering movement is usually transported by pipe when production from the individual well and its group is sufficient to justify the investment. The diameter of these pipes is determined by the volume expected.

The next step is to connect the groups of wells so that the total volume of crude oil reaches

* Reprinted by permission from *Distribution Age,* March 1960.
† Both of Michigan State University.

[1] This illustration is limited to the distribution aspects of gasoline for final consumption in automobiles.

[2] Certain problems in trunk pipeline design are purposely eliminated from the discussion in order to emphasize the fundamentals of the problem. Two of these are seasonality of demand and intermediary delivery problems.

the terminal delivery point (engineering design) of the main pipeline at minimum cost (economic design). Again, it is the volume which is critical in this decision.

Finally, for the isolated low-producing wells, it seems the volume may fall below the minimum required to justify the investment in pipe. At this point, tank trucks may be used. Notice that although collection by pipeline may be feasible from an engineering point of view, the low volume may prevent pipeline construction on economic grounds.

Delivery Program

Turning to the problem of moving the manufactured gasoline from the refinery to the local gasoline station, the principle of grouping local outlets is again employed. Delivery systems are then designed to meet market requirements at each of these outlets.

Because of relatively low volumes sold at each retail outlet, and because market factors are more important in determining locations of stations, the employment of a pipeline system is not ordinarily justified for this level of distribution. Rather, product pipelines connecting the refinery to the major markets are constructed in conjunction with storage depots. From the depot to each individual station, trucks are employed.

Notice that the major determinant of the selection of a pipeline system, rather than truck carriage, is based on volumes for each level in the producing and marketing patterns compared with capital costs that may be supported by the volume for each separate part. When volumes are low, the system chosen usually is the one which requires low fixed cost but high variable expense (trucks). When volumes are high, the alternative chosen is one with high fixed expense and low variable expense.

We now may discuss the pipeline illustration as analogous to any problem in physical distribution.

Diagramming of the physical product flow in a general marketing situation clearly shows certain nodal points. These points take two characteristics. They are either concentration or break-bulk points.

All movements up to the point where they enter into the major intercity trunk lines are essentially the result of combining shipments into larger lots. Movements between any two nodal points occur as a result of the transportation function. But the engineering feasible alternatives may well vary because of differences in physical distribution problems between any two nodes.

All movements beyond the manufacturing node are break-bulk points. That is, the total production of the plant is regrouped to more efficiently serve particular market segments, the total demand of which is less than annual plant production.

For each node, particular and specialized marketing institutions have been developed. Long and detailed listings of the whole array of such institutions could be shown. However, this would be of no particular value.

Physical distribution functions of marketing institutions are stressed. At any nodal point in the system, incoming volumes differ from outgoing volumes. Too frequently, purely descriptive marketing functions are stressed as a method of classifying marketing institutions. The analysis above clearly shows that one of the most important factors in determining the classification of a marketing institution is its key position in the marketing system in terms of incoming flows of materials (supply) and its outgoing movement to markets (demand).

Competitive Complexion

When cast in this framework, the physical distribution aspects of marketing take on a dynamically competitive complexion. Assuming the inconsistency of consumer demand, new developments in transportation, changing relative importance of markets, and a continual revolution in technology and products, effective marketing requires a continual assessment and revision of distribution alternatives. The fixity of channels of distribution so easily assumed now becomes a dangerous practice for a firm to follow in its marketing program.

Note that there are two principles outlined in the selection of any alternative to a particular physical distribution problem for the petroleum industry. These are the engineering and economic requirements.

Physical market requirements in large measure pre-determine the engineering alternatives to a particular logistical problem. However, a number of possible engineering alternatives may be available for the solution of a particular movement problem. The selection of the proper engineering alternative in the particular case then largely becomes a question of economics. That particular engineering alternative will be chosen which yields lowest unit cost.

The pipeline problem is easier to solve than a general marketing problem in physical distribution. For example, the connecting link between the major producing areas and the dominant consuming areas in the petroleum industry almost invariably will involve a selection of different pipeline alternatives.

Many Choices

Comparing this with a more general case, the selection of the trunk line transport agency is complicated by the fact that pipelines are only one among many transport alternatives. Rails, motor carriers, parcel post, water carriers, air lines, railway express, freight forwarders, and others may be used.

However, the engineering factors of some of these limit their selection in specific instances. One does not, for example, ship iron ore in commercial quantities via air freight.

In any particular case, some of the alternatives can be eliminated readily on engineering grounds. Once these obvious eliminations are made, a more sophisticated economic analysis must be made involving the others. An example of this type of analysis can be found in the field of inventory and its cost.

Assume that a particular industry has a daily inventory cost in movement of $1000 for every $1 million of inventory. Let us further assume that four alternative systems of physical distribution meet all engineering requirements for the movement involved.

System A results in an inventory in process of one day. For B it is two days; C three days; and D four days. The associated inventory expense for each then will be $1000 for A, $2000 for B, $3000 for C, and $4000 for D.

If inventory costs were the only costs involved, alternative A would be the most logical choice. In effect, drawing on the pipeline illustration, system A in terms of inventory results in reducing the length of our trunk line pipe to one half of B, one third of C, and one fourth of D.

The impact of inventory expense on the final selection provides a clue to the framing of a proper approach to the solution of any general

problem. That is, all costs for each alternative must be included if a properly designed system is to result. Clearly, the old-fashioned concept of minimizing the transportation rate provides, at best, control over only one segment of the entire pattern of distributive costs.

Fragmented Approach

Another interesting aspect of this diagrammatic presentation of the physical distribution concept is that it clearly shows the fragmented approach that firms seem to take toward their distribution problems. Notice that the key to the solution of the problem of controlling physical distribution costs lies in its consumer orientation. This clearly shows the logistical nature of total effort of the firm in satisfying a particular segment of market demand.

However, the run-of-the-mill organizational chart distributes control over this complex logistical problem by its division into separate and, too frequently, compartmented parts. Control generally is divided in varying proportions among the traffic, sales, purchasing, and production departments.

Each of these clearly has a separate and distinct function. However, by placing primary responsibility upon each of these areas for separate segments of the total problem, an organizational invitation is presented to fragmentize actions to suit the immediate ends of the departments.

Achieving balance in the logistical system of the firm in light of this conflict becomes difficult, if not impossible, if the various departments are given equal and correlative powers. Organizationally, therefore, the worst alternative would be to distribute unilateral control over each part of the problem to each department.

If the divisional approach is incorrect on the grounds that complete and integrated control is impossible, then it must follow that centralized authority over this function is essential. Certainly there are strong grounds for such a policy for at least planning.

Probably a strong case may be made for centralized control over both the planning and operations levels. However, with the institutional rigidities inherent in a traditional organizational plan, the more politic alternative may be to maintain existing departmental divisions for operational control. At the same time, a planning function could be superimposed over all of these operational departments.

18. *An Industrial Packaging Transformation**

Charles J. Zusi†

Packaging in the United States never is static; change is its outstanding characteristic. Of course, packaging exists only in relation to the contents of the containers and in a growing economy such as ours the articles of commerce change continually, resulting in a continuous stream of new packaging.

New materials appear and the old familiar materials are improved to assume new properties and, since packaging uses most materials, new forms result. Storage methods are affected by new materials, both those inside the packages and those providing the desired surrounding atmospheres, all of which may require different kinds of containers.

Transportation methods on land, sea and air have altered radically within the memories of those who are comparatively young, requiring new kinds of packages to meet the new hazards. The principal purpose of packaging is to permit the safe movement of the contained articles and the methods of accomplishing this purpose must be altered as the methods of handling are altered, a ceaseless process.

Self service in selling makes continuously greater demands on packaging, illustrating the increase in the functions the package must perform. Furthermore, competition makes it necessary to offer similar products in a great variety of packages. Finally, packaging is a factor on both sides of the profit equation: it can be used to decrease production costs and to increase sales income, and thus it is subject to constant scrutiny for the purpose of discovering changes to improve one or the other of these functions.

The most striking uses of new materials are occurring in interior packages, that is, consumer packaging rather than industrial packaging. Nevertheless, these are important because they result in changes in the exterior containers and, often, they appear as interior packing in shipping containers. Outstanding materials are foil-fibre cans, aluminum cans and shrink film wrappings. Soon to appear are blow-molded plastics bottles, bottles made of two sheets of plastic material sealed around the contents, generally liquids, and blown aluminum containers.

A good illustration of how a material of this sort, in this case, stretch film, can affect the shipping container is provided by the packaging of DuBarry Hair Shampoo of Warner-Lambert Pharmaceutical Company. The two-bottle unit is attached to a paperboard display card with stretch film. The cards, standing vertically, are held apart a distance slightly greater than the diameter of the larger bottle by fitting them into slots in a V-shaped corrugated pad, then placed into a corrugated box with an inverted V-shaped corrugated pad over the entire interior assembly. Thus the packing is simple, protective, convenient and economical. There are many other effective uses of films as interior packing, such as attaching ceramics to corrugated pads, or slinging fragile parts in hammocks between supporting pads.

Corrugated box manufacturers have been investigating anxiously the use of foamed plastics as interior packing or even as complete shipping containers. These containers have made some progress, especially in the field of photographic equipment. Foamed plastics interior packing pieces molded to fit irregularly shaped articles, or into which such articles can be pressed, have several distinct advantages. They provide excellent cushioning protection, if properly selected; their shipping weight is minimal; often only two pieces per package are required, thus reducing packing labor considerably; they are not destroyed upon removal of contents, making them suitable for use in subsequent storing of

* Reprinted by permission from *Distribution Age,* November 1963.
† Packaging Consultant.

the enclosed article. There even is a portable set of equipment now for foaming polyurethane into the container with the contents in place.

The need for minimizing the use of high-priced labor of packing has spurred a merry battle of materials in interior packing. Molded pulpboard is an inexpensive material which can be shaped to fit and hold in place almost any irregular article, provided that it is not too large or heavy. It also has advantages similar to those of molded foamed plastics. However, to counteract the inroads of these materials, corrugated box manufacturers have developed methods of making economically built-up, multiwalled corrugated pads in all kinds of shapes and faced with various soft or smooth materials.

A new material designed to make a shipping container as well as an attractive unit package is a corrugated sheet called "E-flute" which is like other corrugated board but with flutes or corrugations only about half the height or thickness of B-flute. This sheet takes less space in storage when the box is flat or unassembled and the facings, supported by numerous and rigid flutes are suitable for taking excellent printing impressions. In general, boxes made of this material find their best use as containers for small household appliances such as toasters, irons, electrical frying pans, Christmas tree lights, small sets of tools, etc.

Another corrugated board, not particularly new but expanding in use, is triple-wall corrugated. With three corrugated walls or sets of flutes, this type of board is especially rigid and difficult to puncture, yet it can be scored and formed into a box. Its use is primarily for extra large or extra heavy items or for those destined for export shipments. The railway classification permits its use for weights up to 350 lbs.

Increasing in use are polyethylene shipping bags, especially for some powdered chemicals and for fertilizers. These bags are of great strength but they are affected by certain materials, yet their very low water vapor transmission rate is an attractive property.

Treatments and coatings of fibreboards and laminations with other materials, such as films and foils, have given improved characteristics useful in certain applications. Boards can be made to shed water, to resist the penetration of moisture, to be especially smooth or to have anti-skid properties, to protect enclosed articles, as for example highly finished furniture or enameled surfaces, against abrasion.

Mixtures of polyethylene and wax can be ap-plied to corrugated boxes to make them capable of withstanding water used in hydrocooling fruits or vegetables and the melting ice during shipment in a refrigerator car. Foil can be laminated to corrugated board to improve its insulating qualities or to make it resistant to water.

A brewery in Canada ships cans of beer in a corrugated box having the inner facing made of a sheet composed of two sheets of kraft paper laminated together with one mil of polyethylene. The box is intended for picnic use when two of the cans are removed and replaced with cracked ice.

By the use of special designs and methods, many unusual types of containers can be developed as systems which often include the kinds of handling to be used. There is an increasing use of double-wall corrugated board for heavy items made possible by such schemes. An example of a container and a handling method designed together is General Electric's corrugated boxes for Hotpoint ranges and refrigerators, some weighing as much as 350 lbs. The basic scheme of the container is a vertical flanged tube with cap and bottom having flanges which interlock with the tube flanges and are held in place with metal strapping. A crane equipped with V-shaped hooking plates can lift as many as four of these heavy containers at a time and pile them four or five high in a warehouse.

Mead Corporation is one of the package suppliers who have groups of engineers trained in correlating containers and machines into packaging systems. One of these is a device for packing cans into end-opening corrugated boxes, designed to take various arrangements of cans or of multi-packs of cans, automatically place them into the box and deliver the box to a conveyor leading to an automatic sealer. The end-opening cans are more economical than the regular type but they are awkward to fill manually. Another system of container and machines packs nails into corrugated boxes, arranging them parallel with magnets during the process to make the pack more dense.

The box-plus-machine principle has been used by West Virginia Pulp & Paper Company in a system for packing a group of cartons tightly together automatically in a package lighter than an ordinary corrugated box. The wrapper, or outer carton, is made of 69-lb. linerboard, which binds the contents together tightly to make a strong package. A variation of this system makes the outer package of kraft paper with the edges or scores reinforced with heavier paper or board.

New machines which make boxing with corrugated containers more rapid and economical are closing devices that will seal, tape or stitch boxes of random sizes delivered to them in succession. Such machines of a practical nature have been sought for a long time but it is only within the past few years that success has been attained. Self-adjusting sealing machines came first but they have been followed by somewhat similar stitching and taping machines.

Notable improvements have been made in the marking and printing of containers as they move along a conveyor line. Corrugated boxes can be printed on sides or ends, or both, as they are conveyed, and they can be printed also on top and bottom.

An important new accessory is the non-metallic strapping for bundles, bales and containers, especially corrugated boxes. This strapping is made of kraft paper, rayon, nylon or polypropylene. Among these materials are important properties for the strapping function, such as ability to absorb shock, to maintain tightness on a shrinking package, to be cut with a scissors and to be readily disposable by burning. They do not tend to cut into the bundled materials.

Nylon and polypropylene have the greatest tensile strength, while kraft paper is the cheapest. Nylon is very resilient, will stretch as much as 15% and tend to regain its original length. During the past few years tensioning and sealing devices of satisfactory character have been developed for non-metallic strapping.

There are many advances and changes in areas which, while not actually packaging, have a strong influence on the packages themselves. In addition to the new materials, these developments indicate the trends in packaging, even though it may be difficult to assess them relatively.

One of these is the formation of containers in the plant where the contents are made. This comes largely as a result of the increase in the mechanization of the packaging operations where, for example, a machine or a household appliance is carried through the assembly line on a platform or skid which later becomes part of the shipping container, and then is held, revolved, inverted or tipped by devices along the conveyor while other parts of the package are added.

In other operations, the container is received

as a flat sheet which is formed, stitched, glued and closed around the contents as it moves through suitable machines.

A serious problem encountered in many plants is the packaging of miscellaneous orders of widely varying shapes and dimensions for shipment to customers. Small machines capable of producing corrugated boxes of every size and shape, within the capacity limits, have been developed for this purpose. The articles to be shipped may be arranged on a platform so that guides brought to bear upon them will set the machine automatically to produce the desired container from a flat, rectangular sheet of corrugated board fed into it. A single box or a run of a hundred or more can be made and, although waste may be high and production rate low compared with regular commercial runs, the set up cost is so low that the operation is economically feasible as well as convenient.

The integration of the shipping container into the production and packaging lines makes it more important that it be manufactured to closer tolerances and more uniformly. This tends toward the use of more devices for measuring the partially completed material or container while it is in process and of more controls to insure a uniform result. Inevitably, such instruments are likely to be electronic and it is probable that, within a short period of time, they will have a revolutionary effect on manufacturing processes which have not changed basically for scores of years.

A fascinating development is electrostatic printing, now in its infancy but obviously possessing tremendous possibilities due to the fact that the surface being printed is not touched in the operation by anything except the pigment and that the surface can be curved or irregularly shaped in any way. A corrugated board, for example, can be printed without any indentation at all reducing its strength, even if it is only single-faced material.

Pressure-sensitive adhesives will be used to greater extent. Their full capabilities in many situations outside of the ordinary manufacturing plant normal operations have not been realized fully. A similar device still in its infancy is ultrasonic sealing, which, allied with coatings, could produce some startling effects in the closure of containers. Hot melt adhesives have attracted the attention of boxmakers for some time, especially in the corrugated field, since a revolutionary reduction in the amount of drying of board and adhesive required could eliminate many of the problems of corrugated box manufacture.

Adhesives, in general, have been changing in a fundamental manner providing new properties of extensive consequences in packaging. A basic weakness in wooden boxes, to mention just one field, always has been the joining of the edges of the faces of the container. Nailing is the process generally used, with stapling and gluing also important. With some of the new adhesives it is not inconceivable that the edges could be formed at high speed and also be changed from a box weakness to a point of strength. This could be important in many fields as, for example, in that of fresh fruit and vegetable containers.

If any one material does not produce all of the desired properties in a container, it is logical to think of combining it with another. This has been happening at a rapid rate in recent years, especially as container-manufacturing companies are widening their fields to include several kinds of packages instead of the traditional one type.

Corrugated boxes fitted with plastic bags have found acceptance in the shipment of powders, pastes, semi-liquids and liquids, including many products going to hotels, hospitals and public institutions. Molded polyethylene drums inside of corrugated containers now are familiar to most automobile drivers and every gas station attendant as carriers and dispensers of battery acid. A few years ago it would have been considered ridiculous to think of a corrugated box as a container for acid, a fact mentioned to emphasize the situation that changes appearing preposterous can and do occur in packaging. Foamed plastics of rubber are being attached to corrugated sheets or wood or metal to form cushioning pieces or shock mounts in paperboard, wood and metal containers.

Extrusions of polyethylene and other plastics onto stiffer substrates result in fascinating and useful combinations of properties. An interesting example is the extrusion of a plastic sheet over each side of wood veneer used in wirebound boxes, sealing the wooden piece completely. This makes possible the use of undried veneers in which the moisture content is of no particular importance and warping is eliminated while providing an attractive, smooth-surfaced material. Wirebound boxes are employing other combinations of materials such as veneer laminated on both surfaces to kraft paper and also

corrugated board to form the mat and ends, with wooden cleats and the usual binding wires.

"Corrugated boxes" without corrugations are being formed from boards composed of sheets of expanded polystyrene with kraft paper laminated to each side. High insulating value is obtained and improved qualities of resistance to the weakening effects of high humidity. Resistance to water is reached to a phenomenal degree in corrugated boxes treated and immersed in wax and polyethylene.

Coatings lining metal drums have been developed to the point that this type of container can be used for the shipment of almost anything, including the most corrosive liquids. Cushioning materials and antiabrasive surfaces of all sorts are laminated to corrugated boards and to wood for use inside of containers. In flexible materials to be used as barriers or to form multi-wall shipping sacks, the combinations of materials laminated together are practically without limit.

Since packages are for the purpose of protecting their contents while they are being moved from the maker to the consumer, it is apparent that changes in shipping and handling methods affecting the hazards to which the containers are subjected will be reflected in corresponding changes in the box designs. The changes will vary from possible elimination of the container to slight modifications to make them better suited to the revised handling methods.

Included among such new environments are new freight cars and trucks with better suspension devices and coupling methods and various systems for holding containers in place and for cushioning them against shock and vibration, as in the so-called D.F. or damage-free cars. Even electrically controlled marshalling yards should be included. Palletizing is a powerful influence.

Most important of all is the growing trend toward containerization. As this concept of the movement of packages becomes more prevalent, the time-worn idea of the dropping of a container by a handler as the principal hazard against which the box must be designed loses all significance. A completely new look must be taken at the shipping packages. The containerization idea probably began seven or eight years ago when the New York Central Railroad, searching for some modification of the crude idea of carrying motor trucks "piggyback" on railway cars, devised the idea of large cargo boxes which could ride equally well on a motor trailer or a rail car without possessing any wheels of their own. It was inevitable that this should be extended to include ships and aeroplanes.

Thus a collection of packages can be packed and loaded into a "container" by the manufacturer or shipper of the articles, sealed inside and moved by highway, railroad, ship and aeroplane to its ultimate destination without any handling of the individual packages. Aside from reducing handling charges drastically, containerization makes feasible the redesign of the individual containers from those capable of resisting former export hazards to a type somewhat like a domestic box but modified to fit the new circumstances. Those packages used in purely domestic containerized shipments probably can be changed also to less expensive types.

19. *Analyzing Warehouse Costs**

William J. Meehan†

Why did you add an additional charge for unloading our "D-F" car? This was asked of us by one of our West Coast principals.

He had just sent us his first Damage Free car and had felt he would reduce his costs. He would. But innovations have a way of creating their own smaller cost problems. This was one.

"How can you so readily ascertain that this charge is right?" he asked. Car cost analyses, made on every car arrival, had alerted us. Our car report form showed that it took more time to prepare, unload, and complete a D-F car than a regular car. Observations made us believe that it was taking extra time. The report proved it. The added cost was not covered in the original negotiations with our shipper. Thus, we charged an extra-services charge.

Modernization had reduced car damages so the shipper could reduce his cost. Cost analysis protected the warehouse operator from a loss in handling revenue.

We wrote to our principal, explaining our ability to ascertain this cost. He checked his own warehouse operation. His own plant had found it to be true. This had alerted him to a hidden cost. He allowed the increase to stand—a specific nominal charge assessed only against a specific expense.

The car handling report is a simple one. It is so set up that each employe handling it supplies pertinent facts. The car unloader writes in the car number, account, number of employes and their starting and finishing time. He also enters its proper distribution. He forwards it to the billing clerks with the completed car papers.

The billing clerk enters the handling-in portion of the revenue earned by that car. It is taken from the invoice. The units and the weight handled are added to the form.

Next stop is bookkeeping. The cost breakdown, into fractions of man hours and cents per unit cost for unloading the car and into the warehouse, is calculated to four decimal points. Combined, they give us the cost of handling. The cost is also converted to a cost per hundredweight.

The arithmetic is finished. The result is transcribed to a cost analysis pad. It is listed by individual principals to allow comparative cost analysis. What good is all this? The car handling report shows what a form can do:

- Tells the story and builds the history.
- Immediate recognition of cost trends.
- Instant appraisal of handling cost to revenue procured.
- Surveillance of operating time.
- Relationship of unit cost to hundredweight cost.

Simplicity Key

Simplicity is the key to a form. Simplicity can be explained. The several employes compiling these figures have been informed of why the form is filled out and its importance to our operation. One should not underestimate the importance of explaining the purpose and the ultimate result in compiling a form of this sort by the employes. Once they know the whys and wherefores, its function becomes just as important to them as it is to management. The amount of clerical work of each worker involved is so minute that it has not added to the work load. Each employe looking for it, as part of his operation, keeps it moving until it is listed on the analysis pad. Now, pertinent facts combined will project any type of analysis of handling cost we wish.

"Your wage rates in the South are lower than elsewhere in the country, yet your charges are almost comparable!" an account remarked to us. That may be true. But a number of employers do not take into consideration that an employe does not work 100 per cent of his eight-hour day.

---

* Reprinted by permission from *Distribution Age,* August 1960.
† General Manager, Ryder Bonded Warehouse.

Converting the basic wage into a touch labor, or productive hour, we find a new light on our wage. Reducing actual hours to productive hours, we find a 25 per cent time loss. We get just six hours of productive labor. This, then, has raised our $1.50 per hour for eight hours to $2.00 per productive hour. This basis is used in costing our handling operations. Wage costs have become relative to other areas as a result of this. Those areas do not recognize productive hours against regular hours. That "coffee break" is expensive, isn't it?

Car Analysis

Information taken from our car handling report and transcribed to the car report analysis form allows us to:

- Analyze cost by unit or hundredweight.
- Compare handling revenues.
- Analyze weights against units.
- Average out all columns.
- Average out various cars of one customer.
- Study handling of bulk units against small lot units.
- See cost in relation to rates quoted.

From the car handling report one can take the factors—revenue, number of units, weights, car underloading time, into warehouse time, or hundredweight cost—and segregate each one into its own analyses or a comparative analysis. We took case units weighing 10, 20, 30, and 40 lb. We arrived at an average handling cost for each one, both by unit cost and hundredweight cost. We took 100 lb bags of sugar, salt, and starch and ran comparative analyses on these. We went a step further on both of these. We combined all the case weights to arrive at one cost for handling the average. We also did this on the hundred pound sacks. This knowledge allows us to quote rates predicated on known costs. The possibilities are unlimited. A plant warehouse manager could make the same analyses on all sizes coming from production lines into the rail cars. In fact, he should.

Another sidelight of the car report analysis was that we were able to find a goal unit count per man hour at a good unit cost. Taking these goal figures, we analyze the inbound car movement daily. We estimate how many cars can be handled before demurrage accrues. An average demurrage agreement also helps. The question, "Do we, or don't we, need extra labor?" is answered immediately.

Finding Cost Answer

The inter-relationship of these forms will tell management what it wants to know. A "seat of the pants" operator can easily be confused by current trends and future trends in warehousing unless he knows the cost answer. The use of these simple basic forms gives an accurate daily report. One can work from one, through another, onto the third to project various simple analyses.

Money is an object. Money is also a constant subject with management when discussing labor costs and other expenses. Therefore a very important form, a daily diary, is our next step. The warehouse cost report will tell us each day whether we made a profit or not. All types of revenue are listed; various payrolls are listed, and a prorated share of expenses other than wages, also are listed. Expenses other than wages has been arrived at from a study of actual expenses over a period of years. We arrive at a monthly figure. This is then broken down into a daily figure by dividing it by the number of working days, including paid holidays, in a month.

Warehouse storage revenue is billed the first of the month for goods on hand, along with accrued extra services (accessorial charges). These two totals are divided, like expenses other than wages. The resultant total is prorated to the number of days in the month. Additional new storage revenue and extra services revenue is added to that prorated figure each day. Drayage and handling revenues are added in for the day on which they accrue.

Reverse Side

Payroll is an obvious fact. But the breakdown will isolate certain facts of cost exactly where you want them. The reverse side of the form shows a more complete and comprehensive breakdown of labor costs.

To the expenses other than wages daily figure, we add a precautionary addition. Ten per cent of the daily revenue is added to this expense factor to allow for any increased expenses created by unusual activity. This allows for any costs not forecast. It furnishes a cushion in case the cost occurs.

One can ascertain immediately whether a profit or loss has resulted in the daily operation. Payroll and expenses other than wages are added. Then the combined total is subtracted from revenues above. These figures are compiled prior to noon of the following day.

More Information

Management wishes more information. We reverse the form. Here we see that drayage shows the actual revenue received from the weight handled. The revenue per hundredweight is found. The truck costs and labor costs are added together and divided by the weight, indicating the cost per hundredweight. There is your picture—an immediate visual fact.

Trucks are leased and daily costs are known as the lease rate is the cost per week plus mileage. No hidden costs here. Leasing has become inexpensive as a result. Handling of goods follows the delivery pattern in its breakdown of costs with one exception. Here we use a unit handling cost factor because our revenue results from a unit charge. Here then are the factors for you to isolate certain costs to particular revenues so you may see where you are going.

Another division of revenue comes from extra services, or accessorial service charges, which accrue over and above the regular handling and storage revenues. These are produced in the office by two clerks. Therefore, their salaries are prorated against this revenue. This gives us the cost per cent. The variance being the profit in an office operation.

Now a pattern of cost control is forming where most leaks occur—labor handling. Trends are noted at once. Soaring costs in any one operation will show up at once. If this trend is noted in the beginning of the month, an effort is expended to produce revenues before the end of the month. One does not have to wait for a month-end profit-and-loss statement to know what is happening. It can be produced daily. The jolt of a loss pattern will activate more sales effort; a review of labor; or a reduction of fixed costs such as maintenance. In reverse, excess profits alerts one to space allotments; need for extra labor or clerical help; or the increase of new services through more efficient material handling or office equipment. The need for new equipment expense is proved and accepted prior to the expenditure through this knowledge.

We find that our study of the warehouse cost report gives us:

- A daily knowledge of revenue and expense ratio.

Formula for Converting Withdrawal Charge to Hundredweight Charge

Total number of withdrawals made will (office transaction page)
Produce total number of units withdrawn which (office transaction)
Divided by number of withdrawals will
Produce average number of units per withdrawal, now

From car analysis report procure average weight per unit, then
Multiply average weight per unit by average number of units withdrawn this will
Produce total hundredweight per average withdrawal.

Divide .25¢ withdrawal charge by this hundredweight.
Result will be charge per withdrawal per hundredweight.

Example: 500 withdrawals totalling 90,000 units
90,000 ÷ 500 = 180 (average units withdrawn)
(average weight per unit was shown to be 23 lb)
180 × 23 = 4140 lb or 41 cwt
.25¢ ÷ 41 = .006¢ per cwt per withdrawal.

Expenses Other Than Wages

Employes Benefit FICA Taxes
Group Insurance
Workmen's Compensation Insurance
Travel Transportation, Hoteling
Supplies Office—Warehouse
Telephone—Telegraph
Postage—Meter Charge
Light—Water
Maintenance Warehouse—Office
Depreciation Building and Equipment
Real Estate Tax
Personal Property Tax
Insurance Building
Mortgage and Amortization
Interest on Real Estate
License
Dues—Subscriptions
Bad Debt Reserve
Administrative Overhead
Donations
Claims
Advertising
Sales Expense

- Control of payrolls.
- Breakdown on important labor costs.
- Relationship of specific labor costs to specific revenues.
- The ability to encompass all expenses into a daily factor.

The accumulation of certain facts, although related, will indicate a further refinement of some of those facts. Another history building form is our office transaction report. This form is so set up that five minutes of one clerk's time daily will produce the report from which many further analyses can be made.

This report shows the number of units handled into the warehouse, whether by rail car or truck. And, it shows the number of units outbound via car or truck. At the top of the form we show the carryover units from the preceding month. By adding the inbound units to this total and subtracting the outbound units, we know daily the number of units on hand.

Handling in and out charges are billed at one time which leaves a debit against the future handling out cost. We can readily recognize this debit because we know the total number of units in storage and we know our average unit cost to handle out. Multiplication will tell us the debit. This avoids the need to set up a reverse for this debit with its attendant fluctuations. We acknowledge the debt through this known count. A further refinement on this carryover count is that we know at the end of the month the average revenue we receive per unit. This allows us to approximate very closely the dollar revenue storage for the beginning of the next month.

Delivery tickets are counted to find the trend of the number of units moving out per ticket. As the 1958 recession ended we could see we were writing more tickets, but delivering less units. This showed that clerks were working harder to process as many units as prior to the recession. It proved that it would be unwise, servicewise, to reduce this force.

An analysis of the written tickets will show us which day is the most active on outbound units. Further study will show what part of the day is active.

Invoices, bills of lading, receipts reported and correspondence written are other activities of the office. We compile these as A, B, C, D, E which will give us a daily and monthly total of this type of activity. It is no problem to take total office salaries and divide it by these totals to procure an office transaction cost.

We can also compile the total number of units handled in and out. Dividing the total office salaries by this figure, we arrive at an office unit cost. This is the cost per unit for processing the paper work, 'phone calls, inventory controls, etc. By adding this unit cost figure to our handling in and out figure, we arrive at a total unit cost for handling. We now have two controls on our office operation.

These figures allow the office manager to see the rise and fall per unit cost, as well as office transaction cost. It will warn him to reduce costs or prove that he needs extra help. Once again management can pull any type of analysis from this data.

Weekly Weight Total

Delivery weight is kept daily from the driver's trip sheet. This will give us a weekly weight total to relate to our truck rental cost. Truck costs are in front of us. Solicitation of extra business by the office clerk is indicated if the delivery weight is not up to the profitable requirements. When the weight is heavy, we add extra trucks. If the weight has been poor previously, we can ask for delayed delivery time to allow us to pick up revenue.

By studying the unit movement, it becomes apparent that one can add the total units handled in by labor at the rail car platforms. Dividing that total into their salaries gives a unit cost for that platform. This is true of the truck platform also. The foreman now knows his cost for each operation, separately. He knows when a man earns a salary increase. Dividing the total number of units handled on both platforms into the monthly warehouse salaries, we can arrive at an average cost as a monthly guide per unit. This one unit figure allows us to look back to the preceding year to see at a glance if our costs are up or down.

How broad is the scope of the analyses which can be procured from these forms? We found that we were able to adapt our inbound unit count to the term "inventory" and our outbound unit count to the term "sales." We projected these monthly totals onto a graph. The U. S. Department in its Business Statistics Report shows the "Manufacturers ratio of inventory to sales." By relating our inbound and outbound count graph to this government form, we can see our relationship to the trend nationwide.

This proved particularly interesting in the fall of 1958. We were making our 1959 forecast. Our graph showed that our outbound units were climbing while our inbound units were declining. By analyzing the government graph back to a previous recession, we noted that the relationship of inventory to sales was in a seven-month lag. Sales had risen. But inventory hadn't made the turn until seven months later. Our warehouse graph was showing outbound (sales) much higher than inbound (inventory). As the sales graph on the government form had now turned upward, we then forecast our 1959 program with a strong spring season because of anticipated increases in inventory by that time. Our business followed the pattern as shown on the Business Statistics Chart.

Do these forms add a burden? Do they produce results? The maximum information has not been gathered yet. As the years go on the guide figures become more important; the history of unit movement reaches greater analytical proportions. Meanwhile, the daily results are like a constant flow of line of neon light—any break in the flow alerts management at once.

We have found that our simple forms give us a broader acknowledgment of:

- Immediate labor costs,
- The proration of all expenses into the picture.
- The analysis of unit or hundredweight costs.
- Office activity costs and efficiency.
- Controlled truck operation.
- That we have made a profit!

20. *This is ADMOS ... Automatic Device for Mechanized Order Selection**

"This isn't a warehouse, it's a machine. . . . with a building around it," says H. C. Blake, general manager of dynamic ADMOS, Inc. (Detroit), designers of the automatic order-picking installation shown here. It's not only a machine, but a darn good one; the pride and joy of Johnson and Johnson's big new warehouse just outside New Brunswick, N. J.

"ADMOS IV" checks product availability at point of selection, picks the number of cases of each item ordered, and counts them as it speeds them to the truck loading docks. Simultaneously, it records the action it took, and reports any shortages to the operator by closed-circuit TV. A central annunciator panel tells which lanes are running low—or are out of stock.

There are better than 650 items on ADMOS now, with plenty of room for expansion. It can handle 100 cases a minute, without breathing hard. (With small orders, of course, belt-clearing time slows it up.) It's already putting out well over the volume J&J expected to be handling in 1964. It selects over 60% of all the goods that leave the shipping center. (Another 30% are full-pallet shipments, and the rest consists of broken-case quantities, special promotion deals, etc.)

Errors were practically eliminated, in spite of a tremendous increase in the volume of goods shipped. This means better customer service; which, after all, is the purpose of a distribution center. Fewer people are needed, and it's quite likely that the space savings alone (30,000 square feet) at J&J could pay for the whole thing, although they weren't even taken into account in the proposal. Flexibility and very low maintenance are designed into ADMOS. Size and

* Reprinted by permission from *Factory*, June 1961.

number of lanes can be changed without tools. Simple, rugged, plug-in components and modular construction are used. And it's electro-mechanical, not electronic.

Picking orders at J&J was hardly primitive to begin with. The last word in draglines was installed when this warehouse was built. But errors were too common, the system couldn't be expanded, and it was too slow. Like a tube —once in, you had to go all the way through.

The cost of scrapping the dragline had to be considered during the systems analysis and planning that went into this job. (Each ADMOS —this is No. 4—is unique; designed for a specific installation.) According to J&J, the ADMOS bid was by far the lowest received. And it would be hard to find a tastier capital investment; it offers over a 25% return.

Low cost of the ADMOS system was one of its big attractions, of course, but far from the most important. Johnson and Johnson is an old hand at pioneering, and is plenty savvy about machine design (the only way to get Band-aid machinery is to build it). So it takes more than a gimmick to make an impression. Among the things that impressed J&J were the simplicity of ADMOS; the low-cost, reliable release mechanisms; the comprehensive systems analysis that was made; and the fact that known, dependable components were used—no razzle-dazzle.

The basic idea behind ADMOS is fairly simple. Goods are loaded end-to-end in inclined chutes, or lanes (2000 of them in this case). At the base of each lane, a release device holds the goods in place until it's tripped by an electric pulse, which frees the lowest case. The released case drops to a moving belt and is whisked away at 450 feet per minute. As it approaches the loading area, the case is slowed to 75 feet per minute by live roller conveyors. Electric eyes count the cases as they come off the belt. They're checked and stenciled on the move, then sent directly into a truck. Two men can load a 35-ft. trailer (some 900 cases) in half an hour.

J&J uses punched cards to activate its system, but paper or magnetic tapes would do just as well. The cards are prepared by a computer, which predetermines the cube volume and weight of the orders and breaks them down by truckload. The card reader is controlled from the ADMOS console in the warehouse. The console operator can also pick items manually with a keyboard, use of which automatically cuts out the reader.

When an item is out of stock, the reader prints out the information, and it shows up on the TV screen at the control console. The operator can then either get on his two-way radio and order the lane refilled, or adjust the bill of lading and enter a back order. At a separate annunciator panel, a series of lights show which lanes are low on stock and which ones are empty.

The conveyor system has been kept simple. Conventional rollers and disks have been used wherever possible, and guards have been kept to a minimum. For instance, at one point, the cases come howling into a 180-deg. curve; but proper banking of the rollers (which conveyor manufacturers said couldn't be done) keeps the cases under control. In two places, cases from three belts are being merged at high speed with no gates, electric eyes, or other ornaments. The cases are slowed for easier handling by simply putting a friction bearing after each three rollers. Tracks from the old dragline were pressed into service to bear the movable mechanized bridge that shunts the cases into the right truck. From the bridge, an extendable conveyor can be poked 40 feet into a trailer and backed off as the trailer fills up. If any conveyor fouls up, the reader stops—to prevent a log-jam.

Blake's passion for simplicity also shows up in the design of the lanes and the release mechanisms on ADMOS. In the case of the release, the ADMOS design uses the solenoid as its own frame, instead of mounting it on a separate piece. The solenoid also starts with a little free travel when it's fired. It's much easier to maintain and more reliable than other devices. It's a plug-in unit, and because of its curved race, it acts as a lock until it's fired. Variable tension protects cases, and ingenious features prevent dumping the whole lane, no matter how heavy

the item. All this, mind you, when other releases cost five times as much.

Same thing with the lanes. Instead of using rollers (except on a few special items), ADMOS, Inc., came up with simple coal chutes that cost about 35¢ a linear foot. Rollers run 10 or 20 times that, cost something to maintain, are much more expensive to install. Quick flexibility is another bonus with the chutes. They're made of sheet metal, about 27 feet long, and come in six widths (from 6 to 30 inches). They just clip on to the main frame. If you decide, for example, to change a unit from two 18-in. lanes to three 12-in. lanes, all you have to do is unplug the limit (stockout) switches, pull out the old chutes, and slip the new ones into place. No tools, no troubles, and very little time.

The chutes also save a lot of floor space. At J&J, there are five elevations, each lane inclined less than 20 degrees instead of the usual 30 to 35 degrees. How come the first cases don't get smashed when a lane is being loaded? Two reasons: The last case in a lane is never picked, so there's always a cushion; and a very crafty (again simple) device slows the descent. The cases ride on a pair of removable plastic runners, rather than directly on the chute. The coefficient of friction on these runners can be varied along their lengths. Staggering the "rough spots" along the runners causes the case to be cocked first this way, then that, against the sides of the chute, slowing it down.

Simplicity and economy are reflected even in the main structure of ADMOS. The framework is modular, and boasts a "keyhole" assembly that makes erection and expansion a lead-pipe cinch. Four men, armed with a lift truck, put up a 200-ft. section in just two days. Each of the 50 bays came pre-wired as a harness, and the limit switches were popped into place by hand.

Flexibility and ease of maintenance are designed into all the electrical features. Each lane is essentially its own circuit. If one lane malfunctions, you simply "jump" it out, and the machine will automatically start picking from another lane carrying the same item. Electrical trouble shooting can be done by feeding a special deck of cards through ADMOS—it quickly checks itself for shorts, grounds, open circuits, etc. Each junction box serves two bays in tandem, and every box is exactly alike. A man working at one of the boxes can see every change in mechanical performance caused by his changes in the wiring. Changes can be made by hand, since the connections are all plug-in units, like an IBM panel's. Each junction box cover carries the circuit diagram. Main control and switchgear are centralized, and the entire machine can be maintained by a man with only basic electrical skills.

Like the actual truck loading, replenishing the lanes is done manually. Two men are now replenishing on each shift, but better organization of the items is expected to reduce wasted motion enough so that one man can handle the job. The lanes hold over a week's supply of about 85% of the items, and another 7% have to be filled only twice a week. Each lane has two foolproof limit switches—"reload" and "lane empty"—connected to a central stock control panel. Radio-dispatched lift trucks feed stock into storage racks just behind the lanes, so the replenishers have a convenient supply to work with.

The warehouse kept right on working during the installation of the new system, but the changeover was rough. For one thing, the switch in paperwork threw off the dragline set-up. And the men were naturally edgy. Errors went up for a while. There were breakdowns in replenishing, faulty cases caused jams, and at first the best release wasn't being used with every item. Fortunately, once the mechanical problems are resolved, they don't come back. But they do extend beyond the walls of the warehouse. For example, J&J had to improve its case-sealing equipment, and sell the idea of much more uniformity in packaging. Electrical problems were confined almost entirely to the modified tabulator that was reading the cards (it's being replaced). "ADMOS itself is an electrician's dream," according to a J&J engineer.

Most of the trouble can be blamed on two factors that couldn't be controlled at the warehouse. First, the system was put in at a bad time and put to use immediately. As luck would have it, volume set new records during this period. A sales contest hit right in the middle of it, and several new products went over like ten-dollar mink. The heavy volume that resulted from all this really complicated the necessary debugging and retraining.

The other difficulty was that J&J was really breaking new ground. Machinery was being put in where it had never been before. However old-hat it may be in a plant, installing a major machine is a completely new experience to warehousemen. At J&J, it took a while to reorient the warehouse staff. Sales, of course, objected to temporary mix-ups, and accounting wanted quick payback. They expected the new system to give instant results, like a vending machine. Everyone knew the system should have been debugged before it was used for output, but service to customers won't wait. You can't build up an inventory of orders in a warehouse the way you can in a plant. When an order comes in, it has to go out, period. So ADMOS was in harness before it was tamed.

In spite of a few growing pains, the system is now doing fine. J&J's target volume was 14,000 cases a day by 1964. ADMOS is regularly picking far more than that right now. Maintenance has been negligible. Besides space savings and fewer errors, customer service is much better. Load times are more predictable, and it's easier to schedule trucks. There's a fringe benefit here, too; the outside carrier is now in on the final count, and signs the bill of lading. Before, with 10 dragline teams working, 10 checkers would have been needed. But ADMOS pulls only one order at a time, so the carriers can do their own checking.

The new system provides better control and involves much less walking than the dragline set-up. And it's far more flexible—and expandable. Before, the bays were fixed by the dragline. When a new product came in (if there was room for it), the other items had to play musical chairs. There was no way to expand. But ADMOS can handle J&J's planned expansion through 1965. It also makes product loading in the truck possible for the first time.

Fewer people will be needed with the new system. So far, because of abnormally high volume, debugging, training, and so on, J&J hasn't been able to cut back much. But about half as many men should be able to do the job ultimately. This will also mean fewer—but higher caliber —supervisors. They'll have to know scheduling and maintenance; be concerned with machine utilization, instead of acting like KP pushers.

21. *Equipment Lease Financing**

Vincent M. Jolivet†

Equipment lease financing is becoming more and more commonplace in the United States. Leasing, of course, is not new; it has been used in America for over a hundred years. Certain types of equipment, such as shoe-building machinery and data processing machines have been leased for many years. What *is* new is the fact that almost anything can now be leased, in such a manner that the difference between leased equipment and owned equipment is negligible, and the decision to own or to lease is almost entirely a financial decision. The object of this article is to examine the so-called "straight term" equipment lease now being used so frequently, and to explore the desirability of such leases from the point of view of the user of equipment.

Who Leases What, and From Whom?

First of all, what can be leased? A partial list includes automobiles and trucks, beer kegs, soap racks, locomotives, electric typewriters, wall-to-wall carpeting, crawler tractors, executive aircraft, jet engines, cash registers, electronic computers, turret lathes, extrusion presses, decorative plants, grocery counters, tug boats, and dredges. Almost any piece of equipment desired can be leased.

Who are the lessees? Probably about half of the large corporations in the United States lease some equipment. A lower percentage of the smaller firms employ leased equipment. From whom do they lease the equipment? Equipment can be leased from the manufacturer, such as General Electric, IBM, or Jones and Lamson; from leasing companies, such as United States Leasing Co., or Boothe Leasing; from factors or finance companies and their subsidiaries; from individuals acting as lease brokers. Regardless of who the actual lessor is, however, the money

used to finance the equipment comes principally from commercial banks, insurance companies, and pension funds or endowment funds.

Leases Other Than Straight Term

There are several basic types of leases. One is the short-term lease, such as the lease involved in renting a tractor for a period of one month, or an automobile for a weekend. Another type is the so-called lease-purchase, used when a prospective purchaser does not have the required downpayment for the purchase of equipment. In this case, the buyer rents the equipment for several months and is given credit for a certain percentage of the paid rentals toward the purchase price; once the amount accumulated becomes equivalent to the required downpayment, the transaction is converted to a regular conditional sales contract.

The Straight Term Lease

A third type of lease is one which is often called the "straight term" lease. Generally speaking, the basic lease covers a period equal to about 75 percent or more of the useful life of the equipment (typically less than 10 years). Over the period of the basic lease, the rental payments will equal the purchase price of the equipment plus the financing charges—in other words, the lessor gets his money back plus interest. On occasion, if the basic lease is much shorter than the useful life of the equipment, the value of the used equipment at the end of the lease will be taken into account and the rental reduced, but this is the exception rather than the rule. The lessee pays for all maintenance, insurance, taxes, and similar expenses, although in certain cases the lessor agrees to service the equipment. The inclusion of service in the rental charge is restricted to a few special types of equipment, such as data processing machines, shoe-building machinery, and automotive equipment. This discussion of equipment lease financ-

* Reprinted by permission from *University of Washington Business Review*, February, 1961.
† University of Washington.

ing is restricted to straight term leases which do not include service.

The straight term lease during the basic period is either noncancellable or includes a "rejectable purchase option" which allows the lessee to cancel the lease by offering to buy the equipment for a specified amount approximately equal to the remaining principal invested by the lessor. The lessor is free to reject such a purchase option if he feels the equipment is worth more on the open market, but if he does, the lease is canceled. If the lessee is an excellent credit risk, only monthly payments and no downpayment may be required; if the customer has a lower credit rating, he will be required to make a downpayment ("advance rent") at the time he receives the equipment, although this downpayment will normally be less than the downpayment required for a conditional sales contract or a chattel mortgage. If the customer has a poor credit rating, he may be required to make an even larger downpayment and the monthly payments may be increased to shorten the term of the lease, or he may be turned down altogether. At the end of the basic lease period, the lessee sometimes has an option to purchase the used equipment for a nominal amount, although such an option can endanger the tax deductibility of the rental payments. More often, at the end of the basic lease period, the lessee has the option of renewing the lease at a greatly diminished rent, often as little as 1 percent of the original value of the equipment per year. Although the latter type of option has been used more frequently than the former, it too can endanger the tax deductibility of the rental payments if the renewal rental option is at an extremely low figure compared to the actual value of the equipment at the time the lease is renewed.

New Approach—or Hidden Debt?

Is lease financing a really new method of financing, or is it merely a variation of borrowing? The author is inclined to agree with the latter view. The lessee enjoys the same use of the equipment over its useful life as if he owned it. He makes regular payments which are basically equivalent to the interest and amortization payments for other types of debt. The ability to lease, like the ability to borrow, is based principally on the lessee's credit rating. There are some differences from the point of view of taxes, but these are often of negligible impor-

tance under the 1954 Code. Another difference between the lease and debt is in their treatment as liabilities in case of bankruptcy or reorganization. In bankruptcies, the lessor's claim is generally limited to one year's rent, and in reorganizations it is limited to three years' rent, but only if the trustee rejects the lease. On the other hand, of course, the debt holder would be allowed to claim the full principal amount owed to him. Once this undesirable situation is reached, however, the difference between the lease and conventional debt is probably of little consolation to the lessee. The main difference between using debt to buy equipment and leasing the equipment, in the author's opinion, lies in the fact that in the former case both the asset and the liability are reflected on the balance sheet, whereas in the case of a lease, nothing is shown on the balance sheet, or, at best, the fact that the lease exists appears as a brief footnote to the balance sheet. Because of this "balance sheet difference" lease obligations may be overlooked or not fully understood by prospective lenders, and a greater "borrowing" capacity (debt plus lease) achieved by the lessor, as discussed later. In some cases, this situation may come about as a result of using lease financing *after* having already borrowed from other sources, unless the lenders prevent this by a clause in the loan agreement.

Pros and Cons of Leasing

Let us now look at the pros and cons of leasing equipment as opposed to financing its ownership through conventional debt. Undoubtedly, one important factor which affects the decision to own or to lease is habit. Although by now many businessmen are reconciled to using a leased automobile, very few would think of leasing their desks. Some period refer to pride of ownership, which in a sense is merely an extension of habit. However, profits are not realized from the ownership of capital equipment, but rather from its use. Thus, pride of ownership or habit are hardly rational bases for decision.

Tax Aspects

Until 1954, the major inducement to using the straight term lease was probably its tax advantage. Since reasonable lease payments are tax deductible, leasing makes it possible to "write off" the equipment over the basic lease period, which is shorter than the period permitted for normal depreciation. Faster write-off does *not* save taxes ultimately, however—it merely postpones their payment. To the extent that taxes are postponed, of course, the firm benefits by having the temporary use of these funds at no cost (effectively, this amounts to an interest-free loan). With the advent of the two methods of accelerated depreciation allowed by the 1954 tax code, the tax advantage of leasing was greatly diminished. Although the lease still allows the write-off of equipment over a shorter period than normal depreciation, accelerated depreciation of owned equipment concentrates the tax deduction in the early years, thus offsetting to a substantial extent the tax advantage of the lease. The tax revision of 1958, allowing a depreciation deduction of 20 percent (up to a maximum of $10,000 for a corporation) during the first year in *addition* to the regular first year depreciation, further offsets the tax advantage of the lease for a small firm. The tax advantage of the straight term lease, if any, can be ascertained only by knowing the terms of the lease agreement, the depreciation allowed if the equipment were owned, and the tax bracket of the firm contemplating the lease. By calculating the tax deduction allowed each year under the two alternatives and the amount of taxes saved as a result in a particular year, the *difference* in cash outlay for taxes between the two can be obtained. If this annual difference is then cumulated (with due regard for algebraic signs), the advantage of one method over the other (as far as tax postponement is concerned) can be measured accurately. One additional step is possible: by assuming a suitable interest rate on the funds temporarily obtained through superior tax postponement, a dollar value can be placed on the tax advantage of the lease (if any). This latter figure will rarely be very large.

Cash Flow Aspects

The principal advantage of lease financing over borrowing which is currently advanced is its superiority from the point of view of cash flow—in other words, it makes more cash temporarily available to the user. Whether this is true or not depends on the circumstances. One leasing company, for example, says, "Leasing permits the user to pay for fixed assets out of earnings which those assets produce." Thus, by implication, the money that would otherwise be tied up in these assets is available for other profitable uses. However, this can be equally true of financing by means of a sales contract or a term loan. Proponents of leasing may retort that at least the elimination or reduction of the downpayment by means of the lease frees some cash, but this answer is valid only when compared to a secured loan. In other words, 100 percent financing by means of a lease frees funds only when compared with a secured loan which provides less than 100 percent of the cost of the assets. If the firm is in a position to borrow the full amount, either on an unsecured loan or a loan secured in part by the asset and in part by other assets, this "freeing of the downpayment" advantage does not exist.

Unfortunately, many firms cannot borrow all they could use from banks or from the sale of debt securities; here the advocates of leasing make their most telling point. If the borrowing capacity of a firm is not adequate to meet all of its needs, can leasing be used to finance equipment without impairing the firm's borrowing capacity? Can this borrowing capacity be saved to finance other needs? The answer is a conditional "yes." Suppose a corporation's bank is willing to lend it $200,000 on a term loan basis. If this company can obtain another $150,000 worth of equipment through leasing without impairing its ability to get the term loan, it is very possible that the company will benefit from leasing, because it will be able to expand more rapidly without resorting to the sale of stock (which in any case might not be feasible). This advantage, however, is conditional upon the banker *not* realizing that lease financing is fundamentally a form of debt. Otherwise, knowing that the firm plans to lease $150,000 worth of equipment, the banker will probably reduce his offer of a term loan from $200,000 to $50,000, and leasing will lose its foremost advantage.

The question then becomes, do lenders in general realize that lease financing is basically another form of debt? It is important to remember at this point that the leased asset and the lease obligation do not appear on the balance sheet, except perhaps as a brief footnote. If the company used as an illustration had just borrowed $150,000 on a term loan from another bank, the banker would immediately perceive this from the balance sheet and reduce his offer of a $200,000 term loan to $50,000. Will he be as perceptive in the case of the lease, which is a hidden form of debt? This depends on the banker. Professor Robert Anthony and Richard F. Vancil of the Harvard Business School did some exploratory work in this area. They found that formal techniques of capitalizing leases (to show them on the balance sheets being analyzed) are being used by some of the larger banks and insurance companies, although often not too well. Such formal techniques are little used, if at all, by smaller banks and insurance companies and by other institutions such as mutual funds, investment banks, and pension funds.

Profitability of Leasing Equipment

Let us now examine a situation, making two assumptions: (1) a firm has greater need for funds than its normal borrowing capacity can provide, (2) those who lend to the firm do not fully understand leasing and tend to overlook it in appraising the firm's credit position. In such a case, leasing can provide additional funds in the form of hidden debt. Whether leasing is desirable now boils down to one principal question: Can the additional funds provided by leasing be invested to return more than their financing cost? This question can be subdivided into two others: What is the anticipated return on the investment of the additional funds, and, what is the cost of the hidden debt obtained through leasing? The first of last two questions should be answered by the individual firm in the light of its own investment *opportunities*. Leasing companies may very well mislead potential lessees by implying that the rate of return on the funds obtained by leasing equals the percentage ratio of past net profits (before taxes) to net working capital. This is erroneous, because profits are not exclusively derived from the use of working capital, but rather from the use of all of the firm's assets, and in any case, the mere fact that a firm is making a certain percentage return on its assets does not necessarily mean that this return is possible with the investment of additional funds. (On the other side of the coin, it is possible that a better return is available from the investment of additional funds.) Hence, the firm should assess its own actual investment opportunities.

Cost of Leasing

Turning to the cost of straight term leasing, we find that financing charges included in the rental payments usually amount to 10 to 15 percent simple interest. This is more than the normal cost of bank or insurance company credit, or the normal interest rate on debt securities. This should come as no surprise, inasmuch as the leasing companies obtain a very large percentage of their funds from banks and insurance companies, and obviously a middleman's profit must be added to the interest cost. In this respect, leasing companies are similar to finance companies (most of the larger finance companies are branching out into the equipment leasing field), and the financing costs of leasing are comparable to the charges made by finance companies under similar circumstances. If the financing cost of leasing is greater than costs of funds from some other sources, why then do firms use leasing? The principal answer to this question is probably that firms use leasing as a *supplement* to bank and insurance company debt (if available) rather than as a substitute. In some cases, other advantages of leasing, as listed below, may also influence the decision to use leasing despite its higher cost. A further cost of leasing which should also be kept in mind is the loss of the equipment at the end of the basic lease, unless the lessee continues to make rental payments. In the latter case, despite their sharply reduced amount, these payments are still an additional charge.

One thing that has confused the issue is the fact that both the proponents and opponents of leasing, in arguing their cases, have typically resorted to mazes of figures based on all kinds of assumptions, many of which are questionable or misleading. In other words, they overwhelm you with figures. The author thinks that the whole problem can be reduced to simple proportions by relating it to the cost of capital. Generally speaking, debt capital is cheap (particularly with its tax advantage) and equity capital is expensive, but the amount of debt capital that a firm can obtain relative to its equity is limited. If the firm can obtain additional hidden debt through lease financing, which increases the proportion of debt to equity, then the average cost of capital will be less (except, of course, in the unusual case where the cost of lease financing is greater than the cost of equity financing). If, on the other hand, lease financing merely replaces conventional debt, without increasing the proportion of debt to equity, then no advantage is gained. Which situation prevails will depend on the sophistication of the lending agencies which lend to a given firm.

Other Advantages

In several minor ways, equipment lease financing can have advantages. It can simplify budgetary control and reduce accounting costs slightly. It allows "piecemeal" financing of new equipment. It can make the factory manager more aware of the cost of using equipment, because the financing charge is included in the rental. Leasing can also have an advantage over term loans or bond issues in that it does not usually involve any restrictive agreements. These advantages are usually minor, although in some individual cases they may become rather important.

Conclusions

Equipment lease financing has been growing rapidly in popularity. No longer is its tax advantage a principal reason for the use of lease financing. Basically, lease financing is a form of hidden debt, and situations quite often arise in which lease financing allows a firm to "borrow" more than it could otherwise. A firm which can borrow all it needs from conventional sources at reasonable rates will normally find lease financing unprofitable. The firm which cannot borrow enough to satisfy all of its needs will probably find lease financing advantageous as long as the leasing does not interfere with its normal borrowing, and as long as its investment opportunities are more profitable than the financing cost of leasing. Other less important advantages of lease financing can lead to its use in individual instances. Equipment lease financing will probably continue to grow in popularity, but as it becomes a more important method of financing,

lenders will tend to realize more fully that leasing is a form of debt, and as this happens leasing will lose its foremost advantage. Accountants have been studying the treatment of long-term leases on balance sheets, and it is possible that some day recommendation of the accounting profession will cause firms to follow the practice of capitalization of straight term equipment leases. If this comes about, both the equipment and offsetting lease liability will appear on balance sheets, in much the same way as railroad equipment leased under equipment trust financing appears on the balance sheet of the lessee. At this point, the amount of lease financing will probably level off, although it will undoubtedly remain with us as a common means of financing equipment.

(For those who wish to learn more about leasing, the writer suggests two articles which appeared in the *Harvard Business Review*, one by Frank Griesinger, entitled "Pros and Cons of Leasing Equipment," in the March–April 1955 issue, and the other by Donald Gant, entitled "Illusion in Lease Financing," in the March–April 1959 issue. Information on the tax aspects of leasing may be found in Internal Revenue Bulletin Number 35 (August 29, 1955) and Revenue Rulings 55-540, 55-541, 55-542, and 60-122. A suggested procedure for showing the lease on the balance sheet may be found in the *NAA Bulletin* of June 1958, in an article by Gordon Shillinglaw entitled "A Lease Capitalization Proposal." A more extensive bibliography on leasing is available from the author.)

Section V.   Inventory Management

In the study of inventory management we find a series of trade-offs and compromises. As we investigate inventory management we find that a direct relationship exists between inventory levels and customer service levels. As inventory levels are reduced in order to reduce inventory carrying costs, customer service levels fall correspondingly. What is necessary for the firm to achieve the optimum balance between these two factors is for research to determine the ratio of this direct relationship. At that point where customer service is satisfied, and inventory levels are at their minimum, the firm will find its most profitable position.

Because of this important impact on the quality and cost of maintaining satisfactory customer service levels, the management of inventory is particularly deserving of close and continuous managerial scrutiny. All five articles in this section do much to point up the difficulties involved. Robert G. Brown's *Less Risk in Inventory Estimates,* together with the Baumback and Konopa collaboration, *Inventory Control: How EOQ Can Help,* bring out critical areas and useful methods in attacking the problem. J. L. Heskett's *Marketing Time Lags: Their Impact on Logistics,* is particularly helpful in understanding the nature of the demand for items as a basis for improving the estimate with regard to the size of demand for them in the future.

22. Less Risk in Inventory Estimates*

Robert G. Brown†

The future is uncertain. Only a company with a monopoly in an unsaturated market can be sure of what the future demand for its products will be. For managers concerned with inventories and customer service, this situation poses obvious problems. Accordingly, I shall discuss these questions:

How can the uncertainty facing a company be kept to a minimum?

How can that minimum be measured and accounted for in a well-designed inventory control system?

Forecasts and Predictions

Demand for a product is generated by the complex interaction of many factors. If it were possible to understand the effect of each of these factors, and how they interact, we could build a mathematical model that would give a very accurate estimate of future demand. Usually, however, this is not possible, since we do not fully understand the effect of competition, advertising, service, and substitutes for supplying the demand or for using the product.

We can nevertheless visualize some mechanism, some system of interacting factors, that does generate the demand; and we can use statistical theories to build a useful model of the total effect. For example:

A physicist studying a gas cannot know all the forces acting on a single, specific molecule, to predict its movement. He can, however, make very precise statements about the behavior of a large collection of molecules. Although the behavior of individuals is random, the ensemble has very stable statistical characteristics.

* Reprinted by permission of the publishers from Edward C. Bursk and John F. Chapman, editors, *New Decision-Making Tools for Managers,* Cambridge, Mass.: Harvard University Press, Copyright 1963, by the President and Fellows of Harvard College.

† Arthur D. Little, Inc.

We might think of all the factors in our model that will generate the total demand during the next month. Some might be important, some unimportant; some might be fairly predictable, some unpredictable. But any factor could be put into one of two classes: (1) factors that generated customer demand in past months and are not new to the future; (2) factors that appear for the first time in affecting total demand.

There are many industries, and many types of products, for which the factors in the first class have most of the effect on total demand. In such cases, routine methods can be developed to forecast the effect of those factors, leaving management free to predict the effect of the few new influences. For other industries, by contrast, the future is almost entirely a change from the past; management predictions are more difficult and occupy a more central role. Here, as elsewhere in this article, I use the term "forecast" or "routine forecast" to mean the projection of the past into the future; and the term "predict" to mean management's anticipation of changes and of new factors affecting demand. While in practice both forecasts and predictions must be used, I shall concentrate my discussion on new developments in routine mathematical forecasting.

The difference between routine forecasting and prediction is important. Essentially, in forecasting we take a sequence of numbers and try to guess what the next number will be. Later we know what that next number was, and try to guess the following one, profiting by our mistakes in previous guesses. On the other hand, a prediction requires one to know a great deal about what the numbers represent—what the item is, how it is used, future marketing plans, the probable effect of competition, the economic climate, and so on.

Some people seem to have the ability to predict the future sales of an item, commodity, or stock fairly accurately if given enough time to study all the pertinent information. But it is not at all uncommon for a company to make hundreds or even thousands of items; and when one considers all the package sizes, colors, and locations, there may be a half-million SKUs (stock-keeping units) to be controlled. And the control of total investment, total service, and total cost is based on the control of the replenishment of one SKU at a time.

Since there are not enough skilled people who have the time to *predict* the demand for each SKU, the men who have the job must *forecast* instead, extrapolating past experience and making any necessary adjustments to account for predictions of general economic or competitive factors (e.g., a strike or recession).

Playing the Averages

In the routine forecasting of demand for hundreds or thousands of SKUs we must necessarily "play the averages" as best we can. There are different ways of doing this.

Suppose that, in effect, we have a game in which we are given a sequence of numbers—say, 64, 115, 101, 65, 126, and 111—and must guess what the next number (or numbers) in the sequence will be. We guess 97 (the average of the six numbers), actual demand turns out to be 150, and we sit down to guess again. What method shall we use?

We could take the average of all seven numbers that we have now—104.6.

We could take the average of the most recent six numbers—111.3.

Or—a little more complicated—we could adjust our next forecast on the basis of the difference between the last forecast (97) and the actual demand which materialized (150).

The first two ways of estimating are familiar averages; the third is newer. In some circumstances the first two are adequate, but frequently—especially in expanding markets—they are not. To illustrate:

Let us suppose that the sequence had been 64, 65, 101, 111, 115, 126. Although the numbers are the same as before, the problem is different: each month the demand has been greater than the demand the previous month, so that it might be plausible to assume that the demand in the seventh month is going to be at least 126, and probably higher. Thus the simple aver-

age 97 would be a poor estimate of the next value in the sequence. Some allowance for trend must be made.

Many of the conventional procedures in use for routine forecasting do, in one way or another, compute an average; and a few recognize the problem of systematic trends by asking an analyst to "be on the lookout for a trend, and make the necessary adjustments." But, as we shall see shortly, routine computations can detect a trend more quickly than the eye can, and the necessary adjustments can be made automatically. There are a number of new procedures that can be helpful in this regard, and we shall discuss them in some detail.

Probability and Uncertainty

There is a further dimension to this problem where conventional procedures are inadequate. It is the common practice to estimate a single number, which may represent the most probable or the expected eventuality—for example, 268,100 passenger miles or 23,500 conveyer belts. But this number is almost certain to be wrong, if only by a few units. On the other hand, by specifying a range of possibilities and making the range wide enough, we could achieve any reasonable percentage of successful estimates, even in markets subject to great change.

We shall see later how to estimate the expected value for future demand, and how to estimate the range necessary to ensure any desired probability of being right—right, that is, in predicting that demand will not exceed a number equal to the expected demand, plus an allowance for uncertainty.

Warmdot Case

To illustrate the new, improved methods that can be applied to these problems, I shall use the fictional, but realistic "Warmdot Appliance Company." Through the article I shall refer to four products that typify the problems posed by the thousands of SKUs stocked:

1. Copper tubing is used by both heating and air conditioning contractors; and the demand for it is affected by strikes, the weather, building activity, and competitive sources. The demand for 3B1676, heavy duty $5/8''$ tubing, stocked in 10-foot lengths, is plotted in Exhibit 1. On the average, in the past four years, Warmdot has sold 343 lengths of this item a month.

Exhibit 1. **Demand for ten-foot lengths of copper tubing**

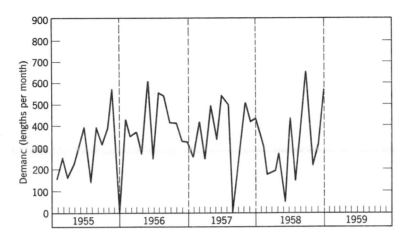

The maximum was 657 in September, 1958, and there were two months with no demand.

2. A new line of general-purpose thermostats was introduced in 1954, and the demand has been growing steadily, as shown in Exhibit 2 for the 1D9120 model. The average demand in the past four years has been 77 units a month, and the maximum was 126. However, since there has been a steady upward trend in demand, the four-year average would be of little value in estimating demand during the first quarter of 1959.

3. Evaporator plates are used only in furnaces, but need to be replaced every two or three years. Exhibit 3 shows how the demand for 1A9375 plates has a definite peak when cold weather sets in. The low sales level of about 30 is a good estimate of summer demand, and a peak of about 700 has occurred every fall—although in different months. So the long-term average of 338 plates a month must be modified according to the season of the year, if we are to have a useful forecast.

4. Warmdot's fan belts are used primarily as replacements on furnace motors, but they are occasionally sold for all sorts of other uses. Exhibit 4 plots the demand for the 2F2828 ½″ x 18″ V-belts. The average of 518 a month might at first glance seem to be a reasonable representation of the demand. Closer examination, however, reveals a tendency to peak during the summer with demand reaching 1,000 to 1,100 belts when most of the maintenance is done, and a winter low that reached zero in two years.

Exhibit 2. **Demand for thermostats**

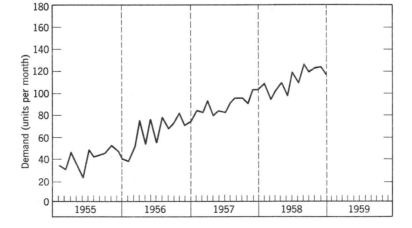

Exhibit 3. Demand for evaporator plates

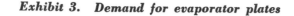
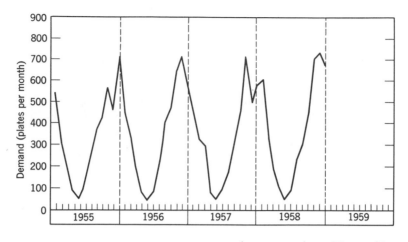

Components of Demand

Note that demand for these four items, like so many other products and services sold by business, is characterized by:

Average demand, both long- and short-term.
Trends in the average, that may continue for a long time, or that may occasionally change direction.
Cycles, which repeat peaks and valleys in demand at nearly the same time every year.
Noise—i.e., the unpredictable fluctuations around the basic pattern described by the average, trend, and cycle.

The demand for any item manufactured at Warmdot can be thought of as a time series made up of the foregoing four components in

varying proportions. The problem of statistical forecasting is to try to isolate and measure each component to that its sum can be computed for future months.

This brings us to the problem of computing trends and averages. I should like to outline this problem in a general way first, before returning to our case example.

Average Demand

When an inventory control system includes an objective method of forecasting demand item by item, the method is usually some form of moving average. Thus, one sixth of the total demand in the past six months may be a very good estimate of the average rate of movement for an item in coming months. This method is straight-

Exhibit 4. Demand for fan belts

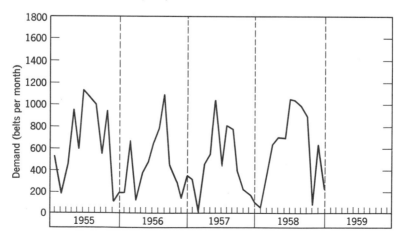

forward, and easily programed for punched-card machines or for electronic computers. Its disadvantage is that a record must be kept of the demand in each of the past six months—which can mean long files.

An alternative method is what I shall call "exponential smoothing." This is a very special kind of weighted moving average with these features:

The new estimate of the average is updated periodically as the weighted sum of (a) the demand in the period since the last review and (b) the old average. Thus it is not necessary to keep any record of past demand, and the data processing becomes more economical.

The average is a weighted sum of all the past demand, with the heaviest weight being placed on the most recent information.

The method can be extended, with little additional data processing effort, to detect, and compensate for, trends.

It can be made to respond smoothly, automatically, and accurately to any anticipated changes in the pattern of demand.

Using exponential smoothing, it is also very simple to calculate the necessary and sufficient allowance for uncertainty in management estimates of the future.

Allowing for Trend

The longer our series of numbers for past demand, the more accurate an estimate based on averaging should be—*if* there is any reason to believe that the market remains stable for a long period of time. But usually it does not, as we know only too well. If the average is computed over a short period of time, it is subject to a large "sampling error"; if it is computed over a long period of time, we may be averaging together several different markets.

Conflicting Objectives

In this situation the moving average is an attempt at compromise. A stock record for each item may show the actual demand in each of the past several months. Although a longer record may be available, we deliberately compute the average using only the most recent six months, or the most recent twelve months, or some other interval. The objective is to take a long enough base period to allow random fluctuations in demand to cancel each other out, but

a short enough period to discard information that is no longer relevant to current conditions. (Items with a significant seasonal pattern of demand are a special case, which will be covered in some detail later.)

Further, even if conventional moving averages serve for smoothing out the fluctuations in a demand history to get a stable estimate of the expected rate of demand, they have the practical drawback of requiring extra work. Not only must the company keep extensive records of past demand, but accounting for trends, changes in trend, and the distribution of forecast error requires cumbersome computations.

Useful Constant

Here we can put our special kind of moving average, exponential smoothing, to work.

Suppose that in our record we had stored only the average past demand computed last month, but had not stored any of the data used in computing the average. This month we have a new value for the demand, and so we want to get a new value for the average. It seems logical that if the demand this month is higher than the old average, we ought to increase our estimate. Conversely, if the demand is below our previous estimate, the new estimate should be lower. Furthermore, if the difference is small, the adjustment ought to be small; but if the new demand is far above the average, the new estimate ought to be increased by a sizable amount.

Now suppose we adopt a rule such as this: to get a new estimate of the average demand, take the previous estimate and add to it a fraction of the amount by which demand this month exceeds that estimate. (Demand below the estimate "exceeds" the estimate by a *negative* quantity; adding a fraction of a negative quantity would, of course, decrease the estimate.)

The fraction used is called a smoothing constant, and is conventionally represented by α, the Greek letter alpha. The value for the smoothing constant must be a fraction between 0 and 1. We can abbreviate our rule as an equation:

New estimate =

old estimate $+ \alpha$ (new demand $-$ old estimate)

It can be shown mathematically that we are justified in calling this estimate an average in the same sense as we use the term "moving average." Therefore, proceeding to rearrange the terms a little, we can write down the basic rule of exponential smoothing as:

New average =

$$\alpha \text{ (new demand)} + (1 - \alpha) \text{ (old average)}$$

The data-processing simplicity is obvious, because only one number has to be recorded instead of the actual demands in each of the past several months. For the typical large company, with 100,000 or more SKUs, a saving of only one-tenth of a second in the time required to process one item can reduce the total running time by almost three hours. In smaller companies, some of the other advantages listed above may have greater relative importance.

Exhibit 5 compares the actual monthly demand for Warmdot's copper tubing with the average computed by exponential smoothing, using a constant, $\alpha = 0.1$. Notice that this estimate is stable, in spite of wide fluctuations in demand, but that it does change gradually when the demand changes.

Corrections for Lag

The average thus computed by exponential smoothing will lag behind a demand that follows a steadily rising (or falling) trend. If we can estimate the magnitude of the trend, however, we can make the necessary correction to eliminate the lag.

An estimate of the trend is the difference between the new average and the old average.

Random fluctuations in demand are, to be sure, bothersome; but a simple method is readily available for estimating the average of a fluctuating quantity. The formula for the new trend therefore looks very much like the basic rule of exponential smoothing:

New trend =

$$\alpha \text{ (new average } - \text{ old average)} + (1 - \alpha) \text{ (old trend)}$$

This method of computing the trend is in fact the least-squares estimate of it, if the weights given to the demand in each previous month are the same as those used in computing the average.

The correction for the lag due to trend can be expressed as:

Expected demand =

$$\text{new average} + \frac{(1 - \alpha)}{\alpha} \text{ (new trend)}$$

Using these formulas, it is necessary only to store the previously calculated values for the average and for the trend, so that the data processing is still simple.

Exhibit 6 shows the results of applying this calculation of expected value, as corrected for trend, to the data for Warmdot's thermostats, sales of which have been steadily increasing in the past four years. Note that, while the expected values computed from month to month were commonly under or over the demand

Exhibit 5. Actual demand for tubing and the exponentially smooth average

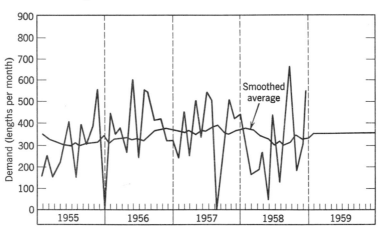

Exhibit 6. *Actual demand for thermostats and the exponentially smoothing expected value*

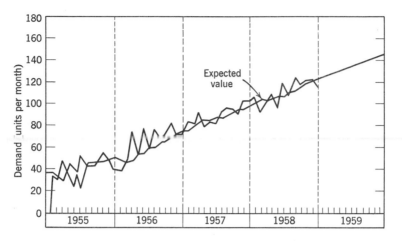

which actually materialized, they stayed with the *trend* of demand all the way.

Choice of a Value

The value chosen for the smoothing constant α determines how much of the past demand figure has any significant effect on the estimate of the average. As in the case of the moving average, the more past data included in the average, the smaller will be the error in the estimate—provided, of course, that the basic pattern of demand does not change during the interval. On the other hand, if fewer past months are included in the averaging process, the response to the changes that do occur will be faster.

If a small value, say $\alpha = 0.01$, is chosen for the smoothing constant, the response will be slow and gradual, since it is based on the average of approximately 199 past months used to compute the expected demand figure. By contrast, a high value like $\alpha = 0.5$, which corresponds to an average of three months' demand, will cause the estimates to respond quickly, not only to real changes but also to the random fluctuations. For instance, in Exhibit 6 the large changes in the first six months of 1955 are due to using a smoothing constant, $\alpha = 0.3$; the remainder of the estimates were made using $\alpha = 0.1$.

In practice, many companies have found that $\alpha = 0.1$ is a satisfactory compromise between a very stable system that fails to track real changes and a "nervous" system that fluctuates with the demand. This value corresponds to a moving average of 19 months' demand. Prediction of major changes in demand, as described below, can help improve the compromise.[1]

Major Changes

Most of the time, demand follows a very slowly changing pattern, so that a small smoothing constant is appropriate. But what if executives think an important change is coming because of the introduction of a new product, a promotional campaign, the discovery of a new use for an item, strikes, or a recession? If management can predict a development of this nature, it can increase the value of the smoothing constant to $\alpha = 0.3$ or even $\alpha = 0.5$, for a temporary period of, say, five or six months.

During that period, the routine calculations will respond quickly to whatever changes do materialize. Later, when the new pattern of demand is established, the smoothing constant can be dropped back to its original value to provide greater stability and accuracy.

Note that it is not necessary for management to predict the magnitude or even the direction of the change. *Management need predict only that a major change will occur shortly.* The routine calculations can detect and correct for the actual change that materializes in the demand for each item. In fact, a computer can

---

[1] For greater detail on this and other aspects of mathematical forecasting, see Robert G. Brown, *Statistical Forecasting for Inventory Control* (New York, McGraw-Hill Book Company, Inc., 1959.

probably make the corrections more accurately than could the men making the prediction.

Getting Started

Once we have recorded values for the average and for the current trend, then the exponential-smoothing formulas tell us how to update these values with the new demand data each month. For the first month, however, special steps must be taken to compute an initial condition for the average and for the trend. The average can be the average of last year's demand. As for the trend, it is frequently practical to assume that it is zero, and to let the system compute its own trend. I recommend starting with a smoothing constant, $\alpha = 0.3$. After six months, when the ups and downs of starting have begun to even out, the constant can be dropped back to 0.1.

Seasonal Patterns

Some products (though fewer than commonly supposed) have a true seasonal pattern of demand—e.g., Warmdot's evaporator plates and fan belts, both of which sell in response to seasonal weather changes.

In deciding to use a seasonal method of forecasting, two principles are important:

1. There must be a known reason for the heavy selling season to occur at about the same time every year, so it can be depended on.

Thus, one company's products have a very definite annual pattern of demand at the plant, even though the actual consumption of the product is known to be remarkably stable from month to month throughout the year. The reason lies in the distribution system. The manufacturer decides on sales bonuses after he looks at the performance against quota for the fiscal year that ends in June. Also, many of the jobbers have to pay a tax on their inventories at the end of December. The net result is a demand on the plant that is light in November and December, and heavy in May and June.

2. The seasonal variation in demand should be larger than the random variations, or "noise."

Failure to observe the first principle may lead management to provide a great deal of inventory when the demand is light, and to cut orders back just before a big, but random, surge in demand. Failure to observe the second may require a great deal of extra work with no results to show for it.

The Base Series

Most common methods of forecasting when there is a seasonal pattern depend on comparing the observed demand this year with historical or predicted figures called a "base series."

The best possible base series, of course, is one that has exactly the same pattern as the demand for the item being forecast will have. Short of this Utopian goal, however, we should settle for a series that is high when demand is high, low when demand is low, and that has about the same relative range of values. Commonly used series include:

Same month last year. Perhaps the most common base series, and the most obvious one, is the actual demand for the product during the corresponding month last year. The pattern of demand should show some *rational* change from year to year; if the changes are not too violent, the pattern observed last year can be used to advantage in forecasting the rest of this year. The evaporator dates in Exhibit 3 have such a demand pattern.

Average of surrounding quarter. If the demand for a product depends on weather, the peak demand may be earlier or later this year than it was last year. Notice the varying peaks for the fan belts in Exhibit 4. If the peak demand shifts back and forth by a month or so from year to year, then the average of the demand in the three months *surrounding* the corresponding month last year may prove to be a more stable base series to use in the case of a seasonal pattern.

Pattern for a line. Suppose that we have a large number of SKUs, that are different sizes or colors of the same basic item (e.g., boys' school pants; pints, quarts, gallons, and drums of porch paint; stovepipe sections; or fan belts). There are random variations in the pattern of demand for each SKU, but when we examine the total demand for all related SKUs, we find that some of the upward fluctuations cancel some of the downward ones. Thus, the total demand for all related SKUs appears to provide us with a clearer picture of the basic pattern.

If we can identify such related items, we can use their total demand in the same month last year (or perhaps the average of their total de-

Exhibit 7. **Actual demand for evaporator plates and the smoothed ratio estimate**

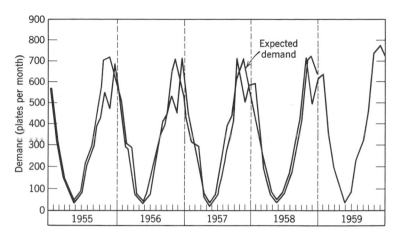

mand in the quarter surrounding that month) as a base series. But note that the items so grouped must in fact be related. It is a mistake to use the total pattern for an entire business (unless only one product line is sold), because different seasonal patterns for different lines may cancel out in the same way the "noise" does, making the base series *too* general. For example, fan belts and evaporator plates should not be grouped.

Demand Ratio

There are several methods of applying the base series to get an item-by-item forecast of demand. A successful one is to smooth the ratio of the demand in the current period to the cor-

responding value of the base series. The procedure is simple:

1. Each month, as the first step, compute the demand ratio. This ratio equals demand in the current month divided by the value of the base series for the current month.

2. Next compute the average, trend, and expected value of the demand ratio, as described earlier for the nonseasonal demand itself. The expected demand for any future month is the expected ratio multiplied by the value of the base series for that month.

Exhibit 7 shows Warmdot's calculations for the evaporator plates, using the same month last year as the base series. Exhibit 8 shows similar calculations for fan belts, but with a base

Exhibit 8. **Actual demand for fan belts and the expected value**

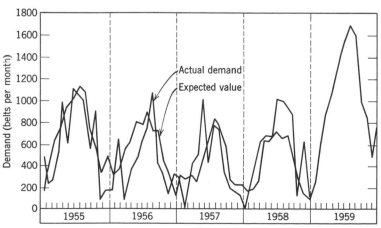

series equal to the total of the quarter surrounding the corresponding month in the previous year. The high forecast for 1959 results from the fact that demand in 1958 was well above the corresponding months in 1957.

Here again, of course, the current demand ratio can be smoothed with a moving average. Indeed, an often cited advantage of the moving average is its applicability to seasonal demand problems. Once more, however, the same kind of results can be accomplished by exponential smoothing—and with less effort and cost.

Forecast Errors

We come now to the question of allowing for errors in the forecast. Barring mistakes in judgment and miscalculations, these errors arise because of the many "noise" factors which make forecasting the problem that it is—factors like the weather, the economic and political climate, competition, marketing strategy, popular styles, and so on.

The first part of this article has dealt with methods of estimating the expected demand that have some advantages over the more familiar moving averages. In an inventory control system it is necessary to estimate the maximum reasonable demand during the replenishment lead time, in order to provide enough stock to meet reasonable demand. The maximum reasonable demand is equal to the expected demand plus an allowance for error.

In most of the current systems, the allowance —commonly referred to as "safety stock"—is equal to a flat "one month's supply" for all items; a more refined system may have different allowances for different classes of items. Such an allowance will be too small for some items with a highly variable demand; it will be too large for others.

By measuring the variability of demand for each item, it would be possible to provide the necessary and sufficient inventory to satisfy demand. In our experience with some 40 corporations, the measurement of uncertainty item by item has made it possible to redistribute the inventory, with an improvement in service and a total reduction of $150 million in investment.[2]

[2] See John F. Magee, "Guides to Inventory Policy: Part II. Problems of Uncertainty," *Harvard Business Review,* March–April, 1956, p. 103.

Probability Distribution

The uncertainty must be expressed in terms of a probability distribution, which may be either a convenient mathematical formula or an empirical curve.

The errors in forecasting demand are limited, of course. Generally speaking, the demand is never negative, and it never exceeds some upper limit; we can write down a number so large that no forecast error will ever be greater. However, it is usually convenient in the mathematical analysis not to have to worry about these physical upper and lower limits. My own experience indicates that the formulas used need only be designed to fit *most* of the errors that occur, and they allow only a negligible probability for very large errors.

In the formula stating the probability that a forecast error will be of any given amount, two numbers will usually be enough to tell us all we want to know about the whole distribution:

1. *The mean or the average value of the distribution of error.* Because with any reasonably good method of forecasting the *average* forecast error should be zero, we need not think of the mean explicitly. (It is of course, a good idea to check that the errors *do* have a zero mean.)

2. *The standard deviation.* This is a measure of how much the errors cluster around the mean value. If most of the errors are very small positive or negative numbers, the standard deviation will be small. If there are several large errors, the standard deviation will be larger, indicating a greater scatter or dispersion of the values.

Exhibit 9 shows the distribution of the errors in forecasting demand for Warmdot's products; the period covered is the same 48 months as in previous exhibits. Thus, for copper tubing, one standard deviation includes errors (in either direction) up to 150 units per month—units in this case being ten-foot lengths. Similarly, two standard deviations include errors of up to 300 units; and three standard deviations, errors of up to 450 units. (In the graphs, one standard deviation is shown by the lightest shade; two standard deviations extend through the bands of medium shade; and three, through the darkest bands). Such figures can be translated in two ways, whichever is more helpful to the forecaster:

Exhibit 9. Distribution of errors in forecasting demand for Warmdot products

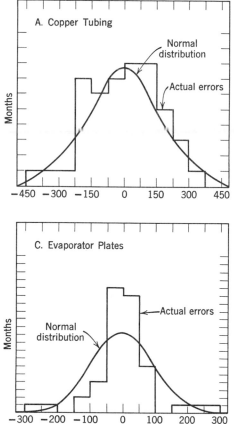

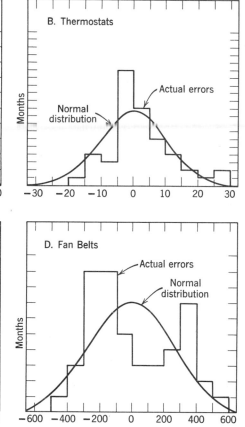

In only 2 or 3 months out of 48—or, extrapolated to a longer period, in only about 6 months out of 10 years, or only 5 times out of 100—will a forecast for copper tubing be off by more than 300 units. Or, stating it in terms of the central tendency rather than of the exceptions, about two thirds of the time actual performance will be within 150 units of the forecast; almost all of the time (95% of all forecasts), within 300 units. And, of course, over the long run, the differences will be distributed evenly between the high and the low sides.

In inventory control we are concerned principally with demand that is larger than forecast —i.e., which may be difficult to service. There is only one chance in a thousand that demand will be 450 units higher than forecast. There is one chance in fifty that it will be more than 300 units above forecast, and four chances in twenty-five that it will be as much as 150 units above forecast.

For the other three products the errors have other normal distributions, i.e., with other values of the standard deviation. Note that only for the fan belts does the normal distribution turn out to be a poor approximation of the actual errors.

Measuring Variability

The standard deviation is an observable property of the demand and the method used for forecasting. The allowance for error is usually proportional to this standard deviation. The number of standard deviations used (e.g., for safety stock) is called a safety factor, which can be adjusted as a matter of policy to give the desired level of service.

Since the normal distribution is evidently a satisfactory approximation to the distribution of errors in forecasting, all we need is an estimate of the standard deviation. With this it is possible to reproduce the whole distribution whenever needed in the derivation of a decision rule, such as one for determining the best level of safety stock.

For the normal distribution, the average value of the absolute difference between the actual current demand and the previous calculation of the expected demand is proportional to this standard deviation. Therefore we can proceed as follows:

1. Subtract the actual demand in the current month from the expected value that was calculated last month (which may be the result of smoothing the demand, or the statistical forecast modified by a judgment prediction).

2. Call this difference the *current deviation*.

3. The new mean absolute deviation can then be expressed in the formula:

New mean absolute deviation =

$$\alpha \,|\text{current deviation}| + (1 - \alpha)$$
$$(\text{old mean absolute deviation})$$

(The vertical bars surrounding "current deviation" indicate that the value is to be taken as positive without regard to actual sign.)

The standard deviation, which will appear in the derivation of safety-stock rules, is equal to 1.25 times the mean absolute deviation.

This method of estimating the standard deviation for each item is the only one that gives a practical current measurement of variation. The most sophisticated studies I have seen else-where depend on a special study of the distribution of error in the past demand, like the four years' history for Warmdot in Exhibit 9, which is used until the next study. (Some analysts assume a Poisson distribution, and take the standard deviation as equal to the square root of the average.) Now, for the first time, it is practical to measure the standard deviation routinely. This extension of exponential smoothing is actually being used in several large corporations today, and it gives a practical, sensitive, and current measurement of the variability of demand, *by item*.

Conclusion

To sum up, the points I have been trying to emphasize in the preceding discussion are:

New methods, especially adapted to modern high-speed electronic computers, can routinely measure the expected demand (including routine detection of, and correction for, trend).

For the first time it is possible and practical to measure the current distribution of error in the forecast, by item.

Sound inventory control systems require independent measurements of the expected demand, and of the distribution of error in these forecasts.

The expected demand, the distribution of forecast error, and decision rules must be used in combination. They are like the legs of a milking stool: you need them all.

23. *Inventory Control: How EOQ Can Help**

CLIFFORD M. BAUMBACK AND LEONARD J. KONOPA†

Despite the fact that the net sales of many firms have increased substantially during the past decade, profits have declined. In its efforts to combat this decline in profits, management has sought various ways to reduce operating costs, and inventory control has been one of the areas getting considerable attention.

Many of the inventory-control techniques that have evolved are quite elaborate and often require the utilization of a computer. For materials that are consumed repetitively, however, economical order quantity (EOQ) purchasing techniques have gained favor as practical inventory-control tools.

Trade magazines and books have discussed various economical order quantity techniques. Some of them have dealt with the application of the "square-root law" or formula; others have shown how to develop EOQ tables; still others have illustrated the graphic approach. It is possible, however, to tie these three approaches together, show how they are related, and provide a do-it-yourself kit for those who may not be familiar with the methods.

The Basic Concept

Theoretically, the most economical amount of material to purchase at a given price is that quantity at which the total cost per unit of purchasing and handling the material is at a *minimum*. This occurs when the unit cost of carrying the material in stores is *equal* to the unit cost of preparing the purchase order for the quantity of material.

* As condensed in *Management Review,* published by the American Management Association, April 1962.

† State University of Iowa.

Purchase Order Costs

To determine the cost of preparing a purchase order, the total operating expenses of the purchasing department are divided by the number of purchase orders written during a given period of time. For example, let us assume that a fictitious firm, the Hawkeye Manufacturing Company, has a purchasing department with total operating expenses of $75,000 per annum. If this department writes 10,000 purchase orders a year, its cost of preparing each order is $7.50 ($75,000/10,000).

The purchase cost per unit of material on any given order decreases as the amount of the material purchased increases. When 100 units of material are requested, the per-unit preparation cost is 7.5 cents per unit ($7.50/100). For 200 units of material, the per-unit cost of preparing the purchase order is 3.75 cents ($7.50/200). Column 3 in the table on page 173 shows Hawkeye's purchase-order cost per unit of material for various order quantities, from 100 to 780 units.

Inventory Carrying Costs

There are two types of cost involved in carrying inventory: (1) taxes, insurance, and interest on average inventory investment, and (2) storage charges.

Each company must determine its particular rate of inventory investment. The Hawkeye Manufacturing Company estimates its rate of taxes, insurance, and interest on inventory investment at 8 per cent per year. If we assume that Hawkeye is buying steel plate at $7.00 per unit, the investment cost of holding this steel plate in storage for one year would be 56 cents ($7.00 × 8 per cent). Since steel plate is being used continuously in production, however, the stock on hand gradually declines from a maximum amount toward zero units. This means that the average investment in inventory is only one-half of the total unit cost. The average annual investment per unit, therefore, is 28 cents (3.50 × 8 per cent).

Turning to storage costs, the cost per square foot of usable storage area must first be determined. The annual cost of storeroom operation is divided by the number of square feet of usable floor area for storage (the total storeroom floor area less the space for office, rest room, aisles, etc.). Let us assume that the annual cost of usable storage area in the Hawkeye Manufacturing Company amounts to two dollars per square foot.

Next, storage costs are allocated on the basis of the area occupied by the material in storage. In our illustration, Hawkeye buys steel plate that is 3½ feet wide, 12 feet long, and ¼ inch thick. The steel plates are ordinarily stacked to a maximum height of 5½ feet. This means that 264 units of steel plate can be stored in a 3½′ × 12′ area. At $2 per square foot, the total cost of storage space occupied by the steel plate is $84 ($2 per square foot × 42 square feet). The storage charge per unit, however, is 31.8 cents ($84/264 units). This unit cost is *not* "averaged" (as was inventory investment), because storage space cannot be assigned below the maximum requirements.

Carrying Cost and Turnover

The total carrying costs per year for each unit of steel plate is found by combining the above costs as follows:

28¢ — taxes, insurance, and interest on the average investment
31.8¢ — storage cost
───────
59.8¢ — total carrying cost

This inventory carrying charge, however, is the unit *cost per year;* the actual unit cost for a purchase order of a given size depends on the yearly inventory turnover rate. For purposes of illustration, let us assume that 20,000 units of the material (steel plates) are normally needed (for production or for sale) each year. If the material is ordered in lots of 100 units each, the inventory will "turn over" 200 times a year (20,000/100), each unit remaining in

storage for only 1/200th of a year. Thus, the realized inventory carrying charge per unit on an order of this size would be .299 cents (1/200 × 59.8 cents). On the other hand, if the material is ordered in 200-unit lots, the inventory turnover rate is 100 times a year. This is only half the turnover rate for the smaller order of 100 units, hence the unit inventory carrying charge for an order of this size is twice as large. Similar calculations are made for purchase orders of 300 units, 400 units, and other purchase-order sizes.

The Tabular Approach

The tabular approach to the determination of the most economical order quantity is given in Table 1. Column 1 represents various sizes of purchase orders, ranging from 100 units to 780 units per order. In column 2, the percentage increases in the number of units purchased over the 100-unit lot size are expressed in decimals. A purchase order for 120 units, for instance, is 20 per cent larger than a purchase order for 100 units; for purposes of convenience in computation, this percentage increase is expressed as a factor of 1.20 in column 2.

Column 3 indicates the unit preparation costs for purchase orders of various sizes. Since the cost is $7.50 to prepare a purchase order, the unit charge for an order of 100 units is 7.5 cents. Tripling the number of units per order would reduce the unit cost to 2.5 cents.

The inventory carrying charges per unit are shown in column 4. As discussed above, they total .299 cents per unit when 100 units are purchased at one time. Since inventory carrying charges vary with the rate of inventory turnover, the data in column 4 are derived by multiplying .299 cents by the respective factor in column 2.

The total unit cost in column 5 is the sum of the unit preparation cost and the unit carrying cost, as given in columns 3 and 4.

Determining EOQ

An examination of the table reveals that the inventory carrying cost per unit increases as the amount of material ordered goes up. Conversely, the order-preparation cost per unit declines as the number of units ordered increases. The

Table 1. *Unit Cost Data, Showing Most Economical Order Quantity*

(1) Number of Units	(2) % Increase over 100-unit lot, expressed as a decimal	(3) Preparation Costs per Unit, in ¢ (7.500 ÷ column 2)	(4) Carrying Charges per Unit, in ¢ (.299 x column 2)	(5) Total Unit Cost in ¢
100	1.00	7.500	.299	7.799
120	1.20	6.250	.359	6.609
140	1.40	5.357	.410	5.776
160	1.60	4.688	.478	5.166
180	1.80	4.167	.538	4.705
200	2.00	3.750	.598	4.348
220	2.20	3.409	.658	4.067
240	2.40	3.125	.718	3.843
260	2.60	2.885	.777	3.662
280	2.80	2.679	.837	3.516
300	3.00	2.500	.897	3.397
320	3.20	2.344	.957	3.301
340	3.40	2.206	1.017	3.223
360	3.60	2.083	1.076	3.159
380	3.80	1.974	1.136	3.110
400	4.00	1.875	1.196	3.071
420	4.20	1.786	1.256	3.042
440	4.40	1.705	1.316	3.021
460	4.60	1.630	1.375	3.005
480	4.80	1.563	1.435	2.998
500	5.00	1.500	1.495	2.995
▶ *501*	*5.01*	*1.497*	*1.497*	*2.994*
520	5.20	1.442	1.555	2.997
540	5.40	1.389	1.615	3.004
560	5.60	1.339	1.674	3.013
580	5.80	1.293	1.734	3.027
600	6.00	1.250	1.794	3.044
620	6.20	1.210	1.854	3.064
640	6.40	1.172	1.914	3.086
660	6.60	1.136	1.973	3.109
680	6.80	1.103	2.033	3.136
700	7.00	1.071	2.093	3.164
720	7.20	1.042	2.153	3.195
740	7.40	1.014	2.213	3.227
760	7.60	.987	2.272	3.259
780	7.80	.962	2.332	3.294

most economical order quantity is that quantity at which these two costs, shown in columns 3 and 4, are equal. It is 501 units of steel plate in this illustration.

The most economical order quantity can also be determined from column 5. It is the quantity at which the total cost per unit of purchasing and handling the material is at a *minimum*. In practice, of course, the actual amount ordered would be rounded off at 500 units.

The Graphic Approach

For those who prefer graphs, the data from the table can be shown in graphic form. Again, the most economical order quantity is derived at that point where the unit carrying costs equal the unit preparation costs, and where the total unit cost of purchasing and handling the material is at a minimum.

Formula Approach

A third approach is to use the "square-root law" in determining the most economical order quantity. The formula can be expressed most simply by the notation:

$$Q = \sqrt{\frac{PN}{C}}, \text{ in which}$$

Q = the most economical order quantity in units

P = the preparation cost of one order in dollars

N = the total number of units of material required per year

C = the carrying costs per unit per year

Using the values that formed the basis for the construction of the table and the graph, it is found that

$$Q = \sqrt{\frac{(\$7.50)(20,000)}{.598}}$$
$$= \sqrt{250,836}$$
$$= 501, \text{ or approximately 500 units}$$

Quite often the practitioner will use the latter approach and plug his data directly into the formula. Although there are many variations of the "square-root law," in the final analysis these variations contain the fundamental relationships expressed in the simplified version,

$$Q = \sqrt{\frac{PN}{C}}.$$

Limitations

Whether or not the practitioner prefers the tabular, the graphic, or the formula approach, he should be familiar with the limitations of this technique. First of all, the material being purchased must be an item that is used repetitively in production. Second, annual consumption of the item must be forecast accurately. Third, the firm must have sufficient cost data with which to estimate valid carrying and preparation costs. Fourth, if either the amount of the material consumed annually or the inventory carrying costs should change significantly, so also will the most economical order quantity. Fifth, in some instances the amount of money tied up in inventory may actually increase. Finally, the derived EOQ figure is not precise, but merely an approximation, and it is subject to limitations of averaging and many simplifications. Despite these limitations, however, the techniques do aid in determining economical order quantities when used with care, and they are far more reliable than intuitive guesses or seat-of-the-pants decisions.

24. *Marketing Time Lags: Their Impact on Logistics**

J. L. HESKETT†

There are basically two major categories of marketing time lags, those associated with the physical handling of goods and the transmission and processing of demand-supply information. They are incurred at each link in an interlocking chain of supply cycles connecting customers and suppliers in a distribution channel.

Physical Handling of Goods

Delays in the physical handling of goods are self-explanatory. They have received an overwhelming amount of attention in recent years. The development of air freight, containerization, and systems of coordinated transportation typify efforts to reduce physical handling time lags.

Demand–Supply Information Transmission

Demand–supply information received by suppliers is imperfect at best. Much of this imperfection is explained by the great interval of elapsed time between the sale of an item to an ultimate consumer and the knowledge of the sale on the part of each supplier of the item in the channel.

Visualize a retail firm in a channel of distribution. The first time lag created here is the delay between the sale of an item and the time when an order is prepared to replace the item. The actual magnitude of the interval depends upon the size of the retailer's inventory, the rapidity with which items are sold, and the inventory level at which a re-order takes place. Order transmission to a supplier constitutes a second lag in time.

Only in isolated cases have attempts been made to create a new, more direct means of transmitting demand–supply information, making no use of the customer order. These have included the use of warranty coupons to be returned by the ultimate customer to a distributor or manufacturer. Inventory audits have served somewhat the same purpose. In the past, both have involved rather lengthy delays mostly outside the control of the user of the information.

Importance of the Problem

According to one source, costs of maintaining inventories average 25 per cent of the value of the average annual inventory in the Nation's warehouses and stockpiles.[1] If this is the case, the annual bill for inventory maintenance is currently over 23 billion dollars.[2] This is approximately 3.1 per cent of the combined sales of manufacturers, wholesalers, and retailers in our economy.[3] The wide swings in economic cycles which are completely obscured by statistical averages lead to even greater total costs, in terms of ill-used economic resources, than those cited above.

In individual industries, effective distribution is based in large measure on the financial health of the middleman. Just as suppliers currently assist their customers at all channel levels in their promotional efforts, they should be aware of the need for assisting customers in matters of business logistics. An exploration of the effects of various competitive strategies, wherever they

* Reprinted by permission from the *Journal of Marketing,* National quarterly publication of the American Marketing Association, 1961.

† Harvard University.

[1] Leon P. Alford (ed.), *Production Handbook* (New York: Ronald Press, 1944), p. 397.

[2] U. S. Department of Commerce, *Statistical Abstract of the United States, 1961* (Washington, D. C.: U. S. Government Printing Office, 1961), p. 494.

[3] *Ibid.*

are maintained in a channel of distribution, will allow a supplier to apply effective inventory strategies in his own firm and supply management assistance to his middlemen-customers as well. If conceived as a project encompassing an entire channel of distribution, the end result will benefit not only individual firms, but the economy as a whole.

Need for Direction

American business firms are spending a great deal of money to reduce physical handling time lags. There is little definitive information which indicates that the attack on this type of lag promises opportunities for reducing inventory levels and fluctuations per dollar of cost any greater than those to be realized by an improved system of demand-supply information transmission. Until this question is solved for various industries and individual firms utilizing a great variety of channels of distribution, little real progress will be made toward a rational allocation of funds to effect the greatest improvement in the physical distribution of goods at the lowest comparative incremental cost.

Clearly, we need to know more about the nature of the physical distribution channels and buyer and seller behavior under competitive conditions in the United States. It is with the purpose of providing some insight into human behavior in the physical distribution channel that the following and other experiments are being conducted today.

The Experiment

Extensive experiments to provide information about inventory levels and fluctuations and demand patterns under a variety of conditions have been conducted by Forrester.[4] His reported work was based on a computer program designed from observations of a channel of distribution. Observed buyer-seller behavior, in terms of time lags, was described in the program. The program was then subjected to varying levels of ultimate demand, under which sales and inventory behavior was observed.

Unlike Forrester's experiments, the one reported below utilized a handscored, functional

[4] Jay W. Forrester, "Industrial Dynamics, A Major Breakthrough for Decision Makers," *Harvard Business Review,* XXXVI (July–August, 1958), pp. 37–66.

management game. Competition of two manufacturers was introduced. Human behavior was observed directly as participants changed inventory management policies to meet changing situations under competitive conditions. The channel of distribution described by the experiment was not meant to portray any one channel currently in existence, although it may have closely resembled many.

Hypotheses

All hypotheses initially established for the study pertained only to the channel of distribution described in Figures 1 and 2. They were four in number:

1. A basic improvement in the amount and type of demand-supply information available to manufacturers and wholesalers can be just as effective in reducing inventory levels and fluctuations, and in improving customer service, as the actual reduction of physical handling time lags.

2. The over all level of inventory in a channel of distribution is not reduced proportionately to a given reduction in the total time lag between the realization of ultimate demand and its supply.

3. Cycles in inventory levels can be self-generating. That is, even with no change in customer demand at the retail level, inventory cycles will continue to occur at all levels in a channel.

4. Fluctuations in inventory levels will increase as one moves nearer the source of supply, in this case the manufacturer.

Research Design

A "before-after with control" research design was used in the experiment.

Three groups of students carried out the exercise. All were M.B.A. candidates with a variety of fields of interest, including marketing and transportation. None had received planned instruction in inventory control immediately prior to, or in connection with, the play of the exercise.

In each group, students represented the firms shown in Figure 1. In the exercise, two competing products, A and B, were manufactured by separate and competing manufacturers and distributed through identical channels of four wholesalers and twelve retailers. Each group carried out forty plays, the equivalent of forty weeks of operation.

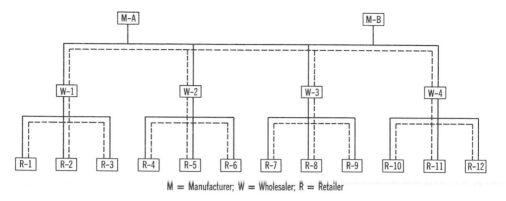

FIG. 1. Type, number, and organization of firms in channel of distribution described in inventory management game.

Each retailer within a group was fed a different customer demand pattern, based on random numbers selected from a distribution with a mean of 8. In other words, the average sale for each retailer in any week was designed to be 8 units throughout the exercise and in all three groups. Corresponding retailers in each of the three groups received exactly the same demand pattern; for example, Retailer One in Group One experienced the same week-to-week demand as Retailer One in Group Two.

Time lags described in the exercise are shown in Figure 2. As indicated, only the lags between receipt of the orders and delivery of products (i.e., physical handling time lags) were known. From production line to retailer and ultimate customer time lags in this half of the supply cycle totalled five weeks. The amount of elapsed time between a sale and the placement of an order to replenish units sold was determined in each case by the individual manager.

At the half-way point in the exercise, or after twenty plays:

1. No change was made in the rules for Group One, the control group.

2. The playing rules for the manufacturer and four wholesalers of Product A only in Group Two were changed as follows: "During the next period of play you will receive a 33 per cent sample of each week's actual sales at the retail level. In other words, four of the twelve retailers selling Product A will report their sales directly to you weekly. In addition, these same retailers will report their weekly ending inventories to you. Each of the retailers in this systematically drawn sample is supplied by a different wholesaler. All other rules and objectives remain unchanged."[5]

3. The operating rules for the manufacturer and four wholesalers of Product A only in Group Three were changed as follows: "During the next period of play wholesalers will be able to receive goods from the manufacturer of Product A immediately after ordering them, instead of waiting for them for two weeks after notification of delivery. The procedure change will be this: As usual, wholesalers will be asked to place their orders for Product A before receiving retailer orders for the current week. However, if the manufacturer of Product A has the ordered goods in stock, he will be able to place them in your hands immediately, meaning that you can fill current retail orders out of goods ordered from the manufacturer before current order levels (from retail customers) became known. All other rules and objectives remain unchanged."[6]

[5] Supplementary instructions for Group Two.
[6] Supplementary instructions for Group Three.

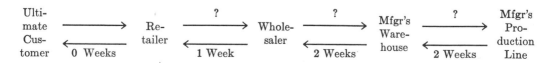

FIG. 2. Time lags in the channel of distribution described in inventory management game.

Mechanics of Play

To the extent possible, play was designed to simulate actual conditions of business. Ways in which this was attempted included:

1. Allowing any system or policy of inventory control which the individual manager might wish to put into practice.

2. Emphasizing the competitive aspects of play, with the ultimate objective of realizing the greatest profit on operations.

3. Prohibiting communication between managers at any one level in the channel of distribution, or between players of different groups.

4. Placing continuous pressure on the players to make rapid decisions. Forty decisions were required in less than 120 minutes once actual play began.

5. Requiring all managers to keep their own inventory control "books."

6. Leaving open, in the minds of the players, the question of shifts in demand patterns at the retail level.

7. Giving no hints about the length of play, thus reducing abnormal behavior near the end.

8. Penalizing retailers for allowing "out-of-stock" situations to develop. This was done by transferring one-half the amount of unfilled demand from the account in question to that of the retailer with the next largest consecutive identification number for two consecutive weeks following the "stock-out." The other half of the unfilled demand was shifted for two successive weeks to the second product carried by the same retailer, on the premise that a retailer with a temporary "stock-out" could induce a customer to buy a brand other than that initially requested 50 per cent of the time.

Compromises with Reality

Compromises with reality, other than those inherent in the design of the exercise, included:

1. The necessity of seating all players in one room with no partitions between them, thus allowing visual observation between players. To alleviate this shortcoming, completed order and delivery forms were required on each play, even when no units were being ordered. These orders were then passed face down between players where necessary.

2. Excluding economic indices from consideration by the players. This was necessary in order to facilitate measurement of the variables actually tested.

3. Placing "bookkeeping" responsibility in the hands of individual managers, allowing math errors to foul the decision-making process. Human errors were natural and desirable to the extent that undetected errors did not affect the performance of other firms by creating impossible stock situations.

4. Confining play to "paper" transactions. No physical transfer of units was possible because of: (a) limited time for play and (b) the visual communication which such transfers would make possible in an unpartitioned room. Consequently, on several occasions errors of bookkeeping were not rectified until after an impossible (i.e., the shipment of goods when none were actually in stock) decision had been made. In the few cases in which they occurred, they were corrected when discovered.

5. The oversimplification, in terms of numbers of firms, of the channel of distribution. Thus, one or two firms making major changes in inventory policy could affect over all inventory quantities at any level in the channel from time to time.

6. The limitation of product competition to two products. This greatly simplified the inventory management task, reducing the number of unintentional errors by managers.

To hold playing errors to a minimum, the written description of the exercise was first passed out to the participants one week in advance. At the beginning of the period of play, a fifteen-minute verbal orientation was given, during which players were given the opportunity to ask questions about the mechanics of play. A "dry run" of several plays then followed, with individual assistance available to the players. A final question and answer period of about five minutes was allowed before play actually began. After the beginning of play, individual tally sheets kept by the participants were checked for accuracy from time to time.

Research Results

Effectiveness of Improved Demand–Supply Information

Inventory Levels. Information in Table 1 indicated that those wholesalers allowed a two-week reduction in time lag between the placement of orders and the receipt of goods (Group Three) reduced their inventories 32.2 per cent below previous levels. Further, the reduction surpassed the 10.9 per cent drop for wholesalers given instead current information (comparable to a two- to three-week reduction in the transmission time of sales data between retailers and wholesalers) about weekly sales and ending inventory levels of a 33 per cent sample of retail outlets. Even more surprising, wholesalers with improved demand–supply information performed less well than those with no aid of any kind, which were able to reduce their inventories by 24.4 per cent as time progressed.

Manufacturer inventory levels for Product A were reduced 46.7 per cent with a two-week reduction in physical handling time. Only a 17.7 per cent reduction occurred when improved demand–supply information was provided. Both of these figures, drawn from Table 1, compare to a 43.1 per cent reduction in manufacturer inventory levels with no change in conditions.

Marked reductions in inventory levels for both Product A and B by Group One indicates that a learning curve was in effect in the problem. After subtracting the variance probably caused by the learning curve, it became apparent that the only improvement in inventory levels after the introduction of test variables occurred among wholesalers in Group Three.

Observation of play suggested that wholesalers and manufacturers in Group Two were not able to make optimum use of the added demand–supply information given them because they didn't have time to use the information, and they weren't sure how much trust to place in it. In this respect, the exercise was probably little different than many actual management situations.

Because no changes in the ultimate demand pattern were allowed to occur, it was not possible to judge the effectiveness of increased information in communicating changes in the level of ultimate demand. The hindrances to the use of the information mentioned previously would probably have reduced its effectiveness even for the latter purpose.

Inventory Fluctuations. Fluctuations in inventory levels were measured by computing the standard deviation of samples of values chosen from the records of individual wholesalers and manufacturers. Performances during the first

and second halves of play were then compared under various conditions.

Among wholesalers, the greatest reduction in inventory fluctuations for both Products A and B resulted when no variable was introduced. Thus, it is likely that the mere introduction of a variable caused an unnatural inventory fluctuation over the relatively short period of time measured. Much the same was true for manufacturers, although reductions in fluctuations when information was supplied were slightly greater (23.2 per cent reduction in standard deviation for Product A, 54.6 per cent for Product B) than those for the control group (12.2 per cent for Product A, 50.2 per cent for Product B). A reduction in physical handling time lags caused a great disturbance in inventory levels of the manufacturer of Product A in Group Three, probably owing to the suddenness with which it occurred.

Level of Customer Service. The level of customer service afforded under all conditions of play was measured by: (1) the number of "stock-out" situations developing at each point in the channel and (2) the amount of lost business or unmet demand, in units, resulting therefrom. This information is shown in Table 2.

Although the level of customer service appeared high under conditions of improved demand–supply information transmission (Group Two), it was even higher among a comparable group of firms when such information was not supplied (Group One). Before any long-run improvement in customer service could occur under conditions of reduced physical handling time lags (Group Three), the reduction itself caused several out-of-stock situations among wholesalers and manufacturers, thus obscuring any comparison of service.

Evidence appears inconclusive to either support or reject the thesis that either of the described changes resulted in any change in the quality of customer service.

Time Lag Change vs. Inventory Level Change

In order to measure the comparative effect of time lag reductions on the over all level of inventory in an entire channel of distribution, it was first necessary to measure the extent to which the total time lag was reduced in the experiment.

Table 1. *Amount and Variation in Inventory, Each Level on Marketing Channel*

Sample No.	Group No.[b]	Product	Half of Play[c]	Retailers Average Inventory (units)	Retailers 2nd Half as % of 1st	Wholesalers Average Inventory (units)	Wholesalers Average Inventory 2nd Half as % of 1st	Wholesalers Average Standard Deviation[d] (units)	Wholesalers Average Standard Deviation, 2nd Half as % of 1st	Manufacturers Average Inventory (units)	Manufacturers Average Inventory 2nd Half as % of 1st	Manufacturers Average Standard Deviation (units)	Manufacturers Average Standard Deviation, 2nd Half as % of 1st
1	1	A	1st	14.8	N.A.	82.1	N.A.	27.4	N.A.	186.3	N.A.	40.3	N.A.
2	1	A	2nd	16.2	109.5%	62.1	75.6%	18.7	68.3%	100.6	56.9%	36.4	87.8%
3	1	B	1st	14.7	N.A.	86.7	N.A.	29.0	N.A.	319.8	N.A.	83.5	N.A.
4	1	B	2nd	17.2	117.0	67.3	77.6	20.2	69.7	234.1	73.3	43.6	49.8
5	2	A	1st	15.3	N.A.	103.5	N.A.	36.7	N.A.	173.8	N.A.	68.2	N.A.
6	2	A	2nd	15.8	103.2	89.5	86.5	31.4	85.7	143.0	82.3	52.3	76.8
7	2	B	1st	15.0	N.A.	94.7	N.A.	26.7	N.A.	139.2	N.A.	102.8	N.A.
8	2	B	2nd	15.7	104.5	84.1	89.4	34.3	127.7	191.5	137.5	46.7	45.4
9	3	A	1st	18.2	N.A.	94.0	N.A.	28.5	N.A.	248.4	N.A.	32.9	N.A.
10	3	A	2nd	18.5	101.6	63.6	67.7	20.4	71.7	132.3	53.3	89.3	271.0
11	3	B	1st	17.5	N.A.	116.7	N.A.	32.8	N.A.	266.2	N.A.	86.4	N.A.
12	3	B	2nd	17.3	99.0	78.5	67.3	25.9	79.0	289.1	108.4	66.8	77.3

[a] Samples were chosen randomly from plays 4 through 17 (for first half measurements) and plays 24 through 37 (for second half measurements) to reduce the effects on measurements of "starts" and "stops" in play; sample sizes for retailers and wholesalers were 40, for manufacturers 10.

[b] Group No. 1 served as a control group; Group No. 2 played the second half with reduced demand-supply information delays; Group No. 3 played the second half with reduced physical handling delays.

[c] The first half of play included plays 1 through 20, the second plays 21 through 40.

[d] Shown as the mean of the standard deviation measurement for four samples of wholesaler stocks (for 10 observations each) from the mean of their individual samples.

Table 2. Level of Customer Service Under Varying Conditions

Group and Product	Half of Play	Retailers: Stock Outs	Retailers: Lost Business (units)	Wholesalers: Stock Outs	Wholesalers: Unmet Demand	Manufacturer: Stock Outs	Manufacturer: Unmet Demand	Total: Stock Outs	Total: Unmet Demand
One, A	1st	6	71	2	31	0	0	8	102
One, A	2nd	6	49	2	24	0	0	8	73
One, B	1st	9	78	1	9	0	0	10	87
One, B	2nd	7	53	2	20	0	0	9	73
Two, A	1st	1	6	0	0	0	0	1	6
Two, A	2nd[a]	4	39	1	7	0	0	5	46
Two, B	1st	7	63	0	0	2	30	9	93
Two, B	2nd	6	52	1	16	0	0	7	68
Three, A	1st	6	51	0	0	2	87	8	138
Three, A	2nd[b]	3	24	2	35	2	55	7	114
Three, B	1st	6	54	0	0	0	0	6	54
Three, B	2nd	9	114	2	10	0	0	11	121
Total		70	654	13	152	6	172	89	978

[a] Group, product, and period for which demand–supply information transmission time was reduced.

[b] Group, product, and period for which physical handling time lag was reduced.

As pictured in Figure 2, the total physical handling time lag from the initiation of a production order to the receipt of the item by the ultimate customer was five weeks. But this only constituted the "feed-out" segment of the cycle. "Feed-ins," in the form of order placements, required time as well.

"Feed-in" time could only be estimated as one-half the number of weeks' sales on hand, less the minimum re-order point. For optimum retailer order quantities in the experiment, "feed-in" time probably approximated ½(3–1), or one week. Comparable times for wholesaler and manufacturer order transmissions were approximately one-half week and one-half week, respectively. Thus, total order transmission time for optimum performance was two weeks. It is likely that it ranged from three to five weeks in actual play. On this basis, the in-and-out time lag approximated 8 to 10 weeks.

Compared to the total marketing time lag, improved demand–supply information transmission brought about a 30 per cent to 62.5 per cent (three- to five-week) reduction in elapsed time. A two-week reduction in physical handling time lag, on the other hand, constituted a 20 per cent to 25 per cent reduction in the total for the channel.

Random samples of average channel inventory values were selected from weeks numbered 4 through 17 and 24 through 37 (to reduce the effects of "starts" and "stops" in play). They yielded the information shown in Table 3.

A comparison of Sample 3 with Samples 1 and 4 in Table 3 provided a range of estimate of the amount of inventory reduction attributable to a three-to-five-week decrease in the time lag for information transmission in the channel. This range was from 0 per cent (actually a negative value for Sample 3 vs. Sample 1) to 18.7 per cent (Samples 3 vs. 4). This range fell well below the estimated time lag reduction of 30 per cent to 62.5 per cent.

A comparison of Sample 5 with Samples 1 and 6 yielded a range of estimate of the amount of inventory reduction attributable to a two-week decrease in the time lag for physical handling. This range was from 1.8 per cent (Samples 5 vs. 1) to 16 per cent (Samples 5 vs. 6). This range fell well below the estimated time lag reduction of 20 per cent to 25 per cent.

Self-Generating Cycles

Information that was graphed indicated that cycles in inventory levels are likely to occur even under conditions where ultimate customer demand remains constant for prolonged periods of time. For this measurement, only the performance of the control group was used to eliminate effects of artificially introduced variables.

Table 3.   Change in Average Level of Inventory in Channel Under Varying Conditions

Group and Product (By Sample No.)	First Half of Play (Average Inventory in Units)	Second Half of Play (Average Inventory in Units)	Per Cent Second Was of First Half
1. Group One, Product A	711	531	74.7%
2. Group One, Product B	857	699	81.6
3. Group Two, Product A	820	701[a]	85.5
4. Group Two, Product B	686	722	105.1
5. Group Three, Product A	830	609[b]	73.4
6. Group Three, Product B	934	815	87.3

[a] Group, product, and period for which demand–supply information transmission time was reduced.

[b] Group, product, and period for which physical handling time lag was reduced.

Only minor fluctuations of little more than 20 per cent above and below average inventory occurred at the retail level for both Product A and B. However, wholesalers' inventory rose to 55 per cent above, and 35 per cent below, average levels for Product A during the same period. Comparable measurements for Product B were 45 per cent above and 40 per cent below the average inventory level. At one point, manufacturer's inventory rose to 62 per cent above average levels for the period and declined to 65 per cent below those same levels for Product A. Comparable statistics for manufacturer's stocks of finished goods for Product B were 42 per cent above and 48 per cent below average levels.

Visual examination of a graph indicated that the greatest interaction between inventory cycles occurred between wholesalers and manufacturers. Levels of the former varied inversely with those of the latter, as might be expected. Further, failure of manufacturers to contemplate changes in order levels of wholesalers resulted in manufacturers' cycles following those of wholesalers by about seven weeks. For probably the same reasons, fluctuations in wholesalers' inventories trailed those of retailers by roughly five weeks.

Inventory Fluctuation vs. Channel Level

Information presented suggested that greater percentage fluctuations in inventory levels could be found as one approached the source of supply. This was in part due to the relatively small quantity of physical inventory serving as a base for percentage fluctuation computations and to greater fluctuations in the volume of wholesalers' orders than in those at other points in the channel.

Conclusions

Validity of Hypotheses

A basic improvement in the timing, amount, and type of demand–supply information available to manufacturers and wholesalers was not as effective in reducing inventory levels as the actual reduction of physical handling time lags. Even under ideal conditions suggested above, it is doubtful whether the first part of hypothesis one would have proven correct. This was contrary to comparable findings by Forrester.[7] Information proved insufficient to assess the effects of variables on inventory fluctuations and quality of customer service. On the basis of the findings, hypothesis one could not be substantiated.

The over all level of inventory in a channel was not reduced proportionately to a reduction in the total time lag in the channel. This appeared to be the case whether a reduction was effected in information transmission time

[7] Forrester, *Op. Cit.*, pp. 47–48.

or in physical handling time. Thus, hypothesis two was accepted.

Cycles in inventory levels were found to be self-generating. That is, they occurred even with no variations in demand on the part of ultimate customers. Further, fluctuations appeared to become greater as one approached the initial source of supply. The findings thus supported hypotheses three and four, and were in general agreement with comparable findings by Forrester.[8]

Other Conclusions

The lack of time for decision-making in inventory management had definite effects on the calibre of the decision. Because of the design of the record-keeping forms used by the participants in the exercise, it was most natural for them to first record statistics and make decisions in the inventory management of Product A. Examination of records of twelve wholesalers in the experiment indicated that in nearly every case performance in the management of Product A was superior to that for Product B. If this relationship is multiplied many times over for the manager faced with the control of hundreds of items of inventory, it becomes apparent that, systematized inventory control is necessary at every level in a channel where improved performance is to be expected.

Especially at the wholesale level, performances in the management of inventories of both Products A and B were markedly similar, even where variables in the system were introduced for Product A but not for Product B. If consistent for repeated observations, this relationship could prove significant for manufacturers in a competitive situation. For it would mean that middlemen tend to gear their inventory control policy for all products to those products on which they receive the best supply service. Results of such action could force manufacturers of competing products to improve customer service or suffer the consequences of repeated distributor out-of-stock situations, and perhaps the loss of distributors.

Limitations of the Experiment

Measurement of isolated variables in a business experiment requires that other variables be held constant. Competition by means of pricing, advertising, and personal promotion was eliminated from the experiment described above. Unrealistic as the rules of the exercise might have seemed, it was this very feature of the experiment that allowed measurements impossible to obtain in many actual business situations.

The mere creation of a laboratory situation removed observed relationships from the realm of reality. The difficulty of assembling participants with backgrounds more closely approximating those of inventory controllers at actual retail, wholesale and manufacturer levels of distribution further reduced realism.[9]

Problems and expense of obtaining repeated observations of behavior under similar circumstances seriously limited claims of reliability for the experiment. No measures of statistical inference could thus be used effectively in assessing results.

Opportunities For Further Research

Despite the shortcomings of business games in research, it is likely that they will continue to provide knowledge about the effects of individual variables on management performance. Better yet, they may serve as a check on conclusions reached by other means.

What are some of the future opportunities in researching the problem described above by this method? The effects of a number of variables can be appraised to gain optimum insight into factors influencing inventory levels, inventory fluctuations, and customer service. Specifically how does time pressure affect the inventory management decision? To what degree does education in inventory control techniques improve management? What is the result obtained from eliminating or adding middlemen to a channel of distribution? How is behavior affected by a change in the costs of placing an order? What are effects of changes in the level of ultimate demand?

The first step in future research of this type is logically the observation, through case studies, of actual time lags and buyer–seller relationships in several marketing channels representative of products of widely differing characteristics. Second, experimentation under laboratory

[8] *Ibid.*, p. 45.

[9] Kalman J. Cohen and Eric Rhenman, "The Role of Management Games in Education and Research," *Management Science*, VII, January, 1961, pp. 131–166.

conditions should be based on observed relationships. Third, results of experimentation should be tested, to the extent possible, under actual business conditions. This repeated interchange of field and laboratory experimentation may develop a set of marketing principles hitherto impossible under more conventional techniques.

Section VI.   Movement Services

Of all the areas of physical distribution management, those of the transportation modes and services are perhaps the best known and possibly the least misconstrued by those in the physical distribution field. However, the meshing and coordination of movement costs with those incurred in other marketing pipeline activities is a frequently observed weakness that has not been given the attention that it deserves. Merrill J. Roberts' "Transport Dynamics and Distribution Management" neatly ties together for the reader the relationship of marketing and movement services. The other articles in this section deal with the characteristics of the several movement services modes, containerization, and shipper cooperatives.

25. Transport Dynamics and Distribution Management*

Merrill J. Roberts†

The drastic changes taking place in transportation today are presenting a great challenge to business management. Carriers and shippers must adapt to alterations in the marketing and the purchasing of transporation services; each group must accommodate to changes on both sides of the transaction.

For purposes of this article, transport dynamics is viewed in these terms: (1) transportation is changing on the supply side as a result of alterations in regulatory philosophy, management attitudes, and technology; (2) these changes in supply are being reinforced by improvements in the criteria governing transport purchasing decisions that spring from the progressively more refined and sophisticated approach to distribution system analysis. This discussion will focus primarily on changes, both actual and potential, in the pricing and marketing of transport services and on the trend toward a coordinated transport network. It will then attempt to indicate some of the implications of these developments for distribution systems and transport purchasing.

Pricing and Marketing

Since public and private responsibility both play a part in our transport system, new approaches to the pricing and marketing of transport services depend on reform of both regulatory and management policies. Policies initiated by carrier management, essentially private business management decisions, must be acceptable to regulatory authorities. The nature of the regulatory veto will, therefore, influence not only the formulation of, but also the disposition and implementation of specific management policies and decisions. It will, moreover, establish the general climate of decision-making and influence the degree and character of initiative that is exercised.

Although initiative does rest squarely with private management and the specifics of regulation do not provide the entire key to rate modernization, a favorable regulatory climate is a necessary condition, even if not a sufficient condition, for reform. Regulation should certainly not discourage, and might conceivably encourage, modernization programs designed to remove the monopoly features built into railroad rate structures in an earlier period and widely adopted by the common carrier trucking industry.

The Regulatory Environment

Many observers believe that by excessive restrictions on competitive rate reductions regulation has, in the recent past, unduly hampered private management in its efforts to eliminate the old value-of-service structures that are anachronistically predicted on commodity values. The Interstate Commerce Commission is guided in rate matters by a statutory provision known as the "rule of rate making." This provision was amended by the Transportation Act of 1958 in an apparent effort to remove the regulatory barriers impeding such rate reform.[1] But the 1958 amendment seems to have been an ambivalent and uncertain enactment. It encourages price competition by explicitly prohibiting the Commission from holding up the rates of one agency to protect the traffic and revenues of another; however, it also explicitly retains the national transportation policy strictures against "unfair and destructive competitive practices."

Clearly, the latitude allowed to management

* Reprinted by permission from *Business Horizons,* Fall, 1961.

† University of Pittsburgh.

[1] Public Law 85–625 (Aug. 12, 1958). 72 stat. 568.

in matters of pricing depends on the Commission's interpretation of this key phrase, and uncertainty reigns supreme. The Commission's approval of the reduced paint rates in Eastern Territory, which is regarded as something of a landmark case, does not provide a very accurate gauge of its interpretation.[2] In that instance, the reduced rates were calculated to increase the railroads' 5 per cent share to only 35 to 40 per cent of the traffic. Aiming as it does at less than half the traffic, this percentage does not begin to challenge the Commission's long-standing conception of "fair" market shares. One can only wonder what the answer would have been if the reductions had been calculated to maximize net revenues by capturing 75 or even 100 per cent of the traffic.

This uncertainty is reflected within the Commission itself. In a statement before a Senate Committee in June, 1960, Commissioner John Winchell said he *thought* that, since the 1958 amendment, the Commission had accorded more weight to management discretion in competitive rate making. Nor is there any unanimity among the Commissioners as to the appropriate interpretation of the 1958 amendment. In a recent case, they were sharply divided on an order requiring rail piggyback rates to be maintained at a level 6 per cent above corresponding truck-water (fishyback) and sea-train rates. Commissioner Howard Freas stated that in his view the order represented "umbrella" rate making of the type that the 1958 Act had specifically prohibited. The "Bartlett bill," introduced in the present Congress, has contributed to the uncertainty by proposing to reintroduce some of the restrictions that the 1958 amendment successfully eliminated.

Although there is evidence of some loosening up of regulatory restraints, it is questionable whether the existing statute as it is interpreted provides the latitude needed for the rather substantial revision of rates that many observers consider essential to an efficient and coordinated transport system. Rates designed to provide shippers with the lowest possible cost and, at the same time, to maximize net revenues for the pricing carriers should not be regarded as "unfair and destructive" because they capture the lion's share of a market. It seems clear that Congress must provide a firm and unambiguous statutory definition of proscribed competitive practices that reflects sound economic principles.

While regulation may be too restrictive to permit the full-scale readjustments that are required, the leeway appears to be generally sufficient to accommodate the sort of competitive reductions that rail management, the leader in these revisions, is presently prepared to adopt. John McMichael of the Traffic Executives Association, Eastern Railroads, reports that the Commission has accepted every one of the rate proposals sponsored by his group.[3] It must be recognized, however, that the boldness of the proposals has probably been tempered by a realistic assessment of the chances for approval.

Carrier Management Policy

At least as significant as any change in regulatory environment is the action taken by carrier managements under present conditions. The growing market consciousness of railroad managements is indeed encouraging; they have become far less inclined to throw service on the market on a take-it-or-leave-it basis. Former Commissioner Owen Clarke, now with the Chesapeake and Ohio Railway, recently told an American Management Association seminar:

". . . in the railroad industry today, we are looking upon shippers as *customers*. More and more in the future, the shipper's slightest wish will be our command (as long as we can make some profit out of it, of course!). We are all quite aware, I think, that this has not always been the predominant attitude among railroad managements in years past, and in some instances, perhaps, it still does not prevail. More and more, however, elements of the modern marketing concept are becoming recognized and accepted by railroad managements."[4]

The changed attitude is reflected in the market research activities recently instituted by the railroad rate committees in several territories

---

[2] *Paint and Related Articles—Official Territory,* I. & S. Docket No. 7027. Decided Aug. 27, 1959. Official (or Eastern) Territory generally embraces the area east of the Mississippi and north of the Ohio Rivers.

[3] Gardner C. Hudson, "Rate Men Ready for Action," *Railway Age,* CL (Jan. 16, 1961), p. 37.

[4] Owen Clarke, "The Rail Carriers," part of a symposium on "The Common Carriers' Part in Product Distribution" in *Management of the Physical-Distribution Function* (Report No. 49; New York: American Management Association, 1960), p. 52.

and by individual companies. This research delves into the economics of the industry producing the commodities whose rates are under scrutiny. It studies competitive relationships, pricing structures, and marketing problems, explicitly recognizing the relevance of total distribution systems for the selection and purchase of transport services. It also establishes close relationships with the shippers and receivers of the freight involved. A number of new rate adjustments have emerged from these activities. The Missouri Pacific has revised its rates on fruits and vegetables to counter exempt truck competition, and some Eastern railroads have reduced rates on insulators (up to 40 per cent), synthetic rubber (up to 30 per cent), and window glass (up to 40 per cent). The research organizations, both of the territorial committees and of the individual railroads, are currently studying many more commodities with a view to further reductions.

While these research efforts are of great importance not only as an indication of a changed attitude on the part of carrier managements but also for the specific rate reductions that they have produced, it is apparent that a commodity-by-commodity approach will be painfully slow. It is true that a certain deliberateness and caution are perhaps called for lest changes do more harm than good, and that the scope for change may in many cases be limited when profit effect is the criterion.[5] Many students of transportation, however, believe that the time of crisis for the railroad industry is close at hand and that its salvation as a private enterprise system hangs in the balance. This suggests a need for a systematic, far-reaching attack on rate modernization based on generalizations regarding transport market behavior as a supplement to the laborious commodity-by-commodity approach.

This generalized approach demands, in addition to inquiries about specific industries and commodities, more basic research into the character and structure of transport markets and costs. It would presumably be carried on at the industry or territorial (rather than company) level since the results would, one hopes,

be of general applicability for sound rate revision. It is the kind of research that the industry might well support in universities and other research centers. It would benefit carriers by hastening the process of reform; at the same time, it would reduce the extent of "selective rate cutting," which may be sound pricing policy (aside from the time problem) but which also has an odious ring in some Congressional committees and elsewhere. And certainly shippers have an interest in such research since it would implement and hasten needed rate readjustments that will improve distribution systems and throw light on market relationships that would be useful for their own transport purchasing decisions.

Other transport industries and firms are also engaging in market research activities. Many airlines have well-developed market research programs that have contributed to an understanding of integrated distribution systems. The REA Express has become a leader in this area and has recently instituted a free consulting service for shippers, which undertakes research to help shippers find out and then make known what they want and need. There is evidence, too, of a growing interest and awareness among motor carriers of the importance of such research, but as yet they have taken little action.

Rate Reductions

As a result of both regulatory reforms and more progressive management policies, transport markets are becoming more competitive. It is apparent from recent transport history that the number of rivals in a market is not the key determinant of its competitiveness; full-scale competition is a result of the aggressiveness of the rivals, which is manifested in their efforts to outdo one another not only in services offered, but also in prices charged. The chief outcome of increased competition on the price front is rate reductions. One railroad official is quoted as saying that, despite the substantial increase in costs and in the general price level since 1946, many rail rates have dropped to 1946 levels.[6] Some examples of drastic cuts in Eastern Territory were cited previously. Clearly, this intensified price competition will bring about especially sharp reductions in rates on

---

[5] For example, if a rate is $1.00 per hundred pounds and out-of-pocket cost is $.80, the revenue contribution or profit is $.20. A rate reduction of 10 per cent to $.90 will not cause gross revenues to decline if volume is thereby increased by only 11 per cent, whereas it would require a doubling of sales to equal the present profit from this traffic.

[6] Kenneth U. Flood, "Questions in Company-Operated Transport," *Harvard Business Review*, XXXIX (January–February, 1961), pp. 128–29.

manufactured commodities as the old value-of-service structures erode; these rates, based on commodity values and born of railroad monopoly, are the most patently obsolete, particularly where proprietary truck transportation exists as a real alternative.

It should be noted that rates need not decrease absolutely to make transport services a better bargain. The new competitiveness is reflected to a considerable extent in rates that are lower in a relative sense but not necessarily in an absolute one. This relative lowering occurs either when the quality of service increases more than rates, or when increases in transport prices fall behind those on other goods and services.

Relative reductions of the latter sort are reflected in the annual indexes of rail rates published by the ICC for a number of the more significant commodity classes.[7] Between 1950 and 1957, the consumer price index rose by nearly 20 per cent; during this same period many rail rates increased by less than 10 per cent according to the Commission's indexes, including rates on such important commodities as baled cotton, crude petroleum, iron and steel pipe and fittings, cement, paperboard, fibreboard and pulpboard, and canned foods.

Incentive Rates. A form of reduction that merits special attention because of its increasing employment is the incentive rates of the railroads. These rates are designed to achieve the economies of full vehicle loading by sharing the cost savings with shippers. A classic example is the reduction on paint and related articles that became effective in Eastern Territory in October, 1959. This scale provided incentives calculated to encourage loadings up to 90,000 pounds in lieu of the prevailing level of less than 30,000 pounds.

Many of the recent railroad rate reductions embrace this same type of incentive feature, including the Eastern Territory reductions on insulators, window glass, and synthetic rubber. To the extent that the rate reductions are effective, their primary impact is to cause a shift in traffic among the modes of transportation. This shift dictates alterations in distribution systems to the extent that it is attributable to the incentive feature. Substantially larger shipments are

apt to occasion heavier inventory costs at the producing plant, in transit, and in the hands of customers. Such a shift not only requires alteration in inventory policy, but as a secondary effect may well lead to heavier warehousing requirements. The ultimate effect is a distribution system characterized by more fixed costs and a loss of flexibility—the reverse of the trends of the past several decades. Carriers must take account of shipper resistance to this development in assessing the potential of incentive rates.

Some of these developments are apparent in the paint industry's response to the new rates on its products. According to one major producer, traffic allocations from at least some of its plants (and on some of its product lines) reflect a substantial shift from truck movement to movement by rail. Rail shipments during 1960 from one plant totaled 170 carloads, which were substituted because of the rate change for 386 truckloads. From another plant, the 1960 rail volume was double the 1959 level. One 80,000-pound rail shipment, instead of three truckloads, is now dispatched weekly to a major receiver in the South. It is important to note, however, that shipments in some product lines and from some plants have been largely undisturbed, showing the influence of nontransport considerations in transport purchasing decisions.

Agreed Charges. Another form of reduction having special implications for distribution systems is agreed charges. Contract rates of this sort, which require shipper commitments of a major share of tonnage, are highly successful competitive devices in Canada but have not yet received regulatory sanction in this country. The Soo Line and other participating companies have put before the Commission a contract rate that would apply on steel or wrought iron pipe and tubing where at least 90 per cent of the tonnage of participating shippers is routed by the rail carriers. Although the Commission recently disapproved a New York Central contract rate on moving rugs and carpeting from Amsterdam, N.Y. to Chicago, it indicated that the veto applied only to the specific proposal and not to the rate innovation itself.

The viability of these rates should be settled promptly on the basis of rational economic criteria rather than legal precedent. If they do receive the Commission's blessing, the associated rate reductions would, like all good things in life, come at a price. Long-term commitments of substantial portions of a company's

[7] Interstate Commerce Commission, *Indexes of Average Freight Rates on Railroad Carload Traffic, 1949–1957* (Washington: U. S. Gov't Printing Office, August, 1959), pp. 1–12.

output would essentially freeze the transport component of the distribution system. The resulting loss of flexibility may be costly as other components of the system—some of them rather volatile—continue to change.

For example, the costs of maintaining inventory may increase, thus dictating shipment by truck rather than by rail. What is a sound transport component when the contract is signed may later prove to be otherwise. Subsequent failure to deliver the required tonnage will then impose penalties on that portion already shipped by rail, and, in retrospect, the use of rail may not represent the best choice at the higher (noncontract) rates.

Rate Increases

We have thus far emphasized rate reductions. Railroad traffic officers, however, are becoming concerned about the need for increases where rates are unduly low. The most obvious examples of such rates are, of course, those that fail to cover the out-of-pocket costs of movement. An examination of the studies on revenue contribution by the Commission's staff confirms that these deficit commodities are, as one would expect, frequently products of the extractive industries, generally the raw materials and semiprocessed inputs of manufacturing industries. There are undoubtedly many other cases in which rates, while not producing deficits, exceed out-of-pocket costs by unduly low margins.[8] These rates may have been economically tenable in earlier years, and, on the whole, they served a developmental purpose in that they encouraged the flow of commerce. Nor were they particularly inconsistent with private profit interests when combined with highly profitable outbound hauls. Now, however, their sanction has weakened with the relatively full economic development of the country and the loss of profitable outbound hauls to competitive modes.

Coordinating the System

The need to effect a fully integrated transport system to meet shippers' requirements and to reduce distribution costs becomes increasingly apparent with the development of more refined (and integrated) distribution system analyses; these often dictate the use of combinations of carriers that are not always available.

Containerization

Because piece-by-piece rehandling is so costly an operation, full transport coordination requires a device to effect interchange economically and expeditiously. The essential tool for this interchange is the container, and the new interest in the old concept of containerization indicates a recognition of its clear-cut advantages, many of which are not restricted to its coordinative possibilities. Multiple-agency service is not required for realizing such benefits as reduced losses from pilferage and damage, faster turnaround for mobile equipment, reductions in warehouse expenses and in packaging costs, and improved customer services.

The integration that has been effected in sea-land and rail-motor services, with the highway van usually serving as the container, is a start in the development and use of this essential tool of coordination. Piggyback services, though still in their infancy, are generally regarded as the forerunners of what is required for a mature containerization system. Despite the comparative newness of these devices, notable gains have been achieved both in the total volume of integrated traffic and in the benefits to shippers. Piggyback loadings in 1960 were up one-third over 1959 and were double the 1958 figure.[9] One company is reported to be saving $100,000 a year just on its Chicago-Denver shipments by eliminating rehandling in Denver.

Certainly these beginnings are encouraging and even dramatic. Progress, moreover, will be accelerated by such innovations as the REA Express trailer pool established recently. But there is a long way to go. Even in 1960, piggyback accounted for less than 2.0 per cent of all carloadings and for only 3.5 per cent of loadings of freight in the "manufacturers and miscellaneous" category.[10] As with the reform of rate structures through the commodity-by-commodity approach, adding a few hundred piggyback cars a year is not going to appreciably advance our development of a truly coordinated transport network. There is a need for refinement

---

[8] Interstate Commerce Commission, *Distribution of Rail Revenue Contribution by Commodity Groups* (Washington: U. S. Gov't Printing Office, 1960).

[9] "Review of Railway Operations," *Railway Age*, CL (Jan. 16, 1961), p. 54.
[10] "Review of Railway Operations," p. 54.

and development of the container tool in the interests of standardization, full intermodal compatibility, and adaptability. But as former Commissioner Anthony F. Arpaia has suggested, these problems are more apt to be handled promptly and efficiently if the environment of and attitudes toward effective transport coordination are healthy and stimulating.[11] In other words, surmounting any technological barriers to effective coordination will not be helpful without appropriate regulatory and management policies to provide the right institutional setting.

Common Ownership

The two basic paths to effective facilitating arrangements are common ownership, as espoused by the railroads, and fuller exploitation of through routes and joint rates, or contractual cooperating arrangements by independent firms (either with or without regulatory intervention). Extensive hearings, designed to ease the path to diversification or common ownership, were conducted in the last Congress on proposed amendments to the Interstate Commerce Act. The issues are also being spotlighted in the John I. Hay case, where the Illinois Central and Southern Pacific Railroads seek to purchase a common carrier barge line; here the interpretation of some important facets of present law is under consideration. The interests of shippers and carriers alike demand a speedy but well-considered resolution of this question.

Without entering into the controversial aspects of the problem, we may note the implications of common ownership for shipper control over the components of the distribution system. It is quite likely that shippers themselves can best determine the superior quality-price combinations of transport facilities and services in given situations.

Most discussions of transport under common ownership presume, however, that such decisions will be made by carrier managements. It is not clear just how important loss of control might be for delicately adjusted distribution systems or how this loss would be offset by gains that might be realized from common ownership. But it is probably sufficiently important to warrant

[11] Anthony F. Arpaia, "Integration of Transportation Systems," address before the Cargo Handling Exposition and Symposium, New York City, Sept. 28, 1960.

the consideration of shipper interests in formulating views on the common-ownership controversy and of carriers in planning for diversified transportation.

Coordination Without Common Ownership

It seems, also, that common ownership represents only a partial answer to the problem of providing necessary facilitating arrangements for the effective integration of the transport system. It would provide the entire answer only if the railroads were to swallow up all independent air, water, and truck lines. The railroad proponents of common ownership vociferously deny both their intention and their ability to achieve this result. Accordingly, coordinative arrangements are still required between diversified railroad companies and independent carriers of all types, as well as between independent carriers and agencies.

It is generally recognized that the interagency coordination achieved by the establishment of through routes and joint rates has been relatively insignificant, despite the crucial importance of these devices for an integrated system. Clearly, drastic changes are required in either management or regulatory policies or both. Advocates of cooperative effort must recognize that voluntary contractual arrangements for the joint production of transport services must have a profit base; vague and general exhortations to broadmindedness and statesmanship are apt to sound rather unconvincing to private management. Perhaps profit opportunities have thus far been limited by the absence of effective interchange devices, particularly containers. To the extent that this is true, the difficulty would be self-correcting as these devices are refined and developed. But it is also possible that available profit opportunities are missed because of biased and myopic management attitudes, such as an undue preoccupation with short-run benefits or an inherent distaste for doing business with a competitor.

The latter attitude may perhaps be illustrated by reference to piggyback operations under which the railroads haul trailers for common carrier truckers to effect the coordination of the two modes. Although there are notable exceptions, one notices suspicion on both sides. "A" will not buy from "B" because if B is willing to sell at a given price he must be benefiting from the transaction in a way that is detrimental to

A; neither will B sell to A because if A is willing to buy at a given price he must be benefiting from the transaction, and therefore it must be against the interests of B.

If this thinking permeated the market place, there would be no transactions and the world's commerce would grind to a halt. Obviously, a transaction can be effected only when both parties benefit, and the gain of one does not represent a loss to the other. There is no apparent reason that such mutual gains cannot be realized in relationships of this sort, even though the companies involved also operate as competitors in other market situations.

The achievement of desirable coordination through voluntary means may serve company self-interest to an extent not fully realized. The following hypothetical example will serve to illustrate the point. Commodity "X" is moved from "O" to "D" via "I" by both railroad and truck, with the market evenly divided at 1,000 tons each per time unit at equal rates of $1 per 100 pounds. Let us say the direct (or out-of-pocket) costs are $.80 by rail and $.85 by truck. With these price-cost relationships, the respective rail and truck revenue contributions per unit are $.20 and $.15 and the total contributions are $2,000 and $1,500. Let us assume further that the cost of the O-I leg is $.40 by rail and $.25 by truck and of the I-D leg $.50 by rail and $.70 by truck. Combined rail-truck service with interchange at I would be the cheapest alternative, amounting to $.75 in comparison with the all-rail cost of $.80.

Even if this cost saving were fully reflected in the governing rate, each cooperating carrier would make more profit by concentrating exclusively on that portion of the total job it could do best. If the rail carrier received $.62 for its portion of the haul, it would realize a revenue contribution of $2,400 from the 1,000 tons, a 20 per cent increase over the $2,000 previously realized. With a $.33 share the motor carrier could net $1,600 instead of $1,500. This level of compensation to the carriers and transfer costs of $.02 at I could be covered by a rate of $.97. In this hypothetical situation, the rate could drop by $.03 while the revenue contribution increased from $3,500 to $4,000, to the benefit of all concerned.

It is incumbent on carriers and on the Commission to determine the applicability of this case and to find the cost-rate-revenue division combinations that will achieve the result outlined in our simple example. Shippers have a

big stake in finding answers to these questions and they should strongly encourage the investigations needed to understand these basic relationships.

If the search for such profit opportunities through coordination should fail, the only path to effective and complete coordination is to grant the Commission more power to prescribe through routes and joint rates and to ensure their effective use. But this cure should be prescribed with caution. Before broadening regulatory powers, we should fully explore the extent to which profit motives might achieve a truly integrated transport system. If there is substantial inconsistency between company self-interest and the public interest in a fully integrated transport system, then the pros and cons of a broader application of mandatory powers in this area should certainly be considered. Perhaps the explicit threat of further government intervention would stimulate carriers to make a wholehearted investigation into profitable coordination. As the preceding hypothetical example suggests, one of the main barriers may be outmoded rate structures that completely divorce rates from relative agency costs. Thus, the emerging reform in rate relationships may be the first step toward true coordination for profit. It is possible also that the reduction in the number of independent firms resulting from the merger movements in both the railroad and trucking industries will be beneficial.

Implications

Having discussed the changing patterns in the supply of transportation services, we shall now consider some of the interrelationships between these changes and the transport purchasing decisions of shippers. The latter adjust their policies and decisions to changes in supply, and the resulting purchasing developments, in turn, alter the character and location of the markets of carriers and require further accommodation by them. Some of the more important interrelationships are revealed by considering the implications of emerging changes in supply and in purchasing for price-quality choices, logistical patterns, and distribution system components.

Price-Quality Choices

An important aspect of emerging tendencies in rate reform and in coordination is the widening range in the kinds of services and their associated prices. Quality variations are reflected in speed, frequency, and dependability; direct additions are apparent in new coordinated offerings such as piggyback. Further additions can be expected from the intensification of price competition. The historical concentration on service competition, particularly between the rail and motor carriers, tended to limit the range of such choices. The general result of service (or quality) competition, whether in transport or in the economy generally, is a progressive refinement in quality, which is, of course, achieved only at a cost and with a corresponding limitation on available alternatives. Active price competition induces lower quality at lower prices, which may often be the best buy when transportation is regarded as but one (albeit a vital) component of an integrated distribution system. Better market choices are available, for example, if railroads do not try to emulate truck service at truck-equated rates, but provide lower quality at lower rates (with, however, the best quality attainable at that rate).

With a better understanding of shipper needs from market research, an agency may further increase choices by offering different combinations of price and quality. Incentive rates exemplify such combinations, but important dimensions other than quantity requirements may be introduced, such as transit time and equipment quality or adaptability.

The growing interest in the system approach to distribution should also have an important influence on the range of price and quality choices as well as on other aspects of transport supply. Increasing carrier marketing consciousness and refined market studies will provide shippers with a better opportunity to make their requirements known. The more precise definitions of transport requirements, which will stem from the more refined and sophisticated analyses of distribution systems, will enhance the effectiveness of the shippers' role in this connection. As former Commissioner Clarke suggested, transportation companies are becoming more interested in what shippers want; at the same time, shippers will be less prone to take what is offered and better equipped to respond to the carriers' interest. This improved response will stem from better identification of the types of services, including relatively subtle variations, needed to provide required market servicing and from better insights regarding the true

costs of alternative systems predicated on different transport components.

The combined pressures from the supply and demand sides should substantially alter the character of transport services and bring about more effective and efficient performance of both transport and distribution. Only partial economy is achieved when the role of the several agencies is determined on the basis of isolated transport costs. True economy requires that each perform the role that will minimize not transport costs but over-all distribution costs. This is a more refined statement of the common reference to the "most efficient carrier—cost and quality considered."

Quality in this context is fully quantifiable since it reflects the nontransport distribution costs associated with the use of alternative agencies. For example, the railroads' chief disadvantage when matched against truck movement is the increased inventory costs caused by larger tenders and longer transit times. Professor John R. Meyer and his associates have provided some generalized measures of quality disability expressed in these terms.[12]

If the calculation is based on average value commodities and average elapsed times, and ten-ton truck shipments and twenty-ton rail shipments, the railroad inventory disability from the transit time differential is $.0299 per ton mile at 50 miles and declines to $.0017 at 1,000 miles. Comparable figures for shipment size disabilities are $.0013 and $.0001. The comparative costs of the two agencies are substantially affected by the inclusion of the extra outlays associated with the inferior service.

According to these illustrative figures, if 500 tons were to be shipped 400 miles over a given time period, the extra inventory costs associated with using rail service would approximate $13,000. Let us assume that the movement costs are $50,000 by rail and $60,000 by truck. If transportation costs are considered in isolation, rail appears to be the most efficient alternative by a margin of $10,000. But if the other relevant costs are included in the comparison, trucks are more efficient by $3,000. Shippers who fail to consider and to compute accurately these associated costs in selecting carriers not

[12] John R. Meyer, Merton J. Peck, John Stenason, and Charles Zwick, *Competition in the Transportation Industries* (Cambridge, Mass.: Harvard University Press, 1959), p. 190.

only inflate their own distribution costs but help to cast the entire transportation system into an uneconomic mold. The more perfectly shippers function in developing integrated distribution systems, the more efficient will be the assignment of the carriers to their various roles and the lower will be the costs of distribution.

Logistical Patterns

The altered rate relationships we have reviewed may also produce changes in the general logistical patterns of business, which, in turn, will affect a firm's locational decisions as well as those of its suppliers and customers. While other factors may prevent any sharp shifts in plant and warehouse location, some changes in the transportation inputs of location decisions require watching.

The general cheapening of transportation, which, it is hoped, will result from rate reductions and improvements in coordination, would weaken the influence of transportation as a determinant in location and give firms greater freedom to locate on the basis of other considerations. But more specific influences on location are suggested by the changed relationship between raw-material and finished-product rates that may be expected as the old value-of-service structures erode from intensified price competition. A cheapening of finished-product transportation would tend to reverse or at least weaken the trends of the past few decades and decrease the influence of markets on plant location. Such a tendency would be strengthened by any increases in unduly low rates on raw materials, which would enhance the attraction of materials sources. Such rate revisions would mean altered delivery costs of materials and perhaps a switch to new sources, with new patterns of logistical relationships and traffic flows.

Taken in the aggregate, changing materials-product rate relationships, in combination with territorial differences in rate trends, exert an influence on patterns of regional development and thus on the logistical relationships of producing firms. Growing regional self-sufficiency is a dominant characteristic of recent economic history that is rooted in a variety of forces independent of transportation. But rate relationships can either abet or hamper this development, and it appears that recent changes have facilitated and hence hastened the move toward regional self-sufficiency. Transportation influ-

ences in regional economic development can be illustrated by the emerging industrialization of the South. Changing rate relationships appear to favor the expansion of Southern manufacturing, primarily for regional markets. Since 1947, rail rates have increased far more on raw materials (on agricultural, mining, and forest products) shipped from the South to the East and on manufactures in the reverse direction than they have on these two commodity groupings within the South.[13] The relatively large increases on materials exports and manufactured imports and the relatively more favorable trends for rates covering internal shipments of both materials and manufactures encourage regional processing. Increasingly favorable short-haul rates on manufactures compared to rates on longer hauls protect Southern producers against Eastern competition in Southern markets. At the same time, the unfavorable trend in long-haul rates on raw materials discourages the siphoning off of Southern staples to supply Eastern manufacturing.

Distribution Systems

Such developments are clearly of great significance for plant and warehouse location and thus for the design of distribution systems. But there are perhaps other ways in which the realized and potential transportation changes we have reviewed will affect distribution-system components and thus the purchase and sale of transport services.

Certainly we can expect changed transport purchasing decisions in terms of transport modes. Some of the ferment in transport supply is reflected in the recent shifts in the shares of total markets handled by rail and nonrail carriers. The latest available data on the relationship between tons moved by rail and total production of various commodities go only to 1957. Much has happened since that year, but even up to that time there were substantial shifts. For example, between 1950 and 1957 the railroad shares of some commodities reversed general trends and increased as follows:[14]

[13] *Indexes of Average Freight Rates on Railroad Carload Traffic, 1949–1957*, p. 6.
[14] Interstate Commerce Commission, *Fluctuations in Railroad Freight Traffic Compared With Production, 1957* (Washington: U. S. Gov't Printing Office, 1958).

Commodity	Railroad Percentage of Total Tons	
	1950	1957
Plastics	1	31
Gases, other than petroleum	8	37
Corn meal	16	41
Iron and steel borings and turnings	41	63
Coke	28	53

Conversely, comparable reductions occurred in other sectors:

Commodity	Railroad Percentage of Total Tons	
	1950	1957
Drugs, medicines, and toilet preparations	50	16
Airplanes, aircraft, and parts	26	14
Asphalt	52	21
Electrical equipment and parts	40	19
Matches	54	20
Chinaware	30	15

Such shifts either reflect or occasion alterations in distribution patterns.

If the forces we have observed continue to intensify, we can expect transportation to become relatively cheaper. Because of the complex interrelationships between transportation and distribution systems, the results of all of this are somewhat uncertain, but some implications may be suggested. The lower cost and improved quality of transport may permit the use of alternatives providing greater regularity, frequency, and speed—a move generally unfavorable to railroad interests. In some circumstances, the new alternatives may make it possible to get by with lower inventory stocks and still maintain or even improve the level of market servicing. In other circumstances, the cheapening of transport may make it economically feasible to increase inventory stocks to improve market servicing. This outcome, which would favor railroads, seems particularly likely when the rate reduction is realized through the application of the quantity incentive feature that characterizes many of the new railroad rates.

Distribution systems will be altered by the increased flexibility resulting from more choices of price-quality combinations of the transport services as well as by their general cheapening. Flexibility would be further increased if the expected rate erosion on manufactured articles were to make proprietary truck transportation a relatively less attractive system component, bringing a reduction in fixed organizational and capital commitments. Increased flexibility from whatever source will permit and encourage further refinement in distribution system design. Shipper responses to the new paint rates is an illustration of the effects of this flexibility. Whereas virtually all movements were formerly by truck, some shipments now move by rail.

We have considered many aspects of transport dynamics and have noted a number of problems, barriers, and implications. Perhaps it would be well to summarize the particularly significant challenges that now face business management.

1. The wider the range of price and quality choices provided by growing price competition, marketing consciousness of carriers, and by the coordination and integration of transport supply, the greater the challenge to traffic and distribution managers. The greater the flexibility provided by alternative choices, the greater the pressure for analytical refinement.

2. Conversely, the more refined the distribution analyses of shippers, the greater the challenge to carrier managers to provide price-quality alternatives that will optimize distribution systems. This will require not only extremely intimate communications with shippers through market research and other media, but also advanced understanding of distribution systems in general and of the distribution problems of particular shippers. The better each side does its job, the lower will be transport and distribution costs and the greater the profits for all concerned.

3. Both sellers and buyers are confronted with the problems of mutual accommodation to change. But as a matter of hardheaded business policy, the carriers must be prepared to be the primary accommodators. Such accommodation will be most successful if backed by intensive research efforts that throw light on competitive relationships and on shipper purchasing policies.

4. We have noted a number of areas where regulatory policy is of crucial importance, both for rate modifications and for coordination. This suggests that all who are concerned with distribution would be wise to take a lively and informed interest in regulation policy. To be effective, this interest must be supplemented by informed judgments, so that regulation will advance the development of a transport system that will best serve the needs of distribution.

26. *A Systems Approach to Transportation**

William Lazer†

The transportation industry and its methods of operation are in the throes of a major transition.

A far-reaching and fundamental change in the philosophy of transportation management, in the methods of improving services, and in decision making is taking place. The major characteristics of the change may be summed up in one word—systems.

Systems Approach

Executives in transportation are embracing the systems approach to transportation's role in company operations and as a solution to distribution problems. The approach interrelates the total complex of transportation and storage activities with other aspects of business operations. Thus it assures company stability, growth, and profit.

This approach, which is now evident in the operation of progressive companies, stresses the interrelationship and coordinacy of all activities in physical distribution. It perceives the transportation function as one segment of the complete system of business action.

The systems approach to transportation management emphasizes the impact of decisions made by this department on every segment of transportation, on all physical distribution activities, or other marketing operations, and on the total business system.

Too often traffic managers regard transportation narrowly. Many of them see it as a functional operation existing largely because of and for itself. In this sense, the performance of transportation functions are viewed as major reasons for the existence of a traffic manager.

* Reprinted from *Distribution Age,* September 1960.
† Michigan State University.

Specialized Activity

From this viewpoint, transportation is considered a specialized operating activity. It falls within the domain of one department affecting one aspect of the organization. Transportation decisions are made and activities conducted largely in the light of transportation dimensions.

This functionalized approach to transportation has serious negative consequences. Companies adopting it are not likely to maximize their profits because:

There will exist a lack of planning and action designed to optimize the use of total company resources and to maximize over-all profits.

Numerous independent decisions will be formulated and implemented without recognizing the consequences for other elements of physical distribution and business operations.

Transportation policies and services will not be designed and adapted to better meet company and customer needs.

A lack of coordination of space and movement strategy will occur which may generate disfunctioning in the total system of business action.

For example, there is often a lack of integration of decisions concerning the types of carriers, warehouse location, inventory levels, storing, and packaging problems. Each may have an impact on the other. As a result, the transportation department may work towards achieving its own specific objectives. They may run counter to the major goals of the company. Profits drop.

In such cases transportation objectives can be achieved. But relatively high costs result for the firm as a whole. Thereby much of the true meaning and value of transportation management may be lost. In such a situation, the total contributions of the transportation department are not as great as they should be. Total profits realized are less than company action warrants.

To overcome these severe limitations, informed traffic managers are becoming adherents of the systems approach. They are viewing transportation problems in terms of operating wholes.

The systems approach does not defend or favor transportation at the expense of the total organization. By adopting a unified and integrated concept of distribution, decisions may be made which will maximize the total output received from all business inputs. It is this coordinated management approach which will lead to increasing efficiency.

Implementation

What are the concrete evidences of the systems approach? Perhaps the most specific evidence is a shift in the organizational title and responsibility of the traffic manager. Several companies have broadened both the "label" and duties to include related activities other than those usually referred to in the field of "traffic."

The position is often referred to by a title such as distribution manager or physical distribution manager. This change recognizes the broader dimensions of responsibility included within the domain of the top transportation executive. It emphasizes the impact of transportation functions on other distribution activities within a company.

The second piece of evidence parallels the organizational evolvement of the position of distribution manager. It is the development of a new concept—physical distribution.[1]

Physical distribution refers to the integration of all aspects of physically handling, storing, and transporting goods on their way to the market. According to this concept, transportation activities in the broadest sense, are regarded as comprising a whole—a system of physical distribution. Management should not think in terms of methods of transportation, warehousing, or handling separately. Management must think in terms of the impact of decisions on each of the other physical distribution segments and on the total company.

Integrated Operations

Third, in recent transportation literature more emphasis is being given to the systems method. Clyde E. Phelps has written in *Distribution Age* that "The warehousing industry today is on the threshold of an entirely new pattern of distribution—distribution center warehousing. Only the beginning phase of a new concept, it encompasses the physical distribution of goods from plant to storage area to point of final consumer market via multi-plant transit stocks.

"This transiting is a system by which the manufacturer can ship a complete order of his entire line of produce at one time, and, on one bill of lading on through rates from the producing point . . . to set up such a program, a sound basis of traffic research coordinated with the production and sales pattern is essential."[2]

Referring to airlines specifically, *Business Week*, March 14, 1959, reported that "The Airline's problem in selling air freight is that the lines have to make their pitch on the basis of distribution as a complete integrated system. . . . The moral is simply that approaching distribution as a total process—and not one made up of separate functions—will sometimes shake management out of long established practices."

In the March 1958 issue of *Distribution Age*, "Lift-On-Lift-Off On the Road to Total Transportation;" explains that "The day of total transportation may be closer than we think. Basically, total transportation is the integration of two or more modes of carriage to provide the shipper with a unified service."

It is evident that the concepts referred to advance systems thinking in distribution. They describe certain basic trends and practices in current transportation management which adopt an integrated, coordinated, and total approach to the solution of problems of physically distributing goods. The writers are expressing forward-looking and practical ideas of managerial significance to the transportation industry.

---

[1] For a definitive discussion of the physical distribution concept, see "Physical Distribution: A New Concept" by Edward W. Smykay and Frank H. Mossman, in *Managerial Marketing: Perspectives and Viewpoints*, by Eugene J. Kelley and William Lazer (eds.) (Homewood, Ill.: Richard D. Irwin, Inc., 1958), p. 360.

[2] Clyde E. Phelps, "Transiting—Revolution in Warehousing," *Distribution Age;* February, 1958, p. 37.

Lack of Clarity

However, since the observations and writings have been offered by several thoughtful people, definitions and meanings are bound to overlap. The same terms are used to designate difference activities.

The materials which follow will present one viewpoint of a systems approach to transportation and warehousing activities. It will include a brief discussion of: The total transportation system, total warehousing system, physical distribution system, and physical distribution as a segment of the marketing and business system.

Total Transportation

The total transportation system is shown in Chart 1. Essentially, it is the integration of two or more modes of transportation to provide shippers with more effective services. Under this concept, various alternative and complementary methods of transportation are coordinated to better meet the shipper's needs. The concept is not as broad in scope as the physical distribution concept. Instead it is one sub-system of the total system of physical distribution.

Specifically, the total transportation system combinates rail, air, truck, pipeline, and water carriers. It is concerned, too, with such facilitating transportation agencies as freight forwarders, railway express, parcel post, air express, and shipper's associations. Management faces the challenge of combining transportation elements in an optimal manner to obtain the most profit. Trailership and piggyback are examples of individual carriers combined to achieve more efficient handling and movement.

The total warehousing concept deals with integration of storing and handling. Under such a concept, the warehouse is no longer just a storage facility. It is an important component of the marketing channel. Its goal is moving goods in the most efficient manner possible.

In the total warehousing system, all the functions performed in storing and handling mer-

Chart 1.   The total transportation system

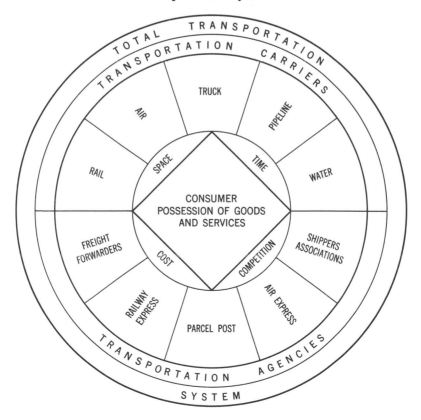

chandise are coordinated. This overcomes barriers of space, time, and competition in getting goods to consumers as effectively as possible. This coordinated approach to warehousing activities is resulting in new and more efficient distribution patterns. Chart 2 presents the elements of the total warehousing system.

The total warehousing system is comprised of two major groups of activities—handling and storage functions and merchandising functions. Included among the handling and storage responsibilities are warehouse location, storing, receiving, consolidation, breaking bulk, handling, packaging, marking, order processing, shipping and delivery, and billing. The merchandising aspects include display, selling, financing, credit, and grading.

Distribution executives are concerned with the integration of storage, handling, and merchandising functions to achieve the optimal warehousing combination. It is in this context of a planned and integrated facility that the warehouse is considered to be a distribution center. Through the use of mechanical equipment, automatic data processing, and by coordinating warehouse-related activities, more effective systems of distribution are being achieved.

Distribution System

To obtain optimal efficiency in physically distributing goods, it is necessary to coordinate all of the company's transportation and warehousing activities. These should be grouped under the authority and responsibility of a major executive. This is the domain of the executive in charge of physical distribution.

The physical distribution manager should be charged with the spatial arrangement of plant capacity and distribution facilities. These two aspects of company operations are linked by transportation systems. As a result the physical distribution manager is concerned with coordinating and combining all aspects of storing, handling, and transporting goods in the most profitable manner.

Chart 2.

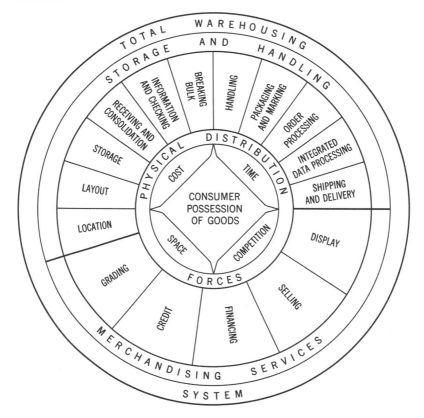

Chart 3.   The physical distribution system

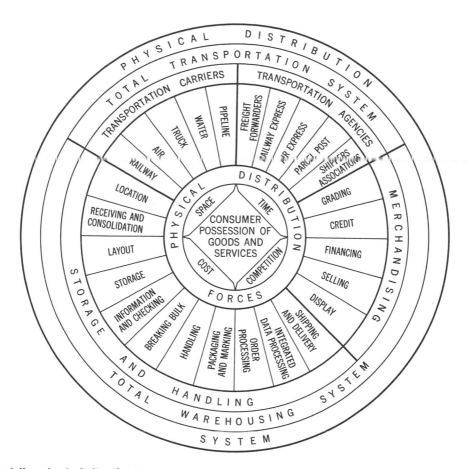

Essentially, physical distribution as a system has two major sub-systems—the total transportation system and the total warehousing system. This is shown by Chart 3.

Under the physical distribution concept, all of the elements of both systems are to be combined to achieve the most efficient over-all system of distribution. This is one of the primary responsibilities of the distribution manager. Clearly the scope of these activities lies well beyond the boundaries suggested by the title "traffic manager."

What do these ideas mean to transportation management? What will the management consequences be for companies adopting the systems approach?

Essentially, these developments emphasize that transportation management has come to recognize that a hierarchy of systems exists in business. First, the company is regarded as a total system of business action—the primary management system. Its purpose is to integrate the production of men, materials, money, machines, and management—whether used for transportation, production, marketing, finance, or other functional purposes, to maximize company profits.

There exists an over-all business system within which transportation and other physical distribution functions take place. This system sets primary limits upon transportation decisions and objectives. It is within the system that the sub-system of physical distribution must operate.

The second implication is that physical distribution is but part of a larger marketing sub-system, which in turn is part of the broader business system. Other components of the company's marketing sub-system are: channels of distribution, pricing and credit, service and product policies, and advertising and selling programs. Decisions concerning physical distribution should be made in terms of their impact on other elements of the marketing system.

Third, the physical distribution sub-system in turn has two major components: the total transportation system and the total warehousing system.

Fourth, the company embracing the systems approach to the solution of distribution problems should benefit because:

Physical distribution assumes an integral position in contributing to the company's over-all profit and efficiency.

Various aspects of transportation and warehousing activities are coordinated for maximum efficiency.

Physical distribution decisions are brought into line with the major objectives and policies of the firm.

The scope and functions of "transportation" executives are broadened to include all of the major activities involved in physically distributed goods.

Physical distribution is recognized as an important company activity in the organization structure.

27. *Transportation Miracles Today**

KARL M. RUPPENTHAL†

At least since the days of Marco Polo, man's imagination has been stimulated by notions of travel. A thousand years ago the wandering minstrels brought exciting tales of the fabulous sights they had seen and of the wondrous places they had been. And, perhaps to prove that their stories were not simply figments of an over-active imagination, they often brought with them spices, jewels, and minerals—tangible souvenirs to show that the far-off places of which they spoke did in fact exist and that the wondrous merchandise which they exhibited was really to be found.

Throughout all of recorded history, few things have been more tantalizing to the imagination than travel. And few devices have exerted a more profound influence on the history of mankind than the machines which have made travel easier and which have made it possible for man to transport the products of the world to his door.

Today the dreams of exotic adventures continue, though in a somewhat different form. Instead of dreaming of a four-month camel ride to see the wonders of the east, boys today dream of a four-hour flight to Paris or a four-day zoom to the moon. Perhaps there are subtle differences in the dreams of today and those of our forefathers a few generations ago. They dreamed of the wondrous products that could be purchased for a song in some distant land. But the modern-day Marco Polos find it difficult even to imagine products that are grown or manufactured on the moon or on Mars that are not already available on earth—and available here at lower cost, with a better warranty, and already packaged in an attractive container.

It has often been noted that in the business world today, change takes place at an ever-increasing rate. A century ago, it was not uncommon for forty or fifty years to elapse between the germination of an idea and its practical application in the world. Today it is estimated that but six or seven years intervene between the idea and its application—and there are firm indications that the pace will continue to quicken.

And in no area of activity is change more rapid, or more important, than in transportation. It would be interesting to note the shock and surprise if we could somehow take a modern-day Rip Van Winkle and suspend him for twenty years. Suppose, for instance, we were to hypnotize a sales manager in early 1950 as he sat in his office in Los Angeles trying to decide whether to fly to New York in a DC-3 to see a customer about a large order he hoped to write. If by some mystic process we were able to put Rip to sleep and then awaken him twenty years later, in 1970, this is what he might find:

He could telephone his Director of Logistics and request his travel advice. Sitting in a small, well-equipped office, the Logistics Director would punch two keys on a Reservisor Machine, one key representing New York, the other Los Angeles. Within seconds a teletype-like machine would begin to operate, printing out all of the possible schedules between the two points, indicating departure times, elapsed time, and fares. It might also indicate whether any particular air line or schedule was preferred because of the quality of its service, the variety of its cuisine, or for reasons of reciprocity. And it would indicate whether seats were currently available.

On request the Director of Logistics would punch another button. That single operation would cause a number of things to happen:

1. The teletype machine would print out a punch card which would serve him as a ticket.

2. It would make the necessary reservation.

3. It would deplete the air line's inventory of available seats appropriately.

* Reprinted with permission from *Transportation Progress*, 1964, Karl M. Ruppenthal, Editor —Part of the Stanford Transportation Series.

† Director of Transportation Management Program, Stanford University.

4. It would order the meal he had selected together with necessary comissary supplies.

5. It would send information to the air line's load control to update its record to accommodate the additional forecast weight.

6. It would revise the air line's revenue forecast for the date in question.

7. It would send specific information to the air line's purchasing department so that napkins, towels, and other supplies would automatically be reordered and in the most economic reorder quantity.

8. And it would debit his bank balance for the price of the ticket, transferring the funds to the air line's account, all the while keeping appropriate income tax records.

Several days later when Van Winkle was ready for his trip, he might step into an automatic elevator which would take him to the street level where he would enter a personal carrier not much different in size from the elevator itself. Punching appropriate buttons, he could then sit down and relax while the electronic vehicle whisked him non-stop to the airport. Its electronic guidance system would take him quickly, safely to the appropriate air line terminal. There he would deposit his baggage on an electronic cart, and his personal carrier would shunt itself automatically to a garage.

Meanwhile the baggage would weigh itself, and be automatically tagged with information concerning destination, density, and shape. Baggage would automatically be loaded in the optimum position in the plane, and the plane's weight and balance records updated accordingly.

Rip could step into an attractive lounge or be moved directly to his plane. Inserting his IBM ticket he would reactivate his return reservation, list his name on the flight manifest, and notify the hostess that he had arrived.

Once on board he could look at a television demonstration of the proper use of the oxygen mask. He could select from a variety of first-run movies, available at his personal TV set. If he were thirsty, he could select a beverage from the Robot Cart. His steak would arrive, as he liked it, when he wanted it, served by a newly developed automatic chef.

If Rip were a stockholder he might well consider the productivity of the air line. Upon inquiry he would find that there were three pilots and one hostess in the crew. Quickly he could compute that the productivity of the captain in a Boeing 707 would be something like twenty

times what it was in the DC-3. And that his productivity would be increased by five hundred per cent in the Mach III. He would also note that work once done by large numbers of reservations personnel, baggage handlers, and clerks could easily be done by machine. He might nostalgically think of the days when long distance flights had navigators, radio operators, and flight engineers. And he might ask himself if he were really ready for the next step—the completely automated plane in which there is no cockpit and the pilot remains on the ground.

Winging its way to New York, the flight's progress would be monitored by computers that would take into account changing winds, weather, and traffic. Before it departed from Los Angeles, its landing sequence in New York would be assigned, thus obviating the necessity for costly waiting at the ramp or more costly circling in the air. . . .

Returning from New York with the order in his hand, Rip could dispense with the mountains of familiar paperwork. Everything necessary could be transcribed onto a single punch card. Putting it into the appropriate machine would cause picking and sorting machines to select the proper quantities of merchandise and to shunt them on carts to the shipping room. There the traffic machine would be queried concerning optimum routes and tariffs. Out of some three hundred possible rail routings and several thousand possible motor carrier combinations, it would select the one that was best for this shipment. It would then alert the appropriate transportation company, manifest, and label the shipment.

Suffice it to say that this freight shipment would be even more automatic than was Rip's own trip to the east. A rail car might be automatically shunted to the Van Winkle siding. When it had automatically moved into place, the robot loading machine would weigh it, load it, and close the door. The car would then shunt itself into the appropriate classification yard where it would proceed to locate the proper outbound track without any need for brakeman or helper. The entire classification yard would be automatic, with perhaps an engineer or two to monitor the control panels.

Once an optimum number of cars had been assembled, powerful electronic units would pull them swiftly to New York City, by-passing present-day classification yards. Such a train could cruise at eighty or ninety miles an hour, automatically opening the necessary switches, sending appropriate passing reports, and making minor repairs while enroute. . . .

Should Van Winkle's order be sufficiently large to warrant shipment by sea, he would discover that the technological revolution had proceeded there equally fast. Nearly automatic Gantry cranes would load sizeable containers into a specially constructed ship that would operate to New York with a crew of five. If Rip would inquire, he would learn that the steamship companies even considered a fully automated ship. And he might be surprised to see that the backbreaking work of the longshoremen had all but disappeared. Some of them might drive a forklift, while another sat in the cab of a monstrous crane. Indeed the longshoreman of the future may sit beside an elaborate electronic console that will control many of the operations of the waterfront. Such a device may simulate the loading of cargo long before a ship arrives in port. In this fashion, the operator will be assured that proper account is taken of the weight, density, and physical characteristics of cargo and that no double handling will be required of a ship that makes numerous calls. . . .

Remarkable as the technological revolution appears, it is important to note that an even more important revolution is taking place in the office. While the hardware side of the revolution may be spectacular, there is no doubt that the paperwork revolution is equally important.

Take for example the common freight bill. Today thousands of clerks write millions of waybills covering billions of pounds of goods. Freight bills invariably are made with multiple copies, and they serve to inspire additional thousands of billing clerks to write additional thousands of manifests, revenue reports, and other miscellaneous forms. Then there are the clerks who check on the clerks, writing thousands more discrepancy forms. And, of course, there are the controllers and the freight bill auditors who make their living by finding mistakes.

One military study recently made indicates that for every parcel that is shipped to our armed forces overseas, there are at least one hundred forms required. And if that study was completely candid, it might add that most of them were really unnecessary, and that civilian shippers are almost as paper prone. Today there are thousands upon thousands of shipments in which the total revenue obtained by the carrier is consumed by the paper work that is entailed. It is clear that as the paperwork revolution proceeds, it should be possible to eliminate thousands of tons of superfluous records and forms.

Of course the other side of the coin is that the modern management devices make it possible for management to have at its fingertips a vast storehouse of information that was previously buried in the stack. Today it is entirely possible for the president of a railroad to know not only how many cars moved along each segment of his line yesterday—he can know their points of origin, their destinations, and their shippers. He can tell what types of equipment were in short supply and which were in excess.

And he can know a lot about costs. Today business devices and techniques are sufficiently sophisticated that it's possible for a carrier to determine precisely how much it cost to move every one of its shipments. It can tell with remarkable accuracy how much it would cost to move additional traffic which presently goes by another mode or which, perhaps, does not move at all. Indeed we have available sufficient mathematical and statistical tools to render obsolete most of the traditional arguments about what does it cost to move a given ton of freight.

It is fascinating to speculate what would happen in the transportation industry if these techniques were utilized as fully as they are in some of the more sophisticated industrial empires. Suppose, for instance, we devoted the necessary resources to a study of the questions of costs. Suppose that we determined to set up a system which would show, beyond a reasonable doubt, the cost of every segment of every movement of every shipment in the United States. Think what a revolution that would be! What changes would be wrought!

Hundreds of thousands of rate clerks and accountants would automatically be displaced. No longer needed, their jobs would be performed by a computer!

Thousands upon thousands of attorneys would be displaced. Since they could no longer argue before the ICC about value of the service and ability to pay, there would be little need for them to argue at all!

And what might happen to the Commission itself! Since there would no longer be arguments about costs, there would be little question whether any proposed rate was reasonable. Instead of listening *ad nauseum* to trivia, the Commission could spend its time discussing long-range policy considerations and other important matters. It would need, for instance, simply to decide what might be a fair rate of return for a trucking company, and that figure—be it five percent or ten—could be easily programmed into the ICC computer to determine whether or not a proposed rate did indeed fall within the pale. There would be no temporary rate suspensions and no lengthy hearings. The computations would be made before your very eyes, and the answer would be swift. . . .

I would be naive if indeed I expected that all the changes I have outlined would really take place in the transportation industry, at least within the next five or six years. I am sure that they will not. However, it is well to remember that within our generation some amazing dreams have come true. Virtually all of the Buck Rogers books that we read as boys have been transcribed as news on the front pages of the *New York Times*. Today when we gamble that anything is impossible or that it will never come to be, the probabilities are high that we are wrong. In this sort of wager, the odds are not equal. The dice are loaded for change.

It is interesting to note that all of the instruments and devices, the gadgets and the guidance systems that would be necessary to build the transportation systems I have sketched are already in being today. To build a completely automated railway, untouched by human hands, would not require one single new invention nor a major break in technology. Every component device that is necessary is already in being today.

And the same is true of computers. Every type of computer that I mentioned, somewhat in jest, has already been built and could be adapted to such use. The question is not *how*, it is, rather, *how soon*. For there is little doubt that many of these "miracles" will be seen in the transportation industry, and their appearance may be fast. The real question is whether the industry will be ready to receive them. And whether it will use them well.

We have long viewed changing technologies through the eyes of the working man—the fireman, the telegrapher, and the stevedore. These men are properly concerned about the effect of technology on their lives and on their jobs.

But today there is another group that might well be concerned. For the evidence is clear that the new business technology will exert a profound effect on the white collar workers in the front office. For it is there that the greatest miracles will take place.

28. *The Role of Railroads in Future Distribution Systems**

HENRY G. HOHORST†

There is a new climate in our economy. This is a time when managements are focusing the same type of attention and techniques on distribution, organization, systems and costs that have been focused in the past on finance, production and sales. Particular attention is being focused on the area variously described as:

1. *Physical Distribution.*
2. *Physical Marketing.* To me, this term is preferable over physical distribution because it connotes the competitive aspects of the service involved in moving the product to the customer. In many fields, especially where the products of one manufacturer are roughly similar to those of another manufacturer, the manner in which the customers' order are serviced and the goods delivered often makes the difference between a sale and no sale.
3. *Logistics of Production and Marketing.* This term is perhaps a better term than Physical Marketing because it points up the fact that we are just as concerned with the in-flow of raw materials and the movement of work in process interplant as we are with distribution of finished products. In addition, the term logistics which is borrowed from the military conveys our all-inclusive concern with materials management.
4. *Business Logistics.* This term appears to satisfy the need for a short phrase which conveys our overall concern.

These terms all include the following functions:

1. Distribution Research and Planning (Channels, order and shipping quantities, inventory planning, plant location, warehouse location, etc.).

2. Participation and translation of sales forecasts into master inventory, production allocation, and schedule plans.
3. Transportation of goods inbound, interplant, to warehouses and for customer delivery involving the traditional traffic responsibilities.
    Equipment
    Routing
    Rates
    Insurance
    Claims
4. Receiving.
5. Plant warehousing and inventory control of raw materials, work in process, and finished goods.
6. In-plant materials handling.
7. Product design.
8. Packaging design.
9. Branch warehouse operation and inventory control.
10. Customer order processing (including liaison with shipping, inventory control, and production planning.)
    Credit Approval
    Order Picking
    Billing
    Invoicing
11. Shipping.
12. Customer service control (including acknowledgements, service monitoring, and tracing).
13. Distribution cost accounting, budgets, control.
14. Optimum plan can only be developed by an analysis of the overall system.
    Component refinement alone is inadequate
    Components must be integrated into system
    The idea phase
    The hardware phase
    Theoretical analysis
    Analysis of all feasible alternatives
    Use of alternatives for creative development

* Reprinted by permission from the *Transportation Research Forum,* 1964.
† *New York Central System.*

Reduction to practice for final evaluation
Competitive decisions without documentation

The major emphasis here is on the overall system. This is becoming an overworked phrase in our defense department but I think it is the appropriate term. In developing programs of this type we are finding that more and more railroads are relying on staff specialists to analyze the major industries that they serve and to recommend those types of services which best fill the needs of the industry they are trying to serve. Our railroad perhaps has a more complete approach in this area than any other.

One example of a complete system which is quite well known is piggyback or as with the New York Central Railroad—Flexi Van. Prior to piggyback a typical rail freight station might look like this.

Let's compare this now with a typical truck freight terminal where trucks come in and material is transferred to smaller trucks for local pickup and delivery operations. Notice that the rail terminal requires 50% more investment, 25% more to operate and service is not as good. Thus, piggyback was born to solve these problems. Piggyback changed not only the type of rail interchange terminal from the expensive type terminal we just looked at to a simplified container operation such as our Flexi Van highway terminal. We have also changed to container trains which run from city to city stopping long enough to drop off some containers, add on others and go through to final destination. Thus, looking at a map of the New York Central System we have high speed container trains moving point-to-point between various load centers with pickup and delivery being handled by truck.

Our multi-level automobile traffic is another example of a complete systems approach to transportation. In this concept we are moving solid trainloads of automobiles from Detroit to our regional transfer terminals such as the ones in Framingham, Massachusetts; Selkirk, New York; Little Ferry, New Jersey, and Sharonville Terminal outside of Cincinnati. Cars are moved in solid train loads on a mass production basis to these terminals where they are transferred to trucks for local delivery. Again, the type of terminal that is used is a crucial ingredient in this new area of handling business. The important thing to realize is that the railroads here are not involved in just moving automobile

cars from one point on the railroad to another; they are concerned with the rail move, the terminal operation and truck delivery to the eventual customer. A complete integrated transportation program.

Grain is another area of change due to complete analysis of the total logistics system. In the past, grain rates have allowed for transit and a typical pattern might be this one. The corn coming in from a farm is assembled in a local silo, moved by a box car to a larger storage elevator, later moved to a mill for processing, then moved to a regional mixing location where it is finally distributed as feed grain for chickens. Although many moves were part of this because of transit provisions, the shipper using a single through rate could in effect end up with a number of moves all for the same transportation price. This has been an expensive way to move grain on a total basis. In addition, some of these moves have been very seasonal in nature. As a result, we have changed the basis of doing business with our customers to a new frill-free low cost method of transporting grain. Now grain is being assembled in larger size country elevators. It will then move directly to a mixing mill. The second and final move will be to the chicken farm. Because this move is oriented to the final consumer (and consumption is essentially constant), we have changed the peak demand for grain cars that has been so prevalent in the past to a more constant year-round need for transportation. This type of program has raised the price that the farmer can get for his corn in the midwest and has reduced the price that the receiver on the other end has to pay for his feed and it has allowed the rails to turn a lost business into a profitable operation.

In all of these operations, the type of terminal involved is the real nut of the transportation business that must be cracked to produce the quality service and carrier profits so essential to a healthy industry. To know where we might go in the future we must consider the basic railroad characteristics.

1. Railroads have the lowest towing costs of any mode of transportation. It is easier to move a car with a steel wheel on a steel rail than it is to push a barge through the water.

2. Rail is a volume operation. Many people have said railroad business is long haul and the truck business is short haul. This is not the basic difference. Railroad is volume and the

truck is non-volume. If there is enough volume point-to-point in a short haul business you can't beat the railroad. In long haul business there are sufficient savings in volume movements that we can frequently subsidize rather expensive pickup and delivery operations by rail. This is why many people think railroads are really long haul rather than short haul.

Let's look at this lowest towing cost aspect. If it takes two men to move a rail car, it takes eight to move a barge and about 15 to move a truck for the same quantity of material. Now if we design cars so that we're moving two pounds of steel for every pound of finished product then we're certainly not taking proper advantage of the rails capacity for lowest towing cost. Equipment design becomes an important facet of how effectively railroads can compete for the business that is available.

Let's look at some of the recent trends in railroad operations that are important in affecting their capabilities. This graph represents the costs per hundredweight versus mileage. The top line represents what costs may have been in the past. Improved turnaround might reduce our costs down to the level of this second line. This faster turnaround is a result of by-passing immediate switching terminals with through trains. Today, for instance, we pick up traffic in St. Louis, move directly on through trains to our key through-train yard in Indianapolis: transfer to a second train which goes all the way to Syracuse, New York: transfer to a final train that might make delivery in New York or in Boston. Thus we have bypassed a number of intermediate switching terminals that we previously used to go through and that might delay cars as much as a day or more. Thus, turnaround on the longer hauls is dramatically improved. In addition, we have eliminated the switching cost at those intermediate terminals and this might be represented by the third line of our chart.

Now the use of bigger cars can further reduce our cost picture and an improved payload to tare weight ratio makes another drop as shown by the last two lines on this chart. It's a continuation of these type trends that we must be aware. It is these trends that affect the railroads ability to compete effectively for the transportation pie.

From the shippers viewpoint, I would like to point out three potential plums for profit improvement. Let's explore how one complete new railroad originated transportation system might help in solving these three profit potential areas.

1. In the bulk versus non-bulk area, bulk trucks are lowering the volume breakpoint which it is economical for the middle-sized consumer to convert to bulk.

2. If the order-to-delivery time can be collapsed to provide delivery when the customer wants the order delivered and still ship directly from the origin plant, warehousing can be eliminated.

3. Recentralization versus decentralization.

The biggest danger in industry today is to build a small plant close to the market and find out in a year or so that the plant should have been larger and perhaps placed closer to the raw material source.

Let's look at the first of these three items. In the past, bags of material might have been transported by truck, unloaded by fork truck, dumped by laborers into a drum and used in the process. The costs of buying raw materials in bag rather than bulk form might vary anywhere from 25¢ per hundredweight to $1.00 per hundredweight. The bag cost alone would probably represent something like 16¢ per hundredweight. By installing a small bin at a total installed cost of $1500, a manufacturer might receive his material by bulk truck where he has no unloading costs of his own because the truckdriver unloads the truck. He has reduced his need for storage within his plant and he has greatly reduced his losses from dumping bags as well as reducing the cost he pays for the raw material. The investment for rail car unloading might run as high as $8000 and the man would still have to unload the car. This is the difference between bag and bulk.

Let's consider the delivery time versus inventory. We might have an operation where material is produced from a central plant. It is warehoused both at the central location and in three other locations where material is delivered to local customers in and around these four warehousing areas. If a satisfactory means can be developed whereby adequate service can be provided from one large central warehouse, this system can be changed to one where there might be three regional sales offices, one central sales office and one warehouse. Material shipped to a point in the local area, transloaded to one or more delivery vehicles and delivered to local customers. Some oil companies are using a system similar to this for shipping packaged lube oils. They load twin-twenty trailers: transport the materials to a local delivery point, split the two trailers into two twenty-foot trailers, have a second truck driver meet him, make their local delivery runs, come back together, hook up and return for another load the next day. By this means they are covering areas with a 400 mile radius.

Recentralization versus decentralization. Let's look at cement. In cement, to be in the market competitively, you must be able to provide a truck delivery to your customer. However, there are real economies in having a large scale plant compared to a small scale plant. Manufacturing costs might differ as much as $1.00 a barrel. Actually, we think that a very modern small plant as opposed to a modern large plant might only have 50¢ a barrel differential but this is still a significant cost differential. If a manufacturer can find a way to reach out to broad enough marketing areas at a reasonable transportation cost and still provide truck delivery to meet his competitive market situation he is in a position to take advantage of the economies of scale in manufacturing. Here are two new technologies available to railroads which can help solve this basic transportation need.

1. A pressure differential rail car which makes possible a very simple rail highway transfer terminal with a minimum cost. This marries the economies of rail transportation with truck delivery flexibility and it eliminates the need for expensive storage terminals.

2. A whopper hopper—this 125-ton cement car which permits longer railroad haul at low cost to permit profitable rate levels so that a large plant can reach a large enough market at a low enough cost to allow it to take advantage of the economies of scale. Here's an example on such a simplified pressure differential rail-highway-transfer terminal. The advantage to a shipper for using such a system is that:

1. It's the lowest cost method of distribution which still meets the truck delivery requirement.
2. There is no investment in the terminal and therefore no risk for the shipper.
3. It allows him to reach more distant markets profitably.
4. By working with one transportation prime contractor a customer does not have to talk with a number of separate transportation people

such as a railroad, a terminal operator, and a truck company.

5. There is faster service to rail-operated terminals because of their key location in the middle of through-train yards, therefore, there is less inventory required to service the market.

Now we think that this type of thing is a very basic system that applies to a large variety of dry bulk commodities. We look at them as three basic products.

1. One where contamination is a problem, such as cement, salt, and similar industrial chemicals.
2. Where contamination is a serious problem, such as flour, sugar and those areas where the Food and Drug Administration is very much concerned with the way in which material is handled.
3. Where contamination is super critical as in the plastics area: where one black pellet in a carload of white pellets can ruin the entire carload.

There is a picture of the New York Central Flexi-Flo car for use in this type of service. This new complete transportation service solves all three problem areas.

1. It allows a distant shipper to take advantage of the economies of a bulk truck delivery to his end customer.
2. Through the use of a complete transportation service, it not only embodies a new car, but also proper train schedules matched with key terminals in the middle of through-train yards that allow a collapsing of order-to-delivery times. Today we are picking up cement from Ravena, New York, just outside of Albany at 5:00 PM and by 7:00 AM the next morning these cars are in Rochester, New York, ready to have the cement delivered by truck to local customers. This is being done on a regular consistent basis.
3. We have allowed for the economies of scale in cement manufacturing by properly pricing so that the large manufacturer can reach out to a broad enough area, meet competitive conditions (i.e., a truck delivery) and still do it more economically than if he had a couple of regional cement plants.

In summary, let's review the trends within the railroad industry that will affect shipper's interest.

1. There is an increasing trend to the complete systems approach by the railroads. These complete systems are being developed by staff specialists in key industry areas.

2. The major advantages of the railroad are—
   a. Lowest towing cost
   b. Volume operation

3. You, as a shipper, must understand your customers total distribution problems as well as your own to properly evaluate the types of services you should be designing in connection with what the railroads do, to best solve your customers problems.

29. Containerization: The Route To Integrated Transportation*

Lassor Blumenthal†

Ever since the mid-Fifties, when the great post-Korean War sellers' market began to wane, one of the American businessman's most valuable defenses against the profit squeeze has been cost-cutting. He has learned to subject both the office and the factory to rigid, scientifically based cost-reducing programs. He has been so successful, in fact, that in the well-run corporation most excess operating fat has long been trimmed off.

But one major cost "frontier" still remains. The troublesome, time-consuming, costly and often precarious business of moving goods from factory to customer has never yielded much to the cost-cutter's disciplines. And as no less than $100 billion a year—almost one-sixth of the Gross National Product—is spent on distribution, any technique that cuts freight costs or handling charges, diminishes inventories or makes faster deliveries, reduces insurance rates or cuts down on pilferage and loss, can bring enormous savings.

Many transportation experts believe that the answer to high distribution costs has finally been found. The method: containerization. As Aaron J. Gellman, planning director of North American Car Corp. puts it: "The objective of containerization is to produce for the shipper transportation and distribution services at the lowest possible cost."

And as more and more shippers turn to containerization, they are finding that this objective is indeed attainable. "A pipeline between factory and customer is the ultimate, but unattainable, distribution system," says one marketing manager. "Failing that, flexible containerization systems are the best way to streamline distribution."

* Reprinted by special permission from *Dun's Review & Modern Industry,* June 1964. Copyright, 1966, Dun & Bradstreet Publications Corporation.

† Vice-President, The Charisma Organization, Marketing and Communication Consultant.

One company that has demonstrated the savings in time and money that result from such versatility is Volkswagenwerk, the world's third largest auto manufacturer. Back in 1960, Volkswagen executives discovered that in order to keep U.S. dealers stocked with spare parts, they had to ship 3,500 wooden boxes a month to the U.S. In an effort to reduce this cost, the aggressive, cost-conscious German company tried containerization, and the number of shipments dropped to 833 containers a month. Recalls Guenter Kittel, Volkswagen of America's general parts manager: "Although we were shipping more parts to the U.S., we reduced the number of boxes we handled to less than 25% of the number needed before containerization."

Moreover, Volkswagen distributors also cashed in on the benefits. "They saved up to 40% of the time it formerly took them to unload," says Kittel. "Six men can now do the work that required ten men when we used boxcars. And by shipping one container to a dealer, the distributor eliminates the handling of 300 individual boxes."

With such tremendous savings in time and money possible for just about everybody, containerization would seem to be the answer to every shipper's prayer. The fact is, however, that there are more boosters than users of the system. The principal obstacle, of course, is the tremendous capital investment in existing transportation facilities. "Nobody wants to admit that the $50,000 trailer bought a few years ago is obsolete," points out one New York freight forwarder. "The changeover to a container system could wipe out a lot of people in this business."

Moreover, the giants of the transportation industry are still locked in a struggle about container sizes and standards. And neither truckers nor railroads can agree on what their role should be in the integrated transportation system that is the inevitable result of universal use of containerization. As North American Car Corp's Gellman puts it: "One of the reasons that waterborne container movements have grown so dramatically is that the role of the ocean carrier has been defined, if only by the enforced limitation of the points between which vessels can be operated. Unfortunately, the majority of carriers have not defined their roles so precisely. Far too many are trying to be all things to all men."

Notwithstanding these limiting factors, experts feel that containerization is well on the way to becoming the backbone of the transportation system. One innovator, President Sol Katz of Strick Trailers, a division of the Fruehauf Corp., believes that his company is about to start a new growth cycle based on industry's greater use of a flexible containerization system. And a West Coast shipping executive detects revolution, not evolution, in the air. The benefits of containerization are so obvious," he claims, "that transportation must now adapt itself to the concept."

The reasons for this optimistic outlook are not hard to find. Consider the Singer Co. for example, which has just discovered that containerization may make possible the complete revamping of its current distribution pattern in Latin America. In a research program, called Project Oasis, the company has hypothesized a situation where components would be placed in containers at the factories in Europe and shipped to large distribution centers in Latin America. With such a system, agents could expect delivery from the Latin American center within ten days of placing an order, and inventory levels could therefore be reduced to about five or six weeks. In actual practice it now takes two to three months for delivery, and Singer agencies in Latin America are forced to carry a costly six to seven months' inventory. Overall, Singer executives believe that containerization could eventually save it between $3 million and $4 million in costs.

Or take Union Carbide Corp.'s plastics division, which has evolved a fully integrated, containerized operation in distributing polyethylene and vinyl plastics from its plants in Texas City and Seadrift, Texas. The chemicals go directly from the production line into aluminum containers; the containers are placed on lightweight truck bogies and taken to a marshaling area at the Texas City docks, where cranes lift them onto one of Union Carbide's container ships, converted T-2 tankers. The ships run to

Perth Amboy, New Jersey, where the containers are lifted out, hitched onto flatbeds and taken directly to customers or to the company's compounding plant in South Bound Brook, New Jersey.

The advantages to Union Carbide from this system have been considerable. First, there are substantial savings in transportation and handling costs. Further, decision on how to package the chemicals (in bags, rigid cardboard containers or hopper cars) can be delayed until the last minute; previously, everything had to be packaged in Texas, then frequently repackaged in New Jersey to meet customer requirements. Finally, the need for silos to hold the plastic powder or pellets as they come off the production line has been eliminated. "For us," says Albert J. Fenaroli, Union Carbide's planning and research traffic manager, "containerization has meant some very handsome savings."

Some experts point out, however, that an artificial brake is being applied to containerization. With the exception of a few carriers that plunged into the containerization business themselves, ocean carriers have made little attempt to attract containerized freight. In fact, early this year several Trans Pacific shipping conferences imposed a $1-a-ton leasing charge and a $3-a-ton loading charge on container cargo going overseas from West Coast ports. A major reason for this hostility, of course, is that the steamship lines have substantial investments in traditional dockside and shipboard loading facilities and are in no rush to declare this equipment obsolete.

To be sure, carrier conferences on some routes, notably the North Atlantic run, do offer a 10% commodity reduction if the container is filled by the shipper at his plant and not unloaded until it reaches the consignee. But many shippers do not consider this incentive sufficient to adopt one of the existing methods of containerization.

Within the United States, however, many major transportation companies have made the tremendous investment in rolling stock and handling equipment, in addition to the containers themselves. The New York Central Railroad, for example, has invested $30 million in its Flexi-Van service. Both Flexi-Van and the Pennsylvania Railroad's Trailer Train are steadily signing up new customers for their systems, and at last count more than fifty other railroads were participating in the services. Growth has been phenomenal. In 1963 Flexi-Van had 7% of the nation's total piggyback volume and accounted for more than 5% of the Central's entire freight revenue. "And this," crows Central President Alfred E. Perlman, "from an operation that turned its first wheel in April of 1958!"

Smart rate-making, of course, made piggybacking the success it is and prompted others to follow suit. Container Transport International, an independent operator of containers in New York, announced the introduction of a new container car whose containers are considered, for rate-making purposes, as part of the car, just as the tank is part of the tanker. The company estimates that goods will travel for 20% less than by conventional shipments.

True, part of their carrier's motivation for rate reductions may be due to the fact that there is a trend among large shippers towards buying or leasing their own private fleets. Nonetheless, benefits accrue to both shipper and carrier. For the railroads, of course, the economics of containerization make it almost imperative; for example, the average revenue from a Flexi-Van car each month is $4,400 compared with a boxcar's average revenue of $407. The prospect of such handsome profits prompted Chicago and North Western Railway Co.'s President Ben W. Heineman to build a million-dollar piggyback terminal in Chicago, designed exclusively for the handling of highway trailers on railroad flat cars. The terminal can handle more than 700 of the largest highway trailers each day. "We now have," says Heineman, "a terminal for piggyback freight in which rail and truck services are integrated."

REA's Success

In freight forwarding, REA Express has been particularly ingenious in developing containerization methods. Within the past few years it has introduced a variety of plans with special incentives for shippers.

For instance, REA's Unit-Pak container—a wire mesh cage—has proved to be the ideal solution for National Distillers and Chemical Corp. in reducing pilferage and damage (always a problem for liquor dealers in less-than-truckload lots) in shipping liquor to customers in Laredo, Texas and Miami. The Unit-Pak is loaded and sealed by National Distillers in Cincinnati and shipped directly to the customers. Says Carl P. Greeley, National Distillers vice president of traffic and distribution: "Pilferage has been wiped out. And the price advantage

has been phenomenal. A 3,000-pound, less-than-truck load from Cincinnati used to cost us $165.90; with Unit-Pak the cost is $82."

REA's newest system is Unit-Haul, a coordinated rail-sea-highway shipment container system. Introduced last fall, the system is being used by REA to ship its own traffic between New York and the San Francisco-Oakland area, via Chicago, and between New York and Los Angeles. Using major railroads such as the New York Central, Union Pacific and Southern Pacific, REA ships the goods coast to coast in van-sized containers on 85-foot-long piggyback cars (four 20-foot containers to a car). By using the railroads' transcontinental passenger trains, says an REA executive, in-transit time is almost 24 hours less than by its regular express service.

Among the water shippers, containerization has made significant progress in coastal shipments and in shipments to such offshore points as Puerto Rico, Hawaii and Alaska. A typical operation is that of Sea-Land-Service, which operates between the East, Gulf and West coasts and Puerto Rico.

Sea-Land owns a fleet of fifteen ships, most of them specially designed to carry van-sized containers, and 8,300 over-the-road vans. When a van is filled at the shipper's loading platform, a Sea-Land tractor hauls it to dockside, where it is lifted aboard and stored. At the end of the run, it is lifted out, attached to another tractor and trucked to its destination. Another service, Seatrain, has entered into an agreement with the New York Central and Pennsylvania railroads to carry their trailers to Puerto Rico from New York.

Last fall Matson Navigation Co. began shipping pineapple-filled containers by rail as far inland as Chicago, an example of coordinated container operations that is naturally benefiting the railroads. "Containers," says Guy R. Glover, vice president for traffic at the Chicago, Burlington & Quincy Railroad, "have brought us new business from companies off our line. A variety of Midwestern manufacturers, notably breweries and tobacco and canned goods companies, are using containers to ship their products to Hawaii, largely because containers eliminate handling costs on the West Coast."

Another example of container coordination was Matson's agreement to ship du Pont's antiknock compound from California to Standard Oil of California's refinery near Honolulu, which serves the Pacific marketing area with oils and liquefied petroleum gas. Socal wanted the material shipped in bulk, rather than in drums, so du Pont had General American Transportation Co. build a unique tank container exactly the size of Matson's containers, similar to a railroad tank car without wheels.

The liquid containers are trucked from du Pont's Antioch, California plant on trailer flatbeds and hoisted onto the Matson ships, where they fit neatly into the "cells" designed to hold Matson boxes. On arrival, they are trucked to the customer.

For du Pont, this elimination of interior packaging in shipping bulk items has been the biggest advantage in containerization—in some cases bringing savings of 35% to 40% of total distribution costs. And its arrangement with Matson proves a most important rule of containerization, in order to render full benefit to the shipper, the container must be a part of an integrated transport system.

For the airlines, with their emphasis on speed in freight handling, containerization is of course made to order—though it is still a fledgling movement. In just the past couple of months, American Airlines has introduced its Astrofreight System and Pan American Airways has brought out its Air Pak system. In both systems, containerized or palletized merchandise is mechanically loaded and locked into jet freighters. American claims that it can load and unload an Astrojet freighter in 40 minutes, compared to the nearly three hours it takes to unload one of its smaller DC-7F piston cargo planes.

But this proliferation of container products and services also points up one of the major obstacles to success: the lack of meaningful standards to govern the sizes of containers, hardware and handling equipment. Truckers can carry higher containers than railroads, which have limited overhead clearance And railroads can carry longer containers than many ships can conveniently place in their holds. Not surprisingly, each carrier wants to maximize its own payload, and the maximum payload for one is usually less than optimal for another.

Overseas, the problem becomes even more complicated, because European railroads have strict regulations governing the sizes of containers that will receive the benefits of lower container tariffs, and they have not looked fa-

vorably on the larger sizes of U.S. containers. Moreover, seventeen European and African nations have already established standards on tariff systems that they want other nations to adopt. John R. Immer, president of management consultant firm World Saving International, and North American delegate to the International Container Bureau, puts it this way: "For practical purposes the European thinks of a 'standard container' as one developed with the capability of universal acceptance. This concept rules out the American van-size container within the foreseeable future."

The main barrier to standardization, of course, is the conflicting interests of the U.S. carriers. Nevertheless, the multifarious elements of the transportation industry are slowly coming to terms with one another. Last year, for example, U.S. members authorized the American Standards Association to announce standard measurements for four sizes of van containers. Although the standards are not obligatory, they are at least a target to shoot for. Too, the International Organization for Standardization, the worldwide association of national standards groups, is meeting about now in Hamburg, Germany, and it is expected to approve at least the 10-foot and 20-foot ASA lengths.

Still to be agreed on are standards for the hardware used to fasten the boxcars to flatcars and bogies and for the container-handling equipment that will make containers interchangeable between all modes of transport in all parts of the world.

Containerization, then, is moving toward complete integration on a world-wide basis. Already, interchangeability of containers among trucks, trains and ships is an accomplished fact. Slowly, each competing type of carrier is being forced to join hands in offering a single transportation service to the shipper. This means that the intricate jungle of commodity rates that governs most shipments today will eventually be replaced by tariffs based mainly on the weight of the container and the distance traveled— whether the shipment contains beef or gold bullion. It also means that the single bill of lading will become the rule, rather than the exception, saving an incalculable amount of paperwork. From the shipper's point of view, such services are long overdue.

30. *What 'Unimarket' Does for Raytheon**

BOYD B. BARRICK†

Too often today, marketing strategy has relegated distribution into a gray area of neglect.

Many customers are becoming disenchanted with the extended lead times manufacturers require for delivery of merchandise—the same merchandise producers spend thousands of dollars to introduce and promote. In many cases, companies are losing sight of a basic marketing truth: no sale is complete until the order has been received in the plant and the merchandise has been delivered.

What is more, a fertile field for cost reduction is lying fallow. The best talent available is being used—in design, manufacturing, assembly, testing, etc.—to get the product to the shipping platform at the most favorable cost.

But, once ready for shipment, the product slips into an uncontrolled, unchallenged distribution method which, in some cases, eats up as much as 40% of the product's cost. It is this segment of manufacturing operations that offers the greatest opportunity for innovation and savings.

Many industries, such as women's hosiery, automotive replacement parts, hardware, drugs, optical goods, wallpaper, electronic components and a host of others, are taking advantage of this opportunity by applying new techniques to distribution.

One of these new ideas, the Unimarket system, was conceived at Raytheon Co.'s Distributor Products Div. several years ago and placed in service early in 1960. Basically, this system eliminates field or regional warehouses and concentrates inventory in one location.

In the Unimarket method, orders are transmitted over leased telegraph lines using data transmitting and processing techniques. Merchandise is transported to a nearby airport and sent to the distributor by air freight the same day the order is received. The entire system, including special communication services, data processing equipment and air freight, is operating at a net saving of 17% compared with the costs of running the older, field warehouse system.

Distribution Analysis

Raytheon's Distributor Products Div. is the marketing agency for the company's manufacturing divisions—the source for all products sold through our more than 800 distributors.

We handle more than 3,000 items, classified into 12 different product lines. The products are compact with high cost-to-bulk ratios.

Distribution of electronic parts is a two-step process: manufacturer-to-distributor, and distributor-to-dealer and/or user. In anayzing our distribution organization, before making any radical changes, we discovered two related problems which apply to both steps:

Inventory Problem

Inventories are expensive for distributors, so they often cannot keep very large stocks of all items. This means the manufacturer must provide assurances of prompt re-supply when needed.

In addition, the products themselves sometimes cause inventory problems. Certain tubes, for example, slowly lose their vacuums and their characteristics vary as a function of time, whether they are used or not.

Obsolescence is another inventory headache. In many cases, by the time a product is needed a newer device, performing the same functions,

* Reprinted by permission from *Industrial Marketing*, February 1963.
† General Sales Manager, Raytheon Company.

may be available. On the average, two years is all an electronics manufacturer can expect for the selling life of a new product.

This situation entails an obligation, and a competitive necessity, for the manufacturer to keep a full line of stock on call. The classic method of doing this is through regional or satellite warehouse systems.

In Raytheon's case, five regional warehouses were stocking approximately $2 million of duplicated inventory. In other industries, dealing in even higher priced merchandise, the value of held inventory soars much higher.

Availability Problem

Inventory problems stem from distributor capabilities and reach down into manufacturer obligations. Availability of products, on the other hand, begins with the manufacturer's abilities and affects the distributor's relations with his customers.

Our analysis showed that maintaining an inventory in the field was still no guarantee a customer would receive the items he wanted when he wanted them. For one thing, it was unsound for us to load regional warehouses with slow-moving merchandise, so only the high-volume, fast-turnover products were kept in duplicate inventory. As a result, our warehouses carried only 60% of the entire line. Nearly half of the orders placed on the regional warehouses, therefore, required subsequent back-order from the main warehouse.

When the element of time was considered, this situation gave distributors a serious customer service problem. Because of their relatively low inventories, 10% of distributors' orders were "rush," not to replenish inventory, but to meet a user's needs for items not on their shelves.

Thus, availability had become an important factor for the specifying influences, procurement personnel and design engineers, and a decisive sales factor for our distributors.

System Analysis

Another analysis we made while considering adoption of the Unimarket principle was a comparative study of regional warehouse and single warehouse systems.

Regional warehouses frequently are annexed

to regional sales offices or are located according to organization, sales or other field activities without regard to the most efficient placement of material handling centers. But, even if we concede that the branch warehouses are properly located, we must weigh their true costs.

Merchandise must be shipped from the home warehouse to the field warehouses at regular intervals. Later, it is reshipped to distributors. Freight costs are invariably greater than they would be for a single shipment to the customer. Raytheon's shipping costs were averaging $116,500 annually.

Operating the warehouses at Atlanta, Los Angeles, Dallas, Chicago, Memphis and Portland, Ore., cost nearly $500,000 a year. Warehouse rentals took $160,000, operating costs $177,000, inventory financing $100,000, and property taxes $48,000.

Although less measurable, the customer service problems incorporated in the field warehouse system are highly significant.

The regional warehouse, with its incomplete stock, was continually on a back-order basis. Every back order multiplied the number of shipping papers and hardened the arteries of distribution.

In the detailed analysis of the one-warehouse concept, it was established that back orders could be reduced substantially if orders were filed originally at the theoretically fully-stocked home warehouse. Experience has proved this out; our back orders have been reduced by 67%.

The order-to-delivery cycle was taking from 10 to 12 days with the time dissipated as follows:

1. Order transmittal by mail: two to four days.
2. Order processing: one to three days.
3. Delivery: one to five days.

The Unimarket system has greatly reduced elapsed time in virtually every area. Today, cycles average two to three days, or a 75% reduction in lead time.

Preliminary Step

Before the Unimarket system was installed, an intermediate inventory control and ordering system had been instituted by Raytheon. Punched data cards were inserted into every package of five electron tubes (the standard wholesale unit) and in ordering units of other items.

Then the Raytheon field sales manager met with each of our major distributors and reviewed purchases and product flow for the previous year. Normal distributor inventories were established which would provide positive order-filling capacity for four-week periods. Once these levels were established, excess inventory was returned for credit and the distributor's existing inventory was codified with punched data cards.

As merchandise leaves the distributor's shelves, the cards are removed, becoming the recording instruments which maintain a constant flow of replacement inventory. This was a major streamlining of the former system under which the distributor and the Raytheon salesman took a physical inventory once a month and prepared an order modified by the distributor's best estimates of volume and product mix.

The intermediate system, which is called RAYCI (Raytheon Controlled Inventory) enabled most distributors to double their inventory turnover. It also provided valuable internal experience in order processing and data identification techniques that proved helpful in reducing warehouse order service time.

Rapid Communication

With the order processing steps converted to electronic data control, our next preparatory step was a thorough analysis of the communications aspects of placing the order.

Raytheon's Distributor Products Div. is represented by 25 district salesmen located in the principal population centers, close to the distributors they serve. In our old system, orders were mailed by the distributor to the district office which then passed the order on to the appropriate field warehouse.

By eliminating the field warehouses, we found, the order could be sent by the district office to the home warehouse. But mail was too slow.

Western Union offered special punched data transmitters that could operate over leased wires in a star network between the selected field offices and the headquarters warehouse at Westwood, Mass. A time and cost study of the leased wires indicated that satisfactory order service could be achieved by assembling the field orders at six order entry points: Los Angeles, Dallas, Atlanta, Baltimore, New York and Chicago.

As adopted, this technique permits ordering instructions from groups of distributors to be assembled at each transmittal point. The headquarters operator then calls upon each office in a prearranged sequence and the orders are transmitted.

The order clerk at the transmittal point uses a prepunched tape for each distributor. This automatically prints the distributor's name, address, credit code and other applicable data and punches a tape that will be used to send the order. Then a punched matrix is used to insert the product identifications on the transmittal tape. These two sources are integrated on a Programatic Flexowriter which produces the tape for final transmission. The operator uses a keyboard to insert variable data such as quantity and price.

When each tape is ready, it is inserted into a Teletype transmitter to await the call from Westwood over a leased wire. The tape transmits automatically as soon as the circuit is clear.

At Westwood, the order is received on a Teletype receiver which prints a punched tape containing the transmitted data. This tape is fed automatically into an IBM machine that simultaneously prints multiple copies of the packing slip, invoice, and inventory control data.

This communications center is manned until 10 p.m. local time each working day to accommodate West Coast orders. Also, this permits paperwork processing required for order-filling to be completed by the time the warehouse opens the following morning.

Transportation Economics

When analyzing the transportation costs involved in moving packaged products to the field, all media were considered and all advantages and disadvantages were weighed.

Considering costs for shipments from Westwood, Mass., to Los Angeles for two typical orders of 20 and 220 lbs., respectively, the following rates and times apply:

Carrier	20 lb.	220 lb.	Time
Air freight (exclusive of pick-up and delivery charges)	$17.50 (min)	$ 54.34	1 day
Air Express	17.08	180.97	1 day
Rail Express	6.88	54.01	5–6 days
Surface	10.35 (min)	22.77	8–9 days

Analyzing similar costs from Westwood, Mass., to New Orleans, La.:

Carrier	20 lb.	220 lb.	Time
Air freight (exclusive of pick-up and delivery charges)	$ 6.00 (min)	$ 35.20	1 day
Air Express	10.05	110.57	1 day
Rail Express	3.19	35.11	4–5 days
Surface	9.12 (min)	20.06	5–6 days

The glamorized concept of air transport pictures an airplane taking off from the front lawn of the factory and landing in the customer's parking lot. But this is strictly a mirage, and some carefully calculated compromises were necessary to take advantage of the rate structures of the various modes of transportation and the times involved.

By analyzing the traffic flow by regions and the minimum rate structure applying to air freight, it was found to be more economical to combine shipments to certain areas and have these shipments broken open for forwarding at 16 break-bulk points throughout the country. The individual orders are packaged at the home warehouse in Westwood where they are addressed and marked with forwarding instructions such as, "Via parcel post Atlanta to Savannah," "Via Greyhound bus New Orleans to Baton Rouge," "Local Chicago delivery via United Parcel Service," etc.

The break-bulk points were established at Atlanta, Birmingham, Charlotte, Chicago, Dallas, Denver, Detroit, Houston, Kansas City, Los Angeles, Memphis, New Orleans, Pittsburgh, San Francisco and Tampa. Most of the orders being trans-shipped from these break-bulk points are less than 50 pounds and are sent by parcel post.

Our study revealed there is a real need still for a low-cost, efficient forwarding service operating on a national basis that could assume forwarding responsibility. In Raytheon's case, it could account for almost 70% of these shipments.

Application to Other Industries

In the Unimarket system we have combined the traditional local market areas and created a single, nationwide market to provide all customers with the same service through data processing, and air freight. The usual array of satellite field warehouses has been consolidated into a single point source for distribution. This system, which has proven its value in electronic parts distribution, is also applicable to other industries which are dealing with products of similar physical limitations, have similar distribution systems, and have similar communications and transportation requirements.

Considering first the product, it should be a packaged item used repetitively. Its size-to-weight ratio can vary from women's hats to miniature ball bearings. However, its weight-to-unit value ratio should be as low as possible. Frames for eye glasses and semi-finished optical lens blocks from American Optical Co. are typical of the high-unit-cost items that are appropriate for this type of distribution.

Product life is a valuable incentive to the air freight concept, too. Parke-Davis Co. uses a similar system to keep abreast of the varying demand patterns for vaccines and perishable pharmaceuticals, while Cole of California ships women's bathing suits by air to keep ahead of seasonal obsolescence and meet retailing demand as influenced by local weather trends.

Some suppliers even use a similar system in selling direct to retailers. Macklanburg-Duncan, a hardware manufacturing firm in Oklahoma City, ships directly, without wholesalers or branch warehouses, to 35,000 retail outlets. The merchandise for retailers in each general area is pre-packaged as in the Unimarket system and sent to break-bulk points where the pre-addressed individual orders are delivered to the post office for parcel post forwarding. Total delivery time from the factory to anywhere in the country has been cut to an average of two days.

The competitive value of prompt delivery and stock replenishment seldom carries an actual price tag, but the advantages are being felt at Raytheon and in these other firms which have adopted similar systems.

In communications, telegraphic dispatch forms a very effective team with modern internal data processing. The time-saving features over mail are obvious and the reduction of error over telephoned emergency orders is quite apparent.

The shrinking of the nation through jet air freight to a market area just five hours wide by two hours deep has put a new factor into the determination of factory locations. Assuming that a product meets the feasibility requirements for air freight—size, weight, perishability and value—it is no longer necessary to locate a factory or warehouse at the center of a distribution pattern or in an industrial complex. As long as a factory is within an hour's driving time of a trunk-line airport, it can be located in an area of skilled labor, favorable wage rates and business climate and still compete very dramatically with plants in mid-country.

The Unimarket system with its automated ordering, data processing and air freight delivery, is opening up a new area of profit improvement in many industries. The grey area of distribution is gradually coming into focus and targets are being defined in black and white. The application of meaningful controls is already retrieving lost profits for many firms whose distribution costs run as high as 40% of total product cost.

By applying these techniques in other specific situations, there are many opportunities for greater profit improvement still before us.

31. *What's the Best Way to Ship?*[*]

THOMAS F. DILLON[†]

Motor Carriers: Emphasis on Service

The motor carrier industry slogan "If you've got it, a truck brought it," was more apt to be true in 1963 than ever before. Motor freight revenues rose to a record high of almost $8.5 billion, up from 1962's $8.1 billion. 1964 looks even better. As railroads curtail less than carload service (down 25% in 1963), as purchasing agents, secure in supply sources and confident of fast delivery, keep inventories trim, 1964 takes on signs of another booming year for truckers.

Advantages

More sophisticated motor carrier representatives calling on purchasing agents. Sharp, young, college grads, anxious to help with problems, know they have to offer more service to get business.

Despite their complaints, truckers realize small shipments are their forte. If they can do a good job handling small shipments, they know they'll probably get the volume. Carriers are improving terminal facilities to speed handling of LTL shipments, buying EDP equipment to cut paperwork.

Carriers continue to experiment with rates, such as COR (Cost Oriented Rates) and constant charge plans, whereby rates are based on weight, not on commodity shipped.

Industry is healthy. With higher revenues, carriers are able to invest in equipment, updating and expanding fleets. Bigger trailers mean lower rates on volume shipments needed to fill them.

Recent I.C.C. decision in piggyback case means truckers will be able to make greater use of this form of transportation. This can lead to lower rates as motor carrier costs drop.

LTL service is being improved. Carriers are

experimenting with batch container system designed to cut terminal handling costs. So far, results have been mixed, with some carriers feeling that containers are more trouble than they are worth. Others are enthusiastic about system. Claim it speeds shipments through terminals, cuts loss and damage, and improves service.

Disadvantages

Carriers continue to raise rates on small shipments, antagonizing influential shippers who claim they are subsidizing low rates assessed on volume shipments. They claim carriers overstate the cost of handling small shipments, run to the I.C.C. for rate increases rather than try to cut costs.

Teamsters Union is powerful. Carriers are no match for Jimmy Hoffa and both sides know it. Carriers cannot stick together in negotiations, but merely rubber stamp Hoffa's demands. This means continuing increases in labor costs. But many truckers feel Hoffa's power has advantages. There has been little labor trouble since Jimmy Hoffa came into power. As long as truckers pay the price, they enjoy labor peace.

Private trucking is growing. Insiders consider this the number one problem. Private trucking is taking business carriers want most—frequent, big volume, easy to handle, moving between regular points. Every time truckers propose rate increase, big shippers threaten to put on their own trucks to handle most attractive shipments, give less attractive ones (low rated, out of the way points) to common carriers.

Illegal trucking poses a problem. Though few say so, many truckers feel private trucking and illegal trucking go hand in hand. Company operating its own trucks cannot make them pay without two-way haul. When legal return load (of company's own freight or exempt goods, such as agricultural products) is not available, there is a stronger temptation and ample opportunity to get a load of "regulated" commodities. Because of shortage of I.C.C. manpower to

[*] Reprinted by permission from *Purchasing*, August 10, 1964.

[†] Associate Editor, *Purchasing*.

221

enforce regulations by stopping trucks and checking cargoes, and lack of interest in enforcing law on part of some states, some truckers have operated illegally (hauling I.C.C. regulated goods without I.C.C. authority) for years without being stopped. Even when caught, trucker can chalk off low fine as "operating expense."

What It Costs

Motor carrier transportation is a huge, fiercely competitive industry composed primarily of small, family held companies. Some observers rate overcapacity as industry's number one problem. Because of competition, purchasing agents will usually find motor carriers more receptive to requests for rate adjustments, service innovations, and general assistance with transportation problems, than railroads who are more apt to be strapped down by tradition.

Almost any motor carrier salesman has close contact with his company's traffic department, and with proper supporting data (tonnage involved, classification, origin and destination points) will be able to get consideration of any reasonable rate adjustment request. Keep track of rates and services your competitors pay and receive. Almost any rate or service can be duplicated provided carrier feels he can make money on it.

What's Ahead

1. Better and faster service as carriers continue to upgrade fleets. Carriers are now seeking authority from the I.C.C. to use the new interstate highway system instead of previously authorized routes. If request is granted, hours will be shaved from many schedules.

2. Continued rate innovations, particularly on small shipments. Carriers know answer to small shipment problem is not periodic rate increase on LTL traffic. They have two alternatives: develop more efficient systems to handle LTL shipments or get customers to ship in larger units by offering greater rate incentives for increased tonnage.

3. Simpler pricing system. Transportation pricing system is out-moded, not in keeping with progress in other areas of industry. Until system is simplified, carriers cannot take full advantage of automation and electronic data processing equipment. Carriers are now experimenting with computer to rate shipments. One

system rates 220 freight bills per minute; a top rate man would take three hours.

4. More mergers. Trucking is no longer a founder-operator business. Industry got its start in 1935 with passage of the Motor Carrier Act (Part II of I.C.C. Act). First generation owners have mostly retired. Though still a closed-family operation, second generation is more sophisticated, college men with broader business background. Now more concerned with finance, industry image, labor relations, training, safety programs, and building empires than with driving a truck. Look for more mergers, better service, and elimination of duplicate facilities.

5. Continued expansion and buildng of terminals. As motor carriers fight to cut handling costs, they are moving away from center of town and toward outskirts where there is more room, less traffic congestion, and lower taxes.

6. Continuing attempts by regulated trucking industry to curtail gray area trucking. Every pound of freight hauled by an illegal carrier is a pound lost to regulated trucking. Acting through CAUT (Committee Against Unauthorized Trucking) and other groups, industry is making all out attempt to curtail such operations through court action, legislation, and turning in violators.

Railroads: They Offer Incentives

Railroads haul well over 600 billion ton-miles of freight (43% of all inter-city freight) annually. While percentage has stabilized following steady decline during the Fifties, mileage and points served have not. Track has declined from 235,000 miles in '39 to 215,000 miles today; points served have dropped by 10%, as marginal stations have been closed.

Nevertheless, railroad executives are confident and anticipate an upswing. They're offering rail users an increasing number of incentives to hold them or woo them away from other transportation.

Cure-all for rail problems, as lines see it, is relaxed regulation, opening door "to compete more vigorously with its competition."

Advantages

Lines are automating facilities, yards, equipment at a growing pace.

Purchases of new cars—many designed to meet special hauling requirements—are picking up, after a lengthy lull.

Piggyback is still relatively limited, but is growing rapidly in scope and service.

Most plants in operation today have a rail siding adjacent or near loading-unloading facilities.

Disadvantages

Railroads lack versatility and flexibility of trucking. They're tied to rail and cannot service off-rail communities directly.

Pilferage is a persistent railroad headache. Ditto for damage, despite strenuous rail efforts to correct situation.

Railroads are in unprecedented state of flux. Considerable confusion regarding rates, service, and equipment works to detriment of rail transport.

What It Costs

Railroads are the most economical way to move materials and components in carload lots over long distances. P.A.'s can effect significant transportation cost reductions by using rail intelligently. Example: average unit costs may be sliced by raising the volume of inbound materials moving via rail.

Operating 24 hours a day, 7 days a week, railroads are not halted by bad weather and related conditions. With proper scheduling of orders, P.A.'s can turn railroads into "rolling warehouses," providing additional savings.

Lending new "zip" to rail operations is plan to introduce diesel engines on all runs. Diesels pull freight trains faster, more efficiently, and with fewer jolts and jars than their predecessors.

Other rail improvements include the introduction of mechanical refrigeration in place of water cooled cars; new approaches to tracing and customer service; and refined bracing and dunnage techniques.

What's Ahead

1. Intensified efforts by rails on all fronts (technological, legislative, etc.) to win back lost freight traffic. Fresh concepts, advanced equipment, and a more aggressive attitude on the part of rail officials will spark this drive.

2. Continued gains for piggyback, as new equipment is built and interest is stimulated.

3. Addition of more mileage to the 26,000 now under centralized traffic control and expansion of push-button classification yards.

4. Serious freight car shortages during peak traffic periods, until replacements fill gaps left by retirement of obsolete equipment.

5. Upped tonnage hauled by unit (shuttle) trains, as rail successes with coal lead to other attempts.

6. Steady pressure for mergers eliminating overlapping lines, duplicated services.

7. Growing reliance on automation, computers, industrial TV to streamline freight handling and hauling, compute rates "scientifically," and roll back operating costs.

8. Increased car-miles per freight train mile (now 70.9); higher average speed (now 20.1 mph); boosted average load per car (now 37.1 tons).

Air Freight: Serves 7000 Communities

Scheduled air freight carriers (combination and all-cargo) now serve 7000 communities either directly or via coordinated air-truck service. Airlifting cargo are 11 major trunk lines, three all-cargo airlines, and a growing array of local service carriers. Cargo total for 1963 (domestic): 63 million tons; 1964 outlook: a higher level, since the tempo of air shipments is running far out in front of last year. Predicted: a spurt to 2 billion ton miles by '67. Despite air freight's 50-fold growth since 1946, however, it still carries less than 1% of total U.S. freight. Estimated air carriage for 1964 is about 1.5 billion ton-miles.

Advantages

Air freight is handling bigger, bulkier items than ever before. Reason? The introduction of specially designed air-freighters (CL-44D, Argosy, Super-Hercules) and the advent of the jet cargo aircraft.

Jets raise air freight's maximum speed to 600 mph (10 times faster than the speediest surface carrier). Range is 3000 miles non-stop; payload, 100,000 pounds. New jets also will have direct operating costs of 3¢ per ton mile once in full operation.

New loading technique and aircraft with straight-in loading speed handling make it possible to load massive pieces quickly and efficiently.

Air freight offers a smooth, damage free ride. Jolts and jars from highways and tracks are no problem in the air. This factor simplifies air shipping's packaging requirements.

Disadvantages

Air freight lacks standards for a variety of systems, containers, etc.

Many airlines still consider passenger service their No. 1 operation; cargo, a poor second. This approach holds back new investments, research; keeps lines from developing needed facilities, techniques, equipment.

Airport delays, freight tie-ups at cargo centers still rank as "prize" air freight problems.

What It Costs

Sky shipping is no longer emergency or special transportation. Machinery, electrical components, and printed materials have replaced drugs, cut flowers, perishables as top airlifted items.

Neither is air freight impossibly costly. The base rate may be considerably higher than other transportation, but there are many savings along the way. They include:

1. Reduced packaging costs, less packing "deadweight" to transport and pay for.

2. Little damage, leading to reduced insurance costs, easier packaging, fewer complaints.

3. Single bill of lading, easing paperwork.

4. Reduced pilferage and theft, stemming from air cargo's speed.

5. Broadened "purchasing horizons." By eliminating time-distance as transport factors, P.A.'s can take advantage of lower costs, better products, regardless of supplier location.

6. Reduced inventory needs. Items may be flown in so quickly that no large inventory is needed. Frees capital for other purposes.

7. Effective interline coordination expedites freight movement.

8. SPEED—and plenty of it.

What's Ahead

1. Expanded jet airfreighter fleets.

2. New appraisals of domestic cargo rates and new approaches to the "overbalance problem" of east-west as opposed to west-east cargo.

3. More, tauter air-truck agreements, extending service to areas not now within air freight's reach.

4. Introduction of short-medium range aircraft capable of operating between smaller communities.

5. Continued experimentation with helicopters and VTOL equipment as cargo carriers.

6. Improved mechanized handling, designed to slash on-the-ground bottlenecks.

Inland Waterways: In a Comeback

Inland waterway freight is riding the crest of a remarkable comeback. Just 10 years ago, freight moving via the nation's river-canal system was down to 2.8% of total U.S. freight. Today, waterway carriers are hauling close to 10% (135 billion ton-miles) over 29,000 miles of navigable rivers. Sparking the "return" of waterways as a key transport mode are: advanced towboats, with power plants of up to 6000 hp; improved, deepened waterways; and the rising cost of competitive transport modes. Outlook: further gains, as industry continues to re-evaluate the cost advantages of inland waterways vs. other surface haulers.

Advantages

New, larger towboats are lifting waterways carriers' hauling capability dramatically. The diesel-powered boats can handle tows as high as 30,000 tons.

Specially designed barges are expediting handling and offering greater in transit protection for a growing array of commodities. Outstanding examples: refrigerated barges for liquid methane; steam-coiled barges for asphalt; tank barges for oil and chemicals.

Improved navigational and communications aids now enable carriers to move despite adverse weather.

Towboat-to-dispatcher radio telephones enable carriers and customers to keep tabs on shipments.

Disadvantages

Industrial dock facilities, loading-unloading equipment, and handling procedures are still inadequate in many areas, despite intensified construction and improvement programs.

Waterways carrier interchanges are limited, despite increased cooperation between operators.

Locks and channels in major industrial areas are overtaxed by mounting waterways traffic, leading to costly delays.

What it Costs

Inland waterways transportation is the cheapest way to move king-sized loads of raw and semi-finished materials on a regular basis and over long-distances. It's slow compared to other transportation, but this problem is far outweighed by the enormous tonnage carriers can move at one time. Best waterways customers include petroleum, construction materials, grains, iron, steel, stone, and chemicals. Types of products moving on waterways, however, are expanding to encompass a broad spectrum of low value, bulky items. Waterway shipments mean substantial savings in overall transport costs for continuous loads. Major beneficiaries are companies with facilities on or close to key waterways. (Nearly 3000 have established waterside sites during the past decade.) Efficient pickup, delivery, and containerization are also substantial cost-cutters.

What's Ahead

1. More powerful, maneuverable towboats, designed to pull "longer strings" of barges with maximum efficiency even through "difficult" waters.

2. Closer coordination of individual carrier operations, leading to an effective interchange system.

3. Improvement of water links to Great Lakes and St. Lawrence Seaway, using Chicago's Calumet-Saginaw Canal as a prime example.

4. Continued movement of industry to waterways, plus expanded construction of dock facilities.

5. Further development of automated hauling systems and mechanization designed to slash loading-unloading-handling costs.

6. Advances in barge specialization. New designs will accommodate commodities not yet carried by inland waterways carriers.

Fishyback: Its Problems are Past

Fishyback transport (trailer-or-container-on-ship) service, problem-plagued in recent years, is afloat once more. Fifteen carriers—Great Lakes, coastal, inland waterways, ocean—currently offer fishyback operations. Outstanding is coast-to-coast trailer-ship service linking New York-Los Angeles, via the Panama Canal, southeast, and Gulf Coast points. Often called "roll-on, roll-off" shipping, trailership operations use 35 ft long trailers. Hauled overland to a port, trailers are detached from their cabs and rigged aboard special vessels. On arrival at destination, they are taken off, linked up to waiting tractors, and driven to the consignee's plant.

Advantages

Fishyback offers door-to-door delivery.

Vans are loaded and sealed at the shipper's facility. They are unopened until arrival at destination, thus eliminating theft and pilferage.

Containerization of fishyback shipments expedites mechanized handling, reduces loading-unloading-handling costs.

Packaging materials and labor costs are cut sharply by fishyback, since containerization cuts the amount and "depth" of protective packing required.

Disadvantages

Fishyback desperately needs standardized containers, procedures, handling systems; closer coordination between land-sea carriers.

Points linked by fishyback are still limited. Many vital areas have no service. The carrier situation is fluid. Sudden carrier dropouts or suspension of service are commonplace.

What It Costs

Fishyback offers many of piggyback's advantages (and disadvantages). It provides low cost water transportation, plus the speed and flexibility of highway transportation. Pickup and delivery are time-savers and efficiency-builders. Thanks to containerization, substantial handling cost reductions are possible. Typical example: in some instances fishyback shippers' costs are 20¢ per ton as against $4 to $5 for standard palletized handling. All types of finished and semi-finished items can move expeditiously via fishyback, provided that in transit speed is not an essential factor.

What's Ahead

1. Increased automation, speeding fishyback load-unloading and reducing costs.

2. Stepped up construction of equipment, development of special ports (Elizabethport, N.J., for example) capable of handling, storing, and transporting fishyback containers.

3. Development and use of modular containers, designed to be made any length merely by fastening individual units together.

4. Mounting pressure to standardize containers, expediting interchanges between carriers and other transportation.

Piggyback: Gaining Momentum

Piggyback (trailer-on-flat-car-service) is gaining momentum. Operations last year hit the 800,000 car mark, 13% above '62. Currently offering piggyback service under one or more of five plans are 63 railroads. Plan 1 involves rail transport of motor carrier trailer; Plan 2, railroad trailers on flat-cars; Plan 3, shipper trailers (owned or leased); Plan 4, rail movement of shipper trailers on shipper flatcars; Plan 5, joint truck-rail transport, door-to-door, under a joint truck-rail rate. Of total railroad freight, 2.8% is now hauled piggyback. New equipment, growing industry interest, settlement of a number of key issues pending before the ICC should lift percentage in the years ahead.

Advantages

Piggyback eases handling, slashes damage, cuts theft and pilferage. Result is substantial savings in key transport costs.

Piggyback service generally includes dependable pickup and delivery, making a complete door-to-door package.

Dunnage and bracing, usually needed in standard rail shipments, are not required in piggyback hauls.

Disadvantages

Coordination of truck-rail piggyback is far from effective, because of motor-rail's fight over regulations, rates, competition.

Absence of container standardization prevents rule-of-thumb planning for piggyback shipments.

What It Costs

Offering the best features of motor freight-rail transportation, piggyback provides high efficiency at reasonable price. Substantial cost reductions are possible, particularly on items moving 200–500 miles. Over 500 miles, rail boxcar may be as effective and considerably less expensive than piggyback. Where services are used extensively, rates are subject to negotiation. Minimum weight per shipment moreover, is generally lower for piggyback than for boxcar.

What's Ahead

1. Tremendous forward strides by piggyback both in technology and tonnage.

2. Clarification of five piggyback plans.

3. Settlement of piggyback cases pending before ICC, leading to new, stable piggyback patterns and concepts.

4. Intensified push toward container, equipment, system standardization.

5. Mounting use of Clejan and turntable-cars as prime piggyback units. (Moved by cable-winch, Clejan units may be shifted from trailer chassis to rail car in 90 seconds.)

6. Growth of piggyback equipment interchanges among railroads.

32. *Minimizing Transportation Costs with Shipper Co-operatives**

EDWARD W. SMYKAY AND IRENE SHIELE†

Increasing costs faced by retail business coupled with decreasing profit margin have made it necessary for retailers to focus more attention than ever on their transportation policies. Engrossed in their primary duty—the sale of merchandise—retailers have neglected the area of savings through improved transportation service and cost reductions. The current business downswing has also emphasized a need for more attention to transportation, and has brought about an increased interest in low-cost shipping methods.

As early as the 1890's, shippers were concerned about the high charges of less-than-carload shipments. It was then that the freight forwarder, specializing in small shipments, came into existence. After a series of disagreements with the railroads, the freight forwarders were brought into regulation under the ICC by the Freight Forwarders Act of 1942, which became Part IV of the Interstate Commerce Act. The freight forwarder operates on a margin which is the difference between the regular carload or truckload rates which he pays and his own published rates. The published rates of the freight forwarder are ordinarily lower than the same movement by the railroad or motor carrier. In this way the freight forwarder became "a transportation agency of function using one or more types of carriers to provide a complete service and responsibility for the through movement of less-than-carload or small shipments."[1]

Today the major innovation used by retailers to fight high transportation costs has been centered around freight consolidation through nonprofit shipping co-operatives. There are several methods which have been employed in the formation of these groups. In some cases, the Chambers of Commerce became interested and formed a chartered association. In other cases, the Retail Merchants Association took a similar course. Finally, in other cities, individual department stores or other businesses combined their effort and secured the services of an agent to supervise the operation and form the organization.

Benefits and Services

These associations are formulated with the following benefits and services for the retailers:[2]

1. Reduction in transportation charges which is the primary reason retailers join the association.

2. Saving in time since the association ships by direct carload shipments which arrive in a shorter time.

3. Reduction in loss and damage due to the loading and unloading of full cars by specialists in the particular types of commodities.

4. Savings in paperwork costs since the association handles all the bookkeeping arrangements and submits single bills to members periodically.

5. Elimination of time-consuming details since the association takes care of all claims against carriers, expedites shipments, and performs other traffic services.

6. Savings in lower insurance premium rates since the association provides broader coverage than is possible by an individual shipper.

* Reprinted by permission from *Journal of Retailing*, Summer, 1959.
† Michigan State University.
[1] *The Retailer's Transportation Manual*, American Retail Federation, Washington, D.C., p. 25.

[2] "Are You Wasting Money in Shipping?" Research Institute of America, Inc. *File*, March 31, 1958, p. 1.

Typical Association

The stated objective of one such co-operative association of retailers is: "to procure for members, through the pooling and consolidation of freight shipments, reductions in landed costs at no sacrifice of transportation service."

This particular association was organized in 1952 and has extended its operation to include a number of cities containing a large number of suppliers and connecting these points with the local area it serves. The association is managed by a Board of Directors composed of employees of member firms. The actual operation is supervised by an executive secretary who receives payment according to the weight of total merchandise shipped.

The association carries all merchandise bought or sold by a member except freezables, order notify, or C.O.D.'s. Predetermined pricing is used; thus the landed cost of any item is immediately known by the member. The association also carries insurance to cover members against refusal of a transportation company to honor legitimate loss or damage claims.

The association guarantees lower landed costs to its members as well as second-morning deliveries from New York and overnight delivery from Chicago. These are the two advantages most often stressed by the association and are considered to be of major importance. A likely question asked by retailers would be: does the association really provide economies to the individual retailer or wholesaler? Another question which concerns the consumer is; are the economies, if any, received by membership in a co-operative association reflected in the store's pricing policy?

Advantages and Disadvantages

In discussing this matter with a traffic manager of a member firm of the association used as a model for this study, it was evident that retailers do effect economies by such affiliation. While this company does not ship the majority of its orders through the association, it is the belief of management that important savings are achieved, especially by the smaller retailer. A large department store usually has a sufficient volume from the major market areas to justify a pool-car arrangement of its own. By this method the shipper receives a lower rate by virtue of the volume shipped. The small independent retailer, however, may find it difficult to arrange a pool-car shipment and consequently he must ordinarily ship by "less-than-carload" rates which are more expensive. A shippers co-operative may offer distinct transport advantages to either large or small retailers on that portion of their freight which fails to reach sufficient volume for full carloads.

The time factor is also important for smaller stores not located in the downtown area. Overnight and second-morning deliveries arrive at the terminal at 6 A.M., allowing delivery before noon of the same day. Regular freight would be delayed at least one more day.

A major disadvantage revealed, however, was the problem of shipping from the resources to the consolidation point. Resources located in outlying areas may cause local cartage costs to the consolidation terminal to exceed savings effected by the association. While some resources will pay for this transportation charge, the majority do not pay any shipping charges at all.

Comparison of Shipping Charges Between Shippers Association and Regular Freight

| | 200 Lb. | | | | 500 Lb. | | | | 3000 Lb. | | | |
| | Freight | | DSA | | Freight | | DSA | | Freight | | DSA | |
	Rate Per Cwt.	Total	Flat Charge	Total	Rate Per Cwt.	Total	Rate Per Cwt.	Total	Rate Per Cwt.	Total	Rate Per Cwt.	Total
Women's Ready to Wear	$4.48	$8.96	$4.50	$5.10	$4.48†	$22.40	$1.85	$10.75	$2.46	$73.80	$1.75	$61.50
Domestics	2.75	5.50	4.50	5.10	2.75	13.75	1.85	10.75	2.46	73.80	1.75	61.50
Pillows‡	5.50	11.00	4.50	5.30	5.50	27.50	1.95	11.25	4.92	147.60	1.85	64.50
Pottery	2.00	4.00	4.50	5.10	2.00	10.00	1.85	10.75	1.79	53.70	1.75	61.50

† Railway Express per cwt.

‡ 10¢ additional charge per cwt. for bulk.

The cost structure established by the Association is in terms of landed cost, which includes both transportation and consolidation and local delivery charges. Transportation is determined by the city from which the shipment originated and the weight bracket for the total of all orders at that city in one day. The consolidation expense covers the cost of receiving, checking, and loading the freight, plus the time used to list on one freight bill the entries covering all orders received on one day. This cost is computed on a weight factor only.

Value Related to Store Size

The question of whether or not savings in transportation charges through shipping co-operatives are reflected in pricing depends, in part, on store size. In a large organization, buyers are not fully acquainted with transportation problems and costs. While large stores are becoming more aware of the necessity for a fuller understanding by their buyers, it is difficult to reflect transportation accurately in pricing.

Many large department stores do not individually assess each shipment since the book work involved would entail considerable expense. Instead, transportation charges are shown on the buyer's monthly profit-and-loss statement. Also the cost-of-service offered by the association is based on the entire day's shipment and is often difficult to assess against an individual order. Thus, savings are reflected in a most indirect way.

In a smaller store, however, it is more customary for the buyer to take transportation into account when pricing the merchandise. In this case, particularly when reorders and national brands are not predominant, savings effected by co-operatives may be directly reflected in the pricing. Since transportation is such an important expense for a small store and control of buyer's action is more direct, knowledge of transportation policy by the buyer is more complete.

This question can also be answered in terms of the type of store operation. It is much more likely that transportation savings would be more important in a promotional store which depends mainly on price appeal for its competitive advantage. A semipromotional or non-promotional store does not depend as heavily on price since it offers service, reputation, and prestige as competitive appeals.

What Effect on Pricing?

It seems apparent, however, that any store could profitably use savings through shipping consolidation. Whether these savings will be directly reflected in price reductions, in the amount and quality of services offered, or in the store's profit margin will depend on such variables as size and type of operation.

As transportation costs continue to increase and stores are forced continually to reduce costs, the future of non-profit shipping co-operatives appears bright. Its benefits in money saved in transportation charges, and also in transit time on less-than-carload shipments are strong advantages today for all progressive retailers.

However, a problem which is presently facing the nonprofit shipper's co-operatives is the possibility of federal legislation that would bring these associations under control by the ICC or might actually declare them illegal. While no attempts have yet been successful, the possibility still looms in the future.

Section VII. Concepts in Physical Distribution Management

The concluding section of this book of selected readings deals with the physical distribution management problem in the Gestalt. At this juncture the reader should have gained an insight into the nature of the physical distribution function, the activities falling within its scope, and the numerous tools and techniques that are or may be used for performing the function more efficiently within the firm.

Some of the articles appearing in earlier sections have presented suggestions and advice on how to organize to carry out the physical distribution function better. So, also, some of the selections in this section touch heavily on matters dealt with earlier. However, it is the total approach in physical distribution management that the reader is expected to achieve as he reads this group of articles which are concerned with organizing for performance of the physical distribution function within the firm.

33. *Rhochrematics and Organizational Adjustments**

Stanley H. Brewer and James Rosenzweig†

Rhochrematics,‡ which is the new science of material and information flow, has many implications for top management. Developed to foster a systematic, integrated approach to managing the flow of raw materials, parts, components, and finished goods, its chief concept is that of maintaining the flow of the product from raw materials to the ultimate consumer.

In maintaining this flow it cuts across the traditional organization chart, and undermines some time-honored management practices, but companies practising Rhochrematics have discovered that it also cuts costs and compresses lead time.

In the case of the Boeing Airplane Company, whose Transport Division adopted this new approach following a survey in June, 1960, savings to date in reduced inventories and lead times are conservatively estimated to exceed $300,000 per year.

Boeing's experience with Rhochrematics and that of the Purex Corporation, another recent convert to the new science, will be discussed in detail later in this article, as cases in point, but the essential thesis here is that managements wishing to profit from this new science

must also be willing to accept its chief concept which is continuous concentration on the flow of the manufacturing process and may involve a complete restructuring of management's accepted channels of authority and ways of doing things.

The term Rhochrematics is a coined word and stands for the flow of things. It comes from two Greek roots, "rhoe" which means a flow as of a river or a stream and "chrema" which stands for products, materials, or things, including information. The abstract ending "ics" has been added here as for any of the sciences, such as mathematics, physics, etc.[1] From the time requirements are established and production planning is accomplished until an end product is delivered to the final consumer, many decisions are made which should be coordinated in order to optimize the entire material flow process.

Aspects of this process are being analyzed continually by almost every producer, wholesaler, or retailer. More and more attention is being devoted to physical distribution, materials management, inventory control, and other aspects of the material flow process. In most cases, however, analyses are carried out in each of these areas with little regard for the effects of changes on other areas. Hence, optimal solutions are often proposed for a segment of the flow process without due consideration for the resultant changes in the total flow pattern. Separate functions are optimized while the total operation proceeds in a suboptimal fashion.

This article attempts to ascertain the benefits that might accrue from a systematic, integrated approach to the over-all problem of material

* Reprinted from the *California Management Review,* Spring 1961, Vol. III, No. 3, Copyright 1961 by The Regents of the University of California.

† University of Washington.

‡ Substantial research on various aspects of integrated approaches to management of material flows has been done at the University of Washington. Sponsorship during the past year of projects which resulted in many of the conclusions reached herein should be credited to The Flying Tiger Line of Burbank, California, and to Canadair, a Subsidiary of General Dynamics, of Montreal, Quebec.

[1] See Stanley H. Brewer, *Rhochrematics* (Seattle: Bureau of Business Research, University of Washington, June 1960), 30 pp.

flow. Since material and information flows cut horizontally across typical vertical organizations, it will be vital to assess the impact on the organization structure of a change in approach. We will point out the benefits that might accrue, set forth some ideas on how organizations might be adjusted, and assess the likelihood of such changes in the future.

"Product Mission"

A total concept, the flow of material and information from the raw material stage through production and distribution to the ultimate consumer, is difficult to conceive and, as such, has not been the target of concerted efforts toward optimization. The total flow is often so complex, involving many separate organizations and agencies, that no one agency has assumed total responsibility for the entire process.

However, when the entire "product mission" is visualized, it is easier to fit the separate parts together and make a systematic, integrated analysis of the entire system of material and information flow. While the time is not far off when such complex systems can be analyzed, via simulation or similar techniques, most attention has been devoted to one or the other of the two major sub-parts of the total flow process, production or distribution.

The flow of material from the raw material stage through the production process to the finished goods stage has been the subject of analysis for management scientists, efficiency experts, and industrial engineers for many years. A great deal of attention has been focused on isolated segments of this internal flow; e.g., costs of acquisition vs. costs of storage, inventory control, production control, expediting, and materials handling. However, little attention has been given to an integrated approach which focuses on the flow process itself rather than on individual functional areas.

Flow Concept

The flow of materials from the finished goods stage to the final consumer also has been the subject of many cost reduction efforts. There has been much furor over the fact that in many cases distribution costs actually exceed costs of production. Accordingly, much attention has been devoted to developing more efficient systems.

However, improvements in the distribution system are often made without reference to possible effects on the production function. More attention must be devoted to analysis of the over-all flow of material and information to optimize the entire process. Continued attention to individual departments, sub-areas, or functions will, of course, develop increased efficiency in isolated segments. However, such increased efficiency may be detrimental to the overall operation.

In this article we will discuss both of the major subdivisions of the material flow process, production and distribution. Attention will also be given to an integrated approach to the over-all flow process, including both internal and external flows.

Organizing for Performance

In all cases, an attempt will be made to show how improvement in isolated functional department areas may not lead to over-all efficiency. Since this problem of optimizing material and information flow is inexorably tied to organization, it will be desirable to set the stage for later analysis by discussing some of the basic concepts of organization, and pointing out their effect upon the problem of material and information flow.

While it is obvious that contemporary organizations must be concerned with multiple goals, the business organization's primary task is that of translating raw materials into goods or services for producers or consumers through efficient utilization of capital and human resources. Business organizations have been growing continuously in size and complexity and undoubtedly will continue in this direction as long as the economy increases in complexity and society becomes more sophisticated.

In their chapter on "Molding of Organization in Modern Society," Pfiffner and Sherwood sum up the factors leading toward greater complexity as follows:

"The many factors that have operated to make modern organizations complex are just those which have served to complicate the entire fabric of society. They include: (1) the liberation of the individual in our social philosophy and policies; (2) the development of new understandings of the nature of human cooperation; (3) the broadening range of organization goals;

and (4) the movement toward task specialization."[2]

Specializing Invites Fragmentation

This latter point is of particular importance for our purposes here. As organizations grow, the many functions that must be performed tend to be split off into various divisions, departments, groups, or units. As this fragmentation occurs, the need for specialists within the organization increases.

Each specialist tends to assume his role and to become more proficient in carrying out his particular duties. The larger the company and the greater the degree of specialization, the more the tendency to lose track of over-all objectives of the firm and to concentrate on strengthening the individual function.

The specialist is motivated by a desire to perform efficiently and move up in the organization; but, for the most part, he is limited by departmental boundary lines. Normally, he can assume more duties within his particular department, but he does not take over functions that are being performed by other departments or divisions unless there is a reorganization. Often, therefore, specialization becomes identified with functionalization. While separating duties and responsibilities on the basis of functions is only one of a number of possible alternatives, it turns out to be an over-riding consideration in many cases.

Work might be divided on the basis of time sequences; for example, planning, execution, and control. However, formal organization structure does not ordinarily follow such a pattern. Equipment is not often the basis for departmentation. Processes such as milling, grinding or heat treating often serve as a basis for organizing work groups. However, process and function are often hard to distinguish and processes might be considered as sub-functions to production.

If two or more classes of customers are entirely different, a company might well organize separate work groups to produce for different customers. Companies producing for both the military and consumer sectors of the economy might be well advised to separate completely their operations in order that entirely different

requirements can be met efficiently. Geographic location of divisions or branches is a typical approach to dividing the work.

Dividing the Work

However, within each of the decentralized units there is also an organization structure which is likely to stem from some more basic factor. Multi-product companies may divide the work according to individual products or product groups in order to focus attention on the objectives of subunits of the organization. In such cases, conflicts may arise between product or product group managers and functional managers who have traditionally been responsible for carrying out the basic functions of the enterprise.

Is Vertical Organization Best?

Traditionally, organization has been predominantly vertical and hierarchical with authority and responsibility resting in individual functions. Typically, superior-subordinate relationships have been established on a functional basis, with orders and instructions going down the line and reports and requests going up the line. Recently, this traditional approach has been questioned as the most suitable for over-all efficiency of the operation.

For example, the flow of material and information in the typical manufacturing operation tends to flow horizontally, cutting across the vertical structuring of functional authority. In discussing new technology and its impact upon organization, Jasinski states:

"But technology, including both integrated data processing and integrated machine production, has developed on what might be called a horizontal plane. That is, the machine cuts across superior-subordinate relationships, affecting the jobs of people in different areas, departments, and work groups. Superimposing a strictly vertical organization structure on a technology which emphasizes horizontal and diagonal relationships can and does cause obvious difficulties . . . Certainly it is management's job not only to recognize these new relationships, but also to take steps to enable them to function definitely and smoothly. A few managers have recognized the discrepancy between organization and technology, and have taken steps to integrate the two.

---

[2] John M. Pfiffner and Frank P. Sherwood, *Administrative Organization* (Englewood Cliffs: Prentice-Hall, Inc., 1960), pp. 14–15.

They have achieved such integration in a variety of ways, which essentially may be classified as: 1. Changing the technology to conform with the existing organizational structure. 2. Changing the organization so as to define and formalize the relationships required by the technology. 3. Maintaining both the existing organization and the existing technology, but introducing mechanisms to reduce or minimize the discrepancies between the two.[3]

Focusing attention on the *flow* of material and information as stressed in Rhochrematics, allows the rethinking called for by Jasinski. The problem, in short then, is that most companies organized in the traditional functional fashion are not set up to take advantage of conceptualizing the total flow process.

The remainder of this analysis will approach this problem by discussing: (1) how differences in orientation result in different emphasis in organization structure; (2) how traditional functional specialization may suboptimize the over-all operations; (3) alternative approaches to controls over material movement; (4) some case studies; (5) some generalizations; (6) developments facilitating a Rhochrematics approach; (7) possible approaches to implementing such thinking in existing organizations.

Differences in Orientation

Regardless of the formal organization structure, the strengths and weaknesses of a company may well depend upon its orientation. Some functions may be stressed with little attention devoted to others, according to the importance of the particular functions to the company's success.

A study of organization charts for companies producing identical products shows that there are often differences in emphasis but that there is a tendency toward similarity, at least formally. A marked similarity can be seen in the way companies producing the same product are organized at the top management or department level, but differences are found within the subdepartments, groups and units.

Intra-departmental differences indicate that similar functions are performed in vastly different ways among companies producing the same

[3] Frank J. Jasinski, "Adapting Organization to New Technology," *Harvard Business Review,* January–February, 1959, page 80.

or similar products. The performance of functions often revolves around personalities, interests and abilities. The background and capability of the departmental manager influence performance, but many times the differences result from physical location with respect to markets, raw material, labor supply, or other factors of importance to the enterprise.

Products Shape Organization Chart

The organization charts of companies producing different products are more likely to be dissimilar than those of companies producing the same product. Yet the pressure of precedent and the similarity of basic functions to be performed tend to set patterns for the organization of all companies. Top management's interests in, orientation to, or any one or combinations of these functions is the greatest stimulus for setting patterns of organization.

The two most basic (or organic) functions of any organization are normally conceded to be production and distribution. As a consequence, they receive the greatest amount of attention, interest, and analysis. Accordingly, greater proficiency tends to develop in the performance of these functions. There also seems to be some interest in integrating the effort that goes into the performance of these basic functions. Other subfunctions tend to be performed (without much integration) by specialists whose role or mission is considered to be support of and service to marketing and production departments.

Should Production Lead Flow?

This is characteristically true of the various phases of the material flow process. Companies that distribute products to almost every community in the United States tend to be sales oriented. Normally, their products are marketed in a highly competitive atmosphere. Without large budgets for advertising and promotion, plus constant pressure to sell stemming from top management, a share of the many markets each company is trying to serve may be lost. Once a competitor captures a disproportionate share of the available customers in any one market, he tends to hold them. This does not mean that production can be slighted, because, of course, availability of good quality products is one of the keynotes to success for the salesman.

Sales are important to all companies, but engineering and production get more attention in companies producing capital equipment and some types of durable goods. Established companies producing airplanes, heavy equipment, and machinery, for example, know that if they develop a superior product their salesmen will be able to capture their considered share of the total market.

Physical distribution of products is often a relatively simple task, maybe little more than delivering orders. The internal flow of material during the production process is of concern to such companies, however. Regardless of orientation, all companies are faced with some aspects of the total material flow process and can benefit from rethinking along the lines of Rhochrematics.

Suboptimization by Specialization

Although many companies tend to be oriented to the finance function, the legal function, the purchasing function, and others, sales and production remain as the basic subdivisions in most organizations. Within each of these organic functions, many subfunctions are set up as separate departments or units.

The resulting fractionalization makes visualizing the total flow process difficult. Each department, in an effort, to protect itself against possible delays and to make a good showing for economy, tends to pad the time schedule in its favor with the result that the entire time schedule, or flow process, is slowed down and paper "economies" prove very costly.

In the average firm, material flows originate with the tool and production planning phase. Although planning may build considerable flexibility into the schedule of production runs, this fact is seldom apparent in the paper-work issued to purchasing.

Padding the Time Schedule

With the schedule in hand, purchasing sets up a program for acquisition of needed materials and builds in safeguards to protect itself against delays in delivery and all other possible contingencies. Next, traffic takes over and builds in a second time "hedge" against unscheduled contingencies regardless of what this may do to slow down the flow of the total operation.

Since both purchasing and traffic are service departments, they are extremely cost conscious. Holding down or reducing costs is a concern to top management, and cost reduction is a way for service units to bring attention to themselves; usually by trying to optimize the particular functions delegated to them. For purchasing this normally means buying at the lowest unit cost consistent with company policies and programs.

Also, the traffic manager is motivated to purchase transportation services at the lowest unit cost, normally meaning large quantity movements, either truck load or carload lots.

Optimization of these two functions normally results in the creation of inventories, establishing requirements for warehousing or storage. This, in turn, enforces requirements for inventory management or control.

Coordinating Material Flow

Within the plant or factory there may be several stops for material—receiving, receiving inspection, storage, processing, quality control, and the production line. From the production line the material—in a different form or as finished goods—is again moved to storage or the shipping dock.

The flow of the outbound material is also influenced by several functional departments or units. Prompt delivery service may be the primary consideration insofar as the sales manager is concerned.

Shipping is normally concerned with getting the order ready and loading it aboard the carrier, after which time it becomes the responsibility of traffic. Other complexities enter the picture when regional company owned or public warehouses are used in the distribution process.

In extremely large companies many of these functions are performed in widely separated departments with a tendency toward optimization of individual functions and little consideration of the total material flow process. This is the concern of Rhochrematics. The further companies go in their growth patterns, the greater the tendency toward functional specialization within each of the units involved in the material flow process, making coordination, integration, and managerial controls extremely important.

The Question of Controls

Managerial controls are normally exercised over departments or functions, by establishing criteria, standards, or expectations. Deviations are analyzed with reference to predetermined tolerances. The greater the degree of specialization and orientation toward a particular function, the more precise the standards for controlling the activity. For small units within major departments, all deviations must be carefully explained.

Extraneous factors or influences are often the only acceptable explanation in the face of pressures from the department manager to increase the output of activities or services rendered by a small unit. And, the efficiency of the unit is judged by its ability to hold costs at the lowest possible level. Such pressures increase the tendency toward optimization of specialized functions. In the absence of good managerial controls, the specialist normally attains his position through loyalty and conscientiousness; traits which might lead to efficient performance of the specialized function.

Rethinking

The larger the company, the greater the degree of organization, resulting in the establishment of standards and procedures for the disposition of discipline. A high degree of discipline normally results in greater efficiency insofar as specialized functions are concerned. It also tends to destroy initiative and this in turn results in more and more suboptimization of the total flow process.

This is sometimes carried on to the extent that individuals within a particular group or unit end up virtually working for themselves and do not coordinate their activities with other employees in their own unit or group. They almost completely lose sight of the over-all objectives of the business organization.

The desirability of managerial controls for the total flow cannot be overemphasized, but the limitations on these controls, cannot be overstated. Controls can only be exercised when standards have been established and information is available to measure deviations from these standards. When functions are so fragmented that information is never brought together at a central source, standards cannot be established and managerial controls can, therefore, not be exercised. Rhochrematics fosters rethinking which may facilitate a fresh, integrated approach to controls.

Managerial Orientation

One approach to better control of material flows is flexible management orientation. Since top management is ordinarily concerned with major functions such as sales, production, and finance, minor sub-functions such as traffic, inventory control, receiving, inspection, materials management, warehousing, shipping, order processing, and purchasing are left to specialists. Specialists tend to establish their own standards, and managerial controls are exercised around these self-imposed standards. There is very little germination of ideas for the integration of interrelated minor functions.

Major pressures that arise in the sales oriented organization seldom develop in terms of a minor function. Problems of the sub-departments often seem insignificant in light of the major objectives of the organization. While material flows are regarded as necessary and extremely important to the conduct of the sales function, the units responsible for this activity are normally regarded as service groups, and the quality of that service is often the only concern of the sales department.

There are constant pressures to give better service regardless of cost, and the most important consideration is probably lost sales or out of stock situations that result from inefficiency on the part of those responsible for material flow. In extreme cases, these service groups begin to incur costs greater than the profits made from individual sales. Since physical distribution is considered a "necessary evil," material flow costs become a disproportionately high percentage of the sales dollar.

Pressures that develop in a production oriented organization will often act as deterrents to good management practices for the control of material flows. Planning in such organizations revolves around the production schedule. An important aspect of the production schedule is the need to meet predetermined load dates; a requirement that is continually impressed upon the minds of the managers of service or support groups that have the job of getting the materials to the load point on the production line.

Distorted Production Schedules

The importance of meeting the production schedule cannot be taken lightly, but side effects should be given some consideration. In order to make absolutely sure that no load date is missed, the many groups that are responsible for managing isolated phases of material flows are likely to build successive high margins of safety which can become extremely costly to the company.

Estimators are likely to be generous on the theory that some of the material may not meet specifications. Purchasers will often have vendors ship early on the theory that vendors may not be able to meet their own production schedules. Traffic is likely to have buyers plan for maximum transit time rather than median or minimum transit time. Receiving inspection will want more than ample time to perform their function.

Rework and quality control are motivated to plan for the maximum amount of time that might be required to accomplish their task. Inventory control and warehousing will normally add a protective cushion of time to allow for unknown contingencies. All these protective cushions of time add substantially to the capital costs of carrying pipeline inventories of the various materials destined for the production line.

In spite of all the effort to the contrary, shortages do occur. The larger and more complex the production activity, the greater is the concern over shortages. This is understandable because a shortage of one small part can conceivably tie up the entire production line. Hence, much effort is devoted to the shortage problem, including the use of premium forms of transportation to expedite needed materials. While some companies consider such extraordinary measures for solving a shortage problem to be a cardinal sin, little thought is given to the fact that hundreds of thousands of dollars worth of material may have arrived weeks or months prior to the time that they were required.

The cost of carrying such inventories and the overages that result from service units protecting themselves against all possible contingencies may receive little attention in the production oriented company. There is often a substantial amount of frenzied activity and many thousands of dollars spent on the shortage problem, but inconspicuous overages may be more costly than shortages that are spotlighted for attention.

Often Takes Drastic Action

Each department manager who has responsibility over some element of the material flow process seems to feel that his special function is more important than that of other department heads. The independence with which people in one department are able to operate is a deterrent to implementation of the Rhochrematics concept. The need for coordination and coop-

eration between departments in the organization is usually stressed, but as long as pressures come vertically down the hierarchical chain and the security and protection of broad departmental boundary lines remains, there is little likelihood that something as complicated as the material flow process can be properly integrated.

Communications Breakdown

Even when there is an extreme desire to work together, there is often a breakdown in communication and flows of information. The many activities related to material flows tend to be extremely complex and require much documentation and record keeping. The many forms and memoranda that are developed in connection with a particular transaction involving the movement of any one of many thousands of items are seldom if ever brought together in one file in a large organization.

Each individual functionally specialized unit has its own records to provide primary information for the activity of the department. Secondary information that is of value to some other unit or combination of units normally is extracted only when something goes wrong. There is seldom any attempt to extract at each stage secondary information that is related to the material flow process.

It is obvious that fairly drastic steps must be taken by companies if controls are to be established around the flow process rather than around the traditional functional departments. These steps include management rethinking and reorientation plus some obvious organizational adjustments which may include authority and responsibility channels cutting horizontally across (flowing) the traditional vertical arrangements. The following section presents several cases where innovations have been made or are being considered to allow the organization to focus on its primary responsibility, the flow of material and information.

How Two Firms Did It

Two examples will be used to illustrate the kinds of innovation that can produce results. In one case, emphasis is placed on the external flow of material and information, primarily the physical distributon of finished goods. In the other case, emphasis is placed on the internal flow of material and information because the company involved is production oriented.

The Purex Story

The Purex Corporation has changed from an organization that could be considered traditional, with many of the materials flow functions fragmented and responsibility divided between several of the major departments, to an organization stressing integrated management of material flow functions. The old organization, as shown in Figure 1, had a traffic manager responsible for arranging transportation of outbound products from major production plants to warehouses and other distribution points.

The production planning function was not formalized at that time and was handled by informal committees with members from sales, manufacturing, and finance. The warehousing function was handled by the sales department for the most part, as was inventory control. Managers of a number of the smaller plants reported to finance.

These plants produced liquid bleach throughout the country and handled some warehousing of finished products produced at other major production facilities. Outbound movements from these plants were the responsibility of the plant manager and, as a result, the lines of authority for these functions emanated from the vice president of finance. Some functional authority was exercised by the traffic manager because it was his duty to furnish routing guides and common carrier rates. Inasmuch as

the sales department was responsible for inventory control and maintenance of stocks at regional public warehouses, it also exercised control over outbound movements from these facilities.

Realignment of Duties

Purchasing in this organization was responsible for control of all inbound movements of raw materials and supplies. Order processing was a function of finance, and shipping reported to manufacturing. There was no attempt to exercise over-all control of the material flow process and, as a result, many inefficiencies developed leading to substantially higher costs than warranted.

Flow System Streamlines Planning

The current organization of the Purex Corporation's material flow function is shown in Figure 2. Production planning has been formalized and put directly under the jurisdiction of the director of traffic and distribution. In addition to the planning function, he has direct line authority over inventory control, distribution services, and traffic.

Regional traffic managers report directly to him and, in addition, he has functional control over the distribution function at the various branch plants. Since these branch plants now

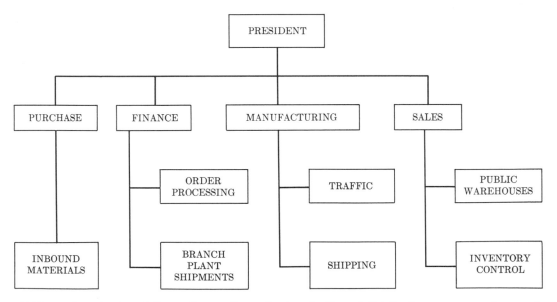

FIG. 1.   Organization of Purex Corporation prior to adoption of distribution management concept.

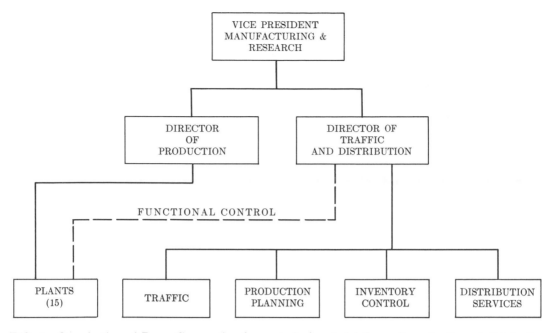

FIG. 2. Organization of Purex Corporation for control of material flows after adoption of distribution management concept.

report directly to the director of production, who in turn reports to the vice president of manufacturing and research, this functional authority almost achieves line status because the traffic director can exercise a great deal of control over all activities affecting materials movement at the branch plant level.

Direct line authority over inventory control now gives him the power he needs to control movement both in and out of public warehouses located throughout the country. Although the chart does not depict it, the director of traffic and distribution also works closely with the director of purchasing in controlling inbound shipments of raw materials and supplies.

Savings Effected

The new organizational arrangement has resulted in many benefits to the company. Although cost reductions are difficult to determine, especially when a corporation is growing as rapidly as is the Purex Corporation, most officials of the company agree that total savings are in the high six figures. Public warehouses have been cut by nearly one-half, from 65 to 35. More efficient management controls are now exercised over inventories and production planning.

Integrated management of many of the func-

tions related to the material flow process is being exercised. Information on all these related functions is converted to punched cards, and the data are analyzed in various ways by means of an electronic computer to obtain day-to-day operating data that are used to plan efficient production, hold inventories at minimum levels, and reduce transportation costs. Continuing attention to and sophistication of the management of material flows is planned by the Purex Corporation.

The Boeing Experience

Investigation of possibilities for better integration of the management of material flows resulted in a case study of the Transport Division of the Boeing Airplane Company in the summer of 1960 conducted by University of Washington faculty members. The initial study resulted in plans to reduce inventories and cut lead times, moves that are conservatively estimated to save the company more than $300,000 per year.

Although reorganization of the functions related to material flows has not as yet resulted, company officials are most enthusiastic about the opportunities and are giving serious consideration to inaugurating a program of reorgan-

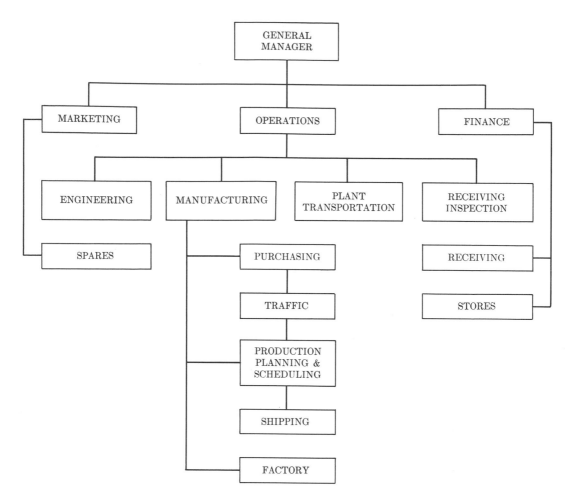

FIG. 3. Present organization of Transport Division, Boeing Airplane Company control of material flows.

ization. Figure 3 shows the manner in which different activities concerned with material flows are now organized in the Transport Division of the Boeing Airplane Company. Serious thought is being given to a plan for realigning these functions into one department.

Here we see two differently oriented companies. The Purex Corporation, with its more than 200 finished products that must be distributed from many plants and warehouses to wholesalers and retailers through the United States, is primarily concerned with outbound movements of finished goods. The heavy moving inbound materials are few in number and consist primarily of bulk shipments of chemicals, oils, and tallow. Packaging materials are also heavy moving inbound items.

The primary concern of the Boeing Company, on the other hand, is inbound and internal move-

ment of the more than 100,000 parts, pieces, and raw materials that go into the production of each airplane. The parts, together with the machinery and supplies that are used in the factory, must be assembled from nearly every state in the country. For the most part, each individual shipment is very small. The end product is the airplane, which is flown away by the customer. Distribution activities are concerned primarily with spares that must be moved to a limited number of airline companies plus the military organizations that purchase airplanes. Boeing is very much production oriented but, of course, sales is an important activity.

System Works in Both Plants

Purex, on the other hand, might be considered sales oriented; yet, production plays a vital role. These companies are the antithesis of one another insofar as their orientation and interest in the material flow functions are concerned. Transportation costs alone in the Purex Corporation amount to more than $8 million a year or approximately 10 per cent of the sales dollar. Boeing, on the other hand, pays out a fraction of one per cent of its sales dollar in transportation costs.

Traffic and distribution play a major role in management of the Purex Corporation, whereas traffic is a minor function in the Boeing Company. However, if the many activities related to the material flow function could be organized under one head at Boeing, and sophisticated approaches developed for managing the material flow process, substantial cost reductions would result.

Other Applications

Many industries should be able to benefit from a Rhochrematics approach to management of their material flows. Service industries such as transportation companies tend to be operations and sales oriented. Since they are not concerned with selling a product, little thought may be given to material flows. The operations oriented company is in many respects like the production oriented organization. An important function is that of keeping the equipment in good condition so that schedules can be met.

These companies often accumulate hundreds of thousands of dollars worth of supplies and spare parts. Since purchasing of supplies and parts plus the various aspects of moving, storing, and issuing them, may be minor functions relative to the primary concern of the corporation, they may get little attention from top management. The fact that a train or truck or airplane or ship cannot move for lack of spare parts would be spotlighted for top management. In order to prevent this, all possible contingencies are planned for, resulting in multiple cushions and an over-supply of many items. Better control and integration of activities could result in substantial cost reductions.

Lumber

Bound industries also tend to be production oriented, with little attention given to company-wide integration of the material and information flows. For example, in the lumber industry when a log is moved to the sawmill it is turned over to a sawyer whose decision is all-important to the operation. Production orientation can influence his decision so that he cuts the best lumber, holds waste to a minimum. Little consideration may be given to the problems of inventory or lack of markets for the end product. Markets might be glutted with the items being produced with shortages developing for other products. Integrated management of raw materials procurement, production, inventory control, sales, and distribution has received little attention in this industry.

Agriculture

The agricultural industry could benefit substantially from an integrated approach to managing of the flows of their products, but since there is very little control exercised by any one individual over the many functions involved in the movement of material from original sources to final consumer, this would be most difficult to organize.

Other industries could be cited whose conceptualizing the total flow could prove extremely beneficial. However, the above examples are representative of the opportunities that can be tapped by rethinking along the lines of Rhochrematics.

Generalists, Not Specialists

The growing need for more scientific approaches to the management of material flows arises out of the increasing complexity of the productive effort of most large corporations. Business philosophy is gradually shifting from concern and need for trained specialists to concern and need for managers with broad perspective and knowledge of a number of related functions. The realization that substantial benefits can be derived from integrating many related functions should result in organization around material and information flows.

The complexity of these functions cannot be overemphasized. The existence of extreme specialists in management capacities in the many fragmented functions and the longstanding efforts that these people have made to professionalize such activities means that innovators will be faced with much inertia and outright resistance to change.

Many traffic managers, warehouse managers, purchasing managers, and others now hold key positions on the management team of most large organizations. Their organizations have been built over a period of years on the theory of functional specialization within the corporation.

There are very few senior people on the American business scene today who have the experience, background, or inclination to take over and manage an integrated approach to material flows. Many feel that the activities are so complex that it will take a long time to develop executives with the proper perspective. However, the tools and developments of the last few years make it possible to reorganize some of these activities in the interest of the over-all corporate objectives.

Facilitating Developments

While innovations stemming from the application of Rhochrematics are likely to come slowly because of the inherent resistance to change, there are a number of facilitating developments which should enhance the likelihood of progress. Separating, for the moment, the two basic elements of the flow process, material and information, we can trace some of these developments.

The technology surrounding the mass production process has been accelerating since the industrial revolution and a typical production line cuts across traditional vertical organizations. Attention in industries utilizing highly integrated production lines is focused on the material flow rather than upon individual functionally specialized units. As more sophisticated mechanization is introduced, the flow of material becomes more and more critical.

Automation Forces Flow Approach

Automation, with its self-adjusting controls over the manufacturing operation, also puts increasing emphasis on the flow process. Typically, the most highly automated operations are those such as processing industries, for example, milling or refining. However, automation is gradually spreading to other operations where concentration on the material flow process has not been as evident. As inroads are made via increased mechanization, integrated machine processing, and automation, management will be forced to think in terms of the flow of material through the plant. Hence, managerial control should be established along these lines.

The external movement or physical distribution of material is also undergoing a number of changes which will facilitate new approaches to

the overall problem of material flow. The elimination of handling through the use of containerization and integration of various modes of transportation is revolutionizing the movement of general merchandise as well as some bulk products.

Air freight is likely to be a new dimension in transportation within the next few years. The cost of moving freight through the air will be cut in half this year as new turbo-prop aircraft are delivered to some of the freight carriers. Several national companies are already using this means to reach national markets from one central production facility. They indicate that elimination of regional warehouses and multiple handling more than repays the added transportation cost.

As airfreight rates are brought down closer to the levels of truck and rail, many more companies will be able to benefit from a revised approach to material flows. Such changes in the external flow of material will often allow rethinking with regard to the internal flow of materials; for example, high-speed movement of finished goods through the normally lengthy distribution pipeline will allow companies to refine production schedules and to control inventories with much less reserve.

Information Flow

While changes in the physical flow of material, both internal and external, have been progressing, some of the most startling advances have been made in the area of information flow. Systems of information flow are critical to the control of the material flow process. The advent of high speed electronic computers has allowed companies to deal with much larger quantities of information.

Fantastic speeds allow computer processing of tremendous amounts of data which heretofore were unusable. More than that, however, the computer has stimulated rethinking on the part of innovative managements with the result being sophisticated new systems of information flow. Real progress has been made where the computer has been used to process information in new and different ways rather than to process the same old data in the same old way, only faster.

High speed data transmission over leased wires or other means has facilitated the use of the computer as a processing device. The most critical problem for systems of information flow as control mechanisms has been the collection and transmission of data rather than processing. Currently, much effort is being devoted to source recording; and once this problem is solved, the goal of integrated data processing will be within reach.

The technology necessary to achieve integrated processing of material and integrated processing of data necessary for controlling the system is either on hand or forthcoming very soon. However, management's ability to utilize these technological advances lags. The organizational adaptations necessary to take full advantage of available technology are slow in coming. Such lethargy is particularly deplorable since many of the advantages or benefits could be achieved through organizational adjustments even without the technological innovations. According to Jasinski:

"The impact of recent technological innovations has forced many managers to take a second look at their organization, particularly with the advent of modern data processing equipment. This equipment requires information in a certain form. Where managers have used it as more than simply a change in 'hardware,' equipment has triggered sweeping revision of data processing departments. To prepare information efficiently for the processing equipment, managers have completely reorganized traditional departments. In this connection there are the telling, perhaps exaggerated, stories of companies that revised their organizations in anticipation of delivery of data processing equipment only to realize such great savings through the reorganization process itself that they canceled their orders for the equipment."

How can such benefits be achieved? How can the ideas embodied in the Rhochrematics concept be applied throughout industry?

Implementing Rhochrematics

The first and most important step in implementing a systematic, integrated approach to managing material flow is awareness on the part of top management that substantial benefit could be derived from changes in orientation. Moreover, if the Rhochrematics concept is to be applied, there must be genuine interest on the part of top management. As is the case with nearly all innovations, there will be considerable initial resistance.

Without support from the upper echelons, proposed changes are usually doomed to failure. For example, if the chief executive merely refers the subject to a committee for further investigation the odds are overwhelmingly against further action unless he maintains an active interest in the project. Committee members, particularly those with vested interests, can ordinarily marshal considerably more "why nots" than "whys."

Since Rhochrematics, the science of material and information flow, stresses the flow process, considerable attention must be given to reorganization in order that controls can be centered around this process. The interrelatedness of and interaction between the various specialized functions must be highlighted. Management attention must be focused on this problem. According to Jay Forrester, "industrial dynamics" must be recognized as an important consideration. He says:

"Our industrial systems are becoming so large and sophisticated that a knowledge of the parts taken separately is not sufficient. In management, as in engineering, we can expect that the interconnections and interactions between the components of the system will often be more important than the separate components themselves.

Managing is the task of *designing* and *controlling* the industrial system. Management science, if it is to be useful, must evolve effective methods to analyze the principle interactions amongst *all* the important components of a company and its external environment. In the same sense that we can analyze complex physical systems, so will it become possible to understand better the interactions within industrial and economic systems.[4]

Management must be willing to step back and re-evaluate its traditional organizational arrangement; it must be willing to restructure traditional arrangements in order to capitalize on the advantages that can accrue by concentrating on the material flow process. The exact nature of new organization structures cannot be pinpointed. For companies emphasizing physical distribution, the distribution manager with au-

[4] Jay Forrester, "Management and Management Science," Unpublished Paper, copyrighted by Dr. Forrester, School of Industrial Management, Massachusetts Institute of Technology, p. 7.

thority over both production and distribution might be the answer. For other companies, where internal flow of material is a more critical problem, a different approach might be appropriate. There will normally be a temptation to impose an additional agency to coordinate or expedite material flows. While this may improve the situation somewhat, it still does not get at the basic problems of empire building in the various functionally specialized departments. Until the concept of primary control based on material flows is accepted, little real benefit will be achieved.

Because of this problem of changing the atmosphere in the company and the attitude of traditionally oriented department heads, it seems that some fairly major innovations are called for in order to instigate a process of rethinking. While the initial stages of such an approach might create considerable turmoil, the long run payoff should be substantial. Management must take some giant strides in the near future if its organizational adjustments are to keep up with technological advancements.

Summary and Conclusions

Rhochrematics literally translated means the science of product or material flows. The term is connoted to mean scientific or systematic approaches to the management of material flows.

Any system is made up of a number of subunits or operations all of which perform functions of major or minor proportions. Any of these functions might be performed independently in optimal fashion, but not necessarily in the best interests of the system as a whole. Focusing attention on the material flow process enhances the probability of optimizing the whole rather than its separate parts.

Over the years, various aspects of the management of material flows have been receiving increased attention. Some companies have recently taken an integrated approach to the basic subfunctions of the total material flow process, production or distribution. More and more attention is being given to "distribution management," "materials management," "industrial logistics," "landed costs," or other segments of what might be called a total systems or Rhochrematics approach.

Organization theorists and practitioners have paid little attention to proposals for bringing all of the activities related to material flows under one head. Traffic, inventory management, in-plant transportation, promotion planning, receiving, storing, and shipping are functions that are often analyzed separately in relatively isolated departments of any one company.

In the past there was little reason to consider a systems approach to the performance of these functions because there were few alternatives and standard straightforward approaches sufficed. In recent years these activities have been complicated many times over by production of many new products, models, sizes, colors, and other variations. There are many new alternatives in transportation that did not exist even 20 years ago; for example, the long haul private, contract, or common carrier truck; "piggy back" and many other innovations in containerization on land, sea, and in the air; and the rapidly developing air freight industry with its promise of much lower rates and improved service.

The revolution that is now going on in information gathering, transmission and processing provides new dimensions for managing material flows. Growing sophistication in the field of management sciences holds excellent promise for developing even better tools for handling and combining the data that must now be used in Rhochrematics. Analyzing the data with simple machine techniques is useful; the application of operations research techniques can prove helpful; and simulation of the material flow process seems to offer additional promise.

Top management must become interested in the Rhochrematics approach before any progress can be made. A thorough study of company goals, plans, programs, and organization will reveal the possibilities for integrating activities related to the material flow function. When such activities are fragmented in different organizational units, there is no way to even approach maximum results.

In the final analysis, serious consideration must be given to adjusting the organization of the company so that many of the interrelated functions become the responsibility of one executive. This executive must be well trained, imaginative, and broad enough in his orientation to make a complex total system function optimally.

34. *An Interfunctional Approach to Promotion and Physical Distribution**

R. Clifton Anderson, William P. Dommermuth, and Norton E. Marks†

Although manufacturers, wholesalers, and retailers aim at the same ultimate goal—increased profits through increased sales—their interests and points of view are not necessarily identical. However, maximum marketing effectiveness depends upon clear recognition by all channel members of their mutual interdependency.

This article questions the traditional view of manufacturers toward functions of channel members, particularly with respect to new products. Whereas responsibility for change must rest finally with manufacturers, other channel members, particularly retailers, have an equally important stake in new products and are in a position to take the initiative in influencing manufacturer attitudes.

The Basis for an Interfunctional Approach

Two major goals of marketing management are to build and maintain a consumer franchise for a brand and to make the brand available when and where consumers expect to purchase it. The activities designed to accomplish these goals are generally designated as the functional areas of promotion and physical distribution.

Much has been written about coordinating the various forms of promotion and developing what can be described as an *intra*functional approach. Similarly, emphasis upon developing a logistical or physical distribution mix constitutes an *intra*functional approach.

The time seems appropriate for a closer look

at increased emphasis upon an *inter*functional approach, stressing the efficiencies available through trade-off possibilities between promotion and physical distribution activities. As background to such an approach, a brief review of the trade-off concept as used in physical distribution management is helpful.

Current Status of Physical Distribution Management

Traditionally, physical distribution was viewed as a group of unrelated functions. Transportation problems received primary consideration, and separate attention was given to problems of storage and warehousing. Decisions in these areas were made independently with little or no attempt to assess the implications of a decision in one area to the operations in another.

The concept of total cost has required management to look upon physical distribution as a total process and to evaluate decisions in all areas according to some goal of total effectiveness. In brief, the total cost approach states that while costs may rise in one functional area such as transportation, costs in another area, perhaps inventory carrying charges, may decrease by a greater extent. Hence, total costs may be reduced.

One major shortcoming of this approach is the danger of isolating physical distribution from other marketing activities in the same manner that transportation problems once had been isolated from other physical distribution activities. Although the scope of physical distribution has been broadened, there is little indication that these activities are being evaluated in relationship to the firm's marketing effort.

* Reprinted by permission of the *Journal of Retailing*, Fall 1966.

† The University of Texas.

Steps Toward an Interfunctional Approach

In order to better coordinate physical distribution and promotional activities, the basic linkage point between the two must first be recognized. The subfunction, storage, *is* that linkage point.

Storage has been recognized as one of the major cost items of physical distribution.[1] However, storage itself is not a unicellular function. At least three separate levels of storage can be identified: manufacturer, wholesaler (including manufacturer-owned facilities, public warehouses, and retailer-owned facilities), and retailer. What is often not considered is that, as the storage function is shifted through the distribution system, its nature changes. At the manufacturing level, storage can be described as *inert* in nature; at the wholesale level, *transitory* in nature; and at the retail level, *active* in nature. *Only active storage, that portion under the control of the retailer, achieves direct results in sales to the ultimate consumer,* and it is therefore imperative that optimum levels of active storage be secured and maintained in an optimum number of retail outlets.

Typically, in aiming at this goal, the manufacturer may give primary attention to promotional strategy: advertising, personal selling, and sales promotion. An optimum *total* strategy does not necessarily result because the relationship of physical distribution and promotion, as linked through active storage, has not been fully appreciated. A more comprehensive approach must include appraising the potential impact of physical distribution policies on the activities of *all* channel members.

For example, particularly in the case of convenience goods, Markov Chain Analysis has revealed interesting patterns of brand-switching which may underlie a surface appearance of relatively stable market shares.[2]

The reasons underlying such switching patterns remain largely unexplained, but we suggest that out-of-stock at the retail level (that is, a lack of sufficient active storage) may be a prime cause of this type of brand switching. The customer seeking Brand "X" and not finding it readily available, will purchase another brand. Advertising dollars spent to build his loyalty to Brand "X" have been wasted, and additional dollars must be invested in an attempt to recapture his patronage.

One survey among housewives, for example, reported that while a certain brand of all-purpose flour was preferred by 31 percent of the respondents, it was actually being used by only 19 percent. Why the discrepancy between preference and use? The analyst suggested insufficient active storage in retail outlets as one probable reason.[3]

The Cost of Lost Sales

Being out of stock at the active storage level means lost sales to retailers, wholesalers, and manufacturers. Because it is difficult to estimate with much reliability the volume of business that is lost, the entire channel of distribution may be expected to approach this problem by examining the costs necessary to avoid inventory shortages, at the retail level. If these costs are significant, the tendency is to assume that the cost of lost sales is smaller.

The cost of lost sales due to out-of-stock situations usually is weighted against the increased inventory carrying charges that would be incurred in order to avoid or minimize inventory shortages. In balancing inventory carrying charges and cost of lost sales, some less obvious but equally significant costs should be considered.

From the manufacturer's point of view, one such cost involves the firm's advertising program, the effectiveness of which can be diluted when adequate inventory is not maintained at the active storage level. A similar dilution can occur in personal selling efforts as well as in the various sales promotion techniques being used. Some degree of ill will can be expected to occur among retailers and wholesalers, and a weaken-

[1] L. P. Alford and John R. Bangs, eds., *Production Handbook* (New York: The Ronald Press Company, 1955), pp. 396–97 as cited in J. L. Hekett, Robert M. Ivie, and Nicholas A. Glaskowsky, *Business Logistics* (New York: The Ronald Press Company, 1964), p. 14.

[2] Solomon Dutka and Lester R. Frankel, "Markov Chain Analysis: A New Tool for Marketers," is Hiram C. Barksdale, ed., *Marketing in Progress* (New York: Holt, Rinehart and Winston, Inc., 1964), pp. 325–30.

[3] George H. Brown, "Measuring Consumer Attitudes Toward Products," *Journal of Marketing* (April 1950), pp. 691–98.

ing of channel support can represent a significant cost to the manufacturer. These and other *hidden* costs associated with lost sales must be incorporated into management's analysis of distribution strategies.

The New Product Example

The introductory phase of new products provides an excellent means for illustrating the workings and benefits of an *inter*functional total cost approach. Several factors exist that make new product introduction difficult.

The large number of new products introduced each year presents the first obstacle. Even the largest retail outlets have limited display and storage space; it is difficult to stock every brand of every product. New entries must overcome the market positions of existing brands by demonstrating to wholesalers and retailers the profitability associated with stocking the new product or brand.

A second factor impeding rapid and successful market entry is "scrambled merchandising." In planning his market coverage strategy, today's manufacturer must often secure adequate representation not only within a given type of retail outlet, such as food supermarkets, but also among several *different* types of outlets, such as food supermarkets, discount houses, and drugstores.

To overcome these obstacles, manufacturers typically rely on a very large and intensive promotional effort, including heavy advertising to consumers coupled with personal selling, to secure active storage in as many retail outlets as possible and to provide for adequate transitory storage at the wholesale level. However, both wholesalers and retailers are reluctant to invest in a new product until its ability to secure a profitable share of the market has been demonstrated.

Although some support has been given to the thesis that heavy advertising can "pull" a product through channels, there is a tendency to overestimate its effectiveness *unless* it is backed by adequate inventories and satisfactory market coverage. Generally, consumers will exert limited efforts to secure a brand that is out-of-stock. Consequently, a dilution of promotional efforts will result because the new product is out-of-stock and/or not enough retailers are willing to invest in the item. This dilution, and the attendant costs, should cause management to apply

a trade-off approach between promotional and physical distribution.

A Case Example

The Marketing Science Institute recently has made available the results of extensive studies concerning promotional decision-making.[4] A digest of one case history will serve to illustrate the effects of the retarding force exerted by current concepts toward active storage. The case involves the Superb Foods Corporation and its strategy in marketing a new salad dressing in an aerosol container under the name, "Presto-Gild." The following excerpted quotations present the sequence of the case:

1. Laboratory development of Presto-Gild was completed in January 1962.

2. Mr. Flint (the marketing manager) recognized that retailers must have an adequate stock on hand when advertising for Presto-Gild appeared, and that they must be sufficiently interested in the new product to give it good visibility.

3. Flint divided the $600,000 promotional budget between sales promotion and advertising. He set aside 25 percent of the total for sales promotion and 75 percent for advertising.

4. From the $150,000 total for sales promotion, he decided to pay 20¢ per case as a retail incentive—the 20¢ per case incentive would cost $75,000 on a national distribution basis.

5. The allocation of the $450,000 budget for advertising was the next consideration.

6. Inventories of Presto-Gild were beginning to mount during the test market period which began September 1, 1961. To avoid spoilage the salad dressing had to be placed on the market and national distribution was ordered. These arrangements required from 30 to 60 days, and before they could be completed substantial spoilage occurred.

7. A review of 1962, the first full year of national distribution, showed that while Presto-Gild had fallen to as low as 75 percent of its goal at one point, it had moved to within 85 percent of its goal by the end of the year. About 60 percent of all stores in the established markets carried the product shortly after the intro-

[4] Patrick J. Robinson and David J. Luck, *Promotional Decision Making* (New York: McGraw-Hill Book Company, Inc., 1964).

ductory period. This has since fallen off to about 50 percent, a figure Mr. Flint considered satisfactory for a product appealing to upper-income groups.

8. Looking ahead to 1963 the advertising agency urged that Presto-Gild's promotional budget be the same as the first year—$600,000.

9. Also recommended in the 1963 campaign were increased trade incentives to boost distribution and additional display material.

A number of factors that would be of interest are not available in the case. We do not know the costs of product development, of setting up the production facilities, nor the amount of capital tied up or lost in the inert storage stage. The statement regarding mounting inventory of Presto-Gild which forced early national distribution suggests that this last factor may have been one of considerable importance.

Another important cost not available is the amount of money expended on personal selling efforts to obtain active storage. Since this was a multiproduct firm, these costs probably were absorbed in the general personal selling expenses of the firm. But even if no new salesmen were added to facilitate product acceptance, the opportunity costs involved in diverting salesmen's efforts from other products is a factor which must be considered and which probably represented a considerable sum.

It should be noted that fully one eighth of the total *explicit* promotional budget was devoted to an incentive plan aimed at easing the salesman's task and securing the retailer's acceptance. Let us suppose that the Superb Foods Corporation had decided to separate the costs involved in the active storage function and to absorb some of these costs themselves. In particular we refer to those costs associated with inventory obsolescence, deterioration, consumer nonacceptance, and inventory carrying charges. In effect, the company would have promoted the product to the retail and wholesale trade under an arrangement whereby dealers added the product without assuming the financing and other major risks usually associated with stocking a new item. Superb Foods would have then said, in effect, "We ask you to put this merchandise on your shelf with the understanding that you will not pay for it until and unless your customers purchase it, and we will back up our gamble with a consumer promotional

program which we believe will assure such consumer acceptance."

The following costs would have been affected by this proposal:

1. There would have been no need for the 20¢ per case dealer incentive thus either saving the $75,000 allotted for this purpose or making it available for increased consumer promotion.

2. The task for the sales force and hence the opportunity cost involved would have been reduced because the proposition now offered by the salesmen to the middlemen would be one which was inherently more attractive.

3. More rapid stocking by more retailers would have increased the efficiency of every dollar in the advertising budget.

4. The spoilage involved through inert storage would not have occurred.

5. The hidden costs of lost sales would have been reduced because a greater number of retailers and wholesalers would have been more receptive to stocking a larger inventory of the product.

While the approach suggested here bears a *surface* resemblance to consignment selling, it is actually quite different in both nature and intent. Consignment selling, in which *the manufacturer retains title* to the merchandise, has been a frequently used tool to retain control over factors such as price and display. This changes the retailer from a merchant to an agent. A guaranteed sale arrangement, on the other hand, clearly recognizes that it is in the interest of all channel members to maintain the retailer's merchant position. The retailer, with his knowledge of local market conditions, is best equipped to make decisions as to optimum selling conditions. To do this, he must be recognized as the *owner* of goods in his possession.

Summary

As interfunctional approach recognizes both the interrelationship between promotion and physical distribution and the interdependency between channel members and manufacturers. Although the interests of these groups are not identical, neither are they incompatible. A problem for one typically involves a corresponding problem for the other.

The uncertainties associated with new products poses serious problems to manufacturers in their attempts to demonstrate to middlemen the product's potential. These wholesalers and retailers, in turn, are faced with the problem of assessing the risk of investing in products whose rate of sale has not been clearly established.

Because of the manufacturer's need to support new product introductions with adequate inventories, his risks of ownership and storage are difficult to avoid. In attempting to shift inventories to the retail level, the traditional approach has been to shift inventory risk as well. While this is an accepted practice for products with established market positions, its use with new products can have a retarding effect upon market acceptance.

An interfunctional analysis, as applied to new product introduction, suggests that the manufacturer retain more of the risk associated with owning inventories at all levels of distribution. Today's market conditions might make it feasible for the manufacturer to extend to middlemen a type of protected inventory arrangement whereby their risk is reduced primarily to that associated with on-premise damage and pilferage and to the opportunity cost of using storage space to stock the particular item. All other risks would be retained by the manufacturer, and although these could increase his costs of physical distribution, they should either reduce promotional costs by a greater amount or improve the effectiveness of promotional dollars.

35. *The Management of Physical Distribution: A Dilemma**

ROBERT E. WEIGAND†

During the last ten years businessmen have increasingly expressed an interest in what might be called an "integrated viewpoint" toward business operations. This term implies two things. First, it suggests that the executive has achieved sufficient perspective to understand the wide range of factors which influence his decision and appreciates the implications of his decisions once they have been made. The factors which are strategic to the success of an operating decision frequently are difficult to identify, complex, and numerous. Accurate evaluation of a problem situation must be preceded by gathering sufficient information about these factors so that an accurate decision can be made. The implications of a decision, meaning the impact it will have on various areas in a business, is difficult to determine both because it involves an element of futurity and because other areas which may bear part of the force of a decision are seldom as familiar to an executive as his own area.

Second, the term suggests that organizational responsibility often accompanies the manager who has such considerable authority to make decisions which influence others. Virtually every executive decision in a firm has at least some small though often immeasurable influence over the other people in a firm. Some decisions are so significant, however, that specific organizational steps must be taken to assure that a decision made in one area does not have a disastrous influence elsewhere within the firm.

The purposes of this article are to demonstrate the interrelationship between what is usually called Sales (or more recently Marketing) and the physical supply functions of transportation and storage, to present empirical evidence which shows that organizational provisions have *not* always been taken to assure a blending of effort of these two areas, and to cite some causes for this lack of integration.

Marketing literature seldom expresses a doubt that the physical supply functions are a part of the marketing process. Implicit in most definitions is the thought that physical movement is as much a part of marketing as the better-known process of selling through a personal sales force, advertising, or sales promotion.[1] Where authors have chosen to list the activities generic to marketing, transportation and storage are virtually always included. From the viewpoint of an academician, there is no question concerning the scope of the marketing process: it clearly includes transportation and storage, which create place and time utility.

A Vital Interrelationship

There is a considerable literary void, however, in specifying the reasons why physical supply decisions are so closely related to the other activities of marketing. The "integrated viewpoint," meaning a reasonably full understanding of this relationship, is not clearly presented in the marketing literature. For an executive to achieve such an understanding through job experience is time-consuming and difficult; some never see the blending of the two areas as they should in order to make fully effective decisions. The following circumstances exemplify the need for appreciating the interrelationship of sales and physical supply.

[1] For example, an American Marketing Association committee defined Marketing as "The performance of business activities that direct the flow of goods and services from producer to consumer or user." Report by the Definitions Committee, *Journal of Marketing* XIII (October 1948), 209.

* Reprinted by permission from *Business Topics,* Summer 1962.
† De Paul University.

Speed of Delivery

First, there is almost universal recognition that ability to deliver goods on the date that they are promised and in the condition implied by the salesman has a substantial influence on the capacity of the sales force to do what is expected of it. The sales force generally views volume as the principal measure of its success. One of the major tactical weapons available to the salesman is the promise of quick delivery. This weapon is particularly important where his customers look upon the product he is selling as substantially the same as that of his competitors. It is really not very important whether either management or the sales force sees differences among brands. If the buyer sees no differences, whatever differences there may actually be are interesting but tactically useless. In an industry characterized by relative homogeneity of product, speed of delivery can be a major competitive weapon.

On the other hand, physical distribution must be attained at a reasonable cost. Attempts to cater to the needs of the market would include, for example, shipment by faster means and the use of regional warehousing through company-owned or public warehouses. These efforts tend to increase volume and consequently are viewed with sympathy by the sales force. Simultaneously, however, they increase costs. The manager of physical distribution obviously acknowledges the importance of sales, but he is held accountable for his own department's costs.

If the sales force manager is not also responsible for physical distribution, the situation just described contains the elements essential to a philosophical and operational conflict. Relatively greater emphasis on volume by the sales manager and relatively greater emphasis on costs by the manager of physical distribution present a dilemma.

Cost of Delivery

Second, the geographic market area a firm can cover effectively is strongly influenced by the costs incurred in making a sale and distributing the product. In heavy goods industries, meaning those groups of firms in which delivery costs are a relatively high proportion of sales price, there is an economic limit to the area that can be served profitably by a single manufacturing plant. But neither the cost of a sales force nor the costs of physical distribu-

tion alone are the determinants of the optimum boundaries of a market area. For example, the sales force may experience relatively little economic disadvantage in soliciting sales a considerable distance from the point of manufacture. But the cost of delivery, if borne by the seller in order to price competitively, may render such sales unprofitable. Therefore the boundaries of a firm's geographic market frequently are determined by its ability to distribute its product economically.

The ability of a manager of physical distribution to manipulate carload or pooled car shipments, to choose the method of shipment, such as train versus truck, and to know when to use central versus regional or "spot" stocking, significantly influences the size of market a firm can serve profitably Again, a dilemma is presented. Central to the dilemma is the fact that there may be little similarity between the optimum sales force territory and the point where delivery costs become too great for the firm to compete with other firms more favorably located.

A Coordinated Inventory

Third, the capital of a firm is used more effectively when inventory levels are closely matched with sales expectations. There is probably considerable temptation in many firms to maintain inventory at about the same level because sales follow no established pattern and are highly unpredictable. To the extent, however, that the marketing executive can forecast either long-term or short-term changes in sales there is merit in coordinating inventory levels with anticipated sales. Except where sales or economic forecasting has become a specialized staff activity, the chief marketing executive often is best fitted to predict what his sales force will sell during the period ahead. (To reduce the likelihood of an overly optimistic bias, some firms have taken the sobering step of holding the marketing executive responsible for selling his predicted volume at a profit.)

The inventory position of a firm not only is affected by the sales forecast, but marketing strategy is also affected by inventory levels. This view carries the unfortunate implication of the tail wagging the dog. In an ideally operated firm, the market dictates what will be manufactured, held briefly in inventory, and sold. But misinterpretation of market tastes and preferences can create undesirable inventory buildup. This build-up, though not planned, becomes a major determinant of short-term marketing tactics. Another dilemma becomes readily apparent. In any firm in which the marketing executive is not fully aware of changes in inventory levels the speed with which he can adjust his department's effort is seriously impaired.

Empirical Evidence

The ideas just presented indicate that there is a close relationship between sales and physical distribution. This relationship, though often ignored in the literature of marketing, must be recognized if profitable decisions are to be made. The individual who consistently sees such relationships is one who has achieved the integrated viewpoint already mentioned.

Such perspective is not likely to be gained, however, unless specific organizational steps have been taken to provide an organization and an atmosphere in which this understanding will grow. These conditions seem *not* to be present in a substantial number of firms. Contrary to what is implied by the definitions of marketing, there is little indication among five industries which were studied that sales and physical distribution are viewed as closely related activities. Furthermore, in relatively few firms have organizational steps been taken to assure that a decision in either sales or physical distribution will not have a serious and unfortunate effect on the other. The evidence presented here is taken from a study of the marketing organization of firms with a net worth of at least one million dollars, operating in the electrical machinery, non-electrical machinery, fabricated metals, chemicals, and instruments industries.

A total of 220 firms replied to a mailed questionnaire.[2] One part of the questionnaire concentrated on the extent of the chief marketing executive's responsibility for traffic and warehousing decisions and the extent of his participation in discussions concerning these activities. Fewer than 10 (9.09) percent of the top marketing executives were fully responsible for traffic decisions, and in only a slightly greater (10.95) percent of firms were they fully responsible for warehousing decisions. These

[2] Additional personal interviews were made, but are not pertinent to the evidence presented here.

figures are probably not too surprising to traffic or warehouse supervisors who are accustomed to reporting to someone other than the top marketing executive. In the majority of firms (50.25 and 53.32 percent respectively) the top marketing executive at least participated in discussions concerning traffic and warehousing although he did not always assume responsibility for these activities.

Although the above is gratifying evidence that efforts are being made to coordinate sales and physical distributions in many firms, a substantial share of the respondents indicated that the top marketing executive neither assumed any responsibility nor participated in discussions concerning physical distribution. The figures were 43.06 and 35.26 percent respectively. (The remaining 6.69 and 11.42 percent indicated that the activities were not a formal activity in their firm.) There is ample cause to wonder how a balanced decision can be made concerning physical distribution when the views of the chief marketing executive are not considered.

Evidence of Change

In order to gain perspective concerning change which may have occurred over a ten year period, the same questions were asked for both 1950 and 1959. There was little indication that the top marketing executive was more frequently assuming full or partial responsibility for these two activities: the figures for 1950 were about the same as for 1959. On the other hand, there was evidence that the top marketing executive was increasingly asked to participate in discussions concerning shipping or storing. The percent of firms in which the top marketing executive participated in discussions (but did not assume any responsibility) changed from 21.54 percent in 1950 to 29.20 percent in 1959 for traffic and from 16.02 percent in 1950 to 21.42 percent in 1959 for warehousing. This appears to be a small but healthy tendency.

Difference According to Firm Size

The firms which responded to the questionnaire were divided into those with sales under $10 million, those with sales between $10 and $100 million, and those with sales over $100 million. There was little difference between the small and medium-sized firms, but the large firms were considerably different. In a greater percent of the large firms the top marketing executive assumed either full or shared responsibility for decisions concerning physical distribution. More specifically, the top marketing executive in 43 percent of the large firms either shared or took full responsibility for physical supply decisions; the figures for medium and small-sized firms were 24 and 26 percent.

This difference is not surprising and can be explained by another significant difference in the responsibilities of top marketing executives in large firms. In about half of the large firms the chief marketing executive was not responsible for supervision of the sales force. His activities were confined to management of staff duties. It would appear that relief from such a time-consuming job as supervision of the sales force affords time for integrating sales and physical distribution.

Reasons for this Dilemma

It has been suggested that there should be a close relationship between decisions made in the marketing department and physical distribution activities. Yet the empirical evidence indicates that in many firms the top marketing executive does not assume responsibility for transportation or storage decisions and only infrequently participates in decisions concerning these areas. The suggestion is now made that the reasons for this dilemma can be identified and that they are not defensible under current conditions.

Complexity

First, traffic decisions traditionally have been considered complex and not easily supervised by an executive trained in marketing. This is an understandable view. It is not easy for a manager to assume responsibility for an area totally unfamiliar to him.

On the other hand, the manager does not need to understand the detailed operations of every individual with whom he is expected to work. It is essential, however, that he have the managerial ability to integrate the actions of the various specialized individuals who report to him. This concept permits a strong argument in favor of the traffic manager reporting to the top marketing executive.

Decentralization

Second, in many firms the top sales executive spends more time working with the sales force than he does managing his marketing staff. Inasmuch as the efforts of the sales force are naturally decentralized the manager of the sales force often feels that he must travel in order to perform his duties effectively. Where such travel is frequent and extensive, management of other activities is impaired.

On the other hand, to an increased extent in recent years marketing executives, particularly those who have achieved the integrated viewpoint referred to earlier, seem to be spending more time planning and organizing a complete marketing system than in daily supervision of marketing activities. Sales supervision is still the responsibility of the marketing executive in the majority of firms, but he often has an assistant who assumes a considerable share of the burden. To the extent that this gives the top marketing executive additional time, he can spend his time managing a wider range of activities than before. And it is suggested here that physical distribution should be among the activities that are within his area of interest. While some will argue that he should not assume responsibility for transportation or storage policies, at the very least he should be consulted because of the influence these areas have on the marketing department.

Interrelationship

Finally, the interrelationship of sales and physical distribution has not always been fully appreciated by those responsible for organization planning. Organizations often have grown with less than adequate regard for structuring activities that should be closely integrated under the same executive. Because most individuals arrive at a middle or top management position through a series of relatively specialized positions this lack of perspective is understandable. Although perhaps understandable, it does not excuse the frustrating results which occur when one part of the organization seems not to know what the other part is doing. Obviously decisions often have an effect throughout the firm; their impact is not restricted to a single department. But some decisions have such a substantial impact on other areas that the interrelationship cannot be ignored. The suggestion is made here that an "organizational audit" would reveal serious structural deficiencies in many firms. One aspect of an organizational audit would consist of reviewing the activities which should be most closely coordinated. The formal organization structure and responsibilities of executives should correspond to this interrelationship. The empirical evidence suggests these steps have been taken too infrequently in American industry.

36. *Improved Efficiency and Reduced Cost in Marketing**

Donald D. Parker†

The Committee on Definitions of the American Marketing Association defines "marketing" as follows: "The performance of business activities that direct the flow of goods and services from producer to consumer or user."[1]

No attempt is made to challenge this definition. Instead, it is presented here to point out that marketing encompasses activities much broader than selling, sales promotion, and marketing research. Emphasis on these functions in current popular business literature has resulted, unfortunately, in a restricted concept of the scope and status of marketing activities in industry.

Marketing management is the exercise of proper management controls over *all* the business functions implied in the above definition. Marketing management, therefore, is much broader than sales management. It includes the exchange functions of buying and selling, the physical distribution functions of transportation and storage, and the other functions which facilitate marketing—such as financing, risk-bearing, and communication.

Substantial progress has been made in improving the efficiency and reducing the costs of production and manufacturing activities. These improvements are major contributors to increased standards of living in the United States. Although we are far from ultimate efficiency in production, there is little doubt that progress there has outstripped improved efficiency in marketing activities.

Yet consumers pay for lost motions in the management and integration of marketing activities as surely as they pay for inefficiency in production. Society can no more afford inefficiency in marketing than it can afford wasteful methods of production; the social cost is no less real. Likewise, companies which fail to improve the efficiency of their distribution activities will fall behind in our competitive economy.

The New Marketing Concept

A significant trend in American industry today is the increased attention being paid to marketing activities by top management. Seldom has business management indulged in such critical examination as is prevalent today in the marketing field.

Companies of all sizes are conducting searching inquiries into consumer habits and motivations, in attempts to determine what they can do to develop or maintain leadership in the marketplace. Serious thought is being given to the proper integration of marketing with the other divisions of the company. Marketing personnel gradually are playing a more important role in product development and production scheduling.

In short, more emphasis is being placed on learning more about the needs, wants, desires, likes, and dislikes of customers and using this knowledge as a primary basis for planning and organizing the entire operations of companies. Significant steps are being taken to improve the efficiency and reduce the costs of performing marketing activities. In far too many cases the steps being taken are restricted only to the marketing research, selling, and sales-promotion aspects of marketing and fail to include the other marketing functions. Until all marketing activities are integrated and until all marketing costs are considered, the potential for improved efficiency and cost reduction cannot be realized.

* Reprinted by permission from the *Journal of Marketing*, National quarterly publication of the American Marketing Association, April 1962.

† Portland State College.

[1] Ralph S. Alexander and others, *Marketing Definition: A Glossary of Marketing Terms* (Chicago: American Marketing Association, 1960), p. 15.

The Cost-Price Squeeze

A recent survey conducted by Dun and Bradstreet asked American business leaders to indicate what they consider to be the most crucial issues facing industry in the 1960's.[2] Responses were received from 1,225 large companies. Many factors were mentioned, but the issue specified most often as most crucial was the "cost-price squeeze" by 27 per cent of the manufacturers and 23 per cent of all the respondents. Other issues—such as taxes, international tensions, and inflation—which have been dominant in the past are considered relatively less crucial today.

Whenever any company faces a squeeze between the costs of doing business and the prices at which they sell, the alternatives for survival are extremely limited. The pattern of prices usually is set by competition, with leadership often assumed by the most efficient competitors. The elasticity of demand or competitors' prices limit the ability of most companies to solve the "cost-price squeeze" problem by price changes. The remaining major alternative is to attack the costs of doing business in an attempt to improve efficiency and reduce costs. These costs may be classified roughly as production costs and marketing costs; and each constitutes about half of the total cost of doing business.

The Last Frontier for Cost Economies

Unfortunately, improvements in marketing efficiency and reductions in marketing costs still lie in the future, representing a major frontier for cost economies. Too many marketing activities do not lend themselves readily to cost reduction, because they are not repetitive and machines cannot be substituted for the human element.

However, there is room for substantial improvement, particularly in the performance of the physical-distribution functions of marketing which constitute a major part of total marketing costs and which are selected for emphasis in this article.

Physical-Distribution Costs

Physical-distribution costs are those costs associated with the physical movement of goods.

[2] "News from Dun and Bradstreet, Inc." Dun and Bradstreet, Inc., November, 1960, pp. 2–5.

The finished goods of a manufacturer or producer—which may be component parts, raw materials, or expendable supplies for another manufacturer—must be moved and usually stored before they have economic value or utility.

There is a tendency to think of the costs of physical distribution as being comprised of transportation and warehousing costs only. Actually, however, there are other significant costs which must be considered when attempting to analyze and improve physical distribution activities. The nature of these costs varies with different companies, but the following list includes the most common costs associated with physical distribution:

1. Transportation by common carrier, contract carrier, or company-owned equipment.
2. Warehousing in public or private facilities.
3. Order-handling, including back-orders.
4. Packing.
5. Inventory insurance.
6. Inventory taxes.
7. Inventory handling.
8. Inventory obsolescence.
9. Inventory capital costs.

It is regrettable that the accounting systems of most companies do not permit an accurate determination of these costs individually. Without this determination, it is extremely difficult to evaluate the alternative methods of performing the physical distribution functions. Also, it should be apparent that any steps that can be taken to reduce the amount of inventory have an immediate and significant effect upon physical distribution costs.

The Important Cost

These comments about alternative methods of performing physical-distribution functions imply that there are varying levels of cost for each alternative. Normally, for example, companies select one or more modes of freight transportation from several alternatives with different costs. Goods may be stored in public or private warehouses. Inventories may be stored centrally or in a varying number of regional warehouses. Various systems for the handling of orders and back-orders are available; different types of packing methods and materials are considered before decisions are made. The prevailing practice is for these alternatives to be weighed and decisions reached which will result in the greatest efficiency and least cost in the performance of each particular sub-function, without regard for the effect of those decisions on the cost of performing other related functions.

Yet the mode of transportation selected affects the cost of packing materials to be used. The location of inventories influences the number of times inventories are handled and the attendant costs. Several of these decisions are related to the amount of inventory required to provide a desired level of customer service; thus, they affect the costs associated with inventories.

The most important cost, and the cost on which attention should be focused in any attempt to improve efficiency and reduce costs, is *the total cost of performing the physical-distribution activity*—not the separate costs of the individual segments. In other words, it is a mistake to concentrate on reducing the cost of one factor only—such as transportation—when to do so has the effect of increasing the cost of another factor by an amount greater than the amount saved. Conversely, it is wise from the standpoint of improved efficiency and reduced marketing costs to increase one cost if, by decreasing other related costs, the net effect is to reduce the total cost of physical distribution.

Organizational Structure and Functional Decisions

All companies are organized to "manage" physical-distribution activities. Most companies place the responsibility for cost-and-service control at the functional level (for example, traffic manager); and the opportunity to look at the total cost is clouded by divided responsibility. Pressures are applied by top management which encourage the separate functional units to control and reduce their costs of operation. Cost reduction becomes the primary way for these functional units to call attention to themselves. Usually, this means taking steps to optimize the particular functions delegated to them.

Thus, the traffic manager, for example, is motivated to arrange transportation services at the lowest possible cost—which usually means concentration on large quantity shipments by truckload or carload lots. Those delegated responsibility for production planning and production scheduling, likewise, think in terms of minimizing unit production costs. As a result,

these and other functions are performed without sufficient regard for the effect of these decisions on other related costs or the total cost. In other words, the optimization of these sub-functions may result in the creation of excessive costs associated with inventory accumulation, inventory control, inventory obsolescence, and warehousing.

The tendency of most companies has been to overlook the potentials for improving service and reducing the total cost of distribution, by failing to co-ordinate and integrate this responsibility at a higher level in the organizational structure of the company.

The result is a condition of suboptimization— a condition of apparent efficiency in the various parts, but less than optimum efficiency in the operation of the integrated whole. As a result, when decisions are made about transportation, warehousing, packing, inventory levels, and the other factors mentioned, they are based on an analysis of alternatives within that specific function, without regard for the possible effects upon other closely related functions. Functional costs are considered, but the all-important total cost of the related functions is ignored. The need, obviously, is for the creation of a position with responsibility for co-ordinating the activities of these various functions and controlling the total cost.

Recently several companies have given serious consideration to revising their organizational structure to achieve more efficient integration of the physical distribution functions. For example, the major appliance division of Westinghouse Electric Corporation last year created a new position titled Manager, Marketing Administration. The responsibility of the executive in this position is to integrate traffic, warehousing, order servicing, inventory control, and production scheduling.

Before anything really effective can be done to implement the total-cost concept and the desired degree of integration, it must have the full support of the chief executive officer of the company. Otherwise, the necessary realignment of responsibility to make it an effective concept will probably never come to pass. The incentive for interest on the part of top management is a desire for improved control over service and costs. Improved control over service leads to expanded markets . . . improved control over costs leads to a lower total cost of distribution . . . and both lead to a competitive advantage and increased profit.

The Function of Inventories

Service vs. Costs

While inventories of finished goods may result from steps taken to stabilize production or to produce economically, the basic function of inventory accumulation is to provide service to customers. In any competitive market, ready availability of inventory plays an important role in customer service, with the critical problem arising in determining the proper balance between service and the cost of providing service. From the extreme viewpoint of maximum service, complete inventories should be immediately available to all customers and potential customers. To provide this level of service, however, would entail unreasonable costs.

The solution, therefore, must be a compromise in an attempt to offer a reasonable level of service—in light of competition—without incurring excessive costs of carrying, storing, handling, and transporting inventories, and without suffering excessive costs of inventory depreciation and obsolescence.

Inventory Problems

In attempting to find the optimum balance between service to customers and inventory costs, many problems arise. No predetermined solutions are available for any industry or company because of substantial differences in inventory variety, the breadth of the market, the urgency of rapid service, the degree of competition, and other factors. Each company should analyze its particular situation and weigh the factors of service and costs which will lead them to an optimum solution.

In analyzing inventory problems, one important factor is the relative rate of flow of different items held in inventory. Studies of the product lines of various industries show a common pattern of varying volume for different classes of items. Typically, a small percentage of items—usually about 10 per cent—account for a high percentage of sales volume—usually about 80 per cent. About half of the items account for a very small percentage of sales volume. This is a critical factor because the slow-moving items usually cause much more than their proportionate share of inventory costs (investment, handling costs, insurance, taxes, and obsolescence).

Alternatives

In most cases, a wide variety of alternatives is available in attempting to optimize inventory location decisions, with each alternative having a different pattern of costs.

Also of importance is the time factor—the time required for inventory delivery from various locations. Different combinations of inventory location and modes of transportation may result in approximately the same time factor, but quite different costs. For example, one company may use inexpensive means of transportation to deliver inventories to a large number of regional warehouses, in order to provide rapid service to its local markets. Another company may centralize its inventories and use faster and more expensive means of transportation, to provide the same level of service to their customers. The former company will have relatively low transportation costs, with relatively high costs of warehousing, handling, and other costs associated with greater inventory levels. The latter company is providing the same service with reduced inventory, but with relatively high transportation costs. The important factors are the levels of service maintained and the total cost of maintaining that service—not the cost of any particular segment.

In the above example, assuming comparable levels of service to customers, the company with the lower total cost is performing the physical-distribution function more efficiently. There is nothing sacred about the maintenance of regional inventories if their elimination or reduction can be accomplished without reducing the level of service to customers.

Tools to Facilitate Progress

Future progress in improving the efficiency and reducing the cost of performing physical distribution functions lies, first, in the integration and co-ordination of the several subfunctions which comprise physical-distribution activities; and, second, in reducing the time required for the performance of these activities.

Much of the inefficiency and excessive cost prevalent in American industry today is traceable to the suboptimization which results from a failure to view physical-distribution activities as a whole. The time lag between order origination and merchandise delivery is the critical factor in matters of customer service, inventory requirements, and the costs of physical distribution.

The solution to problems of maintaining or improving service to customers with reduced inventories lies in reducing the time required for the flow of information and the flow of materials or inventories.

Operations Research

The concepts and techniques of operations research have a great deal to offer in any attempt to integrate the subfunctions and reach decisions about physical distribution activities as a whole.[3] The progress of operations researchers in areas of marketing has been slow because of semantic difficulties and lack of familiarity with the nature of marketing problems; but the future looks bright for substantial improvements in marketing efficiency traceable to the application of operations research techniques. The fundamental contributions of operations research to the solution of marketing problems lie in the following areas:

1. *The systems concept*—considering the elements of related business activities as a coordinated whole instead of a group of independent and unrelated elements. The application of this concept to the subfunctions of physical distribution shows substantial promise for improved efficiency and reduced cost.

2. *The model concept*—which has specific application to the preliminary testing of possible alternatives, in search for improved efficiency and cost reduction in physical-distribution activities.

3. *Emphasis on experimentation*—without which few companies can reach optimum solutions to physical-distribution problems.

Operations researchers are becoming aware of the extreme complexities of marketing activities and the close relationships among the various marketing functions. The foundations have been built for their effective collaboration with management people responsible for marketing efficiency.

In marketing, the greatest success of operations research has been in problems of inventory control, warehouse locations, and other areas related to physical distribution. Out of this success is growing the basis for additional contributions in systems concepts, experimental concepts, and models. Improvement in these areas is the key to the contribution operations research can make to future marketing strategy.

Electronic Data Processing

Much of future progress lies in possibilities of reducing the time required for performance of physical-distribution activities. This includes reducing the information flow time. Communications in a physical-distribution system form the nervous system, providing the feedback necessary to control the system and provide service to customers. Any attempt to reduce the material flow time must be accompanied by corresponding reductions in the information flow time in order to retain balance in the system.

Recent developments and improvements in the capabilities of data transmission and processing equipment have increased tremendously the speed and accuracy of handling greater volumes of data. Progress in reducing the time required for the physical flow of materials actually has lagged behind the advances made in the area of information flow. High-speed electronic computers have made it possible for companies to deal with much larger quantities of information. Increased speeds allow companies to process data which heretofore were unusable.

In addition, computers have stimulated the rethinking of whole new systems of information flow by progressive management personnel. More information may be received; it may be received more rapidly; it may be processed more rapidly; and it may be processed in new and different ways for purposes of better control and improved efficiency.

Air Freight

Recent developments and impending improvements in the air-freight industry represent interesting possibilities for companies interested in reducing material flow time—with reduced inventory requirements and costs—as a means of improving the efficiency and reducing the total cost of physical-distribution.[4]

---

[3] As to the application of operations research concepts to marketing, see John F. Magee, "Operations Research in Making Marketing Decisions," JOURNAL OF MARKETING, Vol. 25 (October, 1960), pp. 18–23.

[4] George M. Shutes, "Airfreight from a Marketing Viewpoint," JOURNAL OF MARKETING, Vol. 25 (October, 1960), pp. 39–43.

Throughout business history, whenever a new mode of freight transportation is introduced, it has developed slowly because the relative cost has been higher. Usually it is considered to be a premium means of transportation, to be used only in cases of emergency. Then gradually the new mode of transportation expands, improves the quality of service offered, and reaches a point of mass acceptance as a routine mover of freight. In each case, the effect has been to revolutionize business practices, particularly in the area of physical distribution.

Today the air-freight industry is in the latter phases of its introductory period, but is approaching rapidly a breakthrough to widespread acceptance as a routine mode of freight transportation. The growth of air freight during the post-World War II period has been quite spectacular, but still represents only a tiny portion of 1 per cent of the total ton-miles of intercity freight movement. Only in a very few cases is air freight considered to be other than a form of transportation to be used in extreme emergency or when unusual speed of delivery is all-important. Although air-freight rates have declined substantially, they still are much higher than rates for surface transportation. The quality reputation of air freight has suffered from erratic and inconsistent service, and from too many examples of unreliability.

Most of the problems which have resulted in damaging the service reputation of the air freight industry are traceable to (1) the fact that air freight has been carried in craft not designed specifically for this purpose; and (2) the fact that the bulk of air freight has been carried aboard passenger airplanes in which passenger operations receive top priority and air freight is incidental.

With regard to improvements in air-freight equipment, steps are being taken which indicate that the future picture is bright. The CL-44, a large turboprop airplane designed specifically for all-cargo operation has been built by Canadair, a subsidiary of General Dynamics, in Montreal. Delivery of these airplanes to the Flying Tiger Line, Slick Airways, and Seaboard and Western Airline began in 1961. Other airlines have converted airplanes for all-cargo use during the interim period before they place orders for more efficient all-cargo craft.

The spread between air-freight rates and rates for surface transportation is destined to become smaller and smaller. The trend in rates for sur-face-freight transportation is upward, while air-freight rates are being reduced. Rates charged by rail and truck carriers have increased sharply during the post-World War II period, and there are indications that this trend will continue in the future.

On the other hand, the trend in air-freight rates is downward, and there are growing indications of declines in the very near future. The inauguration of service by the new and more efficient aircraft will result in decreases in the cost of providing air-freight service. Impending use of new terminals and new cargo-handling equipment, when combined with anticipated increases in volume, will add to the pressures for reduced rates.

Air freight, particularly in light of impending improvements in service and reduction in rates, offers an opportunity for many companies to reduce their material flow time. Increased use of air freight may be related directly to maintaining or improving service to customers with reduced inventory and reduced total costs of performing the physical distribution function. Deterrents have been the relative cost of air freight, the service reputation of air freight, and the failure of companies to conceive of their physical distribution as an integrated whole. Most of these deterrents will vanish in the future.

The Raytheon Case

Several companies and governmental units have taken steps to reduce information and material flow time as a means of reducing both inventory levels and total cost of physical distribution, while maintaining or improving the level of service to their markets.

The example of a company which has received a great deal of publicity as a leader in this area is the Raytheon Company.[5] The Distributor Products Division of this company introduced a data processing system for automatically replenishing distributor inventories in early 1959. This system involved the inclusion of a prepunched data-processing card with each standard package of product shipped to distributors.

[5] This discussion of recent developments at the Raytheon Company depends heavily on a speech by John T. Thompson, General Manager, Distributor Products Division, Raytheon Company at the Distribution Management Conference sponsored by the American Management Association, Inc., in San Francisco, April 13, 1960.

Distributors, in turn, were instructed to mail these cards to regional warehouses on preassigned reorder days for automatic replenishment of items sold during the preceding period. This made it easier and quicker for distributors to place orders, improved their inventory turnover, and made possible lower inventories and improved availability. Also, in 1959 a central warehouse facility was built in Westwood, Massachusetts, and the process of reducing the number of regional warehouses was begun.

Assuming the availability of products at one or more central locations, the place utility of any product can be determined by the amount of time represented in (1) order communication time, (2) order processing time, and (3) transportation time. Raytheon has taken steps to reduce each of these time elements in attempts to reduce inventory requirements and reduce the total cost of physical distribution.

The system of automatic ordering and inventory replenishment making use of prepunched data processing cards reduced the order communication time. At present, the communication order points are regional district offices. Ultimately, data transmitters located in each customer's office will communicate orders directly to central warehouse facilities.

The receipt of orders on punched cards or tapes make it possible to use computers and other data processing equipment in the processing of orders. As a result, the time required for the processing of orders and the accumulation and packaging of orders is reduced from days to a matter of a few hours.

The compression of transportation time is being accomplished by the use of air freight. In a prototype demonstration conducted in late 1959, orders were originated in Los Angeles, Chicago, and Dallas and transmitted to the warehouse facility at Westwood. The orders were processed, filled, and shipped by air freight, reaching their destinations on the same day they were originated. This demonstration proved that the combination of a communications system integrated with an order-processing system and utilization of air freight can provide improved service to customers with reduced inventory and reduced total cost. Raytheon expects to eliminate 50 per cent of its dollar investment in inventory. An annual saving of at least $250,000 in direct out-of-pocket expenses is expected to result from their actions.

Implications

Progress in improving the efficiency and reducing the costs of manufacturing and production activities in American business has outstripped similar progress in the area of distribution. Marketing management faces a challenge to bring about similar improvements in distribution activities. Marketing costs, particularly those resulting from the physical distribution of goods, should be given more serious attention if increased productivity is to continue its contribution to increased standards of living. In our economy, those companies which meet this challenge with organizational change and adjustment to new concepts and new tools will have the competitive advantage in the future.

The costs of physical distribution should be considered as an important segment of total marketing costs, worthy of serious analysis and control. There should be an increased awareness that the important physical-distribution cost is the total cost of performing these activities. Increased attention should be directed to integration of the subfunctions which comprise physical distribution. Necessary organizational changes should be made to place responsibility for these combined activities at a level which will result in optimization of the integrated whole.

Inventories should be viewed by marketing management as a fundamental element of service to customers. But the accumulation, handling, storing, transportation, and obsolescence of inventories represent substantial costs. Alternative mixes of these inventory cost elements are available for consideration in attempts to maintain or improve service to customers at reduced cost. The location and amount of inventories should be determined in light of the time required for service to customers. Recent developments in reducing the time required for order transmission, ordering processing, and transportation should be given serious consideration.

Impending improvements in the quality of air-freight service, accompanied by imminent reductions in air freight rates, represent an opportunity for many companies to improve service to customers with reduced inventory, and thus reduce the total cost of performing physical-distribution activities. Those companies which make the necessary analyses and adjustments and take advantage of this opportunity will be the leaders in their industries.

37. *Total Cost Approach to Physical Distribution**

In recent years, retailers, wholesalers and manufacturers all have exhibited an increasing awareness of the significant effect which physical distribution has on their company's profit picture. The exposure of this long-neglected phase of business activity to scientific analysis is derived from the need to satisfy two objectives.

One objective is to reduce distribution costs, usually brought about by the ever increasing profit squeeze.

The second is to improve marketing effectiveness, necessary to remain competitive.

Accomplishment of these objectives presents a different problem, since each tends to move operating costs in opposite directions. To improve marketing, companies frequently utilize additional field warehouses, commit additional funds to maintenance of field stocks, or make extensive use of premium transportation. However, to reduce distribution costs, companies may restrict field operations and use only the most economical modes of transportation.

Although these and similar physical distribution problems have been analyzed by many companies, most studies have looked only at segments of the problem. Some studies have considered only customer benefits, some considered only warehousing costs, while others have been traffic oriented. These partial evaluations result from responsibility for distribution frequently being spread among numerous functions, including manufacturing, traffic, sales and accounting.

This split responsibility has become apparent to corporate managements as they have devoted more attention to their distribution problems. Thus, there is now a tendency to view physical distribution as a single integrated system stretching from factories to customers with "physical distribution" emerging as a separate function. However, there still remains the question, *"What factors must be considered before altering our present distribution methods?"*

Certain considerations are usually present in varying degrees in most comprehensive distribution analyses. These can be grouped into five categories: operating costs; marketing factors; data processing considerations; mathematical techniques required to obtain optimum solutions to problems; management considerations necessary to make the required decisions and implement the proposed changes.

Together these comprise a total cost approach to physical distribution. Analyzed jointly, a basis for solution to this complex problem is provided. Let's now examine each of these basic considerations.

Operating Cost Consideration

Any proposal to alter distribution methods must deal with the following matters. Transportation is a major expense item in almost every distribution system. The magnitude of this expense is related directly to the number and location of warehouses.

Generally, the manufacturer finds that adding warehouses reduces the distance his goods must travel between his factories and his customers. Cost thus tends to lower as distance is reduced. However, as the number of warehouses increases and the total business is divided among them, the volume handled by each decreases. Hence, the manufacturer finds that where before he could ship carload or truckload lots from his factories to a small number of warehouses, he is no longer able to do this. Consequently, his transportation costs begin to increase.

* Reprinted by permission from *Business Management,* August 1963.
† Booz, Allen & Hamilton, Inc.

Chart 1* illustrates this situation, as shown by the curve labeled "Transportation Cost: Suppliers to Warehouses." As the number of warehouses increases, the inbound transportation cost decreases to a minimum, then begins to increase as the number of carload movements decreases.

Also of concern is the transportation cost outbound from warehouses. As shown in Chart 1, this cost decreases as additional warehouses are added. Theoretically, this cost is minimized when every store has its own warehouse. A critical point, of course, is the number of warehouses for which total transportation cost is minimized.

The retail chain operator faces much the same dilemma as the manufacturer. However, the retailer generally has more flexibility in selecting alternate suppliers. Thus, as warehouses are established in areas of retail store concentrations, suppliers may be located in the vicinity of those warehouses, thereby reducing the distance the merchandise must move and consequently, the cost of transportation. The chain retailer may feel that he requires daily shipments from his warehouses to his stores. However, this restricts the amount of merchandise moved in each shipment and, to the extent that bulk shipments are reduced, transportation costs are increased. Also requiring analysis are the

* The charts contained in this article reflect the situation typically found by the chain store operator.

modes of transportation used and the frequency of shipments.

An important factor effecting the cost of operating warehouses is size. Each warehouse has certain fixed and semivariable expenses. Thus, for a given volume of business, a smaller number of large warehouses will involve a lower total of fixed and semivariable expenses. This is illustrated in *Chart 2* by the curve marked "fixed and semivariable costs."

Also, in larger warehouses, automatic handling devices can be justified with a resulting reduction in operating costs. Thus cost reduction has become quite significant in highly-automated warehouses. For example, devices now are available to perform the following key functions:

Incoming merchandise can be automatically directed by a receiver to an assigned storage area.

Customer orders can be converted to punch cards or magnetic tape to activate a mechanism for automatic order picking.

Outbound customer orders can be automatically sorted and routed to preselected truck or freight car loading docks.

The effect of mechanization is demonstrated by the "direct cost" curve in *Chart 2*. Direct costs, by definition, are those which vary directly with the quantity of merchandise handled. However, on a unit basis, these direct costs are less in a large (high volume) warehouse compared with a small (low volume)

Chart 1. *Transportation cost*

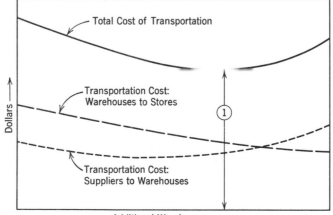

① = Number of warehouses producing total minimum transportation cost

Chart 2.   *Warehouse operating cost*

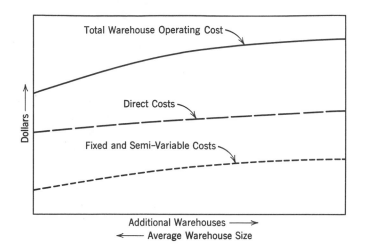

warehouse, since one finds that additional automatic, labor-saving devices can be justified in the larger warehouse.

Another important factor is the location of the warehouses. Factors to be analyzed here are state and local taxes, labor rates, construction costs, and land costs.

Carrying inventory is a major expense item. The components of this cost are: insurance, taxes, space costs (including heat, watchmen and maintenance), spoilage, pilferage and interest on investment, all of which increase with added exposure.

Manufacturers, wholesalers and retailers find that as the number of warehouses increases, the turnover in each decreases. Thus, for a constant sales level, average inventory levels increase with the number of warehouses, because:

1. As the number of customers served by each warehouses decreases, the beneficial "balancing" effect is reduced. To illustrate, a warehouse serving a single customer must be prepared to meet that customer's peak demands. However, if the warehouse serves two customers, it is unlikely that the peak demand of each, for the same product, would coincide. Hence, the warehouse need only be prepared for a peak demand somewhat lower than the sum of the peak demands of the customers.

2. The average warehouse inventory level for each stock-keeping unit can be reduced as the volume through a given warehouse decreases. However, a practical limit is reached when the order quantity is reduced to the minimum factory pack (or to a minimum economic order

quantity). Hence, for some stock-keeping units, subsequent reductions in volume will *not* be accompanied by reductions in inventory.

The retail chain operator also is concerned about the stock levels which must be maintained in his stores. As the number of warehouses increases, the transit time from warehouses to stores is reduced. This permits the stores to operate with lower stocks. This, in turn, produces significant benefits to be discussed later.

Chart 3 illustrates the cost of carrying inventory as a function of the number of warehouses. A critical point to note is the number of warehouses producing total minimum inventory carrying costs.

Marketing Considerations

Warehouse networks generally are expanded to achieve certain marketing values. An evaluation of these benefits normally can be made in these terms:

Service improvement can be equated to changes in time utility and place utility. In some lines, customers have come to expect a given time availability of merchandise. For example, delivery within two days after ordering. Failure to provide this expected level or service results in a competitive disadvantage.

Place utility involves having the goods available where the customer wants them. For instance, in some lines wholesalers know that their customers operate with little or no inventory of their own and consequently, customers must have access to a local wholesaler who stocks a full range of merchandise.

A change in distribution practices intended to improve service must be expressed quantitatively in terms of both added sales to be achieved and the profit engendered by those sales. Contrarily, any change intended to reduce cost must be equated to the possible curtailment of service and the concomitant effect on profits.

A sale may be lost each time an order is presented at a warehouse and is not filled because the requested item is out of stock. This is well recognized by the wholesaler or the manufacturer whose customer may have immediate need for the product and can easily obtain a substitute from a nearby competitor. The retail chain operator knows that when demand for a given item is heavy, he must be able to keep his stores supplied with that item or suffer a loss of sales opportunity.

The risk of lost sales can be reduced by maintaining a high inventory level; yet costs are decreased by keeping inventory levels low. To determine an optimum inventory level, one must assess the probability of a run-out and resultant effect on sales and profits, weighing decreased costs against higher sales.

Turnover is of particular importance to the retailer because of the well-known relationship to markdowns: Namely, as turnover increases, markdowns decrease. Changes in distribution can have a major influence on store turnover since, as noted previously, (1) mode of trans-portation effects replenishment time and (2) proximity of field warehouses can permit reduction of store inventories. Hence, a quantitative relationship is required between turnover and markdowns.

The same problem plagues the manufacturer. The longer merchandise is held in storage, the more susceptible it is to inventory obsolescence. The premium which can be paid to improve turnover should be measured against the possible savings attributable to reduced obsolescence losses.

Data Processing Considerations

The nature and degree of administrative controls frequently spells the difference between a mediocre distribution system and a highly efficient one. Therefore, a comprehensive distribution study should consider the following points related to data processing.

Many automated devices are available, and additional devices are in advanced stages of development for the efficient processing of quantities of orders. These devices may yield economies, not only in the receipt of orders, but also in the physical handling operations. Warehouses can be planned to segregate case lot picking from less-than-case lot picking and to accommodate grouping of items based on their activity, with specialized treatment accorded each group.

Devices also are available to permit manufacturers to offer various forms of automatic

Chart 3. Inventory carrying cost

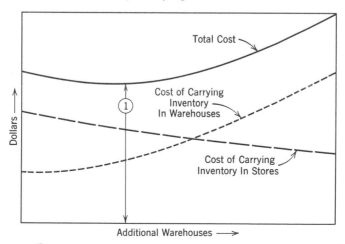

① = Number of warehouses producing total minimum inventory carrying cost

replenishment to their customers. A typical example is the punched card which some manufacturers attach to each unit of merchandise shipped to a customer's sales outlets. When a unit of merchandise is sold, a punched card is returned to the manufacturer. This represents an order to replace the particular item, enabling the sales outlet to maintain pre-established stocks.

The preparation of invoices, shipping documents and accounting inputs also lend themselves to efficient electronic data processing. The costs and benefits of these operations must be considered as an integral part of any distribution survey.

The maintenance of appropriate inventory levels is a major consideration in operating a multiwarehouse network. An approach should be developed to assure that the desired merchandise is available when and where required, while at the same time holding inventory investment to a minimum. Recent data processing system developments permit a degree of sophistication not heretofore obtainable.

Mathematical Considerations

Analysis of the elements comprising the *total cost* approach to distribution is a complex undertaking. It would include analysis of such variables as merchandise in transit from producing points, goods in warehouse stock, products in transit to customers, and store inventories. Until quite recently, required solutions for some distribution problems had not been developed. Currently, better answers are being obtained for these complex problems by using operations research techniques such as linear and non-linear programing and simulation. Some typical mathematical applications are listed below.

It is possible to construct a mathematical model which represents the proposed system. Through use of a high-speed computer, the inputs to the model can be manipulated to produce the equivalent of many years of actual experience with the proposed system. Other proposed systems can be tested in a similar manner to arrive at an optimum solution.

The model design technique can be used to solve complex problems of warehouse design such as determination of: the optimum number of truck spots, or the best width for picking aisles and the optimum material-handling system.

One must usually secure data from some detailed source such as customer orders, invoices, or bills of lading. A mathematically designed sample can reduce the data collection job substantially while maintaining a prescribed level of accuracy.

One frequently needs to determine to what extent changes in variable A and B can be used to predict changes in variable C. Multiple correlation techniques permit this determination. Further, one can determine what change in C is likely to take place for a given change in A or B.

This technique, for example, was used recently to determine the relationship between retail sales and inventory (hence, turnover) and retail markdowns. The result was an expression permitting estimation of changes in retail markdowns as a function of changes in store inventory levels.

Management Considerations

After all of the preceding questions have been answered, there still remain several additional determinations before management has adequate information upon which to make a proper decision.

A major change in a company's distribution system usually requires organizational realignment. If a new distribution network appears necessary, new responsibilities are created and old ones are altered. Management must assign responsibilities for transportation, warehousing and inventory control. These functions must be properly coordinated with manufacturing (or buying) and selling (or merchandising).

Additional warehouses may increase sales and profits for any or all of the following reasons:

1. Improved delivery may open a new market where the company now is not competitive.

2. Sales may be increased by reducing out-of-stock situations.

3. Increased inventory turnover may reduce obsolescence losses.

4. Reduced inventories in retail stores could release space which might be converted to productive selling space.

5. Reputation could be enhanced when customers recognize the consistent early availability of current products. This, in turn, could produce more sales.

These questions are frequently overlooked in the analyses of distribution systems. The reason

Chart 4.   *Effect of additional warehouses on total profit*

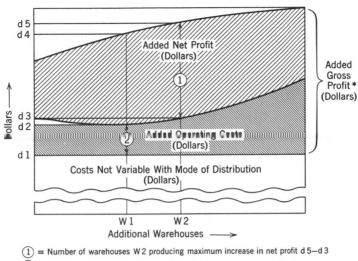

① = Number of warehouses W 2 producing maximum increase in net profit d 5–d 3
② = Number of warehouses W 1 producing minimum operating cost d 2–d 1
* Reflects an improved profit percentage on incremental sales

for this neglect is the difficulty of quantitative analysis. However, techniques now exist for the evaluation of these questions.

Chart 4 illustrates the typical effect of added warehouses on profits. As shown, gross profit increases. Usually, a higher than normal rate of profit can be attributed to incremental sales because of higher volume on the same overhead base. Gross profit will continue to increase with additional warehouses.

As warehouses are added, for example, total operating costs usually will decrease to a minimum and then proceed to rise and accelerate quite rapidly.

Chart 4 permits certain important observations: If the illustrated distribution study has been concerned only with operating costs, the solution would be to operate with w_1 warehouses, since, at this point, operating costs, numeral 2, are minimized.

However, a study of all factors reveals that the optimum number of warehouses is w_2. This results in higher operating costs (d_3-d_2), but also results in higher net profit, indicated by numeral 1.

Added net profit is maximized: (d_5-d_3) instead of (d_1-d_2).

Although gross profit would increase when operating with more than w_2 warehouses, operating costs would increase more rapidly than gross profit, resulting in a diminishing of net profits.

Another critical determination remains. Analyses of each of the preceding questions will have produced an expected economic benefit if the changes in the distribution system are consummated. Management needs next to determine the required investment in additional facilities as well as the one-time costs of implementing the changes. At this point the expected return on the required investment can be calculated and a decision reached on the desirability of pursuing the proposed course of action.

Summary

The cost of distributing merchandise continues to mount every year. As competitive pressures increase, companies will continue to feel the necessity of offering their customers additional services. Yet, in the years to come, the pressure of mounting costs and service demands will cause many companies to consider both modifications and restrictions of their distribution systems. As described herein, the questions arising in the conduct of a comprehensive distribution study are numerous and complex. However, to arrive at a correct conclusion, it is absolutely essential that all of the pertinent questions be answered. It is essential that the ultimate judgment be based upon an examination of the *total costs* involved and their interrelationships. Modern techniques of distribution analysis make this possible.

38. *Quantitative Analysis of Physical Distribution Systems**

JOHN F. MAGEE†

I wish to characterize a physical distribution system schematically. The flow of material and information is illustrated in simplified form by Figure 1. Figure 1 shows how a distribution system is made up of a series of inventory or stock points linked by operations. The stock points may in part be under the same roof—for example, inventories of material in varying stages of completion; the corresponding operations may be manufacturing operations—conversion of items withdrawn from one stock point into new items in another stock point.

The stock points may also be separated by considerable distances, for example, central plant and field warehouses stocking finished goods. Here transportation is the operation separating individual stock points. Transportation in a field distribution system is much like a manufacturing operation inside a plant. In either case, material is taken out of one stock location

* Reprinted by permission from the *Journal of Marketing,* National quarterly publication of the Marketing Association, 1961.

† John F. Magee, Vice President, Arthur D. Little, Inc.

and put into another in a different form. Transporting an item changes it, though perhaps not so strikingly as running it through a manufacturing process. After all, a radio tube in a Chicago warehouse is quite a different item in terms of its utility to customers than a tube of the same specifications in Dallas.

The physical product flow—operations transforming items in one stock location into those in another—is governed by a corresponding information flow, in the opposite direction. Customer or user orders place demands on the last stock-keeping stage. This stage, in turn, must follow some procedure to initiate the replenishment operation. This operation in turn draws on the preceding stock unit for the required material.

This highly simplified display of the interrelationship among stockkeeping units, operations and information processing for an individual item can, in one's imagination, be compounded to represent the highly complex patterns of physical distribution, of material and information flow, which exist in the world today. These complexities arise in part from needs imposed by complex product lines, in part from efforts to bal-

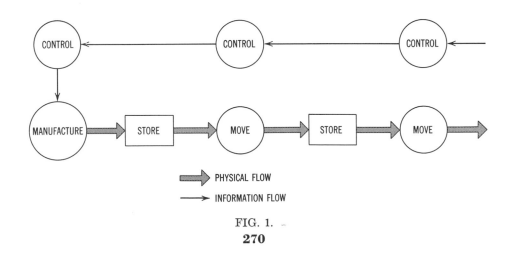

PHYSICAL FLOW
INFORMATION FLOW

FIG. 1.

ance production, transportation and marketing effectiveness, in part from regulation.

The Role of Quantitative Analysis

Quantitative analysis has a significant role to play in the design of physical distribution systems, first, because the proper choice of a physical distribution plan in the circumstances of any particular company depends not merely on theory or generalizations but on facts, significantly on quantitative facts: costs, times, characteristics of the market and customers, product line characteristics, statistics of demand.

In the second place, physical distribution decisions require a reconciliation or balancing of partly conflicting objectives of a business: low production cost, even flow of product, low transportation paperwork costs, prompt response to market needs:

> The production man would like to operate under a level work load with long product runs and minimum disruption. The salesman would like to take selling and promotional action with the comforting knowledge that any demand he might generate would be met, on the spot and without delay. The treasurer would like to keep to a minimum the use of funds to finance plant capacity, inventories, warehouses, and equipment. Etc.

This balancing act poses difficulties for businesses whose thinking and organization often emphasize traditional functions. For physical distribution is a process in which no function has a dominant interest. Quantitative analysis can help businesses work out the balance among objectives and interests in physical distribution.

I will illustrate that quantitative analysis in physical distribution implies observation and analysis of facts, not merely use of mathematical technique. Physical distribution systems are so complex that there is no single elegant technique for organizing all aspects of a physical distribution study. However, theoretical studies in the last decade have contributed greatly to conceptual understanding and technical apparatus available for studies.

Some Issues and Approaches

Here are some of the significant issues to which quantitative studies can make a contribution.

Inventory Investment

How much should be invested in inventory of a particular item at a given location? I do not propose to go into this question in detail, since it has been covered extensively elsewhere.[1] It is sufficient to note that one element of the inventory investment (cycle stock) depends on the size of replenishment shipment—a balance of order handling and shipping costs against the cost of holding stock, including the cost of capital. Another element of the inventory investment (safety stock) depends on policies with respect to capital investment and reliability of service, and on the variability of demand, the size of error characteristic of the inventory control forecasts.

The period over which the forecast error or demand variability must be measured is the response time or lead time of the replenishment system. Consider, for example, a field warehouse. Its lead time is the time needed for it to make a replenishment order, time to process the order, communications time to the source of supply, perhaps the factory, time for the supply source to make up and load the order, time in transit, plus the fixed time interval, if any, between replenishment orders. For example, if the warehouse is on a biweekly reporting or re-ordering cycle, the two weeks must be added to the time for paperwork, communications and transportation.

Quantitative analysis of inventory control systems has contributed substantially (1) in the identification of the system characteristics and costs that must be measured and the policies that must be made explicit, (2) in the use of inventory control theory to set up means for analyzing demand and making routine replenishment decisions automatically, consistent with policies.

There are clearly interactions between the two elements of inventory I have mentioned. For example we may lengthen the review period in a field warehouse to cut paperwork and increase the size of replenishment orders for transportation economy. This may, for example, permit shipment in carload lots and carload rates; lengthening the review cycle, however, lengthens the time period over which demand must be forecast, and characteristically increases the in-

[1] Magee, John F., "Guides to Inventory Policy," *Harvard Business Review,* Jan–Feb, Mar–Apr and May–June, 1956.

LEAD TIME ELEMENT

REORDER PERIOD...........MORE FREQUENT REORDER...........TRANSMITTAL OF DEMAND ORDER-BY-ORDER............

PROCESSING TIME.......EDP-BOOKKEEPING.......ROUTINE DECISION RULES, USING COMPUTERS.......REAL TIME PROCESSING.......

COMMUNICATIONS TIME...........TELETYPEWRITER...........HIGH CAPACITY DATA CHANNELS...........

MATERIAL HANDLING TIME...........UNITIZED HANDLING...........AUTOMATIC WAREHOUSING...........

TRANSPORTATION TIME...........DIRECT DOOR-DOOR HANDLING...........AIR SHIPMENT............

FIG. 2.   Lead time components and some reduction possibilities.

ventory investment needed to protect order service. However, this is not the time to go into such points in detail. I have introduced the inventory control problem to note that inventory control theory is fundamental to physical distribution studies and to point out the relationship between inventory investment and the response time or lead time and the time elements that make it up.

Changing the Lead Time

I have identified the principle elements of response or lead time as (Figure 2) reorder period, processing time, communications time, assembly and loading time, and transportation time. I have also indicated in Figure 2 some of the ways in which the various elements may be speeded up—usually at a cost. For example, we can reorder or report sales from a field warehouse more frequently, daily instead of biweekly; and in the extreme, by customer order. We can use mail, air mail, teletype, or a high-speed data channel like microwave or AT&T's TELPAK. Assembly and loading time may be cut by material handling aids, unitized handling, or possibly mechanized computer-controlled warehousing. You are familiar, I am sure, with

the alternatives in transportation and the time and cost characteristics of these. It is noteworthy how many new technical developments can be brought to bear on the physical distribution process, how each new possibility if treated in isolation will tend to increase the cost of the system, how important it is to analyze the characteristics of each new alternative in the light of the response system as a whole.

Analysis is necessary to measure the time characteristics and costs of the available alternatives, to determine what the relationship is, among well-balanced alternatives, between response time and system operating cost.

A significant advantage of response or lead time reduction is reduction in required inventory. I have already noted how inventory investment, at a given service level, depends on demand variability over the lead time. This variability depends, in turn, on the length of the lead time. For example, Figure 3 shows the observed relationship between lead time and relative size of demand variability for one particular product line. It conforms to the general form of relationship we have observed:

$$\sigma s,t = At\alpha \qquad (1)$$

where $\sigma s,t$ is the standard deviation of demand vs. forecast, observed over time t.

The data in Figure 3 yields a value for α of .62. In some theoretical work, a value of α is arbitrarily assumed, sometimes $\alpha = .5$, sometimes $\alpha = 1.0$. In any real investigation, analysis is necessary to estimate the functional dependence of demand variability on lead time, and if it corresponds to (1), to estimate the value of A and α.

Figure 4 illustrates the balance required between operating cost of the response system and inventory investment. As the lead time increases, operating cost may be reduced (Curve A) while the cost of supporting inventory investment increases (Curve B) leading to an operating point with minimum total cost (Curve C). Since the position of Curve B depends on

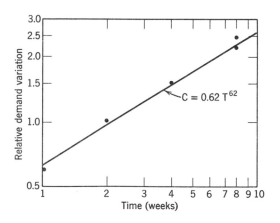

FIG. 3.   Demand variation vs. time.

the cost of capital assessed against inventories and on service policies, the minimum-cost operating method is clearly dependent on managerial policy. Quantitative analysis is necessary to measure and state this dependence and to indicate the consequences of policy change.

Both operating costs and investment affected by the replenishment time will depend on the number of points being replenished.

The Number of Field Warehouses

The minimum number of distribution points—plants, terminals and warehouses from which product is distributed to a customer—will depend on the geographical distribution of product, the acceptable time to deliver an order to a customer, the percentage of the market to be reached in a given time, and the speed of transportation from distribution point to a customer. For example, the following table shows the result of a study of the percentage of the U. S. consumer market that can now be reached by truck in a given time from receipt of order at the stated number of distribution points.

Share of Consumer Market Reached,
Compared with Time to Reach,
No. of Distribution Points

	Distribution Points			
	5	25	50	100
Time				
1 day	33%	90%	95%	99%
2 days	85	99	100	100

These figures have obviously been affected by improvements in transportation techniques and facilities. Many firms, however, are operating distribution systems designed 20–30 years ago, which do not take advantage of recent major advances in transportation, for example improvement of trucks and road systems.

The table of market service vs. time and number of distribution points must be worked out for the particular product line, taking into account its particular market structure. For example, in one case we have found demand roughly proportional to population concentration, with 18 states accounting for 70 per cent of demand. In another case, we found demand highly concentrated, on the West Coast and in a belt from the Great Lakes east, with 73 per

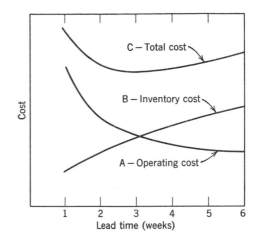

FIG. 4. Illustrative effect of lead time on total distribution system cost.

cent of demand concentrated in 10 states. Analysis of the pattern and anticipated pattern of demand is critical in distribution system design.

Subject to restrictions on service (and also, to test the price of changing these restrictions), analysis is needed to investigate the economic effects of varying the number of field distribution points. The principal cost elements of concern are:

1. *Facilities cost*: We generally find the operating cost of a warehouse including data processing and communication cost, as a function of its normal or design size, to be approximated by

$$C = a + bX$$

and thus, warehousing cost for the system,

$$C_w = aN + bS \tag{2}$$

where N is the number of warehouses and S is demand in total.

2. *Transportation cost*: Within a given mode of transport, transportation cost from plant to field distribution point may be affected only in a minor way by the the number of distribution points. Outbound transportation from distribution point to customer may follow the form

$$C_{TO} = kN^{-\beta} \tag{3}$$

where N is the number of warehouses and β depends on the uniformity of market density. (If the market were perfectly uniformly distributed, β would equal .5.)

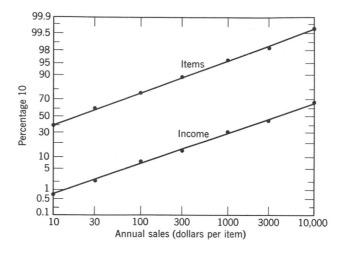

FIG. 5.

3. *Inventory cost*: When distribution point territories are combined, demand variability and thus inventory requirements combine in a complex way. The exact pattern is dependent on the cross-correlation of demand among areas. In practice we find that the variability of demand over a given time interval, as a function of "area" or average demand rate, can be represented as

$$\sigma_{s,d} = gD^\alpha \qquad (4)$$

where D is the total average demand and α may generally take on values between .6 and .9.

Clearly, the costs will depend on the modes of operation—for example, degree of warehouse mechanization, type of transportation used, type of communication and data processing system, etc. Thus, the cost balance and economy of operating more or fewer distribution points must be studied in relation to the replenishment system used.

Even at this level of complexity, in the physical distribution study, it is clear that we are dealing with a host of alternatives: in policies—for example, policies with respect to capital cost, service standards; in operating modes—for example, transportation medium, communication and data processing technique; and in extensiveness—for example, the number of distribution points. These alternatives interact; service standards affect relative economy of operating modes, the choice of operating mode influences the cost of expanding or contracting the number of distribution outlets. This condition cries for quantitative analysis to explore these alternatives, subject to the particular statistical characteristics of the market and cost characteristics of the business.

Impact of the Product Line

So far, we have considered physical distribution alternatives as if we are dealing with a single item while at the same time we are examining alternatives for distribution of the product line as a whole. In most businesses, however, we find a product line in which demand is highly concentrated in a few items while most items account for only a modest proportion of sales (Figure 5). The top curve in Figure 5 indicates the fraction of total items

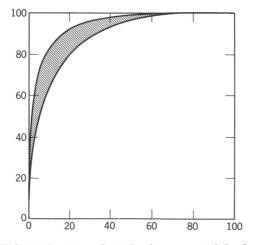

FIG. 6. Fraction of total sales accounted for by fraction of total items.

(vertical axis) with annual sales equal to or less than the amount shown on the horizontal scale. The lower curve indicates the fraction of total demand indicated by these items. We find this pattern, the lognormal distribution, to be characteristic of most product lines, though the slope (the standard ratio) may vary. This product demand distribution leads to the relationship shown in Figure 6, which illustrates the characteristically high degree of concentration of demand among a small per-cent of the items in the line.

Other significant characteristics of the prod-uct line will also show wide differences. For ex-ample, we usually find that inventory require-ments increase as the .7–.9 power of average demand. Thus the cost balance underlying the choice of system will depend on the level of demand of the item in question. Figure 7 illus-trates some of the alternatives available; we may use programming methods such as the transportation and transshipment models[2] to study alternate routings for items in the prod-uct line, and to define the breakpoints, or con-ditions which define the boundary between those items to be distributed one way, for ex-ample, direct plant-to-customer, and those to

[2] Hetrick, James C., "Mathematical Models In Capital Budgeting," *Harvard Business Review,* Jan.–Feb., 1961, Appendix, p. 58 ff.

be handled another, for example, stocked in regional warehouses.

Planning for the Future

So far I have discussed the problems of dis-tribution systems planning as if the planning were static, as if we could make our plans to meet a static (and presumably well-known) market requirement. In many cases, this is a reasonable assumption; the anticipated rate of change of the market is low enough and the ability to modify the distribution system great enough so that a static view is useful. In many other circumstances, however, we must take a dynamic view of the distribution system.

1. Because change in the system may be ex-pensive and laborious.
2. Because anticipated future needs may be inconsistent with present needs.
3. Because we may not be able to see the future too clearly.

Under these circumstances we may want to give up some immediate advantage in order to be in a better position either to have a sys-tem better suited to the future as we anticipate it, without expensive changes, or to be in a more flexible position to deal with the future as it unfolds.

In these problems quantitative analysis can

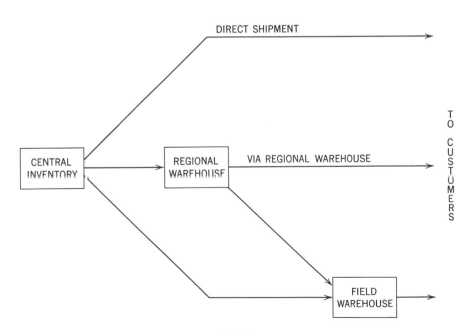

FIG. 7.

be of great value in working out the consequences of alternative systems under various possible market conditions, a series of static solutions under alternative conditions hypothesized for various future points in time. Our concepts and techniques are still weak, however, for evaluating the consequences of these alternatives with respect to immediate moves.

Let me try to use an illustration to make the problem more explicit. The illustration is taken from Hetrick[3] although the analysis is not identical. He states the problem as:

"A problem arose because of the existence of a manufacturing plant which, though physically adequate, was technologically obsolete and unable to supply the quality of products required in today's market. The plant in question was rather small compared to those then being built. Since it was argued that a plant of this size was at an inherent disadvantage for economic operation, there was considerable managerial contro-

[3] Hetrick, James C., *op. cit.*

versy over the proper course of action—whether to modernize the operation by construction of better facilities or to scrap the existing plant and supply the area involved from facilities elsewhere, e.g., plants in adjacent states."

Hetrick notes that when the problem was studied using the transportation model of linear programming, under conditions anticipated in the near future, and five and ten years hence, the following pattern of solutions arose (Figure 8).

The table shows, for example, that program "A" gives an optimum balance of operating cost and investment, under the conditions anticipated in the near future, while "C" is optimum under the conditions anticipated ten years hence. In theory there are 27 plans over time that might be considered, although in practice some are excluded. For example, it was concluded that if program "B" were adopted, it would be impractical to go to "A" or "C", reopening the plant in question.

There are 11 program sequences that are

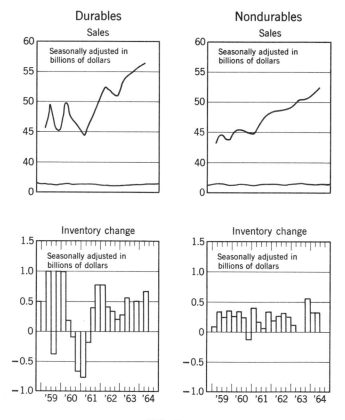

FIG. 8.

		Time		
		Near future	5 years hence	10 years hence
Program				
A	Modernize plant in question Expand elsewhere	"Optimum"		
B	Close plant in question Expand elsewhere		"Optimum"	
C	Modernize and expand the plant in question			"Optimum"

reasonable, each with its own pattern of investment and operating cost. (In addition there are conceivably other possibilities, represented by solutions intermediate to programs "A" and "C".) On the assumption that conditions in future years are well known, these patterns of investment and operating cost may be evaluated, perhaps by discounted cash flow or present value techniques, although these are not entirely satisfactory.

The situation becomes considerably more difficult, however, if we are seriously uncertain about the market or costs five to ten years hence. Then, though the number of alternative programs may not increase, the evaluation of these alternatives becomes difficult. This is not simply a matter of computational volume, but of conceptual fuzziness. The value of flexibility, the value of avoiding current commitments where there is a significant element of risk due to inflexibility, becomes high. While a number of interesting approaches are being taken to evaluation of risky investment programs, I believe we have a good way yet to go.

I do not mean to imply that the conceptual problems of dealing with uncertainty and risk make quantitative analysis valueless; quite the contrary. Analysis can help bare the consequences of alternative plans. I believe, however, that development of concepts for analyzing uncertain returns from investment programs is a most intriguing and challenging research field.

Conclusion

Interest in physical distribution systems is growing widely. I have suggested that quantitative studies can help clarify conflicts in policies and functional objectives, and have indicated some of the concepts I believe are fruitful in a systematic study of physical distribution. I have tried to show these concepts can be brought to bear on many issues in a distribution system, and to demonstrate that quantitative studies of physical distribution must rest on detailed observations of the particular system and market. Development of study concepts and techniques is a vital topic; though much progress has been made to develop methods having practical value now, we have opportunity for a good deal of work particularly in development of long-range programming techniques.

39. *The Logistics of Distribution**

JOHN F. MAGEE†

American business is awakening to a new, exciting opportunity to improve service and reduce costs—better management of the flow of goods from plant to user.

Capitalizing on this opportunity means:

Thinking of the physical distribution process as a system in which, just as in a good hi-fi system, all the components and functions must be properly balanced.

Taking a fresh look at the responsibilities, capabilities, and organizational positions of executives in traffic, warehouse management, inventory control and other functions which make up the overall system.

Re-examining the company's physical plant and distribution procedures in the light of technical advances in such areas as transportation, data processing, and materials handling.

In this article I shall first examine the pressing need for improved management of companies' distribution systems. Then I shall outline some of the most promising ways by which progress in "industrial logistics" can be achieved, with special attention to the implications of technological advances for policy, the problems of getting started with a new look at a company's system, and the steps that should be taken in making a good distribution study.

Stubborn Pressures

The need for progress in distribution is a product of not one but several trends—trends in costs, in product-line policy, and in the market place. More often than not, the challenge posed is to the system as a whole, not just to the particular part or function where trouble is most obvious.

* Reprinted by permission from *Harvard Business Review,* July/August 1960.

† Vice President, Arthur D. Little, Inc.

Rising Costs

For years, businessmen and economists have looked with mixed feelings on the increase in distribution costs in our economy. Over the past half century, tremendous strides have been made in reducing the costs of production, but these feats have not been duplicated in other areas. If the over-all efficiency of companies is to continue to improve, management must turn its attention increasingly to holding distribution costs in line. Physical distribution costs in particular, estimated by some to represent the third largest component in the total cost of business operation, are a logical center for management attention.

The problems of cutting these costs pose certain new and interesting questions for business. Whereas in many production operations it has been possible in the past to substitute a machine for human labor and to cut the cost of one operation without seriously disturbing the rest of the production system, this is hardly the case in efforts to cut physical distribution costs. Indiscriminate cost reduction in any one of the individual cost elements, such as inventory maintenance, warehousing, transportation, or clerical activities, can have a disastrous effect on the efficiency of the system as a whole. To illustrate this point:

Suppose we cut inventories. Certainly a reduction in inventories will save capital investment and the costs of supplying capital, and it may save some expenses in storage, taxes, and insurance. On the other hand, an indiscriminate reduction in inventory levels may seriously impair the reliability of delivery service to customers and the availability of products in the field. An inventory reduction which saves money but destroys competitive position is hardly a contribution to a more effective distribution system.

We can cut transportation costs, perhaps, by changing to methods showing lower cost per ton-mile, or by shipping in larger quantities and taking advantage of volume carload or truck-load rates. But if lower transportation costs are achieved at the expense of slower or less frequent movement of goods, we face the risk of: (a) cutting the flexibility and responsiveness of the distribution system to changes in customer requirements; (b) requiring greater field inventories to maintain service; (c) creating greater investment requirements and obsolescence risks.

Similarly, blanket refusal to allow cost increases in any one part can wipe out opportunities to make the system as a whole more efficient. For instance:

New methods of high-speed data communications and processing may in fact increase the clerical costs of operating the distribution system. On the other hand, they may cut down delays in feeding information back to govern production operations and to control lags in getting material moving into the distribution system in response to customer demand. Thus, they may actually cut *total* distribution system costs because of their impact on improved production and inventory control.

It takes a careful analysis of the total physical distribution system to know whether net costs will be increased or decreased by efforts to cut the cost of any one component.

Proliferating Product Lines

Physical distribution systems in recent years have been put under tremendous pressure induced by changes in product-line characteristics. Until recently, for example, products like typewriters, light bulbs, appliances, and plumbing fixtures were largely utilitarian, with differences in product characteristics rather closely related to function. A typewriter manufacturer did not have to worry about matching typewriter color to office decor or type style to company "image." Light bulbs used to be white and sometimes clear, and they varied by wattage. Now, however, typewriters come in pastels and two-tones. Light bulbs are sold not only to provide light but atmosphere, with a corresponding increase in the number of products that have to be shipped, stocked, and controlled.

Appliances and plumbing fixtures are available to customers not only in the classical antiseptic white, but in a wide range of color and style combinations. In short, style and individuality have become strong competitive weapons.

In an almost unending list of products in the consumer field, variations in color, packaging, and other features have imposed heavy burdens on the distribution system. In the marketing of industrial goods, variations in grade, color, and size have had a similar impact. In paper manufacture, for example, the wide variety of package sizes required for consumer products has led carton manufacturers to demand correspondingly wide ranges of kraft board roll widths from paper manufacturers, and these demands have created difficult problems of scheduling, inventory control, and distribution.

The growth and change in product-line characteristics in both consumer and industrial products have meant that manufacturing plants have had more items to make, and the distribution system has had more items to handle and stock. More items mean lower volume per item and correspondingly higher unit handling inventory and storage costs. Take, for example, just the impact on inventory requirements of substituting three items for one:

Suppose we have substituted items B, C, and D for an old item A. If sales among these items are broken down 60% to B, 30% to C, and 10% to D, with no over-all increase in sales compared to the volume on the old item A, then Exhibit 1 shows what is likely to happen to field inventory requirements—an increase of more than 60%. This figure is based on characteristic relationships between inventory and sales in companies with which I am familiar. In general, the larger the sales, the lower inventory can be relative to sales. Thus, product D with 10% of sales needs a much higher proportion of inventory than product B, with 60% of the sales.

At a carrying cost of 20% a year, this increase represents a handsome expense for maintaining competitive position.

Let us be optimistic, however, and assume that items B, C, and D do more than yield the same total volume; let us assume that total volume increases by 50%. Even so, the inventory requirements would double, and inventory cost per unit sold would increase over 30%—a substantial source of pressure on the distribution system.

Exhibit 1. What happens to inventories when the product line is broadened?

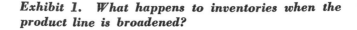

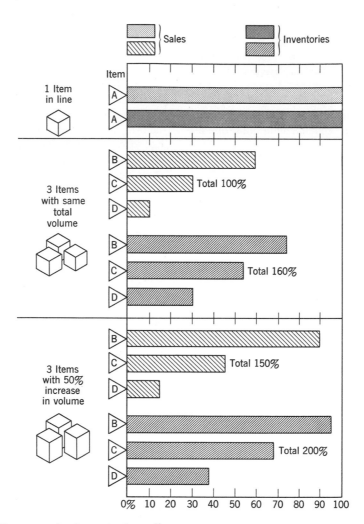

These figures illustrate the impact of small-volume items on the cost of operating the distribution system. Yet diversity of product sales is characteristic in American businesses, whether selling in consumer or industrial markets. Exhibit 2 shows the typical relationship between the number of items sold and the proportion of sales they account for. The figures are based on the records of a large number of firms in the consumer and industrial products field. The exhibit reveals that while 10%–20% of total items sold characteristically yield 80% of the sales, half of the items in the line account for less than 4% of the sales. It is the bottom half of the product line that imposes a great deal of the difficulty, expense, and investment on the distribution system.

Alternative Courses

Increased cost, selling, and product-line pressures suggest that management should take a hard look at alternative distribution patterns, as a means of cutting logistics costs without a major sacrifice in service. Here are a few of the possibilities:

The company can carry central stocks of low-selling items only. To get the right balance of transportation costs, handling costs, and service, it may be necessary to stock these items at one central point and ship them against individual customer orders as the latter arise, perhaps by expedited service or air freight.

For many items in the line, a good compromise may be to carry some low- or middle-volume items in only a few large regional warehouses, as a compromise between the excessive storage costs incurred from broad-scale stocking and the transportation and service penalties incurred by attempting to meet demand from manufacturing points alone.

Warehouse points can be consolidated. With improvements in transportation and in mechanical material- and data-handling methods, large opportunities exist in many businesses for cutting down on the number of field warehouse points. With increased volume through the individual warehouses, carrying a broader product line at the local points begins to make greater economic sense.

Sales-Generating Capacity

The first and most basic job of the distribution system is to get customers, to turn interest and orders into sales. As business has grown more competitive and the public has become harder to please, management has focused increasing attention on the *quality* of its logistical operations. What can be done to make products more readily available for purchase in local markets? What improvements can be made in backing up product merchandising and advertising programs with adequate deliveries and services? Obviously, questions like these are affected by cost considerations, but as marketing objectives they deserve individual attention.

In analyzing the capacity of a distribution system to produce sales, executives will do well to examine three key characteristics:

1. *Location.* It has been estimated, for example, that from 5 distribution points a company can reach 33% of the U.S. consumer market within a day; while from 25 warehouse locations, 80% can be reached in one day.

2. *Inventories.* Judging from my own and associates' experience, approximately 80% more inventory is needed in a typical business to fill 95% of the customers' orders out of stock than to fill only 80%.

3. *Responsiveness.* The ability of a system to transmit needs back to the supplying plant and get material needed into the field determines how quickly the business can shift with changes in customer preferences to meet demands with minimum investment and cost.

Revolution in Technology

The pressures on distribution methods have led to exciting new technological advances for getting goods to the user at lower cost to the company—with less labor and materials expended and less capital tied up in inventories and facilities. When these advances are introduced in proper balance, the distribution process can better meet the needs of the consumer. Major technological changes are now taking place in transportation, information handling, and material handling. Let us examine each of them in turn.

Costs vs. Transport Time

Transportation thinking has been dominated too long by preoccupation with the direct traffic bill. Too much attention has been paid to transport cost per ton-mile and not enough to the contribution transportation makes to the effectiveness of the distribution system as a whole.

Railroad rate structures are to an outsider an eye-opening illustration of what can happen when a transportation system is put under the cost-per-ton-mile pressure for too long. Rail rate structures, despite frequent attempts to introduce some rationale, have degenerated into an unbelievable hodge-podge of unrealistic and uneconomic rate compromises as the roads have

Exhibit 2. What fraction of the total sales is accounted for by what fraction of total items in the product line?

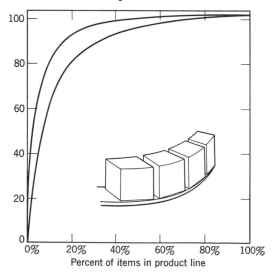

Percent of items in product line

succumbed to the pressure of giving each shipper the lowest cost per ton-mile, often at the
expense of service. While improvements in
equipment, such as the introduction of the
diesel locomotive, have led to greater efficiency
on the track, in some cases at least the longer
trains and increased classification problems that
have resulted have meant little or no net increase in over-all distribution efficiency. The gap
between traffic and marketing thinking is painfully evident in many companies' distribution
methods; little has been done to relate transportation methods and service to the objectives
of the distribution system in support of marketing efforts.

Transportation costs are important indeed,
but they are only part of the story. For example, think of the value of materials in transit:

Data collected on sample shipments in various parts of the country indicate that material
may spend one to two weeks in transit and that
the capital value of assets tied up in the transportation system may, depending on the pressure for capital, add as much as 1% to the
economic cost of the goods.

Service, or reliability of the transport system,
is also important. Goods must get to the user
promptly and reliably, to permit him to operate systematically with low inventories.

The direct and indirect costs of damage in
transport are another large item in the traffic
bill that at times gets overlooked in the pressure for low cost per ton-mile.

Clearly, transport time is one of the key
determinants of the efficiency of the distribution
system. Its impact is not vivid or dramatic, and
executives do not always appreciate what a difference it makes, but in a great many companies it is a significant factor in financing. To
take a simple illustration:

Suppose that in a company doing an annual
business of $100 million, time in transit is re-
duced from 14 days to 2. Time between reorders
is 14 days, communication and processing time
is 4 days, and field stocks average $12.5 million.
In such a situation the reduction in transit time
might well lead to a reduction in distribution
inventory investment of $6 million, made up of:
(1) a reduction of $3.3 million in transit, i.e.,
12 days' sales; (2) a reduction of $2.7 million in
inventories required to protect customer service
resulting from a faster, more flexible distribution
system response.

Speeding up Service

Changes in transportation leading to improved
opportunities in distribution have been truly
revolutionary since World War II. Major super-
highway systems have been built, truck speeds
have increased substantially and so have trailer
capacities. The growth in the use of trucking for
industrial distribution is now well known. The
stimulus from subsidies is only part of the
story; trucks have been able to compete at
characteristically higher ton-mile costs because
they have offered speed, reliability, and flexibility to shippers.

Without doubt, railroads are responding to
this challenge. A recent survey showed that almost all Class I railroads are offering some form
of piggyback or expedited motor-carrier service.
At least some railroads are showing new merchandising awareness in concentrating on customer service. Whether the industry will be able,
in the face of inherent limitations, to reverse the
decline in its share of manufacturers' freight
business is still an open question.

Air freight represents a challenge to both rail
and over-the-road haulers. Today most industry
executives still tend to view air freight as a
luxury, as a service available for "orchids and
emergencies." However, the trend in air freight
rates has been sharply downward in recent
years. With new planes coming into service,
even further reductions can be projected—down
to 8 cents to 12 cents a ton-mile from present-
day rates of approximately 22 cents. Much depends on the success of efforts to develop aircraft equipped for freight handling and for
flexible operation under a wide range of conditions (for example, modest runway lengths),
and to build up the ground service needed to
match air-handling speeds so as to avoid the
danger faced by the railroads—the collapse of
service as a result of concentration on mass, low-
cost, terminal-to-terminal movement.

Impact of New Methods

What is the significance of the ferment in
transportation methods? For one thing, improvement in local truck service opens up opportunities to serve wide-flung markets through
fewer and larger distribution points. With larger
distribution centers, the chance that mechanized
material handling and storage systems will pay
off is enhanced, and inventory requirements are
reduced through consolidation.

To suggest the size of the opportunity, one analysis with which I am familiar showed that cutting the number of field distribution points for a national product line from 50 to 25 would increase total transport costs 7% but cut inventories 20% and cut *total* physical distribution costs 8% (the latter representing roughly a 1% cut in the total cost of delivered product). This was accomplished at the cost of serving a few small markets—about 5% of the total—with second-day instead of first-day delivery.

Rapid truck or air service increases the feasibility of relying on shipments from a few central points to back up service. Here are two ways in which this can be employed:

1. The many low-volume items in the typical product line, the items on which local storage and handling costs outweigh the penalty costs of expedited shipment, can be held centrally and moved to the market where they are needed, as needed. For example, the bottom 50% of the product line, which as Exhibit 2 shows often accounts for only 4% of sales, may require 25% or more of the warehousing costs and inventory capital charges. Turnover of the stocks of these items is often only one eighth that of the high-volume half of the line. In a *relatively* high number of cases, special shipments could be made at a cost well below that of storing the items at local distribution centers.

2. If there are substantial reserve stocks designed to protect customer service located in the field, it is possible to pare them down in the knowledge that additional supplies can be moved in promptly to meet sudden customer demands.

In a typical distribution system a large share of the inventory—as much as 90%—is carried to protect delivery service to customers in the face of fluctuating demand and system delays. This safety stock is most likely to be used at the end of the reorder cycle, when stocks hit their low point before new receipts.

How much of safety stocks is actually used depends on the reorder system and level of service maintained. Typically, the last 10% may be needed only once or twice a year—a turnover rate roughly one sixth the average; and the last 30% may be needed only two to four times a year. Warehouses and inventory carrying charges on this portion of inventory, then, may easily run to 10%–20% of the sales they make possible.

There is an opportunity in many companies for management to cut material held in the field and back up customer service through regularized high-speed delivery service. This possibility will deserve increasing attention from management as the costs of high-speed transport, communication, and data processing drop.

Information Processing

Revolutionary data-processing methods were noisily battering at established business methods some six or seven years ago, but the impact was more in noise generated than in accomplishment. Now that a lot of the superficial excitement has died away, however, a broad and solid structure of accomplishment in modern data-processing techniques is quietly being built.

For one thing, computers seem to have become much more broadly accepted than anticipated. When the earliest internally programed machines were announced, computer manufacturers' optimistic estimates were in the dozens. Today the number of machines installed or in the process of installation is in the thousands. In support of computing or processing facilities, great improvements are taking place in communications systems, especially systems designed to feed into or out of computers. In distribution management, fast, reliable communication is equally important as fast, reliable processing.

The *use* being made of modern information-processing equipment in distribution is just as significant as its broad market acceptance. For instance, machines are being used to maintain local inventory balances, forecast near-term demand, employ forecasts and inventory balances as inputs in calculating item orders, prepare tentative purchase orders, allocate item balances among stock points, and draw up production schedules and work force requirements. These are not mere compiling and accounting functions, nor is it fair to call them "decision making." In these functions, the machine systems are interpreting rules or procedures to work out the decisions implicit in them in light of the facts of the situation. In other words, the equipment is doing what we would like intelligent clerks to do: diligently following policy and weighing costs to arrive at day-to-day actions.

The forecasting function in particular deserves special attention. I refer not to the longer term economic forecasts, annual business forecasts, or even short term (e.g., quarterly) business predictions, but to short-term forecasts of sales, item by item, over the replenishment lead time. These forecasts are made implicitly or explicitly in every inventory control system. In most companies they are left up to the individual stock clerk or inventory controller to make as best he can, usually with little or no training or guides. Management will spend hundreds of hours of industrial engineering time simplifying or improving a job method here and there to take a few pennies out of labor cost. Yet the stock clerk making inventory control forecasts may, through his control over product distribution and assets tied up in inventories, be costing his company many pennies indeed.

Many people still argue that one cannot forecast routinely because intuition and background knowledge count too heavily. They fail to recognize that objective procedures for short-term prediction of item sales have the same merits as, say, routing and tooling lists in a shop. Experience leaves little doubt that great gains can be made by substituting powerful systematic methods for casual or unrecognized ones.[1]

Changes in Material Handling

Mechanization is slowly spreading from the making of things to their handling in distribution. For instance:

One company in the clothing industry has installed a new data-processing system first to handle sales orders and then inventory control and production scheduling systems. At the same time, it has been developing a bin-and-conveyor system which will permit economical mechanization of order-filling activities. The goal toward which both of these efforts are directed is a unified system in which the customer order not only serves as an input in automatic order handling but will also, after suitable internal mechanical processing, activate the warehouse system to select and consolidate the customer's order. This customer order data will also be processed internally for inventory management and production planning purposes.

How will such changes in warehousing and materials handling influence the planning of distribution systems? The effects will take at least three forms:

1. *Integration of systems for* (a) *material storage and transport and* (b) *information handling.* This development should create opportunities for significant "automation" of the distribution function and for reduction of manual drudgery. Ultimate full-scale mechanization of materials handling will not only require redesign of warehouse and transport facilities, but will have an impact on design of products and packages as well.

2. *Pressure to reduce the number of distribution points or warehouses.* Mechanized warehouses cost money. One way to improve the efficiency of capital utilization is of course to increase throughout.

3. *Pressure to concentrate ownership of warehousing facilities.* Mechanization takes capital. This factor will be another force behind the tendency for manufacture, distribution, and maintenance service to become integrated under one ownership roof.

Getting Started

Some managers view the opportunities presented by changes in distribution technology with about the same air with which a bear views a porcupine: the possibilities look interesting, but where can you start to get your teeth in?

Improvements in distribution efficiency cost money. Higher speed, more flexible transport generally costs more per ton-mile. Mechanized warehousing systems or material-handling systems are not cheap. The cost of working out, installing, and testing new information-processing systems may make direct clerical cost savings look like a rather thin return on investment. In fact, direct payoffs from distribution changes (e.g., modified transport methods leading to a direct cut in transport costs) may often be small or nonexistent. The payoffs, often handsome ones, are likely to be indirect, coming about from "tradeoffs" such as paying a higher transport bill to save material investment, putting in warehouse investment to cut over-all shipping costs, and so on.

Because tradeoffs so often are involved, it is not always easy for management to get an aggressive, functionally operated group of people to think *through* the problems. It is not easy for men in production, sales, warehousing, traffic, merchandising, and accounting to grasp other functions' needs or express their own needs in terms which make the advantages of tradeoff and balance clear. Many times the distribution *system* has been run too long as a collection of more of less independent *functions.* Any changes, any tradeoffs to get the system

[1] See Robert G. Brown, "Less Risk in Inventory Estimates," *Harvard Business Review*, July-August, 1959, p. 104.

into better, more economical balance, any modifications to take advantage in the whole system of new technical developments—these are bound to be disruptive and to some extent resisted.

The difficulties in facing up to a searching look at the distribution system are not confined to the individual functions concerned. Some of the toughest questions arise at the general management level. For example:

What degree of sales service is the system to provide? How far will the firm go to meet customers' service desires?

What standards are to be used to judge investment in facilities and inventory so that it can be weighed against any cost savings that are made possible?

What policy will the company take toward ownership and operation of the distribution, transport, warehousing, and information-processing facilities? Will the company operate its own facilities, lease them, contract for services, or rely on independent businesses to perform some or all of the necessary distribution system functions?

What is the company's policy toward employment stabilization? To what extent is the company prepared to pay higher distribution costs to absorb demand variations and to level employment?

Approach to the Issues

Grappling with all of these problems is like untangling a tangled skein of yarn. Each decision has an impact on other choices and for this reason is hard to pin down. The distribution problem is a system problem, and it must be looked at as such. If it is examined in total and if the experience and methods available for studying it are used, the issues just mentioned can be resolved in an orderly, mutually compatible way.

In my experience, three key conditions have, when present, made for a sound distribution system study and an effective implementation program:

1. Recognition by company management that improving distribution means examining the full physical distribution system.

2. Use of quantitative systems analysis or operations research methods to show clearly the nature of tradeoffs and the relation between system operation and company policies.

3. Cooperative work by men knowledgeable in sales and marketing, transportation, materials

handling, materials control, and information handling.

In the following sections we shall see the need for these conditions asserting itself again and again as we go through the steps of making a good distribution study.

Making the Study

How should a distribution system study be made? What principal steps should be taken? As far as I know, there is no formula for the approach. The relative emphasis put on different phases of the study can vary, as can also the degree of detail; the order of analysis can be changed; and so on. But there are important steps to take at some point in any study, and I shall discuss them in logical order.

1. *Data on the company's markets should be organized in a helpful way.*

The distribution system study starts with a study of customers. This does not need to be a field interview program; to a large extent what is required is the organization of market facts which are available. Occasionally, a moderate amount of skilled field interview work may be desirable to obtain customers' estimates of service requirements and their comparision of the company with its competition.

A great deal of useful information can be obtained by analysis of sales data. Here are some of the key questions of interest:

Are we servicing several fundamentally different markets through different distribution channels? Are these markets located differently? Do they buy in different patterns, in different quantities, and with different service and stock availability requirements?

How are our sales distributed among customers? We have found that the top 10% of a company's customers characteristically account for from 60% to 80% or even more of its business.

Do the same customers tend to buy our high-volume items as well as slow-moving items? The answer to this question has an important bearing on how the slow-moving items, for which distribution and sales service costs are often relatively high, should be handled. Few companies seem to have really examined this problem, though strong opinions on it exist in most.

2. *Statistical analyses of product characteristics should be made, with special attention to the nature of sales fluctuations.*

Sometimes the facts about products can be established fairly readily. An example is the susceptibility of items in the line to spoilage or damage. The degree to which sales volume is concentrated among a few fast-moving items (as illustrated in Exhibit 2) can often be ascertained rather quickly, too. But data of this kind do not tell us nearly enough.

Statistical analysis is needed to establish certain key sales characteristics of the product line, all related to the *variability* of item sales. The significance of variability must be emphasized. Business managers are used to thinking in terms of averages or average rates, but the answers to many important questions affecting distribution system design depend on the characteristics of short-term sales variation about the average.

Most items exhibit unexpected day-to-day variations in sales about the average or expected level. In some cases the fluctuations are extremely wide and short-term in character; in other cases they are quite steady and predictable. The statistical characteristics of these variations determine in a very significant way how a distribution system will work and how it should be designed to operate economically.

3. *In analyzing sales variations, special attention should be paid to size, time, area, and volatility.*

Executives interested in the practical implications of short-term sales variations might focus on the following questions:

How big are the ups and downs? The magnitude of sales variations *over the replenishment lead time* will determine how large the inventory of an item must be to maintain a desired level of delivery service. The amount of an item on hand at a field point or on order must always equal the maximum reasonable demand over the lead time. Thus, the bigger the sales fluctuations, the more inventory of an item must be carried in the distribution system—at local warehouses, at the factory—to provide a given level of delivery service.

Are the variations correlated from one time period to the next? If one day's sales are above or below average, are the chances considerably better than 50–50 that the next day's sales will be above or below average, too? If sales are highly correlated from one week to the next, or from one month to the next, this means that the range of accumulated variation over the replenishment lead time increases nearly in proportion to the lead time itself. Doubling the

warehouse lead time would nearly double the range of sales variations and the inventory requirements, while cutting the lead time in half would cut inventory requirements nearly in proportion. If sales are *not* correlated from one period to the next, chance variations tend to offset to some degree; doubling the lead time would increase inventory requirements only 40%–50%; while cutting it in half would cut inventories 30% or so.

High correlation in sales puts a premium on cutting lead times to make the distribution system react faster, perhaps through more expensive but higher speed transport, communications, and sales-information processing. By contrast, lower correlation means it may be more economical to let lead times lengthen and save expense in information handling and transport at the cost of somewhat higher inventories.

Are sales variations correlated between areas or markets? Is an unexpected increase in an item's sales, in, say, the Pittsburgh area likely to coincide with an increase in Cleveland, or are variations unrelated from one market to another? Some causes of expected sales variations may affect a wide geographic region (e.g., weather, rumors); others may be related entirely to local conditions (e.g., individual customers' plans).

The degree of cross-relation in chance sales variations occurring in different markets has a significant influence on warehouse location decisions. For example, if the cross-correlation is low, so that chance variations in sales in one market tend to offset those in another, there is a potentially substantial economy in consolidating warehouses, in having fewer distribution points to serve the same total market. But if the cross-correlation is high, little would be saved to offset possibly greater transportation costs.

How do sales variations compare among items? Are sales of high-volume items relatively more stable than sales of low-volume items? Generally (but not always), one finds evidence that the higher the sales volume of an item, the more stable will be sales, relatively speaking. Differences in the sales volatility of products influence distribution system choices. The more changeable the sales of an item, other things being equal, the better the chances that centralized stocking in regional distribution centers or plants will be advantageous.

4. *Inventory functions should be examined and related to other company needs.*

Characteristically inventories are made up of: (a) stock in transit; (b) supplies arising from periodic shipments; (c) reserves carried to protect service on the face of unusual demand (safety stock). In some businesses, inventories are also carried to accommodate seasonal sales patterns and to permit a smoothed load to be put on manufacturing. These inventory functions and methods for analyzing have already been discussed in HBR[2] and there is no need to outline them again here. Suffice it to say that one important job in a distribution study is to identify the functions actually served by inventories and to characterize the factors—e.g., transport times, reordering principles used, and service requirements—that are responsible for existing inventory levels and costs.

5. *The costs of warehouse storage and handling, traffic or freight, and clerical procedures should be determined.*

Many of these costs are difficult to obtain from normal company accounting records or engineering studies; direct unit costs often just are not maintained in these records. However, statistical analyses of operating cost records can often serve quite adequately.

Warehouse costs are as good an illustration as any of the approach I have in mind. Included here are:

a. *The costs of holding inventory*—These are generally related to the average or maximum inventory level in a distribution center and include space rent (including maintenance and janitor services, heat, and so on) and inventory costs (taxes, obsolescence and spoilage, and especially the cost of capital tied up in inventory). In our experience, careful study of the storage bill typically yields costs of 20%–35% per year on the capital value of the inventory, depending on the financial resources and policies of the company.

b. *The costs of handling*—These include the costs of physically moving material into and

[2] See John F. Magee, "Guides to Inventory Policy: Part I. Functions and Lot Size," January–February, 1956, p. 49; "Part II. Problems of Uncertainty," March–April, 1956, p. 103; "Part III. Anticipating Future Needs," May–June, 1956, p. 57; and Robert G. Brown, *op. cit.* See also John F. Magee, *Production Planning and Inventory* (New York, McGraw-Hill Book Company, Inc., 1958) and Robert G. Brown, *Statistical Forecasting for Inventory Control* (New York, McGraw-Hill Book Company, Inc., 1959).

out of storage or through terminal marshaling areas.

What is wanted here are cost factors which can be used to calculate the warehousing and handling costs under different system plans. These factors usually take the form of:

A fixed charge per warehouse per year × number of warehouses (the fixed charge is generally $5,000–$10,000 per warehouse per year, depending on the character of the space).

Warehousing cost per year per unit in inventory × average inventory in the system.

Handling cost per year per unit through the warehouse.

These cost factors can be built up from an engineering study or derived from statistical analysis of existing cost data. They will, of course, differ for different types of facilities and operating methods. For example, a mechanized warehouse operation will of course have a quite different order of costs from a nonmechanized operation.

Clerical cost factors for alternate operating systems can be derived in similar fashion. Transport costs must also be collected, usually in the form of specimen rates collated with shipment volumes for alternate transport methods. Such possibilities as in-transit privileges, "marriage" of shipments, and forwarding schemes should be reviewed.

6. *Management should analyze distribution plans on paper.*

The effect of alternative numbers of warehouses, changed locations, different transport methods, and different response times should be tested, using the methods of inventory analysis and programing techniques. Existing manufacturing capacities and locations may be used as a starting point. Alternatively—or as a second step in the analysis—the effect of changes in manufacturing facilities, in capacities, or in the product assigned to individual plants can be tested.

The first broad system studies are used to see where the biggest payoffs or traps may be. On paper, it is possible to make some arbitrary changes in lead times, warehouse locations, plant capacities, flexibility, and so on to see what the gross impact on distribution costs will be and thus whether detailed implementation studies are justified. It is important that the system study be based on current demand conditions, such as gross volume, product mix, and regional balance, as well as demand conditions projected roughly five to ten years ahead.

The facilities analysis is a step-by-step process. As the studies proceed, they will indicate potentially useful modifications in the distribution system. For example, a high concentration of sales among a few customers may indicate the need for special distribution plans, or the degree of concentration among products and the statistical characteristics of demand will suggest the need for regional stocking, changed warehouse numbers or locations, or similar alternatives. Again, an inventory study may indicate payoff possibilities in reducing lead times, in modifying service standards, or in introducing new, more flexible transport and handling methods.

Generally, as a result of broad analyses of facilities and operations, special studies will be indicated. Such studies as these may be in order:

Detailed analysis of the information-processing methods and costs to (a) take advantage of advancing technology to improve forecasting and control and (b) cut replenishment lead times.

Investigation of the costs of employment variations and manufacturing changes. Additional inventory—or changes in production technology—may be justified to minimize these costs. If so, however, the additions or changes should be clearly recognized; "manufacturing cost" is too often a lame excuse for careless, inefficient management of materials in distribution.

Study of product redesign or regrouping, especially where the product line may have evolved without much thought having been given to logistics concepts.

Analysis of special ordering procedures, stock locations, and transport methods for handling low-volume items.

Organization Plans

Distribution system management poses some puzzling organization problems to the typical, functionally organized firm. Distribution is not a sales function; it is not traffic management; it is not a manufacturing responsibility. It is an aspect of *all* of these functions. At the same time, the effectiveness of its managers will determine the conditions under which men in the individual functions must work.

Most companies prefer not to put all aspects of distribution management—sales order processing and analysis, field stock control, warehouses, traffic, production control—under one organizational unit, but to divide responsibility among several interested units. Such a division leads, however, to difficulty principally because of failure to (a) recognize the need for specific coordinated distribution systems planning, (b) specify planning and control responsibilities, and (c) set up performance measures consistent with over-all system efficiency and with assigned responsibilities.

In revising an organization to meet current needs and in keeping it up to date, executives should try to have five questions uppermost in their minds:

1. What are the necessary planning steps, policy decisions, and operating decisions to be made?

2. Who is the right person to make each of the decisions?

3. What information does he need, and how can he get it most expeditiously?

4. Does each person know how to recognize an emergency calling for nonroutine action? Does he know how to resolve it?

5. What performance measures reflect what is expected of each person in terms of the operation of the whole system?

Conclusion

To sum up, a number of pressures have piled up on today's distribution systems. As manufacturing efficiency has increased and product cost has come down, costs have grown. Physical distribution costs are a significant share of these.

Business in many fields is becoming increasingly competitive, with competition taking new forms, including availability of goods and reliability of delivery. Product changes are forcing new pressures on the distribution system—more items to carry, faster obsolescence, lower unit sales and inventory turnover. In particular, changes in merchandising practices, such as the introduction of style as a merchandising weapon, have significantly complicated the distribution problem. Pressures for improvement in logistics also include internal forces—for example, the need to stabilize production and insulate production levels from short-term fluctuations in sales.

In the face of these trends, a number of revolutionary changes have taken place. Substantial improvements have come about in essentially all forms of transportation methods. Tremendous strides forward have been made in information-handling methods, including schemes for assimilating and processing data dealing with product demand and with the need for replenishment. Materials-handling methods, ranging from mechanized stock keeping to extensions of the pallet concept to eliminate item-by-item handling, have been gaining acceptance. Finally, and perhaps as important as improvement in physical facilities and concepts, there has been progress in ways of looking at the logistics problem and at methods for analyzing distribution systems.

Long-Run Implications

So far, we have seen farsighted companies taking advantage of the changes I have described by redesigning their distribution systems to cut costs and increase the support given to sales programs. The next step is now beginning to be felt—the insinuation of distribution concepts into certain aspects of long-term planning and capital budgeting, especially the analysis of facility requirements, the location of distribution points, and the determination of financial requirements to support distribution.

Of course, we must avoid the trap of thinking that all management problems will be resolved in terms of efficient distribution. Nevertheless, the long-range impact of distribution-system thinking on production, on product design, and on manufacturing location may be substantial. Perhaps one of the most significant changes will be in concepts of organization, in the assignment of functions and responsibilities. Efficient physical distribution poses a challenge to business in integrating what is essentially a system approach with the functional approaches that hitherto have tended to govern business organization planning.

In the long run, at least two possible directions are open for making a wide variety of products available in local markets. On the one hand, manufacturers can move toward centralized manufacture, with the specialty or small-volume items being made in enough volume to permit reasonable manufacturing economy and then being moved rapidly, perhaps by air freight, to the local markets as needed. On the other hand, management can try to achieve diversity through superficial differences built into a few basic product lines. Low-cost mass transport methods, perhaps rail freight, can be used to move parts and components from centralized manufacturing points with heavy equipment into widespread local assembly or modification plants. At the local points, the final touches can be put on the product to meet customer demand.

One thing seems sure, the choice of distribution system each company makes will have a significant impact on product design, plant investment, and organization. Industrial logistics and trends in logistics technology will receive increasing attention from business, along with markets, capital resources, and product development, in the formulation of corporate plans for the decade ahead.